McGRAW-HILL SERIES IN EDUCATION
HAROLD BENJAMIN, *Consulting Editor*

TEACHING SECONDARY ENGLISH

TEACHING

SECONDARY ENGLISH

JOHN J. DeBOER
Professor of Education
The University of Illinois

WALTER V. KAULFERS
Professor of Education
The University of Illinois
and

HELEN RAND MILLER
Teacher of English
Evanston Township High School
and Community College
Evanston, Illinois

GREENWOOD PRESS, PUBLISHERS
WESTPORT, CONNECTICUT

To

W. WILBUR HATFIELD,

for his distinguished service as educator of teachers of English in the nation through the classroom, the *English Journal,* and his leadership in the National Council of Teachers of English, and for his unfailing guidance and friendship, the authors gratefully inscribe this book.

PREFACE

A number of excellent books on the teaching of English have been written in recent years. This book is not designed to duplicate them. While it is addressed to the classroom teacher, the administrator, the curriculum worker, as well as to the prospective teacher in advanced undergraduate and graduate classes, it concentrates upon the role of English in the total school program in a period of social change and educational reorganization. Without neglecting the practical concerns of classroom procedure, it places chief emphasis upon the over-all design of the English curriculum. It draws upon the data supplied by recent studies in child development, linguistics, the psychology of learning, curriculum development, and the effects of the mass media of communication.

Throughout the volume, the discussion is based upon the assumption that educational programs should take into account both the needs of the individual learner and the demands of the democratic society. In the field of language communication the individual and the social objectives of education tend to merge. The individual who is emotionally secure, able to communicate clearly, and discriminating in his reading and listening is also most likely to be an effective participant in the democratic process. The problems of instruction in English are here considered in the broad context of the developmental tasks of youth and the constantly changing responsibilities of the school which attempts to provide education for *all* American youth.

The authors have undertaken in this book to trace the changing emphases in the teaching of English in American schools and to set forth in concrete terms the chief concerns of the educational profession with respect to the language arts today. Interest in the newer concepts of linguistics and language teaching, the significance of semantics for the teaching of English, the uses of reading and literature and of creative writing in aiding young people to meet the problems of personal growth and of interpersonal relations, the role of English in the development of humane attitudes, aesthetic appreciation, and devotion to the democratic way of life, the ability to read and to listen with critical discrimination, the development of independent judgment in utilizing the mass media of communication, the effective classroom use of audio-visual aids, and the function of English instruction in integrated programs, illustrates the impact of modern curriculum theory upon the field of secondary school English. All these concepts, problems, and objectives are described in detail in this book.

Acknowledgment is made to Miss Lillian Novotny and Mr. William A. Jenkins, who supplied materials relating to the mass media of communication and audio-visual aids in the field of English, to the many secondary school teachers, particularly those participating in the Illinois Secondary School Curriculum Program, for the information and inspiration they have provided, and to fellow members of the Curriculum Commission of the National Council of Teachers of English, whose stimulating discussions have sharpened numerous issues in our thinking. Our thanks go also to the following publishers, who graciously extended permission to quote from their publications: Baxter Seminary, Baxter, Tenn. (for a quotation from *Literary Cavalcade*), the Evanston Township High School, the Oak Park-River Forest High School, the *English Journal*, the National Council of Teachers of English (for quotations from *Elementary English*, particularly two articles by Professor Kaulfers, which form the basis for the chapters on the teaching of grammar), the National Education Association (for a passage from an NEA *Research Bulletin* on the teaching of reading), the *School Review* (for quotations from an article by Professor DeBoer, which formed the basis for a section of the chapter on the teaching of reading), the American Council on Education (particularly for quotations from *Reading Ladders* and *Literature for*

Human Understanding), the *Phi Delta Kappan*, the University of Chicago Press, The Macmillan Company, Rinehart & Company, Inc., Appleton-Century-Crofts, Inc., Harper and Bros., the *United Nations World*, and the World Book Company.

JOHN J. DEBOER
WALTER V. KAULFERS
HELEN RAND MILLER

CHAMPAIGN AND EVANSTON, ILL.
February, 1951

CONTENTS

Chapter 1. CHANGING AIMS FOR THE PROGRAM IN ENGLISH

Modern youth face problems in communication far greater than those faced by their fathers or grandfathers. Radio programs, motion pictures and television, magazines, pamphlets, books, and other media assail the eyes and ears of adolescents with trillions and quadrillions of words each day. Not all of these words are gracious and lovely; not all of them convey truth. It is the business of the school, not merely of the teacher of English, to help young people understand these words and make judicious selection among them.

Guidance in the understanding and selection of words is of especial importance to citizens in a democracy. Words express ideas, and ideas lead to action. Since policies which govern actions in a democracy are ultimately decided by the people, the schools have the grave responsibility of aiding the people in understanding and judging words and ideas.

Understanding and judging words are processes involving all the aspects of language—speaking, writing, reading, and listening. This book will consider all these aspects, or "facets," of language. It will deal with them from the point of view of the modern young person himself, and from the point of view of the society of which he is a part.

As the problems of modern life grow in complexity, young people in secondary schools face developmental tasks of increasing difficulty. Family life, particularly in cities and towns in which at present a large proportion of American young people live, has changed markedly in our generation, and now frequently fails to supply the emotional security which

1

in earlier times it offered. International tensions and the continuous threat of war are reflected in the anxieties of high school boys and girls who respond to questionnaires and problem check lists. Personal conflicts, interracial and intercultural hostilities, and the uncertainties of employment opportunities after graduation further complicate the lives of modern adolescents. All of these, added to the normal perplexities of growing into adulthood, challenge the best abilities of parents and teachers in the guidance of youth.

Particularly the teachers concerned with the teaching of communication understand the impact of changing social conditions upon the lives of youth. The conversations and discussions of adolescent boys and girls, their confidential remarks in individual interviews with teachers, and their ventures into creative expression reveal the seriousness with which they regard their own problems and those of their peers. Their reading, whether in the more worthy forms of literature or in the pulp magazines, and their observing and listening to television programs, radio, and motion pictures bring them face to face with the triumphs, conflicts, frustrations, blandishments, stereotypes, and fears of our turbulent times. The modern school aids the young in interpreting what they see and hear. It helps them to express the emerging conceptions of their own part in the complex scheme of modern life, to find relief and help through spoken and written language, and to meet competently and gracefully the diversified language demands of the adult society which they are entering.

Modern schools consider, too, the needs of society as a whole in the communication program. The democratic society requires an informed electorate, a well-read electorate. It requires a citizenry which is capable of exercising independent judgment as it reads the newspapers and magazines and listens to the radio or views the movies or television. It requires the capacity on the part of citizens to discuss problems of public interest with intelligence and with respect for differing views, and to express their opinions coherently and persuasively in letters to their representatives, the press, and other agencies which influence public opinion. It needs leaders who can use language with honesty and power.

TRADITIONAL PROGRAMS IN COMMUNICATION

Traditionally, the school has viewed its responsibilities in the area of communication in much narrower terms. It has thought, and in too large measure still thinks, that its major task consists in the development of acceptable English usage, the cultivation of a minimum reading ability, and the promotion of a knowledge of a limited number of literary classics. These goals it did not generally succeed in achieving with a high degree of efficiency. The broader goals of personal development and of social understanding though more important from the point of view of human progress, have been generally neglected.

English as a subject of instruction is a relative newcomer to the curriculum of the American secondary school. Preparatory schools in the first half of the nineteenth century still confined themselves largely to Latin and Greek, mathematics, and formal grammar. Grammar was thought to have a certain disciplinary value in the training of the mind. Not until 1873, when Harvard College established English composition as a part of its entrance examinations, was there widespread effort on the part of preparatory schools to develop abilities in English communication. At about the same time, numerous colleges began to require a knowledge of certain English literary masterpieces. In order to standardize these requirements, the National Conference on Uniform Entrance Requirements in English was formed in 1893. As time went on, the requirements in literature were liberalized, so that by February, 1916, high school graduates who sought to enter colleges were given a choice of the books on which they were to be examined. Nevertheless, the college entrance requirements, while not intended to dictate the content of high school English courses, had great influence upon secondary school curricula, and tended to focus English instruction upon literary history rather than the needs of youth.

The phenomenal rise in the high school population, which approximately doubled every decade from 1890 until 1930 and which far outstripped the increase in the population as a whole, created new problems for the English curriculum as it did for secondary education in general. Much of the content of the English program had little relation to the abilities, needs, or interests of the adolescent. Little of it took into account the far-reaching social changes that were occurring. The requirements of the colleges were setting standards of achievement quite inappropriate to the needs of that majority of high school youth who were not expecting to attend college. Unfortunately the effects of these requirements are still too widely felt in the English programs that we have inherited from earlier generations.

Meeting Life Needs in Communication

The revolt against tradition. For the reasons described in preceding paragraphs, efforts were made from time to time by influential educational groups to bring about reform in the English program. Too many young people were making low or failing grades in English and were dropping out of high school. In order to make high schools truly the schools of *all* the children of *all* the people, and so to realize an ideal to which the American people were increasingly committed, various investigations and committee reports concerned themselves with the problem of adapting English instruction to the changing social demands and the needs of individual learners. These successive investigations and reports reflected the changing conceptions of the role of English in modern secondary education. Let us examine certain of them briefly in order to trace the development of a modern philosophy of the English curriculum.

The Report on Reorganization of English in Secondary Schools. One of the earliest and best efforts at reform of the English program was made by a national joint committee on English representing the National Education Association and the National Council of Teachers of English. Dr. James Fleming Hosic was chairman. The report, which was published by the U.S. Bureau of Education in 1917, emphasized that the subject matter of English consists primarily of activities, not of information. "The relating of items of knowledge to the pupil's daily experience," declares the report, "is more important than the relating of these items to each other in his memory." In this emphasis upon activities and on pupil experience, the Hosic Report was well in advance of its time. It classified the desired outcomes of English under the headings of cultural, vocational, and social and ethical values. It did include under the cultural outcomes such factors as knowledge of a few of the greatest authors and understanding the structure and style of the literary types—outcomes which had been heavily stressed in the traditional curriculum and which are still dominant elements in high school English courses—but these were accompanied by other objectives such as reading for meaning, ability to find needed information, and the ability to express oneself with clarity and persuasiveness. Efficient participation in the affairs of the community and the nation were, perhaps for the first time, included as important goals. The study of biographies and of the requirements of various vocations further reflected the new interest in the genuine personal and social needs of youth. The present trend toward an integrated curriculum was anticipated by the Commission's insistence upon cooperation between the English department and the other departments of the secondary school.

One recommendation made in the Hosic Report is thought today to have been ill-advised. In order to ensure adequate attention to the important area of oral and written communication, the Commission urged that the work in "practical English" be separated sharply from the work in "literary English." While the purposes which prompted this recommendation were laudable, the effect has been to create in many high schools an artificial separation between the activities of expression and those of reading and listening. At the present time the trend is in the direction of an integration of all the facets of language communication.

In general, however, the Hosic Committee may be said to have made an enormous step forward in shifting the emphasis in English programs from subject-matter mastery to the needs of young people. In many ways it anticipated the historic pronouncement of the Commission on Reorganization of Secondary Education, which appeared the following year under the title, *Cardinal Principles of Secondary Education*, and which set forth the following objectives of secondary education:

1. Health.
2. Command of fundamental processes.
3. Worthy home membership.
4. Vocation.
5. Citizenship.
6. Worthy use of leisure.
7. Ethical character.

The Report of the Committee on the Place and Function of English in American Life. In 1926, a committee of the National Council of Teachers of English, headed by John M. Clapp, issued a report called *The Place of English in American Life*.[1] It found, after studying communication in everyday life, that oral expression predominates, and recommended that the schools give increased attention to oral expression. Its findings were supported by Paul T. Rankin, who, reporting in the *English Journal* for October, 1928, made the following comparison between the relative importance of the four types of language experience in everyday life and the emphases upon these types in the schools:

[1] Also reported in summary in "Report of the Committee on the Place and Function of English in American Life," *The English Journal*, 15 (1926), 110–134.

	Life use, per cent	School activities, per cent
Expression		
Oral	32	10
Written	11	30
Understanding		
Oral (listening) ...	42	8
Written (reading)..	15	52

It will be seen from Mr. Rankin's figures that, at the time he made his investigation, the schools were emphasizing the activities least common in everyday life and neglecting those which are most common in everyday life. Recent studies of current practice in secondary schools suggest that the proportion of time devoted to each of these types of language activities has not been altered substantially in the period since the publication of the Clapp and Rankin reports.

An Experience Curriculum in English. Influenced profoundly by the educational philosophies of John Dewey, Boyd H. Bode, William H. Kilpatrick, and others, and the writings of such curriculum workers as Bobbitt, Rugg, and Charters, leaders in the field of English undertook in the early thirties to draft the outline of an English program which would be in harmony with the newer educational approaches. In this period the National Council of Teachers of English organized a commission of 100 teachers of English, representing all parts of the country, all school levels from kindergarten through college, and all phases of the English program. W. Wilbur Hatfield, secretary of the Council, was named to head it. Its report was published in 1936 under the title, *An Experience Curriculum in English.* A separate report on the college level was issued at about the same time.

The report exercised considerable influence upon the thinking of leading teachers of English throughout the United States. State and local curriculum makers used it as a model in the preparation of courses of study. Writers of language textbooks insisted that their books were based upon the recommendations of the Commission. To what extent actual practices in the majority of classrooms were affected by the report is difficult to say. Certainly at the present time the recommendations of the Commission are still far in advance of typical practices in English classes.

An Experience Curriculum stressed the *continuity* of growth in language and reading abilities, rather than specific grade placement of individual items. It placed heavy reliance upon actual experience with reading and language expression, in lifelike situations. It advocated the use of "instrumental" grammar, to be taught directly as an aid in the improvement of individual learners' speaking and writing, in the place of systematic grammar-in-isolation, even such grammar as had been reduced to purely "functional" elements. Its approach to language expression is illustrated by the fact that it substituted the term *communication* for the term *composition*, stressing social interaction rather than artistic design in writing. It gave impetus to the free reading movement by advocating a wide variety of reading experiences, with nonliterary as well as literary materials, placing understanding and enjoyment above factual knowledge and familiarity with the structure of literary types. Its recommendations for the English program were bolder than those of the Hosic Report, in that they departed further from traditional forms and came closer to the lives of young people in contemporary society. They were more influential, partly perhaps because they were translated into an actual pattern of school activities, and were followed by an implementation volume, *Conducting Experiences in English.*[2]

Efforts at integration. An Experience Curriculum in English dealt specifically with the responsibilities of English departments. However, even at the time of publication of this report there was a growing realization that English instruction, to be genuinely effective, calls for the cooperative efforts

[2] Angela M. Broening, *Conducting Experiences in English.* New York: Appleton-Century-Crofts, Inc., 1939.

of the entire school staff. Moreover, since the subject matter of English is drawn from many fields of knowledge and experience, it was felt that teachers of many types of preparation should be drawn into the planning of the language arts program. A committee of the National Council of Teachers of English was therefore appointed to explore the relations of English to the rest of the curriculum. Its report,[3] edited by Ruth Mary Weeks, chairman of the committee, included elaborate descriptions of various kinds of correlated and integrated programs at the high school level.

Meanwhile other efforts were made to secure the assistance of representatives of the other subject fields. In 1938, the Council appointed a Committee on the Place of English in American Education. Its task was to appraise the existing trend toward an integrated curriculum, and the probable effect of demands by some generalists that English as a separate subject be replaced by a common learnings course in which English would be taught in relation to the study of life problems. It was the responsibility of the new committee to discover ways in which teachers of English could serve most effectively in the changing school organization.

The first act of the committee was to invite approximately twenty-two national and regional organizations of teachers in the subject fields to attend a conference on the place of the subject fields in general education. All but one or two accepted. At the first meeting, held in Detroit in February, 1939, the National Commission on Cooperative Curriculum Planning was formed, with John J. DeBoer, representative of the National Council of Teachers of English, as chairman. Its first report, called *The Subject Fields in General Education*,[4] appeared in 1941. Individual chapters describing the role of each of the major high school fields in the general education of youth illustrated the striking kinship and community of

[3] Ruth Mary Weeks, *A Correlated Curriculum.* New York: Appleton-Century-Crofts, Inc., 1940.

[4] John J. DeBoer (Ed.), *The Subject Fields in General Education* New York: Appleton-Century-Crofts, Inc., 1941.

interest among the subject fields when the starting point is the youth himself rather than the subject matter. The outbreak of the Second World War interrupted the program of the Commission, which had planned to build further on this basic volume.

The basic aims of English instruction. With the entry of America into the Second World War, teachers were demanding guidance in giving more effective support to the war effort. Nationwide conferences were held on the subject; representatives of English groups met in Washington under the auspices of the U.S. Office of Education; the National Council hurriedly issued a pamphlet called, *Teaching English in Wartime,* by Dr. Neal Cross. In this period a Committee on Basic Aims of English, with Dr. Dora V. Smith as chairman, was appointed by the National Council of Teachers of English. In its report, it enunciated the following principles for the teaching of English in secondary schools:

1. Language is a basic instrument in the maintenance of the democratic way of life.

2. Increasingly free and effective interchange of ideas is vital to life in a democracy.

3. Language study in the schools must be based on the language needs of living.

4. Language ability expands with the individual's experience.

5. English enriches personal living and deepens understanding of social relationships.

6. English uses literature of both past and present to illumine the contemporary scene.

7. Among the nations represented in the program in literature, America should receive major emphasis.

8. A study of the motion picture and radio is indispensable in the English program.

9. The goals of instruction in English are in the main the same for all young people, but the heights to be attained in achieving any one of them and the materials used for the purpose will vary with the individual need.

10. The development of social understanding through literature requires reading materials within the comprehension, the

social intelligence, and the emotional range of the pupils whose lives they are expected to influence.

11. English pervades the life and work of the school.

12. English enriches personality by providing experience of intrinsic worth for the individual.

13. Teachers with specialized learning are needed for effective instruction in the language arts.

The Commission on the English Curriculum. New knowledge of the facts about child and adolescent development and a keen awareness of pressing new social demands upon the school accentuated in the decade of the forties the need for a large-scale sequel to *An Experience Curriculum in English.* The National Council of Teachers of English undertook to supply this need through the appointment of a Commission on the English Curriculum, with Dr. Dora V. Smith as director, and Dr. Angela Broening (for the high school), Dr. Porter Perrin (for the college), and Dr. Helen Mackintosh (for the elementary school) as associate directors. The Commission set about at once to organize an elaborate series of vertical and horizontal committees representing all school levels from kindergarten through college and all the aspects of language arts instruction. The first volume of its report, which will set forth the over-all philosophy of the Commission, is in preparation.

The general viewpoint of the Commission may be noted from its list of desirable outcomes and experiences in the language arts, which is available from the office of the Council, Chicago, Ill. The Commission defines the objectives of English instruction in terms of its conception of the major purposes of education: (1) the cultivation of wholesome personal living, (2) the development of social sensitivity and effective participation in group life, and (3) preparation for vocational competence. It proposes that English programs contribute to these major purposes by aiming at the following:

1. Mental and emotional stability.

2. Dynamic and worth-while allegiances through heightened moral perception and a personal sense of values.

3. Growing intellectual capacities and curiosity.

4. Increasingly effective use of language for daily communication.

5. Habitual and intelligent use of mass modes of communication.

6. Growing personal interests and enjoyment.

7. Effective habits of work.

8. Social sensitivity and effective participation in the group life.

9. Faith in and allegiance to the basic values of a democratic society.

10. Vocational efficiency.

It will be seen that these purposes are in harmony with those set forth in the report of the Educational Policies Commission of the National Education Association on the *Purposes of Education in American Democracy*,[5] but go beyond them, particularly in their concern for the mental health and personal enrichment of the individual. The English Commission's statement may therefore be considered in advance of the Educational Policies Commission's report, since it has profited by the more recent professional studies in human development.

Education for All American Youth. A later, and widely discussed, report of the Educational Policies Commission, called *Education for All American Youth*, proposed a secondary school curriculum which would include a course known as common learnings, to meet two hours daily and to be required of all youth. This course was to provide most of the learning experiences which all young people need for a happy and useful life during the period of adolescence. It was not to include education in vocational skills and knowledge, mathematics, foreign languages, or other subjects required for vocational purposes or for advanced study. The purposes of the course were to help all youth grow in six areas:

[5] Educational Policies Commission, *The Purposes of Education in American Democracy*. Washington: National Education Association, 1938.

1. Civic responsibility and competence.
2. Understanding of the operation of the economic system and of the human relations involved therein.
3. Family relationships.
4. Intelligent action as consumers.
5. Appreciation of beauty.
6. Proficiency in the use of language.

Other more general purposes of the course, shared with other courses in the school, were to include growth in

1. Ability to think rationally and in respect for truth arrived at by rational processes.
2. Respect for other persons and ability to work cooperatively with others.
3. Insight into ethical values and principles.
4. Ability to use time efficiently and to budget it wisely.
5. Ability to plan one's own affairs and to carry out the plans efficiently. This objective extends to groups of young people as well as to individuals.

While the common learnings course was not intended to be a combination of the English and social studies courses, since its proposed organization did not resemble that of the traditional course in English or the social studies, it is clear from the description of purposes that it was intended as a substitute for separate courses in these fields. Moreover, the statement of purposes strongly suggested that its subject matter was to be chiefly within the area of the social studies.

It should occasion no astonishment, therefore, that many teachers of English looked with suspicion if not hostility upon the new proposals. Some of these teachers, to be sure, were moved by a fear that the subject matter in which they had a vested interest would be threatened. Others, however, felt a sincere apprehension that certain genuine values contributed by existing English courses would be lost under the new organization. The Commission did include specific reference to such objectives as the appreciation of beauty, but the essential emphasis was to be on social problems.

Observation of common learnings courses in operation in some secondary schools lends a certain plausibility to the reservations expressed by teachers of English with respect to the new program. It is true that the problem method employed in many of these courses provides excellent opportunities for language learning. Further, many literary selections have greater significance for young people when they are read in relation to the study of vital human problems. Motives for worthy reading may also be increased. Moreover, there is nothing sacred about the traditional organization of English as an independent subject. Nevertheless, unless the teacher of a common learnings course possesses the necessary interest in the language and reading development of youth, and the necessary competence to provide appropriate guidance in these areas, there is genuine danger that important educational values will be neglected. If the excellent program described in broad outline by the Curriculum Commission of the National Council of Teachers of English is carried out in common learnings courses, this danger can be avoided.

The Stanford Language Arts Investigation. An example of the application of many ideas embodied in the English Commission's philosophy to classes in English and common learnings is the volume called *English for Social Living,*[6] a report of the Stanford Language Arts Investigation, carried on in a number of California schools by staff members of Stanford University, under a grant from the General Education Board. This volume contains reports of twenty-five classroom projects illustrating ways in which English classes may help young people to understand themselves and their peers and to develop appreciation for the values of the democratic society. The volume contains abundant material from the speaking and writing of young people and demonstrates the

[6] Holland D. Roberts, Walter V. Kaulfers, and Grayson N. Kefauver (Eds.), *English for Social Living.* New York: McGraw-Hill Book Company, Inc., 1943.

possibilities of employing communication activities in building emotional security, social adjustment, and devotion to our finest democratic traditions. It provides dramatic contrast to the narrow, dull, and futile drills which predominated in the traditional classes in language and literature.

The eight-year study of the Progressive Education Association. A great many educators and laymen expressed serious doubts concerning the newer type of curriculum, as proposed in the reports and investigations described in the preceding pages and in "The Emerging Curriculum in English." [7] Aware of the need to prove that the more functional curriculum can secure results in the form of skills, knowledge, and capacity to succeed in college, a number of educators undertook an extensive investigation of the effectiveness of the newer procedures. Under a generous grant from the General Education Board and through the sponsorship of the Progressive Education Association, a study of the results of the new education was launched on a nationwide scale. Thirty secondary schools, situated in communities distributed over the entire country, participated in the experiment. Comparisons were made over a period of eight years of the performance of thousands of young people in the thirty schools and in the more conventional high schools. At the conclusion of the study, described in *The Story of the Eight-year Study*,[8] it was found that students in the newer type schools performed at least as well as the "control group" in the skills and in knowledge of subject matter and far exceeded them in the more intangible qualities of leadership, appreciation of literature, critical thinking, social sensitivity, and the like. The investigation, which is not nearly so well known as it should be, proved overwhelmingly the superiority of the more modern curriculum.

[7] "The Emerging Curriculum in English," *Bulletin of the National Association of Secondary School Principals*, 30 (February, 1946).

[8] Wilford M. Aiken, *The Story of the Eight-year Study*. New York: Harper & Brothers, 1942.

PRESENT PRACTICES IN ENGLISH CLASSES

Two detailed studies of current practices in English classes have been made in recent years. The first, a study of enormous scope,[9] was a part of the Regents' Inquiry into the Character and Cost of Public Education in the State of New York. It was directed by Dr. Dora V. Smith. The second and more recent study, by Professor Robert C. Pooley and Dr. Robert D. Williams of the University of Wisconsin, was a survey of English instruction in the state of Wisconsin. More recently, a less ambitious sampling was made of practices in Illinois high schools by Professor John J. DeBoer and Miss Jean Ruth Jones, of the University of Illinois.

The findings of these studies reveal, of course, that there is the widest variation in the quality and effectiveness of English instruction in the schools of the nation. Clearly there is no equality of educational opportunity, either for the youth within the nation or for those within an individual state. In the smaller high schools, particularly, there exist an acute lack of suitable reading materials and a pronounced tendency toward regimentation in instructional procedures. The mechanical skills of reading and of language expression are still quite commonly taught in isolation from the situations in which genuine communication is needed. The resources of motion picture and radio have been left relatively untouched. Listening as one of the language arts is apparently neglected in most high schools.

While numerous examples of advanced practices in English instruction may be cited, therefore, the need for curriculum development in this area remains acute. The work of the English Curriculum Commission of the National Council of Teachers of English, and of many state and local curriculum groups, will, it is hoped, contribute substantially to this much-needed development.

[9] Dora V. Smith, *Evaluating Instruction in Secondary School English*. English Monograph No. 11. Chicago: National Council of Teachers of English, 1941.

COMMUNICATION AS AN ALL-SCHOOL FUNCTION

The accomplishment of the aims of English instruction will depend ultimately upon the degree to which these aims are adopted by the entire secondary school organization. The English teacher or the English department alone cannot assume full responsibility for the development of literacy and the other values which teachers of English set out to achieve. The communication arts are learned wherever they are used. Since they are used in all phases of school activity, all teachers have the obligation to cooperate in the improvement of young people's reading, writing, speaking, and listening, and in the understanding of the role of communication in modern society. "Every teacher a teacher of English" should become more than a slogan.

IS ENGLISH MERELY A TOOL SUBJECT?

Certain educators, particularly among the generalists, have considered English a subject without a content of its own, a mere tool subject designed to develop skills needed in other fields. Such a conception ignores numerous values in the process of human development which should be served by the teacher of English. Quite probably these values may be preserved in the more promising experiments in the common learnings, in which English and other subjects are replaced by an integrated course. But whatever curriculum organization is adopted, these values should remain in the focus of teachers' consciousness. The understanding of the nature and function of the mass media of communication, of the motives which account for many types of human behavior, of the role of words in human relations, resources for aesthetic enjoyment, and one's own unfolding ideals for living are examples of the kind of subject matter which modern programs in communication should embrace.

For Further Reading

Aikin, Wilford M., *The Story of the Eight-year Study*. New York: Harper & Brothers, 1942.

Broening, Angela M. (Ed.), *Conducting Experiences in English*. New York: Appleton-Century-Crofts, Inc., 1939.

DeBoer, John J., and Jean Ruth Jones, "Some Current Practices in English in Illinois High Schools," *Illinois English Bulletin*, 36 (May, 1949), 1–26.

DeBoer, John J. (Ed.), *The Subject Fields in General Education*. New York: Appleton-Century-Crofts, Inc., 1941.

Educational Policies Commission, *Education for All American Youth*. Washington: National Education Association, 1944.

Educational Policies Commission, *The Purposes of Education in American Democracy*. Washington: National Education Association, 1938.

"The Emerging Curriculum in English," *Bulletin of the National Association of Secondary School Principals*, 30 (February, 1946). Entire issue.

Hatfield, W. W., *An Experience Curriculum in English*. New York: Appleton-Century-Crofts, Inc., 1936.

Hosic, James F., *The Reorganization of English in Secondary Schools*. Washington: Government Printing Office, 1917.

Pooley, Robert C., and Robert D. Williams, *The Teaching of English in Wisconsin*. Madison: University of Wisconsin Press, 1948.

Roberts, Holland D., Walter V. Kaulfers, and Grayson N. Kefauver (Eds.), *English for Social Living*. New York: McGraw-Hill Book Company, Inc., 1943.

Smith, Dora V., "The Basic Aims of English Instruction," *The English Journal*, 31 (January, 1942), 40–55.

Smith, Dora V., *Evaluating Instruction in Secondary School English*. English Monograph No. 11. Chicago: National Council of Teachers of English, 1941.

Weeks, Ruth Mary (Ed.), *A Correlated Curriculum*. New York: Appleton-Century-Crofts, Inc., 1940.

Chapter 2. COMMUNICATION THROUGH SPEAKING AND WRITING

LANGUAGE COMMUNICATION A PART OF LIFE

What can an-English teacher do to put boys and girls on the way to developing their abilities in speaking and writing? How can they be encouraged to go on improving themselves and be ready to take their parts in life situations and to enjoy life in its fullest possibilities?

If the lessons of the classroom are to carry over into life, we must bring life into the classroom. The teacher can carry on continuous investigations watching how people want to talk and write and then thinking how young people can practice in the classroom the skills they will need.

The teacher's mind may work like this as she goes about the community and lives with the people: People do like to talk! What can we do in a class so that the boys and girls will get the maximum pleasure in talking? How will their lives be hampered if they are afraid to talk or if they have any other talking handicaps? How much richer and more enjoyable their lives will be if they can talk with ease!

In how many different kinds of situations do people want to be able to talk? Aren't quiet talks with friends the best moments of our lives? We give all that we are in these moments. How can we let boys and girls know that there are such moments?

How do people talk in the business and the traffic of the day? How do clerks in stores and customers speak to each other and how would they like to speak? When a bus driver is irritable, he has reason, but he spreads irritation and fails to get cooperation. There is a pleasant spirit of cooperation when a bus driver calls out cheerily, "The side door goes the same place the front door goes. Everybody please move back." What can we do in class so that bus drivers will be like the second one?

Community leaders need to know how to speak effectively in small groups and in large meetings. Everyone should be able to take his turn at being a leader. How can we help our students to be effective citizens?

When we look at our work this way, we can see that it is a part of life; we can continually become better human beings ourselves and can help young people to be the best people they are capable of being. We will never speak in a classroom as we do not want people to speak outside a classroom. We will consider how we can make opportunities for talking in class as people want to talk in other life situations.

Writing? It is true that people use language to speak much oftener than to write; therefore we must put most emphasis on speaking. But are we giving students the opportunities to learn to do the writing they will need to do and will want to do? How can writing help them to live and grow? In writing, as in no other way, we can grasp our experiences, analyze them, understand them. We can communicate with people to whom we cannot speak.

We have not realized how much people want to write. A teacher of composition many years ago began to test a theory that everyone would like to write and at every opportunity has carried on an investigation that others may check for themselves. The best opportunities come while traveling. It is amazing how little reserve and personality make-up people take with them when they leave home. On all kinds of conveyances, at all hours of the day and night, to all kinds of people, this teacher has asked, "Why don't you write that?" or "Have you ever thought of writing?" The seat partners, without exception, have confessed that they had wished they could write and at times had wished it intensely. Most of them said that they were afraid to try because they had not been trained. Writing was a magic mystery for the genius born but not for them. Their attitudes were like those of medieval serfs who accepted the superstition that castles were for those who were born in them. Teachers must not let the superstition persist that they are the high keepers of sorcerers' tricks, which anyone can see in a handbook and which are just dry-bone rules. In a democracy we should know that everyone can write. The great satisfaction and pleasure in writing should be available to all.

If it is true that all people would like to write, this truth is the light to guide a teacher of composition at every step. The wish to write is an inherent part of the desire to be alive in situations, to respond to them, to feel the life in them, to see them in a pattern.

It is probably true that every person in America has lived and is living a story that, if written with insight, would be a novel interesting as a human document and significant in the history of our country. If we realize that truth, all people are interesting and everyone has something of interest to write.

If boys and girls in school realize that American literature has hardly begun, that only a small fraction of our story has been told, and that our literature is theirs to make, they can be stimulated to look for what is significant everywhere.

We have much to tell, much to write.

SPEAKING EXPERIENCES

A teacher must be constantly thinking how there can be the greatest variety of situations in which the students talk with each other as people would like to talk everywhere. None of us ever learns to talk with others as pleasantly as we should like to; we must give the students all the practice we can. A teacher should never say or do anything in class that the students can say and do as well. Here are a few suggestions for providing speech experiences.

The class president can be the chairman every day at the beginning of the period. The teacher may give him an

agenda, which he will present to the class. He may call on
the teacher to explain the assignment for the next day or
week and to take charge of the class. This simple method sets
the stage for the practice of democracy.

When a lesson is assigned, two or more students may be
given the responsibility of teaching special parts of it. They
will not recite what is in the book but will try to think of an
effective way of presenting the information so that the
students will really learn what they need to learn.

A lesson may be stated as a problem, and three to five
students may be chosen to discuss it around a table in front
of the room. One will be the chairman. They will not talk
merely for the sake of talking or argue for the excitement of
it; they will be responsible for analyzing the problem so that
all the members of the class can learn as much as possible.

There may be different kinds of panel discussions. Some
may require several weeks of preparation and be special
events. Others may be less elaborate. Often there can be im-
promptu panel discussions.

It is to be hoped that the students will not ask to have a
debate. Debates belong to the past when men fought duels
with words. Now we try to think together to decide what
to do.

We want to develop speaking readiness. When there are a
few extra minutes, a student chairman can call upon a member of the class to walk to the front of the room and speak for
two to five minutes. Three students may suggest subjects.
The chairman will choose one of them. A stop watch adds
interest to this exercise.

We want to develop the ability to talk *with* people, not
merely *to* them, to tell them what they will be interested in
hearing. We must think of many ways of doing this. Each
student may look for a piece of information that will be interesting to the class. He will speak from the front of the room
even though it is for only a minute or two. He will try to
speak so that there will be a response from the audience. He
can judge his success by the interest in hearing more about his

subject. If it is time for the students to learn to use reference books, the assignment might be: "Find one thing in a reference book in our library that you think will interest the class."

The class might like to tell original stories. Here is a group activity to use at any odd fifteen minutes or longer. It will give practice in speaking, in thinking on one's feet before an audience, and in exercising one's imagination to weave a story. It will help develop a sense for what makes a story.

The class may tell "ingredient" stories. To get the ingredients everyone writes on a slip of paper a word that is the name of something: *toadstool, window, icebox, red hair,* or anything else. A student collects the papers and acts as chairman. He calls on another student to draw five slips. He lays them out before him and reads the words so that everyone will know what the ingredients are. Then he tells a story that he makes up as he talks. He must mention all five ingredients in his story, but they do not have to be important parts of the story. Sometimes it is a good idea to limit the time of the storyteller—to say that his story must last at least three minutes or not longer than ten minutes.

Because people need self-confidence to speak well, there should be every effort to give it to students, and there should be nothing to take it away. All criticisms should be positive. If a teacher says, "Do not say *and-a, and-a,*" that is a way of increasing the hesitation that manifests itself in saying "and-a." As students gain confidence, they speak confidently.

Experiences in spoken English may take many forms. Students should have opportunity for participation in panel discussions, class discussions, forums, radio programs (real or pretended), dramatizations, conversation, storytelling, giving directions, presenting oral book reviews, making reports of experiences to a group, presenting committee reports, assembly programs, making announcements and notices, and interviews. All these activities require specific instruction, with planning and practice by the group as a whole and by individuals.

The interview is one of the most interesting and valuable

of all the forms of spoken English. It provides opportunity for learning how to approach human beings of various ages with tact and courtesy, how to introduce oneself, how to conduct a conversation, ask questions, take notes, and how to report to the class afterward. The interview illustrates most effectively the close relation that exists between competence in speech and social maturity. Class discussion of the skills involved in interviewing, and preparation for specific interviews, are among the most rewarding of all the types of language instruction.

Interviews, like other forms of spoken language communication, can best be taught in relation to units of instruction which deal with real problems. Language experiences for their own sake are lacking in the kind of motivation which leads to genuine competence and ease in speaking with people under varying circumstances and for various purposes. Finding the problems which are of greatest interest to young people and of greatest significance to society—problems such as intergroup relations, boy-girl relationships, community activities, a personal philosophy of life, and vocations—and using them as centers of interest form the most effective way of teaching the skills of communication.

WRITING ORIGINAL STORIES

How can students learn most in writing original stories? Let us give them all the encouragement we can to write as the writers of real stories do. We should not put them in a situation in which no real writer could write.

We are in danger of doing that. If a teacher marks the stories, the students know that, no matter how exciting their stories are, the teacher will devaluate them according to the number of red pencil marks for mechanical errors and that all that really counts is absence of errors. No adult writer would show his story to the kind of person who would scan the pages in search of misspelled words.

If a teacher evaluates the stories, the problem is to write

the kind of stories the teacher likes. That certainly dampens the spirits of a young person. The teacher may read the best stories to the class and ask for criticisms. Then perhaps the stories should be written for the classmates. The conflict and confusion of aims in writing baffle, if they do not paralyze, students.

Every writer should know why he is writing and for whom. Let the students write for their classmates; they will have a single aim and know what it is. The assignment, made a week or two in advance, can be to write an original story. Each student will read his own story to the class. The only requirement for mechanics and form will be that the author must be able to read his own writing. The story is the thing. It will be judged by the students as they hear it read. The teacher may never see the paper.

When this assignment was given to one class, a boy asked the familiar question, "How long does it have to be?" Several in the class said, "Let us write as much as we want to." In a few days a boy asked, "Is eight pages too much? I have written eight pages, and my story isn't finished." Then it was agreed that the class could stop any student while he was reading his story if they were bored. It took five class periods to read twenty-five stories. Every teacher will probably find that in all kinds of work students like to work if they are free and encouraged.

A class after writing individual stories decided to vary the assignment and write a novel of thirty chapters for one lesson. Of course there would be discrepancies, but it would be fun to see what they would be. A committee submitted a plan. The class voted for the name of the hero as they voted for officers. It was Michael. The boys wanted him to be fifteen years old, that is, a year younger than they were. They said that if he was fifteen he would be young enough to have fun and not quite old enough to have good sense. The girls wanted him to be twenty-one in the last chapter. Michael was fifteen in the first chapter and twenty-one in the last. Each student chose the number of the chapter he would write. The girl in the novel was Nancy. The thirty chapters when read in sequence were an amazing story of wild adventure.

One class decided that each student could write a story alone or with others. Four girls wrote a story about four boys who had the names of boys in the class but were very different. They planned the reading to make it most effective. The story was typed, illustrated, and presented to the teacher. The teacher, who had not demanded careful form, found greater accuracy than she had been accustomed to expect in regular themes that were written for her red pencil.

After a class has written stories with all attention and interest concentrated on the subject, the teacher may make duplicated copies of any one for a lesson in analyzing stories; in rewriting parts, for exercises in improving sentence structure or punctuation. This method is more effective than marking all the errors in all the papers.

Lessons on narrative writing techniques may be centered around planning a novel and writing parts of it. Every student may work at a novel he knows he probably will never finish. He may see everything he writes in relation to a larger pattern.

There is a great deal of pleasure in imagining a novel, in rearranging it, in putting people we see in stores, on busses, and anywhere else into situations. We can see significance in everything and are never bored when we are alone. Everyone may enjoy thinking about a novel that he might write though he knows he probably never will write it. If the truth were known, most people dream of writing novels.

The time of the novels should be near the present, and the setting should be the town in which the students live so that they can be looking for material wherever they go.

The teacher may make any assignments that will be useful to the class. They may include any of the following:

1. Write the title of your novel and the titles of some of the chapters.

2. Write the names of your main characters and a brief

description of each. Tell what part each will take in your novel.

3. Write an announcement of your novel that might appear in the papers at the time it is published. Tell prospective readers what they would be interested in knowing before they buy or read your book.

4. Write a conversation that may appear in any part of your novel. Try to manage the conversation to do one of these four things: (*a*) The characters show what kind of people they are by what they say. (*b*) The characters talk about one who is not present so that the reader understands him. (*c*) The characters tell about something that has happened and so advance the plot. (*d*) The characters talk with each other while something is happening so that the reader gets the story as they tell it.

5. How are you going to manage your story so that the reader will know more than some characters know? What will the reader and some characters know that other characters do not know?

6. Write a chapter. It need not be the first but one from any part of the book.

7. Where are you going to begin your story? Remember Horace's advice about beginning *in medias res.* You know that people like stories that begin in the midst of action. How do the movies begin late in the action and then use flashbacks? Are you going to use flashbacks? Write the first page of your novel. Perhaps you will want to ask the class for advice as to where to begin your story.

EVERYONE CAN WRITE POETRY

The writing of poetry can be creative pleasure. It demands accuracy to communicate meaning and feeling as no other kind of writing does. But every teacher knows that if the assignment for tomorrow were an original poem, there would be the opposite of happy results. Poetry isn't written that way. How are poems written, and what can a teacher do to encourage the students to write them? The students who write verse should and will write it when they want to. The best a teacher can hope for is that scribbled poetry will be left on her desk. Perhaps all she can do in the beginning is to say that she hopes to find a poem some day.

When a teacher found the first poem, it was not written in poetic lines, and the spelling was so poor that she could hardly make out the words. On papers of appropriate size she made as many typed copies as there were students in the class. Privately she gave the copies to the author. He was happy when he saw that his poem looked like a poem. For the first time he was interested in the exactness of words, what they looked like, and in punctuation to convey meaning. The teacher said that he might keep the copies, but she would be glad if he would give them to the members of the class. He walked around the room very slowly bestowing his gifts with dignity.

Day after day for weeks the teacher found poems on her desk. She began to wonder if it might be about time to distribute books of poetry to see if the students would like to read poetry in private and aloud in class. That must not be a day too soon. The most important thing about poetry is that it must not be imposed on anyone.

There is a great deal of pleasure in looking for poetry everywhere, in feeling the pulse of poetry in life about us. Poetry should spring eternally in every human heart and imagination. One class compiled a poetry notebook—notes for poems that might be written. Here is one selection.

> Written poems are words in books.
> They are always the way they've always been;
> But the poems that come to me
> Are light as the seeds of a cotton-wood tree.

An interesting poem could be written about a city with its business section, its various industries, its traffic, and its people. There are movies about cities which gain much of the effect through the music that accompanies them.

Have you ever just closed your eyes and listened to all the

sounds around you? You'd be surprised how much you can tell just by listening.

When students like to write poetry, what can a teacher do? A teacher knew that studying forms and technical intricacies would not help anyone in a slow class. The writing of poetry must seem easy and come naturally. She turned the pages of a book of selected poems that the students did not have and copied a line or two here and there, leaving blanks for the students to fill. They were not supposed to guess what the original might be, and she did not tell them. The purpose was to complete lines and add original lines—to write with poets as it were.

Then she discovered that the students thought rhyme was the essential characteristic of poetry. Writing poetry was twisting words into lines that rhymed. To show them that the way poems look is important, she made two assignments. First she gave them duplicate copies of Emerson's *A Fable for Critics* about the mountain and the squirrel and asked them to copy the words in prose form. What was the difference in looks? The lines gave the reader ideas and impressions that he was to see separately. When the students read the two forms aloud, they read the form in poetic lines so that it was more interesting. The second assignment was to find a poem and copy it as it was written and then to rewrite the same words in prose form. Did they see that the lines in poetry express something that can not be expressed in prose?

If the lines of poetry did not have to rhyme, everyone could write poetry. A student would experiment with lines of different length and arrangement. In doing this he gained a sense for words, for writing. He gained more than that, a creative sense for literature.

This poem released some students from old tensions and antagonisms to poetry and gave them confidence:

I COULD NEVER BE A POET

I could never be a poet
for I could never bring myself to

rhyme *love* and *dove* and *woo* and *coo*
and I never punctuate
and my spelling and capitalization
    would be all wrong
and my meter would never be right
and I know nothing about couplets
    and elegies and rondeaus and feet
    and I mix my metaphors
and words like *assonance* and *hyperbole*
    and *onomatopoeia* are Greek to me
and I can never stick to one subject
and I invariably bring in everything
    from the moon to poets to elm trees to ships
in one poem
and my vocabulary is so limited
that I cannot say *intrepid* when I mean *brave*
and I call a magician a *magician* and
    not a *necromancer*
and my imagination is evidently abnormally weak
for I always think of the moon as being
    the moon
and not a beautiful lady smiling
    warm and refulgent on blue-mirrored
    lakes
and touching white-canopied mountains
    with her fingers
and fog to me is just annoying stuff
    that slows down traffic
when I am in a hurry to get somewhere
and positively never do I think of it
    as a huge lion stalking its prey
so considering all this I think
that I shall be a soldier
or a mechanic or a farmer or perhaps
    a doctor or a lawyer
but not a poet

                       —H. M. MARLOWE, JR.[1]

[1] From *Literary Cavalcade*, January, 1950 (Baxter Seminary, Baxter, Tenn.).

Everybody Writes Letters

Since all people write letters, and letters are almost the only compositions many boys and girls will write after they leave school, what should a teacher do?

In writing letters, as in everything else, we need to know upon what basic principle we are working. A letter is nearly always a communication between just two people. The whole purpose in writing it is to communicate with a person; therefore the only thing to do is to think of that person, of what he will want to know, and of how to tell it to him.

There is no perfect letter or even perfect form for a letter in the abstract. If we begin with absolute rules, we become stilted and confused. We use rules for form only to be considerate of another person.

In a friendly letter we put the address and date in the upper right-hand corner, not because of a rule in a book but because the friend might want the information and might like to find it where he is accustomed to look for it.

When we write a business letter, we must remember that it will go through the routine procedure of an office. It is in consideration for the people who will handle it that we put the addresses and dates where people expect to find them.

Perhaps the main reason why we have failed to teach boys and girls to write respectable letters is that we have taught rules instead of helping them to be human beings in their relations with other human beings. Because every letter involves special relations between two people, a teacher as a third person is an intruder who cannot judge it. Letters written as class exercises cannot be expected to have the life that is the essence of a good letter.

One reason for the unsatisfactory results of teaching letter writing is that we have taught a whole letter at once. There are different problems that we can take up in class.

1. How do you ask a person to do something? It is important to cultivate the ability to do that. We know that it is

necessary to tell a person exactly what we want him to do and why it is important. But how? Students can tell what it is they want to ask people to do, and then the class can experiment with different ways of making the request. The test of the writing is the answer to this question: What will the person who gets this letter think and how will he feel?

2. How do you ask a person to reply or act promptly? You do not write "Please attend to this at your earliest convenience," because that implies that he is not businesslike and because it is presumptuous to write in such a commanding way. If you really do need a reply sooner than it might normally come, you can explain why you need it. But how? That is a problem for class experimentation.

3. How do you thank a person who has done something for you? You think why you are thankful, and then you think of the pleasantest way to tell him. Everyone needs practice in learning how to do that.

4. How do you write a letter applying for a job? You think what you would do and say, if you went to see the employer. What would he want to know about you? What questions would he ask? You must answer them in the letter. What questions would you want to ask him? You may ask them.

Because letters written for class exercises are artificial, it is good for students to write those that they will mail. Among the many possibilities are these: letters to boys and girls in other countries or in other parts of our country; letters to moving-picture producers, radio announcers, editors of newspapers; letters requesting information and materials for class projects.

How to Learn to Write Anything

We want students to be prepared to do the writing they will need to do and will want to do. How can we do that when we do not know and they do not know what kinds of work they will be doing? It has been said that the only way to learn to write is to write. That is true, but the statement should be qualified in many ways. There are many kinds of writing. A person cannot learn to do all kinds of writing by learning only one kind.

Can we prepare boys and girls to write anything and everything by requiring weekly themes and wearing out red pencils till we are blue in the face? No. That is probably not even the best way to prepare them to write college themes. Too much proofreading by the teacher is worse than wasted time and nerves. It is confusion and frustration for the students. If a student corrects all mistakes and rewrites all themes, that will impede his progress in learning to write. That means putting the emphasis on errors, and the game should be to avoid errors. He will hesitate to write words he cannot spell and to use new varieties of sentences. His attitude will be negative, or defensive and hostile. He will not have the live stimulation of experimenting. We need to think how people learn by experimenting.

Surely a student must learn to express what he has to say accurately. How will he learn accuracy? Shall we begin with mechanics, with rules? No. If we begin with mechanics and make mechanics our aim, we shall get only mechanics and very poor ones at that.

We have not produced good mechanics in writing. People in offices and colleges complain that the letters and reports young people write are pitiful exhibits of childish blunders. College students make the same mistakes that seventh graders make; they cannot spell *too, athletics,* or *losing.* Surely we must do something, but let us reflect that there may have been something wrong with our methods. Our intensified drills have not produced the results we want. We have drilled on mistakes; mistakes have been our business; and mistakes are what we have.

We have been like the driver of a car who looks only at the instrument board when he should look ahead and know where he is going. He is in danger of becoming entangled in the machinery.

We may remember George Eliot's criticism of education in *The Mill on the Floss:*

Perhaps it was because teaching came naturally to Mr. Stelling, that he . . . set to work at his natural method of instilling the Eton Grammar and Euclid into the mind of Tom Tulliver. This, he considered, was the only basis of solid instruction. . . . He very soon set down poor Tom as a thoroughly stupid lad; for though by hard labour he could get particular declensions into his brain, anything so abstract as the relation between cases and terminations could by no means get such a lodgment there as to enable him to recognize a chance genitive or dative. This struck Mr. Stelling as something more than natural stupidity: he suspected obstinacy, or, at any rate, indifference; and lectured Tom severely on his want of thorough application. "You feel no interest in what you're doing, sir," Mr. Stelling would say, and the reproach was painfully true. Tom had never found any difficulty in discerning a pointer from a setter, when once he had been told the distinction, and his perceptive powers were not at all deficient. I fancy they were quite as strong as those of the Rev. Mr. Stelling. . . . But Mr. Stelling took no note of these things: he only observed that Tom's faculties failed him before the abstractions hideously symbolized to him in the pages of the Eton Grammar. . . . Whence Mr. Stelling concluded that Tom's brain, being peculiarly impervious to etymology and demonstrations, was peculiarly in need of being ploughed and harrowed by these patent implements; it was his favourite metaphor, that the classics and geometry constituted that culture of the mind which prepared it for the reception of any subsequent crop. I say nothing against Mr. Stelling's theory . . . I only know it turned out as uncomfortably for Tom Tulliver as if he had been plied with cheese in order to remedy a gastric weakness which prevented him from digesting it.

SOME PRINCIPLES OF WRITING INSTRUCTION

Is there a fundamental principle for all writing? Yes. Always begin by thinking about what it is we want to say and then find the best way to say it. We can test every piece of writing by answering the question, Does it communicate the meaning we want to communicate? Let us remember that

grammar is not a principle; it is not the foundation of thinking. It is mechanical. We must keep our attention on meaning
and use mechanics as machinery to carry meaning.

To say anything, it is necessary to have something to say.
We do not express meaning unless we express it accurately.
We gain accuracy by using mechanics as a means and not as
the end.

Everyone learns when he can say to himself, "This is what
I want to do and this is the next thing I need to learn in
order to be able to do it." What can we do so that students
will have an active desire to learn accuracy of expression?

Students can write briefly very often. This method has
many advantages over writing long themes.

1. The students can write in class. The teacher can see
how they write while they are writing.

2. The writing will have purpose and can be immediately
useful as it is correlated with the work of the day. The students may write a fact in the lesson studied as a checkup on
their preparation, or they may write an interpretation or
illustration of something they have studied. They may write
their opinions on a subject to be discussed, and then their
opinions can be used and tested in the discussion. They
may write summaries of a discussion or their conclusions
after a discussion. They may write what they think was the
most interesting idea expressed during a discussion. Such
writing develops the art of listening, the ability to select,
assemble, and evaluate ideas.

3. Writing is a social activity. It is nothing unless it is
communication. Each student is making his contribution to
the group undertaking. It is much more stimulating to share
ideas with thirty people than to write a theme in solitude for
a teacher to mark in solitude and return to be worried over
in solitude.

4. Writing can be a better preparation for life activities.
Adults are not often called on to write long themes, but they
are often called on to write brief statements.

5. There can be a greater variety in the kinds of writing.

A student can know what he writes well, and he can find out a few ways at a time in which he can improve.

6. The teacher can mark the papers in various ways so that the students will know what they do well and what they need to learn next. She can judge each paper according to its purpose, which may be accuracy of facts, completeness in a summary, concentration of-thinking, effectiveness in stimulating discussion, directness of statement or tact. She can show the students how mechanical accuracy is necessary to say what they want to say. Sentences may be written on the board to revise.

7. A teacher can help each to know exactly what he can do to improve his writing. She may say to a student, "Everyone listens to your ideas. Your spelling is poor. Can you look at a word after you have written it and tell whether it is spelled correctly? We must think how you can teach yourself to spell." We do not want any student to think or say, "I'm not good in English." Every student does some parts of an English course well, and every student can improve his English.

SOME SUGGESTED EXERCISES

If students think of the meaning they want to express, they will make surer progress toward writing accurately than they could if they thought of rules.

Wordiness shows a lack of attention to meaning. It is using words without thought for the meaning. It may be the result of teaching words as words instead of for their meaning.

Crossing out unnecessary words can be exercises in acquiring accuracy. It is a natural process; as we formulate anything we want to say, we eliminate to concentrate, and as we revise what we have written, we "sometimes add but oftener take away." For an exercise there may be such sentences as these. The directions are to cross out all unnecessary words.

1. Have you seen the murals on the walls in Room 164?
2. The airplane descended down from above to the earth beneath it.

3. The platter fell down off of the table.

4. Let's end up our business meeting.

5. The actors entered into the room dressed in their costumes.

6. Lay the scarlet, red rug down on the floor over the stains of blood and gore.

7 Exterior or outside appearances may be deceiving or give you a false or untrue impression.

8. Scrutinize your paper and look carefully and closely to be sure and certain that you have not left any superfluous or unnecessary words remaining on the page of this paper.

Another exercise in learning to consider the meaning is to rewrite sentences that do not convey the meaning intended because the authors did not think sufficiently of the meaning. There is no one mechanical rule to apply. The following sentences, written by college freshmen, show what blunders may result when the writer does not consider the possibility of the reader's getting *another* meaning than the one intended.

1. With a comb in one hand and a toothbrush in the other, a thought struck me.

2. A big policeman sat on both sides of me in the rear seat.

3. My legs, feet, and arms were numb from standing on them all day.

4. The exercise of the legs should be especially tuff, for without legs a man could not expect to be a good football player.

5. When we saw the Pacific, it was miles from the shore.

6. The next stand we come to we'll eat.

7. Since George Washington, we have had some thirty odd presidents in the White House.

8. Like all great Americans, Lee was called to rest in the year 1870.

9. Men like "Whizzer" White are not born every day but only once in a lifetime.

10. We have seen why a great city (Chicago) grew at the bottom of Lake Michigan.

11. When I first came to the University, I didn't think I was going to like it as well as I thought I would.

12. I expected to see only seven or eight college buildings and to be placed on a hill or knob away from the town and its business.

13. By attending the University one can learn to be unprejudiced and tolerable.

14. I quickly packed my clothes in my suitcase with my roommate.

15. The introduction of the gas-driven motor put the finishing touches on the end of the horse.

16. I little realized why my ancestors came to America before I wrote this theme.

17. Tragedy, of course, has the inevitable sad ending; the lover loses the girl or dies in the attempt.

18. Hawthorne had a very unhappy boyhood as his father died when he was four.

19. Whenever anyone called on the head of the government, the visitor was expected to stand while he sat.

20. Your telephone also brings inconvenience to you by ringing when you are cooking and are near a critical point of being burned or well cooked.

21. After a hard day's work I would return home and there on the table would be a giant dish of corned beef and cabbage, or maybe a plate of Hungarian Goulash, and of course my wife.

22. Every seat was filled to capacity.

23. I had been looking forward to the time when I would be allowed to take civics for a long time.

24. My wife and I are planning a vacation trip this summer. We plan to be away for two months during the month of August.

Let anyone, after spending an hour or so of fun with high school students while they revise the preceding sentences, consider whether thinking of the meaning is not a more direct and effective way to learn accuracy than the traditional way of applying mechanical rules. Take the sentence, "Walking down the street a few blocks from home, there is a large government project." High school students can revise that quickly if they think of the meaning. College freshmen would be confused after they had studied dangling participles and revised twenty sentences containing dangling participles. Recognizing dangling participles is not all that is needed to revise this sentence: "Whether raining, snowing, or hailing, every person in the audience stands, faces the flag, and if it is a man, he removes his hat." High school students can revise the sentence without knowing what a dangling participle is if they think of the meaning.

An eleventh-grade boy wrote, "The reason I don't like to read is when its not interesting over your head or written by women." Is it red marks for errors and another year of grammar the boy needs?

A twelfth-grade young man whose determined ambition is to be a radio announcer and director of radio plays thinks that grammar will give him the one thing he lacks. For a number of years he has studied grammar in schools reputed to be among the best in the country, but he would have only 50 per cent of a chance to get the job he wants if it depended upon answering this question: Which of these two words is a preposition: *if, of?* His job never will depend upon answering that question, but the following sentences that he wrote are evidence that time has been wasted in preparing him for his lifework.

"I couldn't help it," the killer said in a mad voice. he grabed for the gun, and we struded far is and it went of he made with an awful smile and he fell on the floor."

"You stupid fool," said the Boss, "I told you not to have the gun loaded, now get out of here or I'll kill you."

We have been wasting precious years of youth. How can boys and girls learn accuracy and learn it faster? We have been impatient when we have found the very errors in original compositions that we have drilled on in class day after day.

To work with sentences others have written may prepare a person to revise his own sentences, but it is an indirect way of helping him write sentences of his own. Applying mechanical rules to sentences already written and forming ideas into sentences are separate and different psychological processes. Shifting sentences around on paper is not at all the same thing as getting ideas from the head to a sheet of paper.

Student-made Exercises

We know that different skills are required to manufacture a machine and to repair its parts, but we have been teaching as though repairing the parts of a sentence would train a student to manufacture a sentence. To read proof is training in reading proof, but it does not train a person to write a novel, a letter, or an engineer's report.

We must think of ways to help boys and girls learn to manufacture sentences. First, they must assemble materials; that is, they must have something to say. A class offers a social laboratory that we have not begun to know how to use. Many a great writer has said that what helped him most was to have someone with whom to talk about what he wanted to write. Wouldn't any writer be glad to have thirty people who would listen to his ideas and help him put them together?

Perhaps students can learn all the mechanics of composition by working with their own sentences. They can suggest problems or situations in their daily lives about which the class will talk until everyone ought to have an idea. Then each will write his ideas in his own way. A few examples will show how students can learn mechanical skills by using them in their own writing.

When the students need to learn how to use punctuation, they can write short conversations. Punctuation shows what words cannot say, and it is an aid in conveying exact meaning to the reader. It is of no use except to give meaning.

A student submitted a problem to the class. What is the worst way for a boy to ask a girl for a date? What is the best way? A girl suggested that the worst thing a boy could say is, "You won't go to the movies with me tonight, will you?" That is a poor question because it is an embarrassing one to answer. After a number of suggestions, everyone wrote two paragraphs, one on the worst way and one on the best way to ask a girl for a date. Each paragraph must contain the exact words of the speaker, which must be inside quotation marks. What other marks of punctuation are necessary? Why are they necessary to give the intended meaning?

A boy, who was a clerk in a grocery store, suggested a situation. As a woman was walking out the door of the store, a clerk called, "You didn't pay me." How might he have spoken in a more courteous way? After a discussion, everyone wrote two paragraphs, one about what the clerk said and one about what he might have said. The teacher directed the proofreading. She said, "Look at your paper to be sure you have quotation marks around the exact words that were said. Have you put a comma between such words as *she said* and the rest of the sentence?"

The teacher found that some students were not beginning quotations with capitals, and others were using capitals in the middle of interrupted sentences. There were mistakes like these: The clerk said, "perhaps you forgot . . ." and "I am afraid," the clerk said, "That I forgot to ask you." The students then wrote sentences of their own to illustrate how capital letters are used in conversation.

Every day until the students learned how to use punctuation, they wrote short conversations. The subject matter was varied so that they could learn more than punctuation. For example, one day the teacher said that we can all learn to be more courteous if we think how to express what we have to say positively rather than negatively. Late one Saturday afternoon a woman ordered some flowers that were to be sent to a friend. The clerk in the florist shop said, "They can't be delivered today." She might have said that they could be delivered Monday and have asked the woman if that would be all right. What else might she have said?

We all need to cultivate the social skills involved in asking and answering questions. A problem a day will help boys and girls develop their social and writing skills together.

How can students learn to use capital letters by the direct method? They can write a few sentences a day and learn capitalization as they need it in their own writing. They can make up a story, a little at a time, and talk about it. Then each can write a page or a part of a page in his own way and in his own words. Two boys might be taking a trip in an old car. They could cross the Red River and drive west because they want to see the West. They could pass a high school and learn that its name is East Denver High School. In Pueblo the boys could visit Spud's uncle, his mother's brother, whom he calls Uncle Peter. The boys could write home to tell about their relatives and their adventures.

A teacher can take each separate skill the students need and then think how they can use their own ideas and sentences to learn it. Boys and girls can learn more and faster than we have as yet even imagined if learning does not consist of abstractions forced upon them from above but takes root inside of them.

Overcoming the Fear of Words

How can we help boys and girls enjoy their language and their responsibilities in using it? Too many young people, and older people as well, are afraid of words. They are word-shy because their feelings have been hurt when they used words. They are afraid they will make mistakes. Teachers of language, by their fear-of-hell-fire preaching, have killed the natural love of language. Fear of being embarrassed has destroyed the confidence and pleasure many might have in talking with small groups or large audiences and in writing letters.

Words are not governed by some remote and absolute dictator who reveals the mysteries of his ways through teachers. Words belong to people; they are part of the lives of people. Words exist only as people keep them alive; they come when people want them and leave when no longer useful. People make words and change them as they change their own lives; then words influence people. Words are like the people who use them, and people are like the words they use. Loving people have kind, loving words. Words, in all the history of the world, have never submitted to a dictator. No king was ever able to monopolize them. Words have always been democratic. No matter what anyone said about how words ought to be used, they went right along being what the common people, the majority of the people, said. No matter who made rules and laws for words, words lived and died with the people.

How can we give boys and girls a positive rather than a fearful attitude toward words?

One way is to let them see that language is always changing. When people are most alive and their civilization is growing rapidly, they make new words. The students should be on the lookout for new words that are not yet in dictionaries.

A way of helping boys and girls to realize that words belong to the people and change with them is to let them see selections of English at different times in history and then to talk about language and write what they think about it. Each of the following selections represents what was considered good English when it was written. The language of each is different from the language of the others, and all are different from our language today. When we think of that, how do we answer the question, What is good English?

> 1. I was weori of wandering and wente me to reste
>   Under a brod banke bi a Bourne syde.
>   —WILLIAM LANGLAND (1332–1400)

[I was weary of wandering and went-to rest myself
Under a broad bank by the side of a brook.]

> 2. A! fredome is a noble thing!
>   Fredome mayss man to haiff liking!
>   Fredome all solace to man giffs:
>   He levys at ess that frely levys!
>   —JOHN BARBOUR (*The Bruce*, written about 1375)

[Ah! Freedom is a noble thing!
Freedom makes man to have liking;
Freedom all solace (consolation) to man gives:
He lives at ease that freely lives!]

3. Nowhere so bisy a man as he there nas,
And yet he semed bisier than he was.
—GEOFFREY CHAUCER (1340–1400)

[Nowhere so busy a man as he there was not,
And yet he seemed busier than he was.]

Notice the word *nas;* it meant *was not.* It seems strange that people would let that short, handy word go out of use. Try it in sentences we say today. If enough people used the word, it would come back into the language.

Notice the double negative in Chaucer's first line. Perhaps the people in his time thought that the more negatives they used, the stronger their negative statements would be. What do you think?

4. After that I had accomplysshed and finysshed dyuers hystoryes as wel of contemplacyon as of other hystoral and worldly actes of great conquerours and pryness, also certeyn bookes of ensaumples and doctryne, many noble and dyuers gentlymen of thys royame of Englond camen and demaunded me many and oftymes, wherefore that haue not do made and emprynt the noble hystore of saynt greal and of the moost renomed Kyng Arthur.
—WILLIAM CAXTON (the first printer in England, 1485)

[After that I had accomplished and finished different (*divers* from which we get *diversity*) histories as well of contemplation as of other historical and worldly acts of great conquerors and princes, also certain books of examples and doctrine, many noble and different gentlemen of this realm of England came and demanded of me many and often times, wherefore that have not do made and printed the noble history of saint grail and of the most renowned King Arthur.]

Do you notice that Caxton's language is clumsier than ours? People have been learning since his time to say what they have to say more directly. You can take your part in the history of the language by finding ways of expressing ideas more effectively.

5. At length Makduffe to auoyde perill of lyfe, purposed with himself to passe to Englande, to procure Malcolm Camore to

clayme the crowne of Scotlande. But this was not so secretly deusied by Makduffe, but that Makbeth had knowledge giuen him thereof. For Makbeth had in euery noblemans house, one sli fellow or other in fee with him, to rueale all that was sayd or done within the same, by which slight he oppressed the moste parte of the Nobles of hys Realme.

> —HOLINSHED (*History of Scotland*, from which
> Shakespeare took the story of *Macbeth*, 1577)

After students have talked about the following problems, they may write what they think.

1. *Simplified spelling.* What is your attitude toward simplified spelling? If you are opposed to it, what are your reasons? Do you think changes in spelling can be prevented? Do you think that changes in spelling will come naturally? Will you just let them come, or do you want to help them come? The word *ynoh* was changed to *enow* and then to *enough.* Why do we spell a word that way when we pronounce it as we do? Would you be in favor of changing the spelling to *enuf?*

2. *Slang.* What is your attitude toward slang? Do you think we should have different kinds of language as we have different kinds of clothes? Would you call slang the sports clothes of language? Do you want to avoid all kinds of slang, or use all kinds, or choose the kind that you will use? Is there anything that you can say in slang that you cannot say as effectively in other language? Is there a special kind of slang for people of your age?

3. *A universal language.* Do you think there is a tendency in the history of the world, especially at the present time, toward a universal language? Do you think that modern methods of communication will contribute to making a universal language? Do you think that a universal language, made up of the useful words of all languages, will come with the universal brotherhood of man?

At the beginning of the discussion about our changing language, a pupil is almost sure to say, "But if there isn't a right way and a wrong way to talk, why do we have to take

English? If spelling keeps changing, why can't we spell any old way we want to?"

The answer is this: Yes, you can talk and write and spell any way you want to, just as you can wear any old clothes you want to. You can wear shabby, spotted clothes or clothes like those the kings, queens, or serfs wore in 1492, but you might find yourself wearing them in an insane asylum. In the English class we learn the present styles in communicating with others. The language is yours. You can do anything you want to with it. What do you want to do with it?

For Further Reading

Bobbitt, Franklin, *The Curriculum of Modern Education*, pp. 177–200. New York: McGraw-Hill Book Company, Inc., 1941.

Broening, Angela M., *et al.*, *Conducting Experiences in English*, pp. 121–261. New York: Appleton-Century-Crofts, Inc., 1939.

Burton, William H., "Implications for Organization of Instruction and Instructional Adjuncts," in "Learning and Instruction," *Fourth Yearbook of the National Society for the Study of Education*, Part I, pp. 218–255. Chicago: University of Chicago Press, 1950.

Cross, E. A., and Elizabeth Carney, *Teaching English in High Schools*. New York: The Macmillan Company, 1939.

Dakin, Dorothy, *How to Teach High School English*, pp. 3–220. Boston: D. C. Heath and Company, 1947.

Hatfield, W. W. (Ed.), *An Experience Curriculum in English*, pp. 109–276. New York: Appleton-Century-Crofts, Inc., 1935.

Hook, J. N., *The Teaching of High School English*, pp. 274–423. New York: The Ronald Press Company, 1950.

Mirrielees, Lucia B., *Teaching Composition and Literature in the Junior and Senior High School*. New York: Harcourt, Brace and Company, Inc., 1943.

Roberts, Holland D., Walter V. Kaulfers, and Grayson Kefauver (Eds.), *English for Social Living*, pp. 267–283. New York: McGraw-Hill Book Company, Inc., 1943.

Seegers, J. Conrad, "Language in Relation to Experience, Thinking, and Learning," in "Teaching Language in the Elementary School," *Forty-third Yearbook of the National Society for the*

Study of Education, Part II, pp. 36–51. Chicago: University of Chicago Press, 1944.

Seegers, J. Conrad, *et al.,* "Special Tools That Facilitate Expression," in "Teaching Language in the Elementary School," *Forty-third Yearbook of the National Society for the Study of Education,* Part II, pp. 148–193. Chicago: University of Chicago Press, 1944.

Witty, Paul, and Lou LaBrant, *Teaching the People's Language.* New York: Hinds, Hayden, and Eldredge, 1946. (Pamphlet.)

Chapter 3. THE EVIDENCE ON THE TEACHING OF GRAMMAR

WHAT IS GOOD ENGLISH?

Need for instruction in standard usage. The fact that every individual who speaks a language different from our own is likely to be regarded either as a stranger or as a foreigner until we become well enough acquainted with him to overlook his speech shows how basic language is to social integration and national unity. Countries in which large numbers of different languages and dialects prevail among millions of people have experienced exceeding difficulty in maintaining national unity or solving basic national problems. Indeed, a common language is usually regarded as a sociological characteristic of national culture groups as distinct from purely political states. An important reason for teaching English usage as a core subject in American schools, therefore, is the need for educating citizens who can function effectively as a nation. In recent years, science and technology have increased the need for efficiency and accuracy in the use of language. Improvements in means of production, transportation, and communication have extended the area of social and business contacts so far beyond the confines of the village or town that communication on a purely verbal level, in terms of any kind of local dialect, is no longer adequate. A common minimum standard of language usage in grammar, spelling, and punctuation is now a necessity if communication by letter, telephone, telegraph, radio, newspaper, or television is to be not only efficient and convenient, but also accurate enough to prevent costly misunderstandings.

48

For this reason, instruction in standard English is today a personal need of every individual who expects to participate effectively in modern life, whether on the farm, or in the village, town, or city.

Fundamental considerations in teaching English usage. Although societal as well as personal needs require schools to provide instruction in standard English as a means of communication over a nationwide area, the educational task is not so easy as the need is obvious. Any serious effort to meet the responsibility that modern life places upon the school ultimately gives rise to such fundamental questions as What is standard English? How is standard English determined? What recent changes in language should schools recognize as legitimate additions to standard English? How can young people best acquire the habit of using standard English not only in school but also in out-of-school life?

American English usage. Inasmuch as the schools of the United States are charged with the primary responsibility of educating citizens for effective living in this country rather than in other lands, knowing what is considered good American English is of the greatest importance to teachers and textbook writers. For an authoritative guide, the reader is referred to Charles C. Fries, *American English Grammar,*[1] a publication of the National Council of Teachers of English.

This significant work, based on research into current usage rather than on textbook tradition or opinion, deserves a place in every professional library and on the desk of every editor. The scope and intent of the work have been described by the author himself in the following words: [2]

Our study of American English grammar set out to do three things: It tried to present an outline of the three important devices which present-day English uses to express grammatical ideas and a description of the purpose for which each one is used. The three

[1] Charles C. Fries, *American English Grammar.* New York: Appleton-Century-Crofts, Inc., 1940.

[2] Charles C. Fries, "The Grammar of American English in a Language Program," *The English Journal,* 30 (March, 1941), 196–203.

devices are (a) the forms of words (b) function words (c) word order. . . . In Old English at least half the direct objects stood before the verb. . . . The use of six dative-accusative forms remaining in present-day English exhibit the pressures of word order as the grammatical device to distinguish subject and object, and any teaching of rules that tend to spoil the sense for the use of these forms in accord with the pressures of word order will not only be futile but will introduce errors that would not otherwise occur.

The second thing our study of American English grammar attempted to do was to give some proportion to the description of the grammar of present-day English by the use of quantitative information. . . . In a teaching program it seems worthwhile to know, for example, that less than 5 per cent of all instances of noun plurals have forms other than the S-patterns; that only forty-six verbs have *different* forms in the past tense and the past participle; that eight words account for 92 per cent of all the instances of prepositions used (*at, by, for, from, in, of, to, with*) and that twelve words account for 93 per cent of all the instances of conjunctions (*and, that, which, if, as, who, but, when, while, what, where, so*).

The third set of facts our study of American English grammar tried to find were these language items in which Standard English and Vulgar English differ . . . there are many items that are condemned in our handbooks of usage and in our teaching, which are simply matters of divided usage within Standard English and are not characteristic of Vulgar English itself. An effective language program must ignore all such items in the interest of concentrating upon those things that really matter. Examples of items that can thus safely be ignored are:

(a) *None* with a plural verb.

(b) The indefinites *everyone, everybody, nobody*, etc., with a plural reference pronoun.

(c) The indicative form in nonfact clauses.

(d) The use in accord with the pressures of word order of the case forms of the six pronouns which still retain dative-accusative forms.

(e) *As* introducing a causal clause and *so* equivalent to a weak *therefore*.

Our language has been and is constantly changing, but these

changes do not come from the practices of the uneducated or from the foreigners in our midst; and, more important than anything else, the direction of these changes is not affected by the *efforts* of the writers of handbooks and school teachers.

In spite of the teaching hours devoted to *lie* and *lay*, for example, the displacing of the preterite *lay* and the past participle *lain* by . . . *laid*, goes steadily on. We may not like it, but we can do absolutely nothing effective about it.

Textbooks as guides to usage. How sound and reliable as guides to modern English usage are the textbooks commonly used in schools? The most significant investigation to afford an objective answer to this question is that made by Robert C. Pooley at the University of Wisconsin, and reported in *The English Journal* under the title "Grammar and Usage in Composition Textbooks." The following quotations speak for themselves: [3]

I find to my surprise that the improvement in our textbooks is more superficial than a first glance would indicate. In appearance, in organization, in illustration, and in attention to the needs and interests of children they are all the heart can desire, but in fundamental soundness on the English language and its current usage they are fearfully reactionary. . . .

The charges brought against the textbooks in this article are not based on mere prejudice and unsupported opinions. They represent, in fact, the conclusions of a two years' intensive study of the current composition textbooks, including a minute analysis of sixteen of the most widely used texts of the present day. . . .

The textbooks set up artificial distinctions between forms of equal acceptability. Present and past usage prove beyond all doubt that "farther" and "further," "each other" and "one another," "shall" and "will" (first person simple future), the possessive or objective case of the noun preceding a gerund, and the third person condition contrary to fact ("if it were," "if it was") are completely interchangeable in cultivated English. Yet a great deal of space is devoted in the average book to setting up distinctions

[3] Robert C. Pooley, "Grammar and Usage in Composition Textbooks," *The English Journal*, 22 (January, 1933), 16–20.

between these pairs—distinctions not observed anywhere outside the classroom.

The textbooks fail to note current tendencies in speech change. Modern practice has definitely established the much-debated "It is me"; in similar fashion, whether we like them or not, custom is establishing "The reason . . . is because," "due to" in constructions parallel with "owing to," "like" as a conjunction, "data" as a singular collective noun, and "above" as an adjective. While these forms need not be vaunted, their existence and claims to respectability should receive notice. Yet the textbooks give one the uneasy feeling that although English has a glorious past, it has no future.

Although a few textbooks have appeared in recent years which represent a distinct improvement, they have by no means succeeded in making a significant impress on the teaching of English in the large majority of schools. In some respects the textbooks currently in widest use even represent a reaction to predepression times.[4]

Who Is an Authority on Language?

Present-day usage as a speech criterion. If the schools are to succeed in winning the support of young people and their parents for effective English, teachers of language must make certain that their own conception of language, as regards its nature and psychology, is at all times in keeping with present-day fact. Clearly, teachers cannot exert a significant influence upon the speech habits of the out-of-school world if their views of language are so out of tune with sociological fact that people begin to regard them, not as effective human beings who actually live in this world, but as a kind of cult that merely occupies a classroom in it.

Since only dead languages never change, this means that due recognition must be given to all living languages as ever-changing, ever-growing organisms. The proof of this dynamic characteristic of all living languages is to be found on the pages of history.

[4] Harry A. Greene, "Direct versus Formal Methods in Elementary English," *Elementary English,* 24 (May, 1947), 273–285.

The signers of one of the country's most treasured literary and political documents, the Declaration of Independence, for example, spoke of mankind as if the word were plural. They said "mankind are" instead of "mankind is" despite the fact that the singular is more widely preferred today.

Again, how would a modern English teacher grade a student composition containing such a statement as, "The tutor to be supported by the hundred, and every person in it entitled to send their children three years gratis, and as much longer as they please, paying for it," quoted verbatim from Thomas Jefferson's plan for education in Virginia (1799). Note that "every person" is clearly regarded as a plural. Note, too, that the date of the document places it closer to "the King's English" than any modern textbook.

Is "you was" incorrect or illiterate even in referring to *one* person? In the King's English of 1690, the date of the appearance of the *New England Primer,* "you were" would have been used only for the plural. Among "easy questions for children" appear the following:

> Of what was you made?
> For what was you made?

Can anyone cite better proof of the way in which the virtues of one generation can be misbranded as defects by another?

By what authority? Obviously, by the authority of changes in speech habits or usage on the part of those speakers and writers who during the past two centuries have had occasion to use language on the most influential occasions. Dictionary makers and grammarians had little more to do with bringing about such fundamental changes than collecting and reporting convincing proof of them; for language is always made, not by decree or fiat, but by the consent of the governed. As Dean Benjamin once put it, "Language is made by the needs of men, while grammar is made by professors." [5]

Relative criteria for judging language needs. To teach

[5] Harold Benjamin, "Interchange of Cultural Viewpoints," *Phi Delta Kappan,* 24 (November, 1941), 101–103.

English in keeping with the principle of inevitable change in language, one must, therefore, make sure that those usages which are rejected as definitely unacceptable do not have strong support in the speech and writing of able leaders in the professions. In his recent book, *Teaching English Usage,*[6] Professor Pooley draws heavily upon those excellent surveys of modern English which have been sponsored in recent years by the National Council of Teachers of English.[7] The findings with respect to usage he conveniently groups according to the urgency with which they require attention in school. Those expressions which were formerly considered definitely incorrect, but which now have become established by virtue of widespread adoption among influential and respectable people, are obviously listed as no longer requiring correction in the classroom. On the other hand, those usages that have traveled far, but not over halfway to respectability, are listed for consideration after the speech habits to which no literate person would subscribe outside circles of intimate personal acquaintance have been supplemented with thoroughly acceptable substitutes. Unless teachers of English use a similar life-centered criterion for determining what pronunciation, punctuation, or grammar to teach, and when, the danger is always real that the benefits of their instruction will be heavily diluted with nonessential busywork. Unless a clearcut means for making certain that first things always come first is adopted, the English program is likely to seem so irrelevant and esoteric at times as to lose the support of young people and adults alike.

[6] Robert C. Pooley, *Teaching English Usage,* pp. 3–15. New York: Appleton-Century-Crofts, Inc., 1946.

[7] Sterling A. Leonard, *Current English Usage.* Chicago: National Council of Teachers of English, 1932.

Albert H. Markwardt and Fred Walcott, *Facts about Current Usage.* New York: Appleton-Century-Crofts, Inc., 1938.

Charles C. Fries, *American English Grammar.* New York: Appleton-Century-Crofts, Inc., 1940.

Arthur G. Kennedy, *English Usage.* New York: Appleton-Century-Crofts, Inc., 1942.

In an age when the problems of survival itself are as urgent as at present in minority group relationships, purchasing power, and postwar security, the importance of putting first things first becomes especially conspicuous. In such times there is no better way to develop resistance to learning, or even active resentment to language teaching, than to allow the instruction too often to concern itself with what might be mistaken for an elaborate to-do over the aesthetic merit of tweedle-dee over tweedle-dum.

Need for periodic surveys of language usage. An important requisite to success in teaching effective English, then, is keeping abreast of changes reported by the most recent, reliable census of current practice among influential living speakers and writers in all the professions.[8] A periodic census of current speech, taken by the sampling method employed by Charles Carpenter Fries, Sterling Leonard, Albert H. Marckwardt, and Fred Walcott is as indispensable to English teaching today as a periodic population census is essential to effective social, political, and economic planning. Sovereignty in language, as in other aspects of our national life, is vested in the consent of the governed, and the latter are not the writers of last year's grammars, but the transient members of that ever-changing group who successively constitute the most active and influential leaders of the nation's adulthood. Since sovereignty changes hands with each succeeding generation, the watchword is always "from today's facts, not yesterday's textbooks." No language teaching can effectively influence the living if its authority is vested exclusively in the past. Teaching so based often succeeds only in throwing more flowers upon the grave.

Language as an instrument of social control. In his recent monograph, *Four Studies in Teaching Grammar from the Socio-psychological Viewpoint,*[9] Kaulfers has called attention

---

[8] Walter V. Kaulfers, *Four Studies in Teaching Grammar from the Socio-psychological Viewpoint*, pp. 46–47. Stanford University Book store, Stanford University, Calif., 1945.

[9] *Ibid.*, pp. 44–45.

to the way in which control of language can easily become a means of social and political control—a subtle means of disfranchising or disqualifying people from participation in the social, economic, or political life of society. For this reason, language standards in a democratic society should never be allowed to pass into the hands of a single group nor permitted to become more complicated in spelling, punctuation, usage, or methods of instruction than demonstrated necessity requires.

If there is any important criterion by which language can be judged, it is only secondarily one of form. Little beyond self-consciousness, feelings of inferiority, self-deception, and social barriers can be achieved by adhering to an unrealistic philosophy of language based on form exclusively. That such a philosophy can even become destructive of human values becomes clear when one realizes that it was developed and enforced during periods when language was often used as an antidemocratic instrument of social and political control.

On conquering Britain in 1066, the Norman invaders found language an effective instrument of control. They soon made French the official language of the realm. All Englishmen who could not read, write, or speak French were conveniently rendered speechless in the affairs of state. While some might insist that the conquerors did this with the kindest intentions, it is hard to deny that the effects were exactly the same as if their intentions had been vindictive. Are we by any chance still being subtly flattered into making unconscious use of the same device in our own teaching of language? Are we in fact perpetuating a set of literary and linguistic values tailored exclusively for people who, because of their inherited, unworried leisure, could afford to devote a lifetime to exercising their speech and to letting the soul soar through the stratosphere among the masterpieces? If so, can we attain these aristocratic values among any large number of people today without providing the same comfortable, unworried security that is required to put the mind into a receptive mood for spiritual communion with Plato, Virgil, Dante,

Shakespeare, Milton, Corneille, Goethe, or Calderón de la Barca? If we cannot or do not, to what extent can we be successful in setting up these values as requirements, pre-requisites, minimum essentials, or criteria for success and failure in public education without being guilty of uncon-sciously using literature and language as clever instruments of exclusion?

Language standards from the sociological viewpoint. Be-cause of the difficulty of classifying language usage on the basis of form exclusively, Kaulfers has suggested four classi-fications based on the concept of appropriateness:[10]

To facilitate objective, life-centered discussion, the following recommendations are suggested for a tentative platform of prac-tical, long-range, cooperative action by groups representative of, but not composed exclusively of, specialists in language.

Replacement of all classificatory labels for language to which connotations of inferiority are commonly attached (*vulgar, illit-erate, uneducated, incorrect,* etc.) with *labels embodying the con-cept of appropriateness.* In terms of this conception no teacher consciously or unconsciously belittles any speech habits, native or foreign, on the basis of form (pronunciation, spelling, etc.) alone. Instead, she helps young people acquire language that is *appropriate* to specific occasions, without insinuating that every other usage is always inferior per se. Just as people wear different clothes when they work in the garden from those that they wear to church, to the beach, or to a football game, so people often use different language in different life-situations—and frequently for no better reason at all.

What labels can help communicate the concept of *appropriate-ness* as a basis for classifying language? The following are pro-posed merely as practical starting-points for collective profes-sional thinking without pretensions to the untenable absoluteness that present classifications assume.

CEREMONIAL USAGE: The vocabulary and grammar appropriate to formal public address or to ceremonial occasions in which ritual or historical tradition governs language. In prayer, for example, custom still requires the use of *Thee, Thou,* and other

[10] *Ibid.*

forms that would be clearly inappropriate if used in everyday life outside a few religious sects.

AFFECTIVE USAGE: The vocabulary and grammar appropriate to *belles lettres* in which euphemisms, figures of speech, and specialized constructions are used for impressive or emotional effect. Note how inappropriate the following constructions would be in everyday speech: "Oh that I were he. . . ." "Would that they chant not of death!" " 'Deny me not,' protested the maiden." "The Hotel Continental" (title).

NORMATIVE USAGE: The vocabulary and grammar, *apart from technical terms*, that are normally used in carrying on the functions of business, commerce, law, government, schooling, scientific writing, news reporting, public discussions, and semiformal social gatherings. Normative usage derives its importance not from any inherent superiority, but from necessity. People with different speech habits cannot function as a group unless they subscribe to a norm that makes for ready intelligibility over a wide area. For this reason, its standards should never be more absolute than those of *ready intelligibility to the largest possible number of people*.

INDIGENOUS USAGE: The vocabulary and grammar that are completely acceptable among particular groups of people, but too specialized, inbred, or variable from group to group for use on a wide scale. To this category we would assign, under a special subheading, all constructions now branded with labels of inferiority; and, under a separate subheading, all the more highly specialized terminologies of the professions.

How Effective Is Instruction in Formal Grammar?

Results of instruction in formal grammar. Does instruction in formal grammar—nomenclature drill, diagraming, parsing, memorization of rules phrased in grammatical terms, formal sentence analysis, etc.—improve a pupil's ability to use language correctly? Published studies of errors made in schools where instruction in formal grammar is the major concern of the English program reveal that *the same errors are repeated in approximately the same proportion in every grade throughout the elementary grades, secondary school, and college.* In fact, Diebel and Sears found that more mistakes in pronouns were made in the eighth grade by pupils who had received instruction in formal grammar than by third graders who had not had the benefit (?) of such instruction.[11] This fact led the investigators to inquire, Is the present teaching of pronouns leading to a more confused state of mind in the eighth-grade child than existed when he was in the third grade and was entirely unconscious of the rules of grammar governing the use of such words?

The findings of other investigators have confirmed those of Diebel and Sears. A survey of New York State conducted by Dora V. Smith [12] revealed that in small-town high schools which emphasized the study of formal grammar and drill exercises, rather than guided, motivated practice in speech and writing, the pupils achieved a percentile rank of only 8 in ability to write!

The commonly observed failure of work in grammar to carry over into the pupil's own speech or writing led Julius Boraas to investigate the correlation between knowledge of formal grammar and the practical mastery of English.[13] He found that such knowledge correlated *highest with ability in arithmetic, and least of all* (.28) *with ability in composition,* the very skill with which grammar, to be of value, should show a significant relationship. Similar findings were reported by Catherine Catherwood [14] for schools in Minnesota and by Mabel C. Benfer for schools in Iowa.[15]

[11] Amelia Diebel and Isabel Sears, "A Study of the Common Mistakes in Pupils' Oral English," *Elementary School Journal,* 17 (September, 1916), 44–54.

[12] Dora V. Smith, *Evaluating Instruction in Secondary School English.* Chicago: National Council of Teachers of English, 1941.

[13] Julius Boraas, *Formal English Grammar and the Practical Mastery of English.* Ph.D. thesis, University of Minnesota, 1917.

[14] Catherine Catherwood, *Relationship between a Knowledge of Rules and Ability to Correct Grammatical Errors.* M.A. thesis, University of Minnesota, 1932.

[15] Mabel C. Benfer, *Sentence Sense in Relation to Subject and Predicate.* M.A. thesis, University of Iowa, 1935.

Diagraming as a teaching device. Does practice in diagraming improve English usage or reading comprehension? From actual experimentation with equated groups of high school students, half of whom received intensive drill in diagraming while the other half received no instruction or practice in diagraming or sentence analysis, Kenneth C. Barghahn found that practice in diagraming led to nothing but increased ability to diagram.[16] The experimental group made no gains beyond those achieved by the control group in either reading comprehension or command of standard English usage. Later and more detailed studies have proved the uselessness of diagraming as a means for improving student ability in usage, capitalization, punctuation, and sentence structure.[17]

The same lack of carry-over of work in formal grammar, other than diagraming, to ability in punctuation was demonstrated by James W. Evans in an experiment conducted with 831 pupils in nineteen city school systems of the Middle West.[18] Significantly superior results in punctuation were obtained by teaching punctuation directly as an aid to comprehension on the part of a reader rather than by means of grammatically phrased rules and correlated drill exercises.

The investigations reported in the preceding paragraphs are only a small part of the evidence concerning the futility of work in formal grammar as a means of improving a student's own personal use of language, native or foreign. For additional evidence, the reader is referred to the excellent summaries contained in the language arts issues of the *Re-*

[16] Kenneth C. Barghahn, *The Effects of Sentence Diagraming on English Usage and Reading Comprehension.* Unpublished M.A. thesis, University of Iowa, 1940.

[17] James Reece Stewart, *The Effect of Diagraming on Certain Skills in English Composition.* Ph.D. thesis, University of Iowa, 1941.

Claire J. Butterfield, *The Effect of Certain Grammatical Elements on the Acquisition and Retention of Punctuation Skills.* Ph.D. thesis, University of Iowa, 1945.

[18] James W. Evans, *The Social Importance and the Pupil Control of Certain Punctuation Variants.* Ph.D. thesis, University of Iowa, 1939.

view of Educational Research and in the *Encyclopedia of Educational Research*.[19] Not a single objective investigation into the teaching of formal grammar has produced evidence of improvement greater than that commonly achieved by students of like age and ability who receive guided practice in speaking and writing without recourse to grammatically phrased rules, diagraming, parsing, nomenclature drill, or formal sentence analysis. The evidence becomes overwhelming when similar negative findings for the modern languages and Latin are added to the total for English.

Among leaders in the teaching of the language arts who have published critical evaluations and interpretations of scientifically conducted research in the teaching of grammar are Dora V. Smith and Harry A. Greene. In summarizing the findings of thirteen experiments and investigations reported between 1917 and 1938, Professor Smith wrote: [20]

These are not personal opinions concerning the values of the teaching of grammar. The educational world is no longer interested in opinions on this question when unsubstantiated by evidence. These are facts based upon scientific investigation, and *they are all the facts there are available.* Clearly they present a distinct challenge to those who still promulgate the old doctrine [of formal grammar]. The burden of proof today rests with them.

Similar conclusions were drawn in 1947 by Professor Greene [21] in his careful evaluation of eight investigations reported between 1939 and 1941:

The results of the experiments presented here are believed to be convincing. They all point in the same direction. . . . The evidence shows that repeated and spaced habit-forming experiences

[19] Walter S. Monroe (Ed.), *Encyclopedia of Educational Research* (Revised Edition). New York: The Macmillan Company, 1950. See especially the articles on English grammar (pp. 383–395), Latin (pp. 654–662), modern foreign languages (pp. 464–485), and shorthand (p. 118).

[20] Dora V. Smith, "English Grammar Again," *The English Journal,* 27 (October, 1938), 643–649.

[21] Greene, *loc. cit.*

are productive of mastery and should be substituted for formal rules and exercises. . . . Let us reserve the grammar for later adult editorial use.

Limitations inherent in grammatical terminology. Perhaps it is only natural that schoolwork making extensive use of grammatical terminology should have proved less successful in improving English usage than in promoting confusion and a dislike of language study among large numbers of young people. It cannot be expected that students handicapped by limited vocabularies will respond readily to explanations of language usage phrased in such terms as prepositional phrase, subordinate clause, restrictive modifier, or even subject and predicate. The fact, however, that under continuous pressure, reinforced by frequent reviews, they can learn the *verbal* definitions of these terms mechanically by heart, and often parrot them along with memorized examples, has misled teachers to assume that they actually know what they are saying and should, therefore, be able to apply their supposed learning to their own writing and speech. Moreover, the fact that many pupils who have no trouble whatever in using scientific terms acquired from toying with radios, automobiles, or electrical appliances, nevertheless seem to be unable to make effective use of linguistic terminology has been the source of considerable impatience and irritation. Is it sheer stubbornness that prompts boys to speak quite fluently in technical terms about the parts of a radio, car, or electrical circuit and then become inarticulate when asked to acquire what seems, by comparison, a mere handful of grammatical terms?

Perhaps the explanation is to be found in the fact that the terms of applied science and invention deal with specific, concrete things which can readily be seen, touched, or felt, and almost always serve exactly the same purpose, while the terms used in formal grammar, like *noun* and *adjective,* often change their form, position, and even their function from sentence to sentence. For example, the word *orange,* by the usual definition of a noun as a word that stands for a person, place, or thing, could easily be called a noun; but in the expression, "an orange-colored sweater," it assumes all the functions that by definition are usually assigned to adjectives. It must be in this elusive behavior of words in playing hide-and-seek behind a variety of grammatical labels, and in the ability of words, like *go,* to masquerade behind the same generic label in a variety of disguises, from *go* and *goes* to *going, went,* and *gone,* that the locus of the difficulty lies. In view of these complexities, it is probably true that many young people who need personal help in language most simply cannot make effective use of grammatical terminology, or of procedures based upon it, in their own personal writing and speech.

Astonishing as it may seem, careful investigation has shown that even able students from highly privileged language environments, though they often respond to nomenclature drill, diagraming, parsing, and formal sentence analysis as enthusiastically as some people react to crossword puzzles, nevertheless fail to show any superiority in their own subsequent personal use of language over young people from similarly enriched environments who receive no formal instruction at all.[22] Wherever the students come from homes in which like care has been exercised by the parents in pruning and guiding their children's speech from infancy (perhaps by sheltering it from contamination by those "uncouth" boys and girls from across the railroad tracks who say "ain't" and "Me an' him never done nothin'") no difference in language habits, or in writing skills, can be found among those who receive training in formal grammar and those who do not. These observations suggest that all formal grammatical procedures, as well as all terminology beyond the names for the parts of speech commonly indicated after words in dictionaries, belong, like the technical terms used in law or medicine, on the *professional* level of higher education rather than on the consumer level of elementary and secondary schooling. Their function is primarily to make intraprofessional communica-

[22] Kaulfers, *op. cit.,* pp. 16–17.

tion more accurate and convenient among *licensed* practitioners, and to supply grammarians, philologists, and lexicographers with efficient tools of research and classification.

How Valid Is Current Practice?

Obsolescence in present-day practice. Despite the fact that careful investigation and experimentation give no support to formal grammar as a means of improving usage in either English or foreign language, such teaching continues to dominate language instruction in most schools. An examination of the most widely used textbooks allows of no other conclusion. It is inconceivable that any larger number of teachers would adopt basic textbooks that contain so much material that they (presumably) do not use. Because of the blow dealt to the schools by the war, no significant change has taken place since 1938 when Dora V. Smith wrote "more time is being spent in the high-school English classes of America today upon grammar and usage than upon any single phase of instruction." A study of the high schools of Illinois by DeBoer and Jones [23] in 1948 revealed that "more time is devoted to study *about* language than to actual experience in either writing or speaking under guidance."

Formal grammar and preparation for college. Although inadequate programs for the preservice and in-service training of teachers may account for the conditions described in the preceding paragraphs, "pressure of college entrance examinations and requirements" is commonly offered as a justification for the continued use of nonfunctional procedures. Because this misconception is still widespread, special attention is called to the fact that even before the late war, 75 *per cent of all the college placement tests for Freshman English in use in 130 major colleges and universities in Amer-*

[23] John J. DeBoer and Jean Ruth Jones, "Some Current Practices in English Instruction in Illinois Secondary Schools," *Illinois English Bulletin,* 36 (April, 1949), 1–26.

ica did not contain a single item of technical grammar, while over 96 per cent of all the items dealt with usage exclusively. It is significant to note also that the Eastern College Board abolished the old examination in formal grammar in favor of a comprehensive power test over ten years ago.[24] It is safe to say that today no student is required to know formal grammar in order to pass college entrance examinations creditably, provided he can express himself effectively in speech and writing.

The fact that many teaching assistants and instructors in college courses in rhetoric make use of grammatical terminology thus remains the only plausible excuse for teaching formal grammar to prospective college students. That this need can readily be filled by means of a short vocabulary unit, taught exclusively on the *recognition* level to seniors definitely planning to enter a particular college the following term, is obvious. To be functional, however, such a unit must be composed only of such terms as are suggested by the colleges in point, for grammatical nomenclature varies too much from institution to institution, and even from instructor to instructor, to be helpful if selected in any other way.

Formal grammar as a preparation for foreign language study. Is formal grammar needed in order to study a foreign language successfully? All the research and experimentation available—and the evidence is overwhelming—show that such knowledge is neither essential nor helpful.[25] Although some teachers of languages still use formal drill methods, hardly any high school textbooks published since 1940 assume a foreknowledge of formal grammar. One junior-senior high school Spanish series, including an all-inclusive four-year

[24] Dora V. Smith and Constance M. McCullough, "An Analysis of the Content of Placement Tests in Freshman English Used by One Hundred and Thirty Colleges and Universities," *The English Journal* (High School Edition), 25 (January, 1936), 17–25.

[25] Walter S. Monroe (Ed.), *Encyclopedia of Education Research,* pp. 456–457, 532, 654. New York: The Macmillan Company, 1941.

grammar suitable also for use in college, not only makes a foreknowledge of grammatical terminology entirely unnecessary but actually uses fewer grammatical terms in all books combined than are commonly found in one high school English Grammar.[26] Even where used, the terms are a concession to conservative teachers and are not allowed to stand in the way of ready comprehension on the part of students.

The modern viewpoint of the foreign languages regarding the teaching of formal grammar has been summarized for teachers of English by Kaulfers [27] as director of the foreign language programs in the Stanford Language Arts Investigation and as editor of its report, *Foreign Languages and Cultures in American Education:*

Elementary school teachers who provide work in formal grammar merely as a preparation for the study of a foreign language in high school are not contributing to anything significant or promising in modern education, and may at times actually be defeating the major concern of language teaching—that of helping young people grow in confidence, ease, power and honesty in the effective use of language for worthy life purposes.

What Grammar Should Be Taught?

Grade placement of grammar. Which usage skills should receive attention in the secondary school? On the basis of studies made by Rivlin, Charters, Stormzand, and O'Shea, among others, J. Paul Leonard [28] derived a practical outline for a four-year high school course in which the emphasis was to be on the ability that the topics represent rather than on their grammatical names. The following outline is a reference guide or check list for teachers as licensed professional workers and is in no sense a syllabus for high school students.

[26] *Voces de las Américas, Voces de las Españas,* and *Guía al Español.* New York: Henry Holt and Company, 1947.

[27] Kaulfers, *op. cit.,* p. 21.

[28] John Paul Leonard, "Functional Grammar: What and Where?" *English Journal,* 22 (November, 1933), 731–735.

GRADE ALLOCATION OF FUNCTIONAL GRAMMAR

First Year

I. Complete-sentence concept.
- A. Recognition of the sentence as a complete thought. Practice in the recognition of complete thoughts expressed in simple and complex sentences, but no classification into these two kinds of sentences. Differences (not analytical but on the basis of thought elements) between complete sentences and fragments. Understand that subject may not always be stated, as in commands.
- B. Capitalization of first word in every sentence.
- C. Use of period at the end of every sentence except where a question has been asked. (No classification into imperative, interrogative, and declarative.)
- D. Use of question mark at end of sentence asking question.
- E. Division of complete sentences into two parts—complete subject and complete predicate. (This is to be a mere explanation leading into the work in Division II.)

II. Subject-element concept.
- A. Recognition of complete subject and its function. Need for subject in every sentence, difference between complete subject and a sentence.
- B. Position of complete subject in a sentence—normal and reversed positions. Recognize subject when not stated as in command or request.
- C. Single-word subject—subject substantive.
  - 1. Noun.
    - a. Concept of noun—no classification.
    - b. Proper noun (omit common).
      - a'. Recognition of proper nouns.
      - b'. Capitalization of proper nouns.
    - c. Number.
      - a'. Singular.
      - b'. Formation of plurals (spelling).
  - 2. Pronoun.
    - a. Concept of pronoun and its recognition.
    - b. Correct use of pronoun as subject of sentence.

   c. Antecedent of pronoun.
    a'. Recognition of antecedent.
    b'. Agreement with antecedent in person, number, and gender.
    c'. Place of pronoun in sentence in relation to its antecedent.
   d. Capitalization of pronouns referring to God and of the pronoun I.
   e. Changes in forms of pronouns for plural number.
   f. Changes in forms of pronouns for different genders.
  D. Adjectives.
   1. Recognition and understanding of uses in sentences. Comparison of most frequently used adjectives.
   2. Position of adjectives near word explained. May be placed in predicate.
III. Predicate-element concept.
  A. Recognition of complete predicate and its function. Need for subject and predicate in every sentence. Difference between complete predicate and sentence. Subject and predicate relationship.
  B. Position of predicate in sentence.
  C. Verb.
   1. Concept—must be verb in every sentence, and function use concept of complete verb.
   2. Subject of verb.
    a. Recognition of subject of verb and relationship.
    b. Agreement in number, formation of plurals of verbs.
  D. Adverb.
   1. Concept and function in sentence, recognition in sentences.
   2. Relation to verbs and adjectives.

Second Year

II. Subject-element concept.
  A. Noun.
   1. Possessive case (omit nominative and objective) to show
    a. Ownership (stress apostrophe).
    b. Relation or connection.

    2. Collective noun—recognition of and effect on number of verb.

    3. Nouns in apposition—stress comma punctuation.

B. Pronoun.

    1. From the meaning of pronouns derive the understanding of the use of relative, personal, and indefinite pronouns (stress "its" and "it's"). Dwell little on intensive, reflexive, and demonstrative usages. Stress improper use of personal for demonstrative pronouns.

    2. Case forms of relative pronouns.

        a. Nominative—as subject.

        b. Genitive—relationship and ownership.

C. Compound subject—recognition and plural meaning. Comma punctuation of word subjects in series without connectives.

D. Adjectives.

    1. Proper adjectives and the way they are derived from proper nouns. Capitalization of these adjectives.

    2. Understanding of concepts of articles and correct use in sentences for various meaning (no classification into articles or demonstratives because of no inflectional difficulties).

    3. Spelling and meaning of "those," "that," "these," etc., and prevention of errors such as "them books."

    4. Commas with adjectives in series.

III. Predicate-element concept.

A. Verb.

    1. Auxiliary verbs (helping verbs, beginning with the break-up of complete verb concept).

        a. Agreement with subject of "to have" and "to be."

        b. Correct use and meaning of most commonly used auxiliaries—"may," "can," "shall," "will," etc.

        c. Tense sequence (elementary).

    2. Principal parts.

        a. Difference between past participle and past tense. Stress correct use of principal parts of most common irregular verbs.

    3. Understand three persons of verbs for agreement of subject with predicate verb.

    4. Spelling, tenses, and formation of most common ir-
regular verbs.

    5. Tense.

      a. Present.   *b.* Past.   *c.* Future-progressive.

    6. Object of verb—use of nouns and pronouns as objects
of verbs (especially pronoun objects).

    7. Predicate attribute—noun, pronoun, and adjective (add
to concept of pronouns, adjectives learned previously,
objective case, pronouns (objects of verbs), and
verbals.

  B. Adverb.

    1. Position of adverbs.

    2. Use of "more" and "most" with adverbs, context, and
not memorization of comparison.

  C. Agreement between verb and compound subjects.

IV. Modification element.

  A. Concept of modification—qualifying meaning.

  B. Modification by words.

    1. Review of function of adjectives.

    2. Review of function of adverbs.

  C. Concept of modification by groups of words (phrases and
clauses).

  D. Concept of subordination.

  E. Clauses.

    1. Recognition and function.

    2. Dependent clauses (spend no time on others, for they
are simple sentences).

      a. Agreement of subject and predicate within clauses.

      b. Placement in sentence.

      c. Punctuation of dependent clauses.

    3. Complex sentence.

  F. Phrases.

    1. Recognition of phrases.

    2. Use of phrases in sentences.

    3. Use of prepositions with phrases. (Teach prepositions
incidentally.) Teach correct use of prepositions with
phrases. No classification. Correct form of pronoun
after preposition.

V. Connective element.

  A. Review compound subject.

B. Review previous connectives taught (those words serving as connection words but not having been called such).

C. Connecting simple sentences and complex sentence thoughts.
  1. Coordinate clauses.
  2. Conjunctions for connection.
    a. Coordinating.
    b. Subordinating.
  3. Punctuation with use of conjunctions to connect simple sentences into compound sentences.
  4. Punctuation of same ideas when conjunctions are omitted.

Third Year

III. Predicate-element concept.
  A. Verb.
    1. Forms and uses of verb "to be."
    2. Tense.
      a. Present perfect.
      b. Past perfect.
    3. Infinitives.
      a. Concept and function.
      b. Pronouns as objects.
      c. Subject of infinitive and abusive splitting of infinitives (expand under modification).
    4. Participle.
      a. Dangling participles.
      b. Pronoun as object of participle. (Teach more in detail under modification.)
    5. Gerunds.
      a. Case of noun or pronoun used with gerund.
      b. Correct use of pronoun as object of gerund.
IV. Modification element.
  A. Clauses.
    1. Dependent clauses.
      a. Modification of other parts of sentence (adjective and adverbial).
      b. Nonrestrictive (pay no attention to restrictive)
        a'. Placement in sentence.

      b′. Punctuation of nonrestrictive clauses and parenthetical expressions.

      c. Inverted order of clauses and their punctuation.

  B. Phrases.

    1. Position of phrases in sentence (adjective and adverbial).

    2. Use of commas when phrases are out of usual order.

Fourth Year

VI. Refinements of expression.

  A. Review the elements previously taught which have been insufficiently understood or not learned.

  B. Sentence structure.

    1. Practice in analysis for correction of errors.

    2. Use of transposed word order for emphasis and variety.

    3. Variation in types and forms of sentences.

    4. Use of conversation and quotations for sentence variety. Punctuation with this.

    5. Use of expletives for sentence variety.

    6. Sentence variety by proper use of active and passive voices—stress active.

    7. Practice in variation in uses of verb forms and in participial and infinitive phrases.

    8. Practice in variation in construction.

    9. Parallel construction.

    10. Practice in subordinating thought elements.

    11. Freakish literary expressions.

  C. Diction.

    1. Imagery and action in word choices of adjectives and adverbs.

    2. Practice in the use of descriptive verbs.

    3. Style as it pertains to grammatical construction, not as it comes from the innate power of expression.

A more specific guide to expressions which are to be corrected as well as to divided usages which can safely be ignored as having become established through acceptance among educated people, is contained in Robert C. Pooley's book, *Teaching English Usage*.[29] Based on such reliable surveys of current English practice as those made by Leonard, Markwardt and Walcott, Fries, and Kennedy,[30] and arranged in terms of the best experimental evidence available concerning grade placement of items, this publication of the National Council of Teachers of English is of inestimable value as an aid in deciding what grammar to teach from the lower elementary grades through high school. For example, the forms (divided usages established by acceptance among large numbers of educated people) which are to receive *no class instruction* in the senior high school are listed in the accompanying outline. In presenting the list, the author comments as follows:

The expressions . . . are either established in present usage or are still in dispute. If the forms are established, there can be no reason for trying to correct them; if they are in dispute, few pupils have time to bother with them. A more favorable attitude toward good English can be created by concentrating attention upon a relatively small number of language forms. A few defects may be cured, but to be told that nearly all of one's language habits are bad is merely discouraging. Although the forms in the following list do not deserve class attention, individuals who inquire about them should certainly be given as accurate information as possible and should be urged to observe how the forms are used. They may be told that an expression is acceptable for colloquial but not for more formal English, that even for colloquial use a given form seems to be preferred, or that no preference can be indicated.

A. Pronouns.
   1. Case forms.
      a. It is me.
      b. Who did you invite?
      c. Who is it for? [1]

[1] For colloquial use the interrogative *who* may be used instead of *whom* unless the pronoun in the sentence follows immediately its verb,

---

[29] Pooley, *op. cit.*, pp. 177–226.

[30] Leonard, *op. cit.*; Markwardt and Walcott, *op cit.*; Fries, *op. cit*; Kennedy, *op. cit.*

  d. I will work with whoever you suggest.
 2. Agreement with antecedent.
  a. They had a bad earthquake in San Francisco last week.
  b. Everyone was here, but they all went home early.[2]
  c. I failed to answer his question, which was thoughtless of me.
  d. If you are going to make a windmill, you need tools.[3]
 3. Unclassified.
  a. They invited my guests and myself.
B. Verbs.
 1. Agreement with subject.[4]
  a. Athletics are stressed in most schools.
  b. The kind of tools you want are hard to find.
  c. Neither of the boys were here.
  d. None were willing to oppose the bill.
 2. Miscellaneous.
  a. I've got to write the letter.
  b. I got home early.
  c. I will probably be at the party.[5]
  d. Will you want this book tonight?
  e. I would go if I were you.
  f. Would you go if I stayed at home?
  g. He said that New York was a large city.[6]

---

verbal, or preposition. The relative *whom* presents practically no problem because of the common tendency to omit the pronoun or to use *that, e.g.,* "a girl I know," "a girl that I know."

[2] The plural pronoun may have a singular antecedent, if in the sentence the pronoun is far removed from its antecedent, especially if the plural idea is very strong. If the pronoun is placed near its antecedent, good usage follows the grammatical rule for agreement, *e.g.,* "Everyone brought his friends."

[3] In informal speech and writing, the indefinite *you* is permissible. It also appears frequently in literary English.

[4] There is an increasing tendency for a verb to agree with the meaning rather than with the form of the subject.

[5] Very little distinction is made between the uses of *shall* and *will* and *should* and *would.* "Shall I?" however, is regarded as being more courteous than "Will I?"

[6] Such attraction to the past tense is common and probably established.

C. Adjectives and adverbs.
  1. It was awfully kind of you to come.
  2. I feel badly.
  3. He ran further than I did.
  4. Most everyone came.
  5. I only have fifty cents.
  6. Come quick.
  7. It is pretty cold today.
  8. The wind is real strong.
  9. You'd better drive slow.
D. Conjunctions and prepositions.
  1. He isn't as old as Henry.
  2. The reason he wrote a poor test was because he was ill.
  3. Arrangements were made to divide the work between the four girls.
  4. I don't know if I can go.
  5. It looks like it would rain.
  6. I tried to swing the racket like you do.[7]
E. Miscellaneous.
  1. Try and finish the work on time.
  2. What was the reason for Henry objecting? [8]
  3. He tried to thoroughly understand the problem.[9]

[7] *Like* for *as* or *as if* is generally permitted in conversation and informal writing but not for formal use.

[8] Either the possessive or accusative case of a noun seems to be accepted before a gerund. The accusative case of a pronoun in this position is open to dispute.

[9] The split infinitive is permissible except when the use of it produces an awkward construction.

How Can Contradictions Be Avoided?

The fallacy of infallible rules. In the light of the circumstances governing linguistic change, an important requisite to successful instruction in English is acceptance of the fact that language is too fluid to permit of classification on the basis of fixed, invariable rules. Although it might be well, for example, to examine a long sentence to see if a semicolon or two would assist a reader in absorbing the meaning of its several coordinate clauses, surely no one would insist on setting off with semicolons the three clauses of Caesar's famous remark, *Veni, vidi, vici*—I came, I saw, I conquered.

Again, it might be well to avoid tiring people with a monotonous type of sentence pattern in which everything is loosely tacked together with "and" like the prefabricated sections of a henhouse. An absolute injunction against the use of *and* at the beginning of a sentence, however, would require that we suppress the King James Version of the Book of Matthew; for in it, as Professor Pooley has pointed out, almost every sentence begins in this way, and we have it on the very best of authority that the translation is in none other than the King's English! Certainly the only tenable position in cases of this kind is that which cautions against the overuse of "and," or *any other word, phrase, or sentence pattern,* when the speaker or writer has no special reason for repeating it, such as he might have were he consciously striving for a particular effect.

The impossibility of imputing goodness and badness, or absolute correctness and incorrectness to language apart from a specific, real-life situation becomes apparent on comparing the seemingly contradictory standards of usage to which the natives of different foreign countries subscribe. In French, for example, the redundant use of the pronoun, as in *Votre frère est-il plus âgé que vous?* (Your brother is he older than you?) is considered highly desirable in questions that have a noun as subject. Again, even the most illiterate Frenchman would never think of saying "It's I" (*C'est je!*). The one and only acceptable form in French is *C'est moi* (It's me!).

In view of these facts, appropriateness to social needs and circumstances would seem to be the only criterion tenable universally as a basis for judging language usage. Although this criterion does not give language teaching the same authoritarian security as the doctrine of absolute correctness and incorrectness, it does not lead to absurdity when applied to specific situations. Moreover, it can easily be translated into a practical program of effective classroom instruction as indicated in the following chapter.

For Further Reading

Fries, Charles C., *American English Grammar*. New York: Appleton-Century-Crofts, Inc., 1940.

Fries, Charles C., *What Is Good English?* Ann Arbor, Mich.: C. C. Fries, 1940.

Greene, Harry A., "Direct versus Formal Methods in Elementary English," *Elementary English*, 24 (May, 1947), 273–285.

Kaulfers, Walter Vincent, *Four Studies in Teaching Grammar from the Socio-psychological Viewpoint*. Stanford University, Calif.: Stanford University Bookstore, 1945.

Leonard, Sterling A., *Current English Usage*. Chicago: National Council of Teachers of English, 1932.

Marckwardt, Albert H., and Fred Walcott, *Facts about Current Usage*. New York: Appleton-Century-Crofts, Inc., 1938.

Pooley, Robert C., *Grammar and Usage in Textbooks on English*. Bureau of Educational Research Bulletin, No. 14. Madison: University of Wisconsin Press, 1933.

Pooley, Robert C., *Teaching English Usage*. New York: Appleton-Century-Crofts, Inc., 1946.

Pooley, Robert C., "Where Are We At?" *The English Journal*, 39 (November, 1950), 496–504.

Smith, Dora V., "English Grammar Again!" *The English Journal*, 27 (October, 1938), 643–649.

Symonds, Percival M., "Practice versus Grammar in the Learning of Correct English Usage," *Journal of Educational Psychology*, 22 (February, 1931), 81–95.

Thomas, Charles Swain, *The Teaching of English in the Secondary School*, pp. 34–39. Boston: Houghton Mifflin Company, 1917.

Chapter 4. HOW TO TEACH GRAMMAR AND USAGE

ESSENTIALS OF A PROGRAM OF SPEECH IMPROVEMENT

Diagnosis. The first step is always diagnosis of the pupils' strengths and weaknesses in language to avoid spending time and energy on the correction of difficulties which, while common among young people in general, are not always common to more than a minority of a particular class. Objective usage tests are of value in this connection, but since individuals are always on guard in such situations, the scores may not yield a true picture of the pupils' actual language habits. They may measure only their impressions of what they think other people want them to say.

Confirmation. The second step, therefore, involves validating the findings of the diagnostic test to determine to what extent the concepts of normative usage registered thereon actually represent the examinees' own personal use of language outside the English class or testing situation. Since it is seldom practical to follow any sizable number of students around the playground or into the home, opportunities for observing their language habits in informal situations are more easily provided in the classroom. Free discussion of topics close to pupil interests, such as hobbies, pets, favorite radio programs, or interesting personalities in the field of sports, usually afford opportunities to observe and tabulate points of strength and weakness in oral usage, while short autobiographies often yield symptoms of such difficulties in punctuation, capitalization, spelling, vocabulary, paragraphing, or usage, as commonly enter into composition.

Validation on the basis of "first things first." Having secured a list of difficulties common to the class as a whole, or to small groups within it, the teacher is ready to take the third step, *viz.,* comparing the difficulties of her own group with the list of unacceptable usages that in terms of the best available consensus deserve replacement at this particular age and grade level. Naturally, those speech habits which represent the most extreme departure from the norm and are most typical of the class as a whole will receive the highest priority in the order and amount of attention given them in group work. Without a valid basis for putting first things first, instruction in English runs the risk either of attempting too much at one time, or of spending too much time on relatively unimportant details. If a comparison of the scores on the diagnostic test with the teacher's diagnosis shows that the students at least suspect what forms of speech are preferable to others for general use, but obviously do not act in conformity with their better judgment, the problem becomes one of building effective language habits, and not primarily one of learning grammatical terminology or classification. This point is important, for the world is full of proof that neither knowledge nor skill of itself compels action.

Motivation of the transfer of training. If, on the other hand, a comparison of the results of the diagnostic test with the teacher's own observations shows that a large majority neither recognizes effective usage nor practices it, the need is for developing, simultaneously, insight into what constitutes effective English, and the desire to use it on all appropriate occasions. Since almost every group consists of some young people who know better, but don't act like it, and of a considerable number who *don't* know any better *and* act like it, this is the usual situation in all but the more highly selective schools. The fourth step, therefore, involves devising and carrying out plans for helping needy young people gain insight into what is considered standard English in pronunciation, vocabulary, spelling, capitalization, punctuation, and sentence structure, and to develop the habit of applying what they learn, not only when they are under observation in school, but in all life situations where standard English is the most appropriate and effective form of language.

In devising such plans, it is well to bear in mind that habitual and extreme departures from normative usage can usually be traced to a very limited, and often severely underprivileged, language environment in the home or neighborhood. The language habits that young people bring to school reflect the language of almost everyone with whom they come into most frequent contact—including, very often, their parents, relatives, neighbors, and friends. For this reason, only mental barriers, or lines of cleavage between the teacher and the group, are likely to be created if the attitude toward language is one that casts humiliating reflections upon the young people, their parents, relatives, or friends. The result may even be retaliation with a dislike for English or for the teacher, or both. In such cases the task of instruction can obviously become weighted with difficulties, and at times unpleasant for all concerned. For this reason it would seem preferable to approach the problem from the viewpoint of helping young people acquire a varied and serviceable wardrobe in language, especially one that will enable them to feel both at ease and effective in other language situations than those of intimate personal acquaintance. In school we use standard English, not because of any inherent superiority, but simply because we cannot be effective citizens, wage earners, or professional people in a country of this size, unless we all subscribe to an easily understood, common medium of communication that will enable us as Americans to speak or write in Seattle and still be readily understood in Los Angeles, Honolulu, London, or New York. We do this partly as an indispensable responsibility of modern citizenship, partly for our own good in securing and filling desirable positions, and always as a civic courtesy practiced by people who have had the advantages of schooling. We do this because we do not confuse democracy with the cult of mediocrity in speech or manner.

Extension of the area of language experience. If the pupils' language environment has been so underprivileged or restricted, however, that they cannot distinguish between normative and nonnormative language, it is possible that they will see little need for supplementing speech habits that are perfectly intelligible and acceptable to almost everyone whom they meet outside of school. In such cases, enrichment of language experiences with opportunities to hear standard English, and with life situations in which such English is clearly the most appropriate, becomes essential both in developing insight into what constitutes standard English and in building a desire to use it one's self. Recordings by competent actors of stories, short plays, or abridged novels from the pens of well-known modern authors provide excellent means for interesting young people in the effective use of oral English in modern life. Among such recordings are Ronald Colman's interpretation of *Lost Horizon* and *Tales from the Olympian Gods*, and Herbert Marshall's moving rendition of *The Snow Goose*.[1]

Many modern recordings are useful also in relating English to other interests, such as world literature or music, that deserve encouragement in school. For example, Joseph Machlis'[2] anecdotal biographies of Schubert, Beethoven, and Tchaikovsky, beautifully illustrated with excerpts from their better known works, can serve not only to supply models of effective usage in pronunciation and grammar but also to link the study of English with good taste in that more universal form of intuitive or emotional communication called the language of music. Such recordings can also provide models for radioscripts, musically illustrated biographies and stories, or dramatizations of the community's history, that the

---

[1] Ronald Colman, *Lost Horizon* by James Hilton, Decca Records, Album No. DA-402; *Tales from the Olympian Gods*, Decca Records, Album No. DA-475. Herbert Marshall, *The Snow Goose* by Paul Gallico, Decca Album No. DA-386.

[2] Joseph Machlis, *Music Master Series*, Vox Records, Vox Productions, Inc.

group may later wish to produce, under guidance, as a means for securing practice in writing and speaking for an audience —another class, a club, a parent group, or a school assembly.[3]

Selected radio programs, where these are conveniently available during the class hour, can naturally serve much the same purposes. In any case, committees charged with keeping the group informed concerning programs available during out-of-school hours, and with acting as a board of listeners to review the broadcasts for the group, deserve a place in every English class, not only as aids in broadening and deepening language experiences but also as means for promoting good taste in radio listening habits.

Appropriate talking pictures are still another aid wherever the school is equipped to use them conveniently. Even more valuable and convincing, however, are speakers representing the ablest talent that the community has to offer as examples of the vocations and professions which the members of the class profess a desire to enter. In such cases, the need for writing effective letters of invitation, for exercising good taste in welcoming, introducing, and thanking the speakers, and for following up their visits with appropriate notes of appreciation approved by the class, all help to give both knowledge and practice in standard English a practical motivation. Discussion periods following the talks afford additional opportunities for practice in asking worth-while questions that have been thought out and phrased beforehand.

Provision of audience situations. Inasmuch as opportunities that enable young people not only to hear effective English, but also to practice it, are more valuable than those affording only opportunities for passive experience, the organization of the learning program in terms of motivating activities in audience situations is always desirable. Such situations generally include writing intelligent letters of apprecia-

[3] Holland D. Roberts, Walter V. Kaulfers, and Grayson N. Kefauver, *English for Social Living*, Chaps. XII, XVI (1942), and *Foreign Languages and Cultures in American Education*, Chaps. III, V, IX (1943). New York: McGraw-Hill Book Company, Inc.

tion or suggestion to those artists of the radio, stage, or screen whose stellar ratings depend to some extent upon mail from audiences; sending notes of condolence to ailing classmates; carrying on correspondence with young people in other parts of the country or abroad concerning topics of mutual group interest; interviewing adults in class or at home regarding unusual hobbies, experiences, or achievements; staging play readings; giving newscasts; presenting illustrated talks on imaginary travels (perhaps with the aid of a balopticon or delineascope for showing pictures obtained from friends or secondhand magazines); or producing radio dramatizations of some aspect of the community's history or achievements. The guiding principle is always helping young people "find something interesting and worth while to say and building an audience situation which will give them reasons for saying it." [4]

In material prepared for audiences, errors will occur, but they will far more often be symptoms of insecurely fixed language habits or of undeveloped insights, than of flagrant carelessness. In such circumstances few people deliberately misrepresent themselves in public. Moreover, motivating audience situations help at least to stimulate, even if they do not always inspire, effective writing and speech. After all, few young people can long take a genuine interest in learning to speak and write well if the only real destination for their efforts is the wastebasket after a grade has been recorded in the roll book. The grade book and wastebasket seldom inspire greater learning than the fact that "if you write big and leave lots of margin, your paper will look longer."

Although anticipation of an audience response serves to stimulate language learning and to discourage careless handwriting, spelling, punctuation, and usage, it obviously cannot correct departures from standard English if the pupils have no basis for knowing what the most appropriate forms

[4] Holland D. Roberts, "English Teachers Face the Future," *The English Journal* (College Edition), 27 (February, 1938), 101–113.

should be. The need for giving young people models and criteria by which to guide their writing and speech, therefore, requires that instruction be provided in what is commonly known as grammar. In the sense that every language teacher attempts to bring his pupils' speech and writing into conformity with the norms of effective current usage, every teacher of language teaches grammar. Indeed, it is impossible to be against such instruction, for the very obvious reason that one of the commonest meanings of the term is usage in conformity with accepted norms, as in the sentence "His *grammar* is bad."

NONTECHNICAL METHODS OF IMPROVING USAGE

Therapeutic procedures in language teaching. Inasmuch as we can do little to alter the life behavior of language nor change by one iota the fundamental limitations of human minds, our most promising alternative in teaching, as in the profession of medicine, is a continuous quest for more economical and effective procedures. Indeed, therapeutic practice in language teaching, as in all areas of education, might profit considerably from observing how the ablest practitioners of one of our most highly trained and respected professions go about securing improvements in human beings. The first step is always a careful diagnosis to determine the exact cause of difficulty and the probable extent to which it can be removed within a given period of time. Only after careful diagnosis is a special course of therapy undertaken, modified always to suit the individual's particular condition. Even after treatment has begun, there is not the slightest hesitancy about reducing, increasing, or abandoning a particular prescription or course of therapy if it fails to produce the desired result. That is because the real value of a particular remedy or operative procedure is never regarded as residing in the medicine or technique, but in its *effect upon the individual.* The fact that one person may not be helped so much as another by penicillin, for example, does not cause the physician to brand the one patient as superior and the other as beneath consideration. At the same time he can usually distinguish between real needs and malingering, and between external symptoms and internal causes.

Today the failure of an individual to respond to a certain treatment rarely causes an able physician to give up in despair and abandon the case; for his practice is no longer limited, as it was two centuries ago, to a few patent medicines for everything, or to one standard cure—usually bloodletting —for everyone. Let it be noted, too, that the modern physician is concerned always with securing definite, specific improvements in the individual, not with teaching him a course in the theory of medicine. He does not insist that his clientele first master the basic essentials and technical terminology of the profession before they can receive help. Indeed, despite the vast nomenclature of his practice and the rigorous scientific training that it involves, he can talk to his clientele in their own language. Perhaps, as Dr. Luella Cook has observed, that is because he has had time to digest his learning and therefore does not have to give it back exactly as he took it in.[5] Perhaps, too, it is because, if he is a good man rather than a charlatan or quack, he is more concerned with helping human beings than with impressing them with the mysteries of his art.

Grammar books as reference aids. The teaching of language usage might gain much by adopting similar procedures in working with young people. The suggestion implies reserving technical vocabularies and specialized grammatical procedures as convenient professional tools for use only by licensed specialists in language, and cultivating, as does a good physician or lawyer, the ability to talk to our clientele, directly in language that is readily comprehensible to them. Its implementation requires that the building of effective language habits, in the order of their importance, be made

[5] Luella B. Cook, "Teaching Grammar and Usage in Relation to Speech and Writing," *Elementary English Review,* 23 (May, 1946), 193–198, 213.

the constant concern of our teaching, rather than mastery of the theory, classification, and nomenclature of language on a professional or semiprofessional level. So conceived, the teaching of usage does not regard grammars as teaching or learning aids, nor as textbooks, but as authoritative *reference* books, like etymological dictionaries or technical encyclopedias, to be consulted primarily by teachers, and by such advanced students as are definitely preparing to become teachers, grammarians, philologists, lexicographers, linguisticians, proofreaders, or editors. With the help of these suggestions, many unnecessary difficulties surrounding the teaching of English can be avoided. An example of the way in which a teacher can unconsciously create her own "problems" deserves consideration here.

An example of "futilitarianism." Not long ago, an outstanding graduate student, serving as interne in a public secondary school, invited the supervisor to observe her practice teaching in an unselected ninth-grade English class numbering thirty-four boys and girls. The subject of the day's work was the use of the comma as treated in a combination grammar and exercise book. During the discussion of sentences based on the grammatically phrased rules, it became apparent that at least 90 per cent of the group could not distinguish between the use of the word *for* as a preposition and its use as a conjunction. Consequently, few were able to apply the rule that "clauses introduced by the conjunction *for* must be preceded by a comma." As a result, they were putting commas before the preposition in such sentences as "We were waiting for the postman to arrive," and leaving them out in such sentences as "We left after the third act for it was getting late." In other words, the rule and the practice exercises assigned the day before had not helped to improve the pupils' command of written English. Instead, they had actually taught young people to make mistakes!

As a Phi Beta Kappan, well disciplined in advanced courses in English, the student teacher had no trouble locating the apparent source of the difficulty. Obviously, the pupils did not know their grammar. To get them to use a comma before "clauses introduced by the conjunction *for*" thus inevitably meant reviewing the grammatical meanings of preposition, conjunction, and clause. A more discouraging exhibition of well-intentioned "futilitarianism" could hardly be imagined. Although some students could repeat previously memorized definitions quite adequately, few could give examples of what they were talking about. Most students could not recall the definitions accurately, much less offer clear-cut, relevant examples, despite the fact that they had passed tests on all these things in previous grades.

To prevent depressing periods of prolonged silence, the teacher tried to prod their memories by recalling the grammatical definitions herself, and then asking members of the class to repeat them. At this point, the performance, with its dense concentration of grammatical terms, began to suggest the incantations of a voodoo doctor performing rites over the body of the great departed—in this case, the comma "before clauses introduced by the conjunction f-o-r," since by now the original subject of the meeting—the comma—had indeed been lost somewhere among the grammatical labels.

The low point of the performance came during the analysis of the term *clause*. To enable the group to understand the grammatical difference between such expressions as "for the postman to arrive" (which do not require commas) and "for it was getting late," proved an altogether superhuman task. The expression "for the postman to arrive" contained a noun, "postman," that seemed a good enough subject; and it contained a verb "arrive," that even some of the better pupils were perfectly willing to accept as a predicate. Why, therefore, wasn't it a clause? And "Why," asked one of the more precocious youngsters, recalling what had provoked this involved discussion, "Why shouldn't you put a comma before it like the rule says?"

By this time, the teacher, despite her Phi Beta Kappa key, her advanced graduate work in English, her own mastery of formal grammar, and her desire to teach, was at her wits' end.

In fact, a considerable number of pupils had already given up trying to follow the discussion and were seeking relief from boredom, or from their own feelings of inferiority, by acting smart or amusing themselves with irrelevant, distracting conversation. Only the final bell saved the teacher and class from a fate worse than pseudoprogressive education.

A practical alternative for grammatical nomenclature. A few days later, after the young people had been afforded some opportunity to forget their unfortunate experience by transferring their attention to reading, the practice teacher, on advice from her supervisor, wrote on the front board a list of unpunctuated sentences, some of them containing the preposition *for,* and the remainder, the word *for* used as a conjunction. Alongside the list she wrote the statement, "Whenever the word *for* means *because* inside a sentence, put a comma (,) in front of it." With the aid of this simple, unpretentious statement, the group were able to punctuate the entire list of sentences correctly within less than five minutes, and then to write correct examples of their own invention. The most retarded girl in the class did not feel tempted to put a comma in the sentence, "He was waiting for his father to come home," for the simple reason that the word *because* would not make sense here. All of this was accomplished in a very few minutes—almost at a glance—without the use of the term *preposition, conjunction,* or *clause,* and without the slightest risk of losing either the morale of the group or the comma itself under a stack of elusive labels. The procedure simply did not assume that specific language difficulties require generalized therapy any more than a simple headcold requires a semiprofessional course in medicine on the part of a patient.

If no danger of bringing back unpleasant recollections of frustration had existed, the practice teacher might have been advised to conclude this phase of the work with the comma by adding parenthetically, "When *for* can be taken to mean *because,* it is a *conjunction;* in most other cases it is a *preposition.*" By so doing, she would have used the grammatical terms more in keeping with their real function as labels for reference purposes, and also have paid her respects to those parents and teachers who cannot conceive of English teaching apart from its professional nomenclature. By so doing she would also have enabled any student to feel at home in any company—he would then feel just as much at ease on social visits with the most conservative professors of language in later life as any students taught by the most formal method. At a tea or dinner he, too, could do his part to keep the conversation from fainting by fanning up little conversational breezes with such questions as "Professor Post, what progress are you making in restoring the imperfect subjunctive to its rightful place in American English in elliptical dependent clauses contrary to fact?"

Formal grammar as the easiest method. The case just described illustrates a few of the means for replacing formal methods in developing effective usage with more direct, economical, and efficient procedures, quite without denying the utility of formal grammar to teachers and specialists in language as convenient means for professional intercommunication among themselves, or as tools of linguistic classification and research. The case illustrates the very obvious fact that while grammatical terminology, diagraming, parsing, and formal sentence analysis are (and should be) easy for people who earn their living as linguisticians, they are hardly easy for pupils who need help most; and it is probably the latter, as the presumable beneficiaries of instruction in English, who ought to have the final say regarding what is hard and what is not. Adult specialists are much too prone to fall into what Edgar Dale has called the COIK fallacy—Clear Only If Known. The traditional contention that rules and procedures phrased in the professional language of the grammarian are in the long run the easiest way to learn a language is assuredly only half true: true where the truth counts least, and consistently false in the very situations where the truth should count most. It is absolutely true only if the teacher has no other resources at her disposal for treating problems of usage.

When this is the case, the methodology of formal grammar must obviously be, not just the easiest way, but also the one and the *only* way. But in such cases, is not the teacher in much the same position as the physician of old whose limited resources at one time forced him to rely on bloodletting as a cure for almost everything?

Formal grammar as a strictly professional tool. Without denying that the terminology of linguistic science is of great convenience to teachers as members of a licensed profession, cannot teachers prevent it from increasing resistance to learning by using it only as a set of labels for reference purposes after having achieved the language outcomes desired? In the suburban community where this is written, the housewives often take great pride in preserving the fruits that grow in such abundance in the vicinity. They do not begin their canning season by looking up the Latin names for the peaches, pears, prunes, and apricots that they have in mind to preserve. On no occasion have they been known to label their jars before they are sure that they have something in them that will keep. Neither has any housewife ever been known to insist that the contents of the jars with labels taste better than the contents of those without. Cannot the use of grammatical labels be regarded with the same elementary common sense? After all, is not helping people to live more effectively in this world more important than just developing a classroom vocabulary in it?

Usage guide for the double negative. Obviously, an approach suitable for teaching one use of the comma is not always appropriate in teaching another. The problem is always one of analyzing the specific language difficulty, of selecting the particular procedures that are uniquely appropriate in treating it, and of realizing always that some students may respond better to one device and others to another. In general, most problems of language usage can be handled in one of four nontechnical ways. Where the situation involves two sets of linguistic facts, such as negatives vs. positives in sentences like "He never gave me none neither(!)," we can use the usage-guide method by simply writing on the board (for transfer later into the pupils' notebooks) a brief reference outline stating

After	*We say*
hardly	anybody
never	anyhow
no(ne)	anyway
not (n't)	anywhere
nothing	ever
scarcely	any

Then we may have the students change sentences on the board that have been quoted directly from their own writing or speech, using the usage guide as a kind of dictionary. Since *none* and *neither* come after *never* in the sentence "He never gave me none neither," we replace them with the words *any* and *either*, not because the words are called positives or negatives, nor because a textbook tells us to avoid double negatives, but because that is the customary way effective writers and speakers use English by common consent, much as football players have agreed on six points for a touchdown rather than four or forty. We do not mislead young people into believing that we talk and write in certain ways because of what words are called in a grammar; for the truth is that "languages have come into being, and great literature has been written in them, long before a grammar or a prosody was ever thought of."

If a workbook containing sentences phrased in language that the young people will recognize at once as being typical of their own is conveniently available, we may work out just enough exercises to help them clarify the conception in their minds. If not, we may have to supply additional practice sentences, on the board or in duplicated form; for there is no better way to waste time than to ask students to change sentences which they themselves would never think of writing or saying. Unless the students recognize the language of the practice exercises as their own, the carry-over of the work into their personal, independent use of language is destined to be small because of their failure to see any connection between the two.

Use of practice exercises. All work with prephrased exercises, however, may well be limited to the bare amount needed to develop ability to use the usage guide as a kind of dictionary. In order to fix a particular usage in their own speech habits, we would do well to rely for practice more on the composition of short illustrative sentences or questions by the pupils themselves. For example, we may say, "Now let's see if each of us can write ten good questions of our own to prove that we know when to use *never-ever, none-any, nowhere-somewhere,* and the rest of the words in the outline. Then let's try out the questions on each other."

This culminating step can provide oral practice and also furnish an appropriate setting for a group evaluation of the questions later. For variety, the procedure can even be turned into a kind of game simply by setting a time limit. The winner then becomes the person or team that has the most sentences done correctly when time is called. The big point is that no one has ever acquired independent ability in writing or speech merely by doing *other* people's exercises, or reworking *other* people's language, for such practice too often reduces the learner to the level of a ventriloquist dummy— and ventriloquist dummies cannot perform except in the immediate presence of a master voice.

Confusion of past participles with past tense forms. The approach used in dealing with the double negative can also be applied, with minor modifications, to the confusion of past participles with past tense forms in sentences like "We sung a new song," and to almost any other situations arising from the confusion of two or more sets of language elements. In the case of *sang* vs. *sung, did* vs. *done,* and the like, our usage guide might say, "After forms of *to have* and *to be,* we say *sung, done, run, seen,* or *come;* otherwise we say *sang, did, ran, saw,* or *came.*" The list can be expanded to cover all the difficulties noted in the pupils' own writing and speech. If the expressions *to have* and *to be* are too vague, the forms themselves—since they are only twelve—can easily be listed in the summary.

Pronouns as objects of prepositions. Again, if the textbook in current use contains such a rule as, "Personal pronouns that are governed by a preposition must be in the objective case," we may supply a usage guide saying,

After	We say
to	me
for	him
of	her
by	them
with	us
between	whom
but (except)	

For example, It's a secret between *him* and *her.*

Nobody saw it but *her* and *me.*
Are you going with *me* or *them?*

Although more prepositions may be included in the left-hand column, the seven that are already listed will take care of all common errors.

Obviously, only a teacher more interested in covering the grammar than in helping young people would ever introduce the topic *unless* the students' own speech revealed serious difficulties with the use of pronouns following a preposition.

If any precocious student should inquire, "Why do you have to say *me* after *between?*" the answer would come closest to the truth if we simply said, "It is a custom that leaders in language have agreed to make a rule of, much as leaders in football have agreed on six points for a touchdown rather than sixteen or sixty." Surely, such an answer as, "because personal pronouns governed by a preposition must be governed by the objective case," would not explain the reason *why* at all. The alert student could still ask, "*Why* do personal pronouns governed by a preposition have to be in the objective case?" Fortunately for teachers of formal grammar, most

normal people do not indulge in such grammatical grandilo-
quence.

Inasmuch as usage guides of this kind are intelligible to
anyone with the reading ability of a fourth grader, they can
be supplied to parents interested in guiding their children's
speech. Needless to say, such cooperation would be difficult
for most parents if the materials involved several pages of
explanations concerning the use of the "past participle after
auxiliary verbs in compound tenses, in the passive voices in
elliptical passive constructions, and as participial adjectives."

The Meaning Approach to Usage

Transitive and intransitive verbs. Confusions involving so-
called transitive and intransitive verbs, like *sit* and *set,* or *lie*
and *lay,* can usually be resolved simply by helping young
people gain insight into the real meanings of the individual
verb forms. This procedure might be called the synonym
method, though the term "meaning approach" is entirely
adequate. It has already been illustrated in the discussion of
the comma before the word *for* when it can be taken to mean
because. The usage guide in such cases may become a kind
of alphabetical dictionary of near synonyms for testing the
real meaning in specific cases, with the aid of such nontechnical explanations as:

We say *laid* when we mean *placed,* as in "He laid (placed)
it on the table."

We say *lying* when we mean *telling a lie* or *resting,* as in
"The book is lying (resting) on the table."

For the confusion of *sit* with *set,* the guide may read as
follows:

Usage Guide for Sit and Set

1. sat . . . (was, were, been) seated.
   They have sat (been seated) there for two hours.
2. set . . . put, place, hatch (eggs), go (went) down.
   The sun set (went down).

3. setting . . . putting, placing, hatching (eggs), going down.
   The hens are setting (hatching eggs).
4. sit . . . (to) be seated.
   You may sit (be seated) here.
5. sit out . . . remain (stay) seated during.
   Let's sit out (remain seated during) this dance.
6. sitting . . . seated.
   What was he doing sitting (seated) there?

The procedure from here on is very much the same as that indicated for the previously mentioned usage guides. The aim is never verbatim memorization of the lists, but absorption of their content directly into the learners' own language habits through reference to them in testing their own writing or speech in doubtful cases, much as intelligent people use dictionaries to reassure themselves concerning the spelling, meaning, or pronunciation of words. Although the labels *transitive* and *intransitive* can be added in parenthesis alongside the definitions, their use would contribute nothing to the utility of the guide and might even sidetrack the classwork from active practice in the language itself into that unprofitable form of erudite shovel-leaning and academic leaf-raking that at one time characterized so much pretentious busywork in the teaching of the language arts. A good teacher is no more concerned with technical labels when her young people still say "Him and me ain't never seen it," or write fragmentary or garbled sentences, than a good physician is concerned with a patient's mosquito bites when he is obviously suffering from a severe case of malnutrition. A good teacher knows that all the hens in America, as well as the sun, the moon, and the stars will continue to *set,* and that millions of young people will continue to *sit* dances out, without the slightest concern as to whether their behavior is transitive or intransitive. *A secure profession never confuses pretentiousness with scholarship.*

Specific versus generalized methodology. But how shall young people be taught to use complex or compound sentences effectively if they are not sure even of a subject or predicate, not to mention such things as relative pronouns, prepositional phrases, or subordinating conjunctions? Here, as elsewhere, the first step is always diagnosis of the specific need that is to be served. This means finding out exactly what it is that we wish to accomplish—not in general, but in a particular case: to develop ability to use commas with non-restrictive clauses? to avoid sentence fragments? to make straggly, overloaded sentences more effective by learning ways to subordinate minor qualifying elements? We do not aim at everything at once. We locate a particular target and change our aim as the target moves.

Sentence-pattern methods. If the specific need, for example, is ability to write more intelligible and effective definitions, we assume that models of different varieties of definitions may be essential as guides. We may then complete sentences, modeled after the definitions, from which essential parts have been left out. This preliminary imitative practice soon enables students to write acceptable definitions of their own. During a group evaluation of the definitions later, no one says that a sentence is poor because an adjectival or adverbial modifier is misplaced. Instead, he calls attention to the fact that the meaning is blurred, confusing, or misleading, or the wording so muddy that we have to wade through the sentence or to reread it several times. Improvement then takes place by comparing the sentence with its closest desirable model, and changing it until the wording parallels that of the closest example. Dr. Luella Cook has discussed this method in convincing detail in the May, 1946, issue of the *Elementary English Review.* Dr. A. I. Roehm of George Peabody College for Teachers has developed similar sentence-pattern techniques for use in both elementary and secondary schools, and even in college foreign language.

The question test for sentence fragments. What can be done, however, in the case of those young people who cannot even tell the difference between a fragment and a completely stated thought? In such cases, if their insight into language is too limited to enable them to learn from contrasting examples, it is certain that no superimposition of grammatical terminology or formal analytical procedures will do more than induce frustration and resistance to learning. Difficulties of the type involved here may be the result of a variety of different factors, not of any one general cause. Successful teaching, therefore, depends upon accurate diagnosis of the particular difficulty: Are a student's sentence fragments attributable to the fact that he uses periods where he should use commas? If so, the remedy lies in helping him gain insight into the difference between the use of the period as a kind of stop sign at language intersections, and of the comma as a kind of caution signal. Reading his paper aloud exactly as it is punctuated often suffices to indicate both the difficulty and the simplest way to remedy it.

Or are a student's sentence fragments attributable to undeveloped ability to visualize an audience? Does he fail to put down on paper all that he really has in mind, perhaps because he wrongly assumes that, everything being perfectly clear to him, others will readily understand? When this is the case, no mere definition of a sentence as "a complete thought" will obviously be of much help. Whatever he writes *is* a complete thought in his own mind; otherwise, he would not write it as such! The need, then, is for experience in writing for audiences and witnessing their reactions. Without ability to visualize a reader or listener to whom we are trying to make things clear, speaking and writing are seldom effective but often deadening for lack of incentive or motivation. Only by learning to imagine ourselves in the presence of a real audience can we learn to write and speak well. In fact, without a reader or listener, speech has very little excuse for being. Even in personal diaries there is an audience—the author himself a week, month, year, or forty years later.

Occasionally, when ability to imagine a reader is almost pathologically retarded, a simple self-test for sentence fragments may be helpful when other devices fail. This test assumes that *a completely stated sentence can be regarded as the answer to an imaginary question and contains the*

wording of the question inside it. The test, then, is to see
whether or not we can form a question out of what has been
written by *changing always the position of the first word*
so that it will not come at the beginning or end of the statement. For example:

> *Today* is Tuesday. Is *today* Tuesday?
> *He* was here when I arrived. Was *he* here when I arrived?

When a thought is completely stated, as in the examples just
given, the question formed by *changing always the position
of the first word* will sound perfectly acceptable. In the case
of fragments like "When I was young," however, a question
will either be *impossible to form by changing only the position of the first word,* or sound awkward or forced, as in such
strained efforts to beat the test as "I was young; when?(!)"

Note that beyond changing always the position of the
first word, the question test permits of no other changes
except the use of the more emphatic *do(n't)*, *does(n't)* or
did(n't) forms of the action word. For example, to the fragment, "When I was young," we might add "I played (did
play) baseball." The question test would then easily give us
either "Was I young when I played baseball?" or "Did I play
baseball when I was young?" Either question would show
that we have finally achieved a completely stated thought in
"When I was young, I played (did play) baseball."

In a few very exceptional cases involving colloquial or
idiomatic usage, the test may require matching the question
and answer to see if they make sense together. For example,

> *Fragment:* On going home.
> *Question:* Going on home?
> *Test:* Going on home? On going home (!).

Since the reply, "on going home," does not answer the
question in any relevant way, it is a fragment, and something
must be added to it in order to convert it into a completely
stated sentence. This refinement of the test should not be

introduced unless a very specific need for it arises from fragments written by the pupils themselves in their own compositions.

The question test for clauses. The concept of the question test is of considerable value in enabling young people to distinguish between clauses and phrases, especially in relation to punctuation. The following paragraph illustrates its application to the punctuation desired (but rarely achieved) from the study of such rules as "a dependent or subordinate clause which introduces a sentence is set off from the independent clause by a comma."

A group of words that makes a sentence by the question test is usually set off from the rest of the sentence by a comma (,) if the group of words comes right after *if, when, while, although, since, because.* . . .

For example, in the following model, the group of words in parentheses ( ) is a sentence by the question test. Since this group of words comes right after the word *if*, a comma (,) is placed at the end of the group, like this:

If (*I had the time*), *I would go to Europe this year.*

Other key words that commonly introduce "dependent clauses" followed by commas when they begin a sentence can be included in the list as desired. Only one caution need be emphasized in this connection: Schools and textbooks tend to stress overpunctuation. If a school-written composition of 250 to 350 words were published in a magazine or book, correctly punctuated according to all the textbook rules, the printed page would look as if it had the measles. Although editors and publishers are by no means agreed on the details of punctuation, the tendency is to use punctuation marks only where required to assist the reader in grasping the meaning readily. As in other cases involving instruction in usage, examination of various types of effectively punctuated sentences, followed by practice in writing and evaluating sentences written in close imitation of the models, is a more direct and effective way of developing ability in punctuation than the study of grammatically phrased rules or diagraming.

The thought approach in sentence building. Although many pupils can learn to write and punctuate complete sentences correctly, their composition may still show the need for guidance in such matters as coordination and subordination of ideas in clauses or phrases. That "the thought approach" has definitely proved its superiority over the conventional grammar approach in such cases has already been indicated in a previous connection. In her article, "Grammar Approach versus Thought Approach in Teaching Sentence Structure," Ellen Frogner illustrates the method with the following examples: [6]

A primary aim in the first unit was to make pupils conscious of the fact that a mature speaker or writer reveals the exact relationship between ideas. Pupils using the thought method began by noting that a sentence like "Mary plays a good game of tennis, and she makes excellent cake" is not good because the two statements about Mary are hardly related in thought. The class suggested a second idea which would be related to the first, as, for instance, "Mary plays a good game of tennis, and she is also a true sportsman." It was noticed that "and" was used correctly here since one idea was added to another, both of the ideas being closely related and equal in importance. The next step was to have the pupils volunteer with similar sentences, noting words suitable as substitutes for "and". . . .

Another common error occurs in the use of "is when" and "is where" in definitions: "To portage is when you carry canoes and provisions from one lake to another." Instead of pointing out the mistake of an adverbial clause used as a noun (as was done in the grammar classes), pupils taught by the thought method reasoned that "to portage" is not "when" or time, but "to portage" is "to carry." They noted also the parallelism and balance of the second part of the sentence with the first. . . .

. . . a composition contained such statements as the following: "Mr. White is our adviser. He grasped the seriousness of the situa-

___

[6] Ellen Frogner, "Grammar Approach versus Thought Approach in Teaching Sentence Structure," *The English Journal,* 27 (September, 1939), 518–526.

tion. He immediately called a meeting of the officers." How could the ideas be combined to avoid the monotonous childish sentences? Several possibilities were suggested, one of which was: "Having grasped the seriousness of the situation, Mr. White, our class adviser, immediately called a meeting of the officers." Pupils improved the expression of thought by means of subordinating ideas in a participial and an appositive phrase; yet they were not drilled in the recognition of the grammatical constructions used. . . .

Such questions as the following were asked in approaching the many types of sentence fragments: Is the idea immediately clear? Do the words leave you "up in the air" as if something else belonged with them? What seems to be left unstated? What is the main statement to which these words add something as a contributing or subordinate idea? How can the subordinate idea be expressed in proper relationship to the main idea of which it is a part? Thus the pupil was led to consider the expression of the whole thought rather than to search for the grammatical elements of subject and predicate.

Additional examples of the thought approach are contained in Dora V. Smith's article, "English Grammar Again." [7]

Evidence proves that . . . matters of style . . . may be taught quite as effectively without grammatical knowledge as with it, if emphasis is placed upon clarity of thought and effectiveness of expression alone. For instance, a pupil writes, "I like hunting, to fish, and when I go swimming." The teacher points out (in language readily comprehensible) to him that his three kinds of sport are parallel in his thinking and will be better expressed in parallel fashion. Without any hesitation he writes, "I like hunting, fishing, and swimming" or "I like to hunt, to fish, and to swim." No mention of gerunds or infinitives need to enter into the problem at all.

The other evening the members of a church society joined in singing ardently a song written by one of their number. Everything went smoothly until they reached the stanza: "How dear to my heart is the church on the corner. When walking down

[7] Dora V. Smith, "English Grammar Again," *The English Journal*, 27 (October, 1938), 643–649.

Fifth Street, it comes into view." The hilarity of the audience was no measure of its grammatical knowledge. Violence was done to the *thought*, and people recognized that fact instantly. Pupils can correct such sentences readily without any grammatical knowledge whatsoever.

It will be noted in the examples just given, as well as in the reports of experiments comparing the efficiency of direct as compared with indirect methods of teaching usage, that guided practice, based on the students' own speech or writing, is abundantly provided. No reputable writer has ever suggested that good usage is acquired just by letting speech grow like unclipped weeds.

School-wide programs for speech improvement. Attempts to develop effective language habits in young people will naturally be more successful if English staffs can count on the cooperation of teachers of other school subjects in seeing that the pupils apply in other classes what they learn in English. Such cooperation, where lacking, can often be secured by making a school-wide program in effective communication the topic of a series of full-dress faculty meetings. If such meetings can be guided and unified by a concrete project, such as the cooperative formulation of a pupil stylebook containing the indispensable essentials of language usage to be observed throughout the school, the discussions are likely to prove of greater practical assistance and to be more productive of outcomes, than if they deal only with theoretical generalities.

Moreover, if the stylebook is produced by a committee representing all areas of the curriculum and is discussed and revised by the faculty as a whole, the assurance that teachers outside the field of English will not just file it away, but make effective use of it, is greater than if the staff merely ratifies a prefabricated stylebook on persuasion from the English department. The formulation of a stylebook as a cooperative school project reduces the risk of giving teachers of other subjects the impression that they are being imposed upon.

Only one danger must be avoided. It is the almost irresistible tendency to put so much in the stylebook that it becomes too unwieldy for self-instructional, school-wide use. This tendency can be controlled by limiting the body of the book to those indispensable basic essentials on which almost unanimous agreement can be reached, and reserving for an appendix all detailed aids, such as the reference guides discussed earlier, and matters concerning which a very substantial faculty majority cannot be mustered. The most serviceable stylebook worked out independently by a committee of English teachers might, if too detailed or if adopted without a background of collective school-wide thinking, receive no greater attention than a copy of the basic English text presented to each teacher of mathematics, science, art, music, social studies, manual training, or physical education.

The indispensability of life-centered content. To be sure, none of the procedures so far described will suffice to develop outstanding writers or speakers. Perhaps it would be well for young people to learn early in school that the first draft of a letter, story, poem, speech, novel, or play is never so good as the second, third, fourth, or fifth draft made by constantly testing the material with a view to making it clearer, more interesting, or more convincing to readers or listeners. No misconception can be more discouraging to young people than the false notion that effective writing is attributable exclusively to an inherited talent or form of genius. Examination of the first-draft manuscripts of great writers has shown that they often contained as poor handwriting, as many erasures and cross-outs, and sometimes as many errors in usage, as are to be found in the compositions of sixth graders. If Charles Dickens' works have merit as examples of effective writing, it is not because he was successful in producing superior first drafts, but because he sometimes revised his writing as many as twenty times. He was willing to do this because he felt that he had something important to say and knew exactly to whom he wished to say it. Because his message was important to him, only the very best way of expressing it was good enough.

If any considerable number of young people are to be aided in achieving more than normative standards of performance in language, therefore, we must accept motivation as a daily responsibility. This means, as a former president of the National Council of Teachers of English once expressed it,[8] helping young people "find something interesting and worthwhile to say and building an audience situation which will give them reasons for saying it," for as Professor Mary Weeks has so well put it, "if the matter does not count most, the manner will not count at all."

TEACHING ENGLISH AS A SECOND LANGUAGE

Teaching non-English-speaking students. Although this book is primarily concerned with teaching English to young people from English-speaking homes, no discussion of the subject can be realistic unless it takes into account the considerable numbers of young people to whom English is primarily a foreign language. In the Southwestern states from 20 to 39 per cent of the school population come from homes in which little or no English is spoken.[9] Many of our larger cities, such as New York, Cleveland, San Francisco, Los Angeles, or Detroit, include non-English-speaking populations large enough to fill the second or third largest city in almost any of the countries from which they emigrated. Indeed one of our states, New Mexico, has long been obliged to conduct legal business in either Spanish or English.

In situations where English teaching is, for all practical purposes, a process of teaching a second language, books that contain concrete examples of modern practices in foreign-

[8] Holland D. Roberts, "English Teachers Face the Future," *The English Journal* (College Edition), 27 (February, 1938), 101–113.

[9] Algernon Coleman and Clara Breslove King, *English Teaching in the Southwest*, p. 4. Washington: American Council on Education, 1940.

language teaching at the intermediate school level can be of great use to the teacher of English. Among these are *Foreign Languages and Cultures in American Education, Modern Languages for Modern Schools, Modern Spanish Teaching,* and *Twentieth Century Modern Language Teaching.*[10] For teachers of young people who come from Spanish-speaking homes in an American community, Tireman's *Teaching Spanish-speaking Children* is indispensable [11] and will be found useful also in dealing with the language problems of other non-English-speaking groups.

In general, the following principles can serve as guides in diagnosing instructional problems, and in selecting, organizing, or presenting content to young people whose command of English is not so great as their command of a foreign language:

1. True measures of intelligence are almost impossible to secure in the case of bilingual young people. Because their linguistic savings are divided between two languages, a single test of their ability in *one* language fails to do justice to their total achivment. A child from a non-English-speaking home who has acquired 3,500 Spanish words and 1,500 English words (a total combined vocabulary of 5,000 words) surely is not less intelligent than a child of the same age who has acquired a total vocabulary of 5,000 English words and no Spanish words at all. Because schools pay dividends on only one language, however, the bilingual child usually seems retarded by comparison, and is often falsely diagnosed as of inferior intelligence. By the time the diagnosis is corrected, educational malpractice may already have induced such

[10] Walter V. Kaulfers, Grayson N. Kefauver, and Holland D. Roberts, *op. cit.* Walter V. Kaulfers, *Modern Languages for Modern Schools.* New York: McGraw-Hill Book Company, Inc., 1942. Walter V. Kaulfers, *Modern Spanish Teaching.* New York: Henry Holt and Company, Inc. Maxim Newmark, *Twentieth Century Modern Language Teaching.* New York: Philosophical Library, Inc.

[11] L. S. Tireman, *Teaching Spanish-speaking Children.* Albuquerque: University of New Mexico Press.

chronic symptoms of maladjustment and dislike for school-work that problems of attendance and cooperation in class tend at times to eclipse all problems of aims, objectives, or methods. To avoid such complications, or to correct them where they exist, the teacher of English will wish to read the finest treatment of the subject that has so far appeared in professional literature—"We Mexicans," by Eddie Ruth Hutton of the Phoenix Union High School, Arizona.[12]

2. Total segregation of non-English-speaking children is hardly desirable for sociological reasons, but separate group-ings especially organized to serve their special needs are at times indispensable as a temporary means for helping them bridge the gap betwen two different cultures. Otherwise, the school may be far more successful in aggravating symptoms of maladjustment or feelings of inferiority than in achieving anything envisioned in its ideals of democracy. This view-point has been cogently expressed by one of the most suc-cessful teachers of children from non-English-speaking homes: [13]

These Mexican boys and girls have an extremely limited vocabulary in both English and Spanish. Few read or write Spanish. It is a spoken language only. Their English suffers from obvious translation. For this reason we need two periods a day. In English we concentrate on the problems peculiar to the Spanish-speaking child. Double negatives seem logical to the Mexican boy or girl because he uses them, and correctly so, in his own language. When it is pointed out that he says *chico* plainly, little practice is needed to teach the pronunciation of the words *cheek, check,* or *chimney.* Often by the translation of a word into Spanish a whole English idea is made clear and much time saved. In a segregated group the pupil is not embarrassed because of his "accent" and the feeling that he is inferior because he understands less English than other members of the class. When someone says that "adequate" means "something rich people have got" (etiquette) or "something water runs through"

---

[12] Kaulfers, Kefauver, and Roberts, *op. cit.,* pp. 29–41.
[13] *Ibid.,* pp. 34–35.

(aqueduct), no one seems startled. In a class of English-speaking children no one would appear startled or laugh either, for the Mexican child would have avoided that situation by simply remaining silent.

At the beginning of the year one boy confided that sometimes in his social studies class he had something he wanted to say, but that he was afraid because he didn't know enough big words. Then he asked that we learn some. Several times I asked if he had talked in the class mentioned. No, he had not. It was not until several months later that he rushed in and said, "I talked this morning. They were all talking about poverty making criminals of people. I told them it wasn't true."

3. Content and methods must be chosen on the basis of a diagnosis of the specific language needs of the particular young people who are to receive instruction. All study of formal grammar as a subject becomes an absurdity at the elementary and intermediate levels here. So also does any passion for covering a particular classic commonly read by young people of like age in regular English classes. An excellent illustration of the humorous absurdities to which the selection of inappropriate content can lead in classes for non-English-speaking students is contained in Leonard Q. Ross, *The Education of Hyman Kaplan*.[14] A large part of the humor of this well-known book is attributable to the reactions of the central character to literature far beyond his linguistic depth, and even farther removed from his most obvious needs. In a sense, it is a practical demonstration of the use of great literature to make a human being appear more amusingly stupid and comical than the Creator, Himself, intended.

When based on a specific diagnosis rather than on predetermined content, the procedure is in terms of priority of need, and from specific to general. For example, pronunciation of common words and expressions needed in getting about safely and comfortably—traffic signs, directional signs, names of common places and things, expressions of cour-

[14] Leonard Q. Ross, *The Education of Hyman Kaplan*. New York: Harcourt, Brace and Company, Inc., 1937.

tesy, etc. Dramatization of life situations, actual excursions to stores, and the like, are preferable to purely memoriter work or study-for-a-test activities. Although memorization and testing have their place, the primary stress is on *inducting the learner into the life of the English-speaking community* rather than exclusively on English as a classroom subject of study. Conceived in any other way, the teaching of English to young people from non-English-speaking homes is likely to suffer from lack of motivation, and to fall conspicuously short of its opportunities to serve as an Americanizing influence in the interests of improved intercultural relations.

Similarly, reading activities may appropriately center on helping young people find in magazines and books the answers to questions of personal interest and importance to them. By reading to learn, they will learn to read. Obviously, illustrated materials, on a maturity level compatible with the learners' own, are a distinct aid. Of greater value and appeal than kindergarten-primary texts for young people of junior and senior high school age are such illustrated magazines as *Life* or the better comic books. Study of advertisements alone can often be converted into a profitable form of practical vocabulary work for beginners, and lends itself readily to a variety of picture-identification games.

4. The resources of materials used in teaching English as a foreign language abroad deserve to be capitalized in American schools. Michael West's reductions of such junior classics as *Treasure Island* into a 1,000-word vocabulary should prove as successful in American classes for retarded readers, and young people from non-English-speaking homes, as they have been in India. The reductions of many literary and scientific works to Basic English are an additional resource upon which the teacher of English as a second language can draw, especially in the case of teen-aged and adult students. Nothing can be more incongruous in language teaching than the reading of kindergarten sagas at the adolescent or adult level of maturity.

5. Proficiency in such matters as pronunciation is a *habit*, rather than subject matter, and as such cannot be achieved as a unit boxed off for intensive study and thorough coverage in a few weeks devoted exclusively to the topic. In the case of pronunciation, the students will "backslide" or revert to their "foreign accent" if proficiency is achieved through hothousing—that is, in too short a time to allow of the fixation of a new habit to the point where it is automatic. The alternative, therefore, is to make improvement in pronunciation a continuous responsibility in all classes, and an integral aspect of all oral work. Since overintensive emphasis on pronunciation at any stage can induce frustration or intensify self-consciousness to the point where it leads to stammering or stuttering, learning from mistakes, rather than perfection the very first time, should be emphasized to the extent to which the traffic will comfortably bear. Pictures and diagrams showing the relative position of the tongue, lips, teeth, and soft palate are essential in the case of the more difficult sounds. *Demonstration of the exact way the sounds are produced, rather than descriptions of them,* is the key to success, if such demonstration is immediately accompanied by carefully supervised *reproduction* of the sounds as distinguished from imitation of their facsimiles. Recordings of the pupils' speech, by providing a kind of mirror of their pronunciation and intonation, are valuable teaching aids. Because fluency depends on ability to pronounce groups of words rather than isolated sounds, pronunciation exercises should place primary stress on ability to reproduce word groups of gradually increasing length, in interrogative and exclamatory as well as declarative context.

To avoid frustration on the part of the pupils, perfection should be kept in mind as an ideal, but never as an immediate, irreducible minimum for all students. The popular notion that less than perfection at the beginning, and at all times, will ingrain wrong habits of pronunciation so deeply that they cannot be eradicated later, is not confirmed either by common sense or by research. If this assumption were true, many teachers of English would still be saying "muvver" instead of "mother," because they pronounced English so badly and for so long as little children. What progressive standards, then, can the teacher set up as a reasonable group goal?

In the beginning, *intelligibility* to a native American listener may well be insisted upon as a desirable minimum goal. For example, Would a native American understand what the learner is *trying* to say? From here the standard may soon be raised to that of *ready intelligibility:* Would a native American readily understand what the learner is saying? For those pupils who achieve this standard, the teacher may provide special assistance that will gradually enable them to attain the ultimate desired goal—that of normal, accent-free speech. Inasmuch as individual pupil progress in habit formation varies widely, grouping of students for special help within the regular class hour is inescapable. This obviously requires planning the classwork in such a way that the majority of the pupils can be occupied in silent reading or written work at their seats while the teacher works with a group of five or six pupils gathered around her desk, or around a table in a corner of the room. In some cases, responsible pupils who are especially proficient in pronunciation can be enlisted to serve as assistants to referee the practice of small groups.

Where the number of non-English-speaking students in a particular school is too small to justify the organization of special-help classes, the problem is one of placing the students in the English courses most nearly suited to their educational and social maturity levels, and then organizing them into a special working committee within the courses assigned. Since an extra hour of work in English a day is likely to be the minimum required to meet their special needs, other course work will normally have to be reduced in proportion. Responsible English-speaking students in the class can often be enlisted as teaching assistants or tutors on special topics, especially if such service is recognized by the student body and faculty as a desirable way of earning credit toward the school's annual citizenship or service award. If the classroom library includes illustrated magazines and well-known classics in reduced vocabulary editions, the problem of differentiating the work of the non-English-speaking group will be greatly facilitated.

6. Opportunity to secure recognition is essential in all programs for non-English-speaking students. Since inability to compete in language with fellow students of like age can become a very discouraging experience, opportunities to secure recognition without publicly exposing a temporary handicap is of practical importance. If a student's native language is taught in school, utilization of his abilities in the foreign language class or club is desirable. If the student has special abilities as an instrumentalist, dancer, athlete, or vocalist, capitalization (but not exploitation) of these can provide the degree of recognition required. Discovery of such resources is the responsibility of the teacher and school counselor. Few students—least of all, non-English-speaking students—can be expected to violate all rules of modesty by advertising their talents without cause. Many classroom activities, such as choral reading by a verse-speaking choir, or choral rendition of famous poems that have been set to music as songs, provide opportunities for securing recognition within the class, if not always as an individual soloist, at least as a member of a team or production group.

Teaching young people versus covering textbooks. Suggestions of the kind offered here obviously have as their objective the development of effective speech habits in young people, and of building these habits into their life behavior as means for making them enlightened and productive human beings. This objective implies something quite different from memorizing grammatical terminology, labeling the parts of sentences, or "doing" proofreading exercises in a textbook. Although the procedures that have been suggested are easy for young people to follow and, therefore, save time and effort in school for the more important business of guiding

actual practice in language as effective communication to a
reader or listener, it is not assumed that reconstructing life
behavior can ever be so easy as "covering" a textbook with
the aid of devices for gradually disfranchizing those who do
not respond to this kind of instruction. Success in implement-
ing any of the suggestions offered on the foregoing pages can
be achieved only by teachers who are willing to recognize
language as the natural birthright of every child, and to see to
it that the aristocratic slogan of the old English classroom,
"Talk my way, or you can't play" is replaced with a warm-
hearted determination to facilitate rather than encumber the
arts of communication.

FOR FURTHER READING

Cook, Luella B., "An Inductive Approach to the Teaching of
Language," *The English Journal,* 37 (January, 1948), 15–21.

Cook, Luella B., "Teaching Grammar and Usage in Relation to
Speech and Writing," *The English Journal,* 35 (April, 1946),
188–194.

Frogner, Ellen, "Grammar Approach versus Thought Approach
in Teaching Sentence Structure," *The English Journal,* 28
(September, 1939), 518–526.

Hatfield, W. W. (Ed.), *An Experience Curriculum in English,*
Chap. 17, "Instrumental Grammar," and Chap. 18, "Usage."
Chicago: National Council of Teachers of English, 1935.

Hook, J. N., *The Teaching of High School English,* pp. 274–315.
New York: The Ronald Press Company, 1950.

Kaulfers, Walter V., "Grammar for the Millions: If Not Formal
Grammar, Then What?" *Elementary English,* 26 (February,
1949), 65–74, 107.

LaBrant, Lou, "Teaching High School Students to Write," *The
English Journal,* 35 (March, 1946), 123–128.

O'Rourke, L. J., *Rebuilding the English-usage Curriculum to In-
sure Greater Mastery of Essentials.* New York: The Psychological Institute, 1934.

Pooley, Robert C., "Forever Grammar," *Bulletin of the National
Association of Secondary School Principals,* 30 (February,
1946), 45–49.

Pooley, Robert C., *Teaching English Usage*, pp. 191–255. New York: Appleton-Century-Crofts, Inc., 1946.

Salisbury, Rachel, "Grammar and the Laws of Learning," *The English Journal*, 35 (May, 1946), 247–252.

Schlauch, Margaret, *The Gift of Tongues*, Chap. 6. New York: The Viking Press, Inc., 1948.

Chapter 5. SEMANTICS AS A COMMON LEARNING

THE UNREALITIES OF LANGUAGE

Compounding absolutes. "It was a good example of an irresistible force meeting an immovable object," remarked Mr. Johnson on telling his family about the truck that crashed into the concrete wall near Fifth Street. "You should have seen the wreck!"

As a statement giving his *impressions* of the accident, Mr. Johnson's analogy was, perhaps, both effective and appropriate considering the circumstances in which it was made. At least no one was injured by the inaccuracy of his observation if, indeed, it was noticed at all. Few people are trained to detect distortions of reality resulting from the use of descriptive words with absolute connotations, like *irresistible* and *immovable,* in combination. Yet in the world of fact, two mutually exclusive absolutes simply cannot exist together at the same time. If a force is truly "irresistible," no object can remain "immovable" before it; and, conversely, if an object is actually "immovable," no force can prove "irresistible" in its presence.

The fact that both the truck and the concrete wall suffered considerable damage should have been proof enough to Mr. Johnson that his statement was nonsense from a strictly objective point of view. Like many other people, however, he probably thought that his analogy stated the case perfectly, and would doubtless have resented any correction as bickering over the picayune. Inasmuch as his observation was made in circumstances that could not seriously affect the welfare of any human being, most readers, like the writer, would be more inclined to agree with Mr. Johnson than to censure his misuse of words. The illustration merely shows how easily language that is grammatically correct, and at least super-ficially appropriate to the circumstances, can be quite inac-curate as a statement of fact without being classifiable as lying.

Distortions of reality are almost inevitable when words with connotations of the universal or absolute are used with-out qualification. For while absolutes can be manufactured through words, they do not necessarily exist in fact. To illus-trate, the assumption that $2 + 2 = 4$ is about as universal and absolute a truth as can be found on the face of the earth. Yet in reality, two drops of water added to two drops of water are far more likely to yield *one* drop instead of four. Again, two drops of this chemical and two drops of that may even produce an explosion rather than proof of a mathematical truth. The big point is that language used without anchorage in the world of fact can lead to erratic behavior and disillu-sioning results. The appeal which absolutes make to a com-mon human desire for security, or peace of mind, in which everything is settled with finality, renders recourse to such self-disillusionment through language as compelling as it is dangerous. Constant friction between a world in which things are relative, and a mind in which they are absolute and fixed, can easily lead to frustration of such magnitude as to bring about nervous collapse, or mental disorders bordering on insanity. As a commonly accepted basic assumption, "Two plus two equals four," is absolutely and universally true only when we are not talking about anything in particular. When we are speaking about reality, the specific truth about two of *this* and two of the *other* may vary all the way from this to that.

Where no action is contemplated, minor distortions of reality regarding things or events are usually harmless and, in the hands of effective speakers or writers, form the lin-guistic basis of much of the world's best poetry and humor.

Where such distortions concern human beings and affect our attitudes or actions toward them, however, the misuses of language can, by their cumulative effect, lead to such destructive menaces to human welfare as race riots, savage treatment of the insane, sadistic punishment of delinquency regardless of causes, and even world wars. The power of language to accomplish such destruction is attributable to the "emotional voltage" or "feeling tone" that words—especially nouns, adjectives, and adverbs—often carry. The individual who has been conditioned to think of a certain nationality or culture group as "dirty dogs" is a good example of the person whose emotional reactions (no matter how pardonable they may be because of injuries suffered at the hands of one or two members) can easily result in violence against the group as a whole.

The hypnotic powers of language. Language, after all, has hypnotic powers. Hypnotism itself is accomplished through the use of language in circumstances that render the mind readily susceptible to suggestion. Equally great are the autosuggestive powers of language involved in self-hypnosis through the habitual use of certain formulas, a routine often mistaken for thinking or creative problem solving.

Primitive cults have made extensive use of these "occult" powers of language. In our own century, the Coué,[1] system of psychological therapy won a considerable number of converts to its method of inducing improvements in mental and physical health through the autosuggestive repetition of such word formulas as "Every day, in every way, I'm getting better and better." Like other systems making specialized use of the hypnotic and autosuggestive powers of language, his method did not lack testimonials to improvements or cures bordering on the miraculous.

Where used for constructive purposes, the autosuggestive and hypnotic powers of language doubtless have a beneficial therapeutic value. The fact that these resources can just as

[1] Émile Coué, *Self-mastery through Conscious Autosuggestion.* New York: American Library Service, 1922.

easily be made to serve destructive ends, however, places upon teachers of English the responsibility for enabling students to distinguish between the various uses of *affective* language (those which influence the emotions) and the various kinds of *effectual* language that mention actions or conditions without apparent personal bias in the way of emotional coloring. Without instruction in semantics, at least on the consumer level, the best student of English is in danger of becoming as much a victim as a master of his resources in language.

After all, of what ultimate life value is a large vocabulary or superior proficiency in reading comprehension, if these resources merely render their possessor more susceptible to the word magic of irresponsible publishers, reporters, commentators, or dishonest politicians in matters affecting not only his pocketbook but also the good name and welfare of his fellow men—perhaps even the lives of his children and closest friends in case of domestic or international conflict? The objectives of all good teaching must include making people sensitive, not just to the values, but also to the *limitations* of their tools. A student whose proficiency in the mechanical use of language merely provides a well-fertilized field for clever fraud, is a tragedy; a teacher who does not care to what ends his lifework is put, is a disaster. Without adequate vaccination against the malign viruses of language, the most highly schooled intellectual can easily fall prey to that cultivated sickness of mind that causes the mouth to work independently of the brain and all the rest of the body.

Semantics in the classroom. Although the science of semantics, as such, is too complex to be included as a separate subject in the curriculum of the secondary school, many of its resources can be drawn upon effectively in English classes. Indeed, since the present century is witnessing a struggle for the conquest of men's minds, in which the science of propaganda by remote control is concentrated in every country in the hands of that small fraction of the population which has easiest access to the mass media of communication—the radio, television, the newspaper, the magazine, and the sound film —it is doubtful if a single course or unit of work, concentrated in a particular year, can provide more than a very temporary immunity, at the risk of as much confusion as clarity. In dealing with so all-pervasive a medium as language, only insights developed through spaced repetition over a period of years, in direct connection with such problems and issues of group life as fall within the pupil's background of experience, can yield the kind of mind-set that is required if people are to be the masters rather than the victims of language.

At the level of secondary education, the commonest language pitfalls deserve special attention in all English classes, not necessarily as a "unit" in isolation, but in close correlation with the reading of literature, composition, discussion of current events, and the study of the mass media of communication. The commonest language pitfalls that deserve attention in English classes are described in the following paragraphs.

THE QUICKSANDS OF LANGUAGE

Overgeneralization. Such a statement as "Parents insist that the traditional classics be taught in high school" is a good example of remarks that illustrate both the nature and the frustrating effects of overgeneralization. As worded, the statement implies that *all* parents—*i.e.*, every single parent—wants the traditional classics taught, a 100 per cent unanimity that is nonexistent in the social world. Since overgeneralization is common among people who habitually make dogmatic statements without taking time to investigate the facts, it is a distorted use of language that can easily lead to irrational behavior. In reality, the authority for the statement was probably little more than the remarks of a *few* parents which the speaker translated into unanimity. Few teachers ever meet *all* the parents. In large schools it is doubtful if the teacher of English meets more than 10 per cent of the parents, even in communities where a strong Parent-Teacher Association exists. Even if this organized and more vocal 10 per cent were unanimous in their regard for the classics, they would still fall far short of a majority.

The teacher who is misled by such overgeneralizations naturally hesitates to make changes worth mentioning in the literature program, no matter how disappointing the results of his instruction continue to be after years of experimenting with various types of methods and devices. The teacher who is sensitive to the dangers of overgeneralization, on the other hand, retranslates the statement to conform to reality: "Some parents whom I have met want the usual classics taught in high school."

If on the basis of a careful evaluation of the English program, he should decide that a change in the literary content would be beneficial to the large majority of his students, he would then try to respect the wishes of the minority of parents while protecting the interests of the large majority of young people under his guidance. A differentiated, semi-individualized reading program, in which some young people read the traditional high school classics in keeping with their parents' wishes, and others read material better suited to their needs and abilities, would be one solution to the problem of preventing a vocal minority from dominating a silent majority. Whereas, the victim of overgeneralization might risk no change at all, the teacher with insight into the problem would seek ways and means for accommodating differences in keeping with democratic principles, fundamental among which is the protection of minority interests without letting these dominate the group as a whole.

Wherever a generalization of the kind just described is advanced without support in verifiable facts, the individual trained in semantics will almost unconsciously translate it with modifying qualifications, e.g., "Some parents probably want the traditional classics taught in high school." How many parents would have to wait upon facts obtained from an objective interview or questionnaire. The word "probably" would be added in the case of a generalization made by an individual suspected of a personal bias, for example, a teacher in need of a good reason for not changing the books that she finds easy, convenient, or personally gratifying to teach, regardless of their effect upon the large majority of young people.

Translating unsupported generalizations with the aid of such modifiers as "some" and "probably" is a simple device for sensitizing young people to the dangers of overgeneralization, and for neutralizing the distortion that all careless uses of language are likely to involve. Here are a few undocumented statements that young people of high school age should have little difficulty translating into more realistic terms:

1. Englishmen like to drink tea.
2. Mexicans are lazy.
3. Education courses are boring.
4. Americans have little respect for law and order.

Where a generalization involves a group of people treated as a class, an additional modifier involving an analogy to the speaker's own group is desirable in the interests of unbiased social understanding. Thus the generalization "Mexicans are lazy" might well be paraphrased to read "*Some* Mexicans, *like some Americans,* are (probably) lazy."

Emotionally charged speech. A critical reader should have little difficulty deciding which side the writer favored when he wrote "This heroic little band of Anonymians overcame ten thousand of the barbarian horde." The use of words with a favorable feeling tone or positive emotional charge, like *heroic,* in contrast with such unfavorable epithets as *barbarian,* indicates plainly that the writer sympathized with the Anonymians. Perhaps he was right. In the absence of specific facts concerning the cause of the conflict, and the specific manner in which both sides behaved, however, the reader is entirely at the mercy of one reporter, and in danger of absorbing an emotional bias that may be completely unwarranted by the actual facts. While the uncritical reader is in constant danger of absorbing prejudices unconsciously, especially if the exposure to emotional bias in language is continuous and uncontradicted, the reader trained in semantics automatically translates such statements into the most neutral language at his command: "A small number of people called Anonymians won a struggle against an enemy of ten thousand." Whether such a victory should be greeted with sorrow or exultation would depend upon facts not available in the original statement. Therefore, no evaluative judgment would be rendered, nor action taken beyond investigating the facts from all sides if the matter is one of great personal interest or vital import.

By assigning positive numbers of +1, +2, or +3 to words with varying degrees of favorable emotional voltage, and negative numbers of −1, −2, or −3 to words with unfavorable connotations, the degree of emotional bias in speech or writing can be determined with sufficient accuracy to serve all practical purposes of semantic analysis. Words without a perceptible feeling tone in a particular context can be numbered 0, while factual words referring to specific people, places, or things, or to a specific amount or number, can be designated with an F to indicate possible *fact*. In this way, not only the degree of emotional bias can be evaluated, but also the proportion of possible fact to purely emotional voltage that the language contains.

In the case of the statement, "This heroic little band of Anonymians overcame ten thousand of the barbarian horde," the analysis might yield the following results:

```
0     +3     +1   +1   0     F         0    F    F    0
The heroic little band of Anonymians overcame ten thousand of
0     -3     -2
the barbarian horde.
```

Analysis

Positive charge   (sum of all positive numbers) favoring the Anonymians: +5.

Negative charge   (sum of all negative numbers) unfavorable to their opponents: −5.

Degree of bias   (sum of all numbers regardless of $+$ or $-$ signs): 10.

Ratio of fact to bias   (number of F words as compared with the total number of words with numbers above or below 0): 3 to 5.

From the analysis, it is obvious that the sentence is far more an expression of emotion than a statement of fact. Although no two analyists will agree on the assignment of specific number values because of the different emotional associations that people have with particular words and expressions, they will rarely disagree on the preponderance and direction of bias, or the relative proportion of factual to purely emotional words, unless the statement is ambiguous or unintelligible.

The value of the analysis is obviously not in the degree of numerical agreement among different evaluators, but in the habit of semantic analysis that it helps to develop. The variations in numerical assignments are themselves interesting indications of the different degrees to which people are susceptible to the emotional charges that almost all words acquire, either from the context in which they are used or as a carry-over from previous associations. Although the technique is inappropriate for purely aesthetic forms of expression, such as poetry that falls under the classification of belles lettres, its use is well suited to consumer education in language in connection with the study of advertising, news reports of important current events, political speeches or editorials, and the like.

Rubber-band words. Despite the fact that men have for ages attempted to find security in verbally phrased ideals, their success in the present century has been no greater than in earlier times. A large part of the difficulty can assuredly be attributed to the rubber-band qualities of the words in which ideals are so often phrased. Freedom, for example, is an ideal that men have cherished since the beginning of history, but its meaning is perhaps more confused in our own day than in the Golden Age of Pericles. At that time, any man was "free" who was not a slave,[2] and "freedom" was in no small measure synonymous with that release from routine tasks and less attractive forms of manual labor which the possesion of slaves made possible. Release from many of the tasks and chores of daily life "freed" men for participation in the assembly as voting citizens, and for military service when the security of the state required it.

Today, so simple an explanation of the meaning of *freedom* is no longer possible. "Freedom is the opposite of slavery" is not a satisfactory definition for societies that have abolished, at least in law, all forms of involuntary servitude except military conscription and imprisonment for crime. The concept of freedom is in danger of degenerating into a rubber-band word that people can stretch at will in almost any direction that best suits their personal interest. In such circumstances, confusion and contradictory forms of selfish behavior are inevitable outcomes.

When the word *freedom* is used indiscriminately, the individual trained in semantics will attempt to discern what concepts the speaker has in mind. Questions such as the following need to be answered before the meaning of the term can be discerned in any given context:

1. Freedom for whom? The Greeks were free because they had slaves.

2. Freedom at whose expense? The Greeks were free largely because enslaved men released them from certain restrictive types of work.

3. Freedom for what?

Without specific referents, the word can easily be stretched to mean a selfish license to do as one pleases without regard for others; or freedom of rich and poor to die in want; or simply the competitive dog-eat-dog freedom of the jungle that eventually ends in a monopoly for the strong and in fear-haunted insecurity for the weak.

Since misuse of the term can easily lead to the kind of chaos

[2] Ellwood P. Cubberley, *The History of Education,* p. 21. Boston: Houghton Mifflin Company, 1920.

that critically affects the bread-and-butter existence of large numbers of people, irresponsibility in the use of the word is a matter of serious concern. Wherever the needs of survival have forced men to choose between bread and liberty, they have consistently chosen bread for, without it, all hope of enjoying or regaining freedom would be extinguished by death. Perhaps nowhere has the problem of our time been stated more clearly than in the words of the Latin American, Haya de la Torre: "Some men have promised us bread without freedom; others have promised us freedom without bread. Our quest is bread with freedom."

If so complex a problem is to be solved rationally in a society in which freedom is not conceived as the mere linguistic opposite of involuntary servitude, the term will have to be redefined as that by-product of shared responsibility among enlightened, self-governing men which releases each individual from slavery to fear, want, insecurity, and chronic frustration. The greater the degree of shared responsibility, the greater then becomes each individual dividend of freedom.

Since almost all abstract nouns partake of the nature of rubber-band words, care in their use, and sensitivity to the extent and direction in which they are being stretched, deserve especial attention, if confusion and contradictory forms of behavior are not to result from their injudicious application to any of the great social, political, or moral causes with which they are so frequently associated. In reality, almost any virtue phrased in terms of a rubber-band word can be converted into a vice simply by stretching it beyond the point of diminishing returns. For example, *thrift*, carried to psychopathic extremes, can easily be transformed into avaricious or miserly hoarding. Kindness, as in parental treatment of children, can easily be stretched to resemble soft-headed indulgence; and even truthfulness, when carried to extremes, can lead to that vice of which Mark Twain must have been cognizant when he wrote, "An injurious truth has no virtue over a malicious lie. Neither should ever be uttered."

The critical point to bear in mind in dealing with rubber-band words is the point of diminishing returns at which the virtues that they presumably symbolize begin to turn into vices. Because the language of social life has not acquired the definiteness of the natural sciences and mathematics, awareness of the hazards involved in the use of verbal abstractions is essential if disillusionment, futile tugs of war with rubber-band words, or even armed conflict is not to result. Whereas democratic societies have let the voting citizen decide, through the ballot, when the point of diminishing returns has been reached in relation to such concepts as "freedom," "private enterprise," or "rugged individualism," totalitarian societies have consistently placed such decisions in the exclusive control of a kind of supreme grand council responsible only to a *Führer, Duce,* or Generalissimo.

Whether the world's democratic countries can remain so will depend in no small degree upon the extent to which their citizens are sensitive to the language of virtue, especially as used by those who have easiest access to the radio, chain newspaper, and national magazine. The road to dictatorship is paved with chaos and confusion. Since confusion and chaos begin in the minds of men, and can, therefore, be traced to a faulty use of the language medium through which most thinking about social, economic, political, and moral problems is done, the responsibility of the school to give life-centered instruction in semantics is inescapable. At the secondary school level, activities such as the following can make a substantial contribution through the English or common learnings program:

1. *Contradictions.* Such sayings as "Better safe than sorry" put into words the unfortunate experiences which large numbers of people have had in acting hastily or unintelligently. Since it is possible for a person to become so afraid of making mistakes, or running into trouble, that he will hardly do anything at all, people have popularized another expression to balance it, "Nothing ventured, nothing gained." Such seemingly contradictory sayings show that rules regarding be-

havior in life can seldom be as fixed or definite as the multi-
plication table. Like the stop-look-listen signs at railroad
crossings, they do not prohibit us from crossing the rails, but
serve as caution signals warning us to move only after we
have made sure that the tracks are clear. What other common sayings or proverbs do you know that contradict or limit
each other to prevent people from going to extremes?

2. *Extremities.* Almost anything carried to extremes can
lead to unhappy results. Thus *freedom* carried to absurdity
can lead to such confusion, choas, or lawlessness that people
begin to wish for a dictator to restore order. Show how
thrift, truthfulness, or *kindness to animals,* if carried to unin-
telligent lengths, may do more harm than good. Do you know
any story, joke, play, or poem that shows how carrying a virtue to extremes has led to serious trouble? Can you write an
illustration of your own in story, play, or poem form?

Additional projects, problems, and exercises can be found
in abundance in Hayakawa's *Language in Thought and
Action.*[3] Although the textbook is best suited to mature
readers in the upper grades of the senior high school, or in
college, much of the exercise material can readily be
adapted for use in junior and senior high school English
classes.

Euphemism. The use of more pleasing words for the same
act, condition, or thing has a subtle but influential effect on
human behavior. As Hayakawa has indicated, it is probably
true that many people who would not hesitate to pay several
dollars for a *filet mignon* in a fashionable restaurant, would
not order it at all if the menu listed it as a tender piece of
dead cow. Roast beef *au jus,* instead of roast beef *with juice,*
and pie *a la mode,* instead of pie *with ice cream,* are additional examples of euphemism found on bills of fare.

In this case, the early association of euphemism with class
status remains apparent. An aristocracy that lays claim to
special inherited privileges by virtue of superior blood is con-

[3] S. I. Hayakawa, *Language in Thought and Action.* New York: Harcourt, Brace and Company, Inc., 1949.

stantly forced to prove its inborn nobility by distinguishing itself from the mass through the kind of speech, dress, and manners which it adopts. Although many contributions of aristocracy to euphemism are useful in any social situation, schools have too frequently accepted the standards of aristocracy in language as the only criterion of acceptability, without distinguishing between those practices which have values for all, and those which have little use except as external signs of class status or badges of caste.

As late as the turn of the century, mention of any part of the body below the head, except through very indirect forms of euphemism, was certain to brand the speaker as a member of the lower class. In our own day, restrictions against naming the commoner social diseases on the radio or in the public press doubtless did much to prevent a frontal, common-sense attack upon the problem. It is significant to note that after such restrictions were modified and recourse to elaborately indirect forms of euphemism was made unnecessary, a constructive, nationwide program of prevention and cure became possible which, within the space of only ten years, has reduced the incidence of social disease by 50 per cent.

The foregoing example emphasizes the need for distinguishing between those euphemisms which serve the life needs of all, and those which merely prevent people from coming to grips with problems in terms of direct, realistic solutions. To attempt to eliminate euphemism without regard for such distinctions would result in a loss comparable to that which Marshal Foch must have had in mind in his reply to an American who joshingly referred to French etiquette as "a lot of hot air." "It certainly is," replied the Marshal, "but like the hot air in an automobile tire, it makes the riding through life a great deal easier."

Granted that a discriminating use of euphemism is important in life, it is nevertheless important that the actual condition, act, thing, or code of behavior which is euphemized be clearly understood rather than disguised by the verbal label. Otherwise, misunderstandings of a serious nature can easily result. The word *love* in marriage, for example, is understood by many people in its early Christian sense of a lifelong devotion to one person, to the exclusion of all others, capable of evoking voluntary sacrifices on behalf of the marriage partner, and making possible a mutual sharing of responsibilities, joys, and sorrows. Until recent years, long courtships, followed by engagements of six months to a year, served to pretest both partners to determine whether both could abide by the marriage code voluntarily, out of mutual devotion, or whether incompatibilities or weaknesses in the degree of devotion would make lifelong obedience to the marriage code and its associated responsibilities impossible except as a matter of outward conformity to social pressures. Once engaged, both parties felt the force of public opinion in the small town or village sufficient to make them give serious consideration to their vows. Departures from the accepted code could not long be concealed or kept secret.

Since 1900, however, the advent of the automobile, the increase in the number and size of cities, the intermingling of populations through immigration and mass movements from rural to urban areas have served to confuse the meaning of the code and also to weaken the pressures that formerly contributed toward its enforcement through public opinion. The automobile has facilitated travel from farm or village to communities in which departures from convention can easily be concealed. Moreover, the cosmopolitan character of many cities has served to confuse the code by bringing the visitor into contact with Latins accustomed to a double standard, with Asiatics familiar with polygamy, and with nationalities that regard sex behavior from a biological standpoint rather than from the strictly moral viewpoint of the Puritan. The result is that many young people embarking upon matrimony literally do not speak the same language even when they are using the same words. Love, as a word symbolizing a joint way of life, often becomes little more than a sentimental euphemism for a strong biological impulse. It should place no strain upon the imagination to predict the possible consequences of a marriage contracted between two individuals who use the same term in entirely different senses. Among the reasons most frequently given for initiating divorce actions is "incompatibility"—a term that social workers and lawyers commonly regard as a euphemism for inability of the married partners to make the mutual adjustments that each takes for granted as essential in terms of his personal understanding of the words *love* and *marriage.*

Inasmuch as the problem is one of serious and far-reaching significance, the responsibility of public education in promoting worthy home membership and ethical character is proportionally great. In a society in which only a very small percentage of the children attend church with any degree of regularity,[4] and living quarters are often little more than an apartment or cluster of rooms in which to sleep and change clothes, the school is forced to assume responsibilities that in former days could safely be delegated to the church and home. In serving this need, the teacher of English can find many opportunities in connection with character study in literature, especially at the upper levels of secondary education. Independent, differentiated reading programs making therapeutic use of stories, novels, and plays that portray problems akin to those faced by individual members of the group obviously present greater and more varied opportunities than are likely to be encountered in the reading of a single uniform text. Misunderstandings and maladjustments resulting from miscommunication are especially to be noted. Other activities that can sensitize young people to the dangers of uncritical euphemism include the following:

1. Rewriting advertisements that make exaggerated use of euphemism where none is required.

2. Translating magniloquent statements into everyday language, perhaps with the aid of Ogden's *General Basic English Dictionary.*[5]

[4] *Everybody's Digest,* December, 1949, p. 45; *Pageant,* December, 1949, pp. 20–26; *Time,* Nov. 28, 1949, p. 62.

[5] New York: W. W. Norton & Company, 1942.

Given: Siblings manifest tendencies toward mutually antagonistic responses.

Write: Brothers and sisters sometimes fight.

Given: In Spanish, the conjunctive personal pronouns must precede the auxiliary verb in all compound tenses of the indicative.

Write: In Spanish the words for *me, you, him, her, it, them,* and *us* go before the words for *have, has,* or *had* in such expressions as "Have they found them?" or "She had forgotten us."

Ghost words. As common as any of the pitfalls of language discussed in the preceding paragraphs is the danger of unconsciously mistaking the existence of a word for the actual existence in fact of whatever the word is supposed to mean. Words without specific referents, *i.e.,* words that do not stand for something that exists somewhere at some time, are ghost words until real meaning is put into them in the form of specific actions, conditions, or things. Although no invention or improvement of importance has been created without the use of some verbal symbols that project or reconstruct rather than just identify reality, results have been achieved only by making these ghosts materialize by giving them specific referents in time and space. As Korzybski [6] has indicated, language is at best a map of reality; it is never reality itself. In terms of this analogy, ghost words are names of places on the language map that do not exist in the flesh. Anyone who has tried to follow verbal directions and become confused in the process needs not proof of the distortions to which language as a map, or guide book to reality, is frequently subject.

All abstractions, such as *leadership* and *cooperativeness,* and all overgeneralizations in which specific referents are unidentifiable, partake of the nature of ghost words or maps to ghost towns, to the extent to which common agreement is lacking concerning the specific actions or pattern of behavior involved. Rating scales in which such terms appear are not

[6] Alfred Korzybski, *Science and Sanity: An Introduction to Non-Aristotelian Systems and General Semantics.* Lancaster, Pa.: Science Printing Press, 1941.

uncommon in American schools. A high rating on virtue words, like *leadership* and *cooperativeness*, or in terms of such descriptive generalizations as "Works without being watched," is often interpreted to mean desirable and significant growth encouraged by the school. Where the activities in which leadership and cooperation have been manifested are mutually understood among parents, teachers, and students, the terms doubtless carry enough meaning to prevent them from being mere ghost words with favorable feeling tones. Since such a mutual understanding does not always exist, however, the inclusion of specific referents on all rating scales, *i.e.*, specific activities or situations in which cooperativeness and leadership have been shown, is imperative if the scales are to have any semblance of objectivity or real life meaning. Despite the implications of virtue that the words convey, it is not their sound effects but their referents in time and place which determine the degree of goodness or badness involved in any given situation. After all, savages and criminals often *cooperate* without benefit of formal schooling and also develop some form of *leadership*, while safe robbers regularly "work without being watched."

Since discussions that make indiscriminate use of rubberband words, overgeneralizations, emotional symbols, and ghost words commonly lead to verbal activity that is more often a substitute than a guide to action, the development of insight into the language problems involved is a major responsibility of instruction in English. In the case of symbols, such as "democracy," to which varying connotations and emotional associations are attached, recourse to operational definition is desirable. Such definition is in terms of specific action, *i.e.*, in terms of how a democratic person or state behaves or goes about solving problems. The emphasis is upon the act or process as a distinctive characteristic of democracy in real life situations rather than upon descriptive adjectives or synonyms.[7] Activities such as the following readily lend

[7] William Van Til, *et al.*, *Democracy Demands It*. New York: Harper & Brothers, 1950.

themselves to practice in composition and panel discussion centered on crucial issues in individual and group living:

1. To what extent is the following statement true or false?
"In our country every citizen has the same right to disagree. and to protection in expressing his disagreement, as a member. of the Supreme Court in writing a minority or dissenting opinion."
2. What would you do?
The inhabitants of a new subdivision of 500 houses, recently incorporated into the City of Elmtown, feel that they lack adequate fire protection because the nearest fire station is over four miles away. State, in order, the exact steps that they should take to obtain better fire protection from the city.

Life-centered problems, such as the foregoing, obviously bring instruction in English into close correlation with instruction in the social studies. Where these fields have already been unified through the medium of an integrated core program in social living or common learnings, this fact presents advantages rather than difficulties. Since many English courses, however, have laid primary stress on aesthetic materials, best described as "lavender and old lace in a vague and timeless shadowland," the introduction of content dealing with the crucial issues of present-day life is not always welcomed. Many teachers of English are the unfortunate heirs to generations of predecessors who used the language arts—especially belles lettres—as means of escape from the unpleasant affairs of the out-of-school world rather than as means for gaining insight into their nature and possible solutions. Life-centering all instruction given in school, particularly the teaching of the language arts and literature, is a major responsibility if the benefits of the educational program are to be commensurate with the time, effort, and money that such required subjects as English commonly demand. Although literature with a high degree of aesthetic merit is indispensable in building the right emotions in men and, where necessary, in arousing the conscience of mankind, its pertinence or relevance to present-day issues is even more important than its aesthetic quality per se. The greatest contributions to human welfare have not been made by culture sitting aloof upon a monument, but by men of good will toiling in the mud.

Nor are the social studies beyond criticism in their approach to the problems of modern life. In the teaching of citizenship or civic responsibility, the tendency has been to stress the structure or forms of government rather than its function or process, and to deal in virtuous generalizations on a high level of abstraction. Such teaching always contains seeds of danger. Unless the citizen understands exactly how such needs as street lights, improved police protection, more adequate garbage disposal, storm sewers, or street repairs can be secured through democratic process in a particular neighborhood, undesirable attitudes and behavior are likely to develop. These include the discontented grumbling that is a symptom of frustration; scapegoating that seeks to find a culprit and places the blame on others; a suppressed desire for a kind of benevolent despotism that will "get things done"; or simply a meek and resigned let-George-do-it reliance on the supernatural.

Semantic shift. The fact that words change their meaning according to the context in which they are used is a common source of confusion in language, especially when the same term is used in different senses in the same sentence or paragraph. Awareness of semantic shift is, therefore, an important prerequisite to the development of discrimination in the use and consumption of language. Some insight into the range and magnitude of the problem can be obtained from the fact that the 570 most commonly used words in English have approximately 7,000 different uses.[8] Thus the little word *run,* with its compounds, has 800 meanings, from *home run* to *run on a bank* or *run in a stocking.* It should require little reflection to realize that the mere acquisition of the word *run* as a vocabulary item with one meaning does not give a clue to all its many possible implications. A foreign student

[8] "Education," *Time,* 55 (Jan. 9, 1950), p. 42.

of English, for example, is often discouraged when his mastery of the most commonly used words does not always enable him to understand them in context.

LANGUAGE IN WORLD AFFAIRS

Although semantic shift forms the linguistic basis of a great deal of the world's humor, it is also responsible for a sizable share of its misunderstandings. In international relations, where translation from one medium of communication to another is involved, the pitfalls of semantic shift require special precautions lest misunderstanding and ill will on the part of millions result. International tension, bordering on a crisis between England and Germany, for example, is reported once to have arisen over the use of the word *alsbald* in a communiqué from a German chancellor to the British foreign office. The condition which the chancellor indicated would be necessary as a basis for further negotiations was that the German colonies should be restored to German sovereignty *alsbald*. The English interpreters translated the term as *at once* or *right away*, a condition entirely impractical, and not a little peremptory from the British point of view. It was not realized until after several changes of notes that the term had been used in the sense of *as soon as possible* rather than *at once*. Only after misunderstanding of the proportions of a near crisis had developed did the interpreters realize that the source of difficulty was a case of semantic shift in translation.

The misconceptions to which semantic shifts can readily lead are especially to be guarded against in the consumption of news items from abroad. A change in *government*, for example, is likely to be only a change in *personnel*, say a change in ministers at the cabinet level. Most Europeans think of *government* more often in terms of persons than in terms of form or structure, while the opposite is more widely true among inhabitants of the United States. It is, therefore, not hard to imagine what impressions of utter collapse, chaos, or anarchy a youngster might receive from a current event headed "French government falls," if no one had informed him of the phenomenon of semantic shift.

Again, among Europeans and Latin Americans the term *revolution* is more likely to refer to a fundamental change in government policy than to a violent overthrow of the structure of government by rebellious forces. In this sense, the United States has undergone many "revolutions" apart from the war for independence or the war between the states. It is probably unawareness of semantic shift that once caused an American tourist to view with alarm the campaign slogan used by a popular aspirant to the presidency of Mexico, "How the blood will flow in the streets if that man is elected!" She exclaimed, "His slogan is *I shall continue the revolution!*" The thought that the candidate was merely pledging himself to continue putting into effect the democratic principles of the Mexican revolution of 1917 did not occur to her. In reality, the word *revolution* contained no more threat of violent radicalism in the campaign slogan than in the name Daughters of the American Revolution.

The extent to which unawareness of semantic shift in the consumption of sensationalized news can lead to misunderstandings on a national scale can readily be illustrated from our varying impressions of Mexico in the past quarter of a century. At a time when many Americans were afraid to visit the country because of the sensational news reports of banditry across the border, the actual banditry of an entire year did not equal the crime of one night in Chicago. Similarly, all the "revolutions" of a hundred years in Central America have not led to more fatalities than are commonly caused by automobile accidents during a single year in the United States.[10]

Even among speakers of the same language, semantic shift is a common source of confusion. A recent visitor to the

[10] Samuel Guy Inman, *Latin America: Its Place in World Life* (Rev. Ed.), p. 107. New York: Harcourt, Brace and Company, Inc., 1942.

United States from England could not help expressing what she interpreted as being a serious contradiction in the American attitude toward *government.* "You seem almost to worship government *of the people, for the people, and by the people* as commended in Lincoln's Gettysburg Address, and yet from the comments of the most influential editorialists and commentators, one would think that *all* government, no matter what kind, is something to be distrusted and feared." From the viewpoint of semantics, a clearer distinction between the kind of government that is to be revered and the kind that is to be feared would make for greater clarity in our political thinking. The translation of a term with many meanings into a malevolent "spook" is a symptom of immaturity. So, too, is the habit of thinking of government only in terms of its forms, structure, or codified laws without regard for the persons who determine how they are to be interpreted or used.

Language and the State. For the truth is that throughout history the "State," regardless of its written constitutions or external form, has ultimately become whatever the group with easiest access to the means of communication has wanted it to be. Athenian democracy, for example, was limited to that minority of the population whose citizenship rights gave them the privilege of making themselves heard on the floor of the Assembly.[11] Even among this group, civic influence was so closely correlated with ability to communicate to an audience that public speaking, or oratory, was a key subject in the educational program of free men. In fact, so keenly did the Greeks appreciate the inseparable relationship between government and access to the means of communication that the optimum size of the state was defined as the number of voting citizens who could assemble within hearing distance of the human voice.

In this connection it is important to note that, because of developments in the field of radio, television, and electronics, the whole world could today be brought within hearing dis-

[11] Cubberley, *op. cit.,* pp. 18–21.

tance of the human voice, and the wishes of the audience recorded and tabulated by machine, with less difficulty than the election of an American president 100 years ago. Such possibilities are of far-reaching significance for the present and future wherever the nature of the state or the need for world government is under consideration. The possibilities can no longer be regarded as fantastic except among the descendants of the men who said that airplanes would never fly, or that transmission of sound around the world without wires was the rankest kind of nonsense.

The fact that the State, regardless of its form or structure, ultimately becomes whatever those who have easiest access to the means of communication want it to be, is revealed even more clearly by the supremacy of the Church in western Europe during the Middle Ages. For centuries even kings at times had to humble themselves before the power of the Pope. The source of this supremacy is not difficult to trace. Since the clergy were among the few inhabitants who could read and write and had access to books, they enjoyed a long-range advantage over secular rulers who, like Charlemagne, never acquired a comfortable facility in reading and writing. Moreover, the clergy were in control of church auditoriums in which large numbers of people regularly gathered by tradition, while secular rulers had no comparably receptive audience for their communications. The early dominance of the church in colonial America can be explained on much the same grounds. It was not until lay groups acquired adequate command of the means of communication, in response to new life needs, that the secularization of government and public education took place.

To this day, those countries of Latin America in which from 50 to 80 per cent of the inhabitants are functionally illiterate,[12] in the sense of being unable to read a newspaper or write a simple letter, give proof of the fact that in the end the State, regardless of its structure or constitution, becomes

[12] Homer Kempfer, "Illiteracy in the Americas," *School Life*, 32 (December, 1949), 33–34.

what those who have easiest access to the mass media of communication want it to be. Despite the fact that most of these countries have constitutions modeled after our own and commonly include themselves among the democracies, military dictatorships and contests¹ between aspirants to dictatorial powers have less often been the exception than the rule.

Since insights of the kind developed in the preceding paragraphs are indispensable to intelligent living in a world which science and invention have made so small that nothing today is foreign, the responsibility of the English program for developing such insights is one that cannot safely be neglected. The history of the world since 1930 has shown how propaganda, developed into a deadly science, and censorship of the press, radio, church, school, theater, museum, concert stage, and lecture platform can enable a mere handful of men to hypnotize whole nations of mankind as by the gaze of a serpent. Although it is customary to think only of foreign lands as frightening examples of this practice, the same conditions can arise in any country by default of a populace more gullible than discriminating in its use and consumption of language. A nation in which five chain newspapers can reach 85 per cent of the reading public, and also control 400 of the most influential broadcasting stations, is safe only so long as its citizens are enlightened. Although the fact has been frequently denied, the pressure upon the press and radio to favor those groups which contribute from 75 to 95 per cent to their income through advertising is at times irresistible.¹³

In the service of the aims implied in the foregoing discussion, the teacher of English will find the following activities effective to the extent to which they are adapted to the maturity level of the student:

1. Collecting and discussing examples of humor in which

¹³ For recent examples, see *Time*, Oct. 31, 1949, p. 49; Nov. 21, 1949, p. 93; Jan. 23, 1950, pp. 38–39; Sept. 11, 1950, p. 64; Aug. 21, 1950, pp. 52–55; Apr. 10, 1950, p. 47; Jan. 5, 1948, p. 72.

the incongruity depends primarily on semantic shift in the meaning of a certain expression or word.

2. Analyzing points of disagreement in panel discussions to determine to what extent the differences are real, and to what degree they are linguistic. For example, are the dissenters using the same word in different senses?

3. Comparing reports of an important event in two or more newspapers, published under entirely different auspices, to determine the extent of factual coverage and the impression of the event which the readers of one newspaper might receive as compared with readers of another.

4. Analyzing reports in the press or on the radio for evidences of "selective selection of the news." Since all that happens in the world cannot be reported within the limits of time and space governing every commentator and journalist, selection of what is to be printed or reported is inevitable. It should be self-evident, however, that a consistent selection of certain items, such as crime, to the neglect or subordination of other news, can give the reading public a very warped and distorted view of the world. Where "selective selection" is consciously practiced as a propaganda device against certain groups within a society, or against a foreign country, the ultimate cumulative effect can be destructive of the welfare of thousands through the promotion of ill will to the point of hysteria. Surely a newspaper which gives an ax murderess as much attention on its front pages as any victory for the American way of life on the battlefield deserves to be suspected not only of selecting the news without regard for the public interest, but also of sensationalizing and coloring it to serve selfish interests. An English program that merely develops literate, but gullible, ventriloquist dummies for such irresponsible journalism does not represent a high achievement in public education.[14]

5. Reading books which give examples of semantic diffi-

[14] Willey Ley, "Hoaxes That Fooled Millions," *Science Digest*, 27 (February, 1950). 14–19. "What's Wrong with the Newsreels?" *Magazine Digest*, 40 (January, 1950), 84–86.

culties and discuss specific ways for detecting and avoiding them. Although the following books contain passages that presuppose a relatively high level of maturity, as a whole they are well within the reach of juniors and seniors whose reading ability is up to grade average. Voluntary individual reading, with reports to the group, is especially to be encouraged on the part of students with mature reading abilities or special interests in semantics.

Stuart Chase, *The Tyranny of Words*. New York: Harcourt, Brace and Company, Inc., 1938.

Robert W. Desmond, *The Press and World Affairs*. New York: Appleton-Century-Crofts, Inc., 1940.

S. I. Hayakawa, *Language in Thought and Action*. New York: Harcourt, Brace and Company, Inc., 1949.

Irving J. Lee, *Language Habits in Human Affairs*. New York: Harper & Brothers, 1941.

Curtis D. MacDougall, *Hoaxes*. New York: The Macmillan Company, 1940.

Institute for Propaganda Analysis, *Propaganda Analysis*, Vols. I and II. New York: Columbia University Press, 1938–1939.

Commission on Freedom of the Press, *The American Radio and a Free and Responsible Press*. Chicago: University of Chicago Press, 1947.

Clyde R. Miller, *What Everybody Should Know about Propaganda—How and Why It Works*. New York: Methodist Federation for Social Action, 1949.

Education versus propaganda. In view of the extent to which schools depend upon language and the readiness with which they can be intimidated by those who have easiest access to the mass media of communication, the need for distinguishing between education and propaganda cannot safely be ignored. Clearly, such overgeneralizations as "All education is a form of propaganda" do little more than beg the question. Nor do efforts to distinguish between "good" and "bad" propaganda contribute a solution. The likelihood that agreement on what is good and what is bad can be reached in the case of any emotionally charged issue is very slight, indeed. The humorous side of such glib distinctions was well emphasized by the wag who said, "When you try to get me to vote for *your* candidate, it's *propaganda;* when I try to get you to vote for *my* candidate, it's *education.*" Efforts to define abstractions without regard for specific referents can easily lead to such prejudiced definitions as that which was once made of "The Good, the True, and the Beautiful": "Beauty is what I like best; truth is my way of thinking; goodness is the way I think other people should behave."

A distinction between modern education and propaganda, however, can readily be made in terms of historical antecedents. The earliest uses of the term, *propaganda,* in the modern sense is to be found in the efforts of the Church to promote the Faith, especially in competition with Protestantism. Most dictionaries give *Congregatio de Propaganda Fide* (Congregation for the Propagation of the Faith) as the origin of the term. In the Roman Catholic Church, the proper noun refers to a congregation of cardinals charged with the management of missions, or to a college of the kind established by Urban VIII (1568–1644) to prepare priests for missionary work.[15] Since the Church at the time followed the policy of censoring or suppressing contrary points of view, even where supported by demonstrable fact, the distinction between modern education and propaganda can be found in the degree to which *all* relevant points of view regarding an issue, and *all* sides--not just one or two—are given a fair hearing before a decision is made.

Propaganda, then, is the promotion of an idea, program, candidate, or cause by presenting only favorable facts and points of view, and disregarding, suppressing, or maligning those which are contradictory or unfavorable. The learning situation which prevails when propaganda constitutes the dominant or exclusive method of schooling may properly be called indoctrination. In contrast, education in our society is the learning situation that exists when all relevant facts

[15] See "Propaganda," *The Catholic Encyclopedia,* Vol. 12. New York: The Encyclopedia Press, 1911.

and points of view are fairly presented as a basis for making a decision by democratic process. Although it is often assumed that propaganda makes use of emotional language and can thus be recognized by its obvious bias, this assumption is dangerously naïve. Scientific propaganda is more subtle than obvious. Its devices include the following:

1. *Selective selection of the facts.* Only favorable facts are presented and others left out. Anything suggestive of emotional coloring may be rigorously avoided to give the reader or listener the impression of objective, reasoned scholarship interested only in the truth.

2. *The band-wagon technique.* Contrary points of view are occasionally presented to give the impression of fairness but are immediately overwhelmed by what appears to be a very large majority of right-thinking people. Since the opposition is made to appear weak and futile, the tendency among the uninitiated is to "bet on the winning horse." Group pressure is used to put dissenters on the defensive even though in reality they may be a very substantial majority. The slogan for this type of propaganda is "Everybody is in favor of it (or against it); what's the matter with you?"

Since teachers in American schools are educators rather than propagandists, it is their duty to see that all relevant facts and points of view receive a fair hearing. Where problem solving is involved, the notion that a problem has only two sides must be discarded as unrealistic. Because debating, in the old-school sense of winning an argument, is not the same as finding the solution to a problem—and sometimes more productive of heat than of light—this device should be replaced by panel discussions or open forums guided by leaders representative of all relevant points of view. This assumes that both the discussion leaders and the classroom audience will have investigated and evaluated all relevant facts before arriving at a decision. Otherwise, the discussion produces little more than a public pooling of ignorance.

In his capacity as moderator or consultant, the teacher will help the students to diagnose and identify any propa-

ganda devices that they have consciously or unconsciously
attempted to use. However, he will not take a neutral position where none is justified by the preponderance of facts.
It is a peculiar type of mind, indeed, which would make a
few facts, indicative only of rare exceptions, the equivalent
of the vast majority of facts which indicate the rule. Neutrality in such cases comes very close to imitating the spineless
referee who felt that, in order to be fair, he had to call just
as many fouls against one side as against the other. As Van
Til has expressed it, "The middle position is a position, too,
and the would-be impartial leader has no more right to take
it than either extreme."

In his article on the handling of controversial questions,
Wilhelms offers the following suggestions: [16]

1. Focus on the problem, not on the fight.
2. Hunt for common ground.
3. Define the issues.
4. Develop criteria or standards of reference.
5. Be realistic about proposed alternatives.
6. Keep your weight off the decision.

In the light of the foregoing suggestions, it is probably self-
evident that, because of the emphasis which debating places
upon winning an argument rather than upon solving a problem and because of the constant danger that it risks in reducing a problem to only two extreme sides, it is not the best
technique for reaching practical decisions on social issues.

Having provided for a fair presentation of facts and relevant points of view regarding the problem, the teacher should
see that all possible solutions, including compromises, are
evaluated. Finally, a choice of solution by secret ballot should
be made to complete the process of democratic action guided
by education rather than propaganda. There is little point to
discussing a problem that requires no solution. There is even

[16] Fred T. Wilhelms, "Letter to a Teacher on Handling Controversial
Questions," *Progressive Education*, 26 (October, 1948), 8–12. This
entire number is devoted to the teaching of social issues.

less point to devoting class time to problems regarding which no one will ever have to act as a member of a family or citizen. This is not a period in history when men can afford the luxury of making verbal noises just for the sound effects. Training in problem solving thus includes practice in making decisions in the light of the best available evidence—decisions that are obviously valid only for the specific circumstances of time and place that are under discussion, and never eternal and irrevocable, but modifiable in the light of new evidence and of such changes in circumstances as require new solutions.

Putting real meaning into words. The fact that children, like parrots, can be taught to repeat words and phrases far beyond their level of comprehension has misled teachers throughout the ages. Ability to repeat verbal material from memory has often been mistaken for an understanding of it and for ability to apply what the words say. It was not until well after 1800 that catechetical drilling on questions and answers, to be learned verbatim, was gradually replaced by methods that attempted to avoid mistaking vocalization for learning.

Unless words are filled with the content of personal experience, they are likely to remain empty symbols in the mind of the learner and hence be misused or readily forgotten. Early missionaries among the Eskimos, for example, found it difficult to teach the Lord's prayer in view of the unpleasant, foreign associations that the natives had with bread as a food. To them it had no appeal, because it lacked both taste and smell. Hence, the phrase "Give us this day our daily bread" had to be translated by an expression denoting deer, fish, polar bear, walrus, and seal.

The danger of teaching vocabulary without reference to the content of experience is real in all schools where language is taught. The risk is particularly great when new words are introduced in list form for learning through memorization of spelling and meanings without reference to context or need. A methodology sensitive to this risk, and to the requirements of good training in semantics, places primary emphasis on the act or process and introduces the verbal symbol as the need for identifying it arises. In a sense, growth in vocabulary thus becomes a by-product of new experiences demanding the use of new words for describing, identifying, or communicating what *is being*, or *has been, done*. From this background of experience, words whose pronunciation, meaning, or spelling causes difficulties may be lifted for special consideration as separate items, but the procedure in such cases is always from the whole to the part.

Inasmuch as real life experiences are difficult to infuse into many words that young people should learn in school, the resources of the sound film as a means of bringing the world into the classroom deserve serious consideration. Excellent films are now available for concretizing the meaning even of such complex concepts as democracy and despotism. A school that is eager to make effective use of visual aids for strengthening the content of experience behind language will find *The Educational Film Guide*,[17] with its thousands of classified titles, an indispensable aid. As Edgar Dale has indicated, poor teaching of language occurs "when undue attention is given to mechanics and little attention to meaning. If the symbols . . . are without meaning, without rich association, children will merely be 'barking at words'."

Language customs. As important as the semantic vagaries of language are the conventions governing its use. These range all the way from the taboos against certain topics of conversation at the dinner table, or the use of certain words and expressions outside circles of intimate personal acquaintance, to the different style of diction and delivery that is

[17] *The Educational Film Guide.* New York: The H. W. Wilson Company. See latest current edition; also the selected bibliography by Searley Reid, "Motion Pictures on Democracy," *School Life*, 32 (January, 1950), 61–63; also *A Directory of 897 Sixteen Millimeter Film Libraries*, Visual Aids Section, U.S. Office of Education, Government Printing Office, Washington 25. Edgar Dale, "New Media for World Communication," *The News Letter*, Ohio State University, 15 (December, 1949), No. 3.

expected in a prayer or sermon, as compared with a military command or political speech. Lack of social sensitivity here can defeat the purposes of communication as completely as any misuse of words. For this reason, practice in using language appropriate to different circumstances is essential in the English course. Here dramatization of different life situations can provide valuable experiences.

On the international level, differences in language manners and customs present a common obstacle to communication. Latin Americans, for example, value poetic imagery and an aesthetic choice of words in public addresses. That is, perhaps, to be expected of representatives of countries where most educated men write poetry. To cut short an exquisite speech, however long, just because it is past time for lunch, would be regarded either as a symptom of poor breeding or as a lack of appreciation for the finer things in life. In contrast, among the Russians, rapierlike sallies and sarcasm with humorous overtones are prized as attributes of a telling speaker. Among English-speaking people, on the other hand, facts and arguments presented briefly and without oratorical embellishments, but with qualifications bordering on understatement to forestall rather than to invite argument, are generally preferred. The difficulties to which such differences in language customs and manners can lead at the international conference table have been described by a well-known interpreter for the United Nations:

I once heard this particular difference in speech etiquette brought succinctly to the attention of the Assembly, at the meeting of the Social Committee in Paris. The Cuban delegate, tired of the Chairman's constant interruption of the speeches of his Latin-American colleagues, protested:

"Not being all Nordics and Anglo-Saxons, we cannot fit into the pattern of brevity, terseness, and conciseness which you demand of us, Mr. Chairman. Such patterns befit the Northerners, but we like an orator to be imaginative, emotional, moving."

It was a Latin-American delegate who, during the General Assembly meeting in Paris, pleaded for the inclusion of the phrase, "from the cradle to the grave," in the article on the Declaration of Human Rights dealing with social security. He wanted to ensure that a worker should be covered by measures of social protection, in just that manner; the words were his way of saying precisely what he meant.

"Such phrases have no place in a serious document," pronounced a Western European delegate.

"It's a legal document, not a poem," muttered a Benelux member.

A member of the United States delegation whispered darkly into a neighbor's ear, "Why not 'from womb to tomb'? At least it rhymes!"

Again, semantic shift can cause confusion:

"Gentlemen," pleaded the Soviet delegate, "let us not behave like a bull in a china shop!"

He was speaking, naturally, in Russian. The Chinese delegate, however, was listening in English, as no Chinese translation was available that day. He raised his hand.

"Mr. Chairman, I should like the Soviet delegate to explain just what China has to do with his objections."

"Mr. Chairman, I said nothing whatever about China. The Chinese delegate must have misunderstood."

"Mr. Chairman, I distinctly heard my country mentioned. I request an explanation." [18]

Although little can be done to change language customs that are deeply rooted in tradition, insight into their existence and nature is essential to intelligent behavior in social situations where they arise. Awareness of their importance can serve as a vaccine against impatience and frustration, and at times provide clues to ways and means for reconciling potential differences through intelligent preplanning of programs and remarks. In dealing with this problem in the English class, the teacher will find the contributions of colleagues in the foreign languages, and of qualified citizens who have lived abroad, a valuable aid.

[18] Ina Telberg, "They Don't Do It Our Way," *United Nations World*, 3 (September, 1949), pp. 28–30.

Exercises in applied semantics. Despite the fact that semantics has only recently received attention at the high school level, and then only in a very few schools, materials that have been tried out successfully in English classes are available in larger quantity than might be expected. Samples of these are presented in the last section of this chapter. Their ultimate aim is the development of such discrimination in the use and consumption of words in law, advertising, newspaper reading, political discussion, and the like, as will enable the student to become a master more often than a victim of language. Such discrimination implies the habit of testing words, against the hard rock of reality, to see if they have the true ring of steel on granite or just the thin twang of tin on wood.

How Language Affects Us in Daily Life: Law [19]

Below are reports and descriptions of cases which have actually been tried before courts in the United States. Read each carefully with a view to answering the questions which follow it.

I

Crowley v. Chicago, St. P., M. & O. Railway Co., 99
Northwestern 1016 (Wisconsin, 1904)

In Chippewa Falls, Wisconsin, a city ordinance made it unlawful for a train or locomotive to remain standing across a street or alley for more than five minutes.

One day a train was standing so that the head of the locomotive reached slightly into the cross-street. Joseph Crowley, in order to get by started to drive his team of horses over the tracks in front of the resting locomotive. Just as he did so, however, the engineer suddenly let off steam, which frightened the horses so that they tipped over the load, throwing Crowley to the ground and hurting him. He sued the railway company for damages.

[19] Adapted from Walter V. Kaulfers, *Modern Languages for Modern Schools,* pp. 323–327. New York: McGraw-Hill Book Company, Inc., 1942.

1. Just why was the case brought before the court. In other words, exactly on what did the people involved disagree, or what were they trying to settle?

2. Can you find the exact word or words that caused trouble, or on which the decision of the court was based?

3. To what extent was the case purely a matter of law? To what extent was it a matter of settling or interpreting the meaning of words?

4. How would *you*, as judge, decide the case? Why?

5. Would you favor changing the wording of the law to make it clearer? If so, how?

II

People v. Keller, 161 New York Supplement 132
(New York, 1916)

Julius Keller ran a restaurant in New York City, and to make his place more popular he put on a floor show every night during the dinner hour. This show consisted of a small orchestra, with dancing and singing. No admission was charged for the show. It was a free entertainment feature coming with the meal.

Now the city of New York had an ordinance which made it unlawful for anyone to run a theater or to hold a circus performance without a license. Keller was arrested and convicted for violating this ordinance with his show. He appealed to a higher court.

Keller argued that he was running a restaurant, and neither a theater nor a circus (though some of his entertainment acts were like those to be found in a theater or a circus), and that consequently he was not breaking the law.

Questions for discussion same as for Case I.

V

DECISIONS

Below are the court decisions for the cases. Compare your own decisions with those rendered by the judges, and then answer the questions that follow.

Case I: The Supreme Court of Wisconsin decided the case against Crowley simply by pointing out the meaning of the word *across*, which was a vital part of the law involved: "The train in question was stopped and allowed to stand for a considerable length of time on Canal Street in such a way as not to obstruct public travel thereon, yet so that the head and the roof reached slightly into the cross street, called A street. It was not *across* a street in any sense of the term. That being the case, it seems that the charge of violating the ordinance entirely failed." (p. 1017.)

QUESTIONS FOR DISCUSSION

1. Did the judge interpret the meanings of the words in question correctly? What authority can you quote to show that he did or did not? What authority did *you* consult as a basis for making your own decision?

2. In making a decision, should a judge confine himself to the strict dictionary definition of a word, or should he take into consideration what the person who wrote the document *intended* the words to mean? Do all dictionaries agree on the meanings of words?

3. Was "justice" really done in this case, or did the court merely juggle words in someone's favor?

Case II: The higher court agreed with Keller. "It is plain," remarked the judge, "that a restaurant and a theater are different things. It is equally plain that appellant's (Keller's) place was not a circus. A *circus* is defined in the *Standard Dictionary* (Student's Edition) as a large enclosure, with parallel sides, with one end rounded for races; a show in which feats of horsemanship, tumbling, strength, etc., are exhibited." (p. 138.) "The word *theater* is defined in the *Standard Dictionary* as a building especially adapted to dramatic, operatic, or spectacular representations, a playhouse, and in the *Century Dictionary* as a building appropriate to representation of dramatic spectacles, a playhouse, a room, hall, or other place with a platform at one end and ranks of seats rising step-wise as the tiers recede from the center, or otherwise so arranged that a body of spectators can have an unobstructed view of the platform. A theater usually has, among other parts, an auditorium, an orchestra circle, parterre row, dress circle, etc." (p. 137.)

The judge also pointed out that the chief purpose of a circus or theater is to earn money directly for the management, but that the only purpose of the entertainment set up by Keller was to increase the popularity of a business already established—his restaurant. Thus, the law in question did not apply to any of his activities. He was thus declared innocent of the charge against him.

QUESTIONS FOR SUPPLEMENTARY DISCUSSION

1. Do you know of any cases now before the courts that are based to some extent upon disagreement over the meanings of words? Is either party trying to take advantage of certain loopholes in the wording or language of the case or law?

2. Can you think of any particular situations in which a person might get himself into difficulty in life if he were careless in his own use of language, or in signing his name to something that he had not read carefully?

3. How important is a thorough knowledge of language to a lawyer or judge?

4. The following articles in *The Reader's Digest* show how language often gets people into difficulties. Select one of the articles and report your findings to the class.

   a. Olive H. Rabe, "Read—Before You Crash," Vol. 30, May, 1937, pp. 43–46. Condensed from *The American Magazine*, April, 1937.

   b. E. Jerome Ellison and Frank W. Brock, "The Wage Snatchers," Vol. 30, March, 1937, pp. 99–100. Condensed from *Today*, Dec. 26, 1936. (Read before you sign.)

   c. "Lotteries and the Law," Vol. 19, June, 1936, pp. 78–81. Condensed from *Today*, May 2, 1936. (Fraud through advertising, etc.)

   d. "Public Easy Mark No. 1," Vol. 27, October, 1935, pp. 69–71. (Read before you sign—and keep a copy.)

   e. Marc A. Rose, "Law and the Little Man," Vol. 19, February,

1936, pp. 75–76. Condensed from *Today*. (How workers often lose their earnings by failing to read carefully what they sign.)

INFERENCE AND INTERPRETATION [20]

The following article tells about a government project. Read the article carefully and then answer the questions that follow.

Several months ago the central government began work on another of its national improvement projects. It will combine soil conservation with flood prevention. A huge man-made lake, covering thousands of acres, will be made by damming up a river which has been running rampant nearly every spring, carrying fertile soil with it. Little of the region is fertile farm land, but the project will prevent the soil from being washed away, and will allow grass, shrubbery, and trees to grow again.

As is usually the case with such projects, some good bottom land will be flooded. The farmers now cultivating the land will be asked to move to other regions. Government agents, experienced in working with farm families, will help farmers find other land just as good as that which they are leaving. The government will, of course, pay all moving expenses and will repay the farmers for any property lost. Those farmers who want cash for their property, instead of other land, will be paid after government agents estimate the value of their holdings.

Some families have already moved, taking early advantage of the courteous assistance provided by the government. The others will leave soon. It is not surprising that a few of the farmers are stubbornly opposing the general welfare by refusing to move.

A few men living in the region have been given work on the project and thus benefit two-fold from the program. Most of these, however, were selected by civil service examinations, and come from all parts of the country. They live in neat frame houses in a miniature

[20] Adapted from a contribution to the Stanford Language Arts Investigation by Max Schifer and Leif Thorne-Thomsen.

town built near the dam. They are very sociable and democratic, and mix freely with the people living in the region.

The present government was given broad emergency powers when it came into office. It was expected that these would be used to reconstruct the country. Now the government is encouraging brilliant young social engineers to exercise these powers for constructive purposes. Their activities have been introduced into fields with which the government has not hitherto concerned itself. The relatively small amounts of money spent will be well repaid by the sound planning which will save the nation's resources for the people.

Directions

Assume that the article you have just read is *based on descriptions* given both by those who support and by those who oppose the government. Assume also that it appeared in a news magazine which carefully checks the accuracy of all information contained in articles.

Each group of three sentences below refers to an item of information given in the article. Every statement is a possible interpretation of that information. As in reading a newspaper or magazine article, decide *which version or interpretation tells what is probably happening*. Then check the *one* statement in *each set of three sentences* which you think is most nearly correct. *DO NOT SKIP ANY SETS.* You may wish to read the article several times while working with it.

1. _____ *a.* The project will greatly improve the value of the region.

   _____ *b.* It cannot be determined whether the project will conserve good soil and prevent floods.

   _____ *c.* More good land will be flooded than will be saved.

2. _____ *a.* All the good soil in the region will be covered by the lake.

   _____ *b.* Some of the bottom land will be covered by the lake.

   _____ *c.* Only a small percentage of the good soil will be flooded.

3. _____ a. The government will probably give the farmers land which is not as valuable as that which they are leaving.

_____ b. The farmers will get land just as good or better than that which they leave.

_____ c. The government will settle the farmers on other land.

4. _____ a. All the farmers on the land to be covered by the lake will have to move whether they want to or not.

_____ b. Nearly all the farmers are willing to cooperate with the government and move elsewhere.

_____ c. Most of the farmers resent being forced to move.

5. _____ a. The government will pay the farmers as much, or more than their land is worth.

_____ b. The government will pay the farmers the amount that the government agents estimate their property to be worth.

_____ c. The government will give the farmers much less than their land is worth.

6. _____ a. The people of the region get the poorest jobs, although they are capable of doing better-paying work.

_____ b. Some people living in the region are working on the project.

_____ c. All people working on the project have good jobs.

7. _____ a. The employees from other parts of the country are political appointees, who actually passed only a dummy examination.

_____ b. The employees were fairly selected by rigid tests.

_____ c. Most of the employees were selected by civil service examinations, but it cannot be determined whether the examinations were easy or difficult.

8. _____ a. The employees from other parts of the country live apart, but visit with the native inhabitants.

_____ b. The employees are liked by the local inhabitants, and are glad to talk about the project with them.

_____ c. The employees were instructed by the government to spread lies about the project.

9. _____ a. The men who planned the project probably in-

clude government engineers and persons experienced in soil conservation.

_____ b. The planners are impractical theorists.

_____ c. The planners of the project are capable men who wanted to aid the people.

10. _____ a. The government uses emergency powers to experiment with unsound programs.

_____ b. The government is using emergency powers to rebuild the country.

_____ c. The project is being developed under emergency powers.

11. _____ a. The government is promoting soil conservation projects.

_____ b. The welfare of all of the people is being promoted by the government.

_____ c. The government is using its position to obtain still more power.

12. _____ a. Most people in the country probably do not know much about the project.

_____ b. The people of the country would not be in favor of the project if they had an accurate description of it.

_____ c. If they knew what the government was doing, the people of the country would be in favor of the project.

13. _____ a. The government is moving into fields in which it does more harm than good.

_____ b. The extended activities of the government are necessary for the people's welfare.

_____ c. The government is doing things which other governments did not do.

14. _____ a. Government engineers have estimated the results of the project, and have probably concluded that it will be worth more than the money it costs.

_____ b. The project will be of much more value to the people than it costs.

_____ c. The government is spending money recklessly on poorly-planned projects.

15. _____ a. The people will be greatly benefited by the project.

_____ *b.* If such projects conserve soil and prevent floods, they will be of some value to the people.

_____ *c.* The people will be poorer as a result of the project.

EVALUATION OF ARGUMENTS [21]

Name_____
    Last   First

Date_____

Grade or Class_____

Teacher_____

Directions

When people have to make decisions, they usually gather as much information as possible on the problem and then make their decision on the basis of that information. Very often the information is given in the form of an argument or of an explanation stating why certain things should be done.

Arguments are a help in making decisions *if all parts of them are true,* and *if the conclusion*—the part that shows how the problem may be solved—*deals with the same subject as the rest of the argument.*

All the numbered items in this exercise are short arguments or statements about problems. Try to decide whether each argument is helpful.

In each case, put a check in the column headed "Helpful" if you think that the argument would help you make decisions on the problem. Put a check in the column headed "Not helpful" if the argument would not help you. Do not skip any items.

Remember, you are not asked to decide whether the argument settles the problem. You are asked only to decide whether it *would help you to make a decision.*

Now try the first few arguments, and if you find that you do not understand what you are to do, read the directions again.

---

[21] Adapted from a contribution to the Stanford Language Arts Investigation by Max Schifer and Leif Thorne-Thomsen.

Help- ful	Not Helpful	
————	————	1. Since the normal age at which pupils enter high school is between the ages of 13 and 14, we can conclude that it is unusual for a pupil to reach high school at the age of 11.
————	————	2. Statements which are untrue, or which distort the true facts, are called *propaganda* and should not be believed. Any advertisement which states that a product will do things which it will not do is *propaganda* and should not be believed.
————	————	3. The welfare of the country should be safeguarded, even if it be at the expense of a minority of the people.
————	————	4. Capitalism is an ideal which has never been attained. For this reason, the arguments against the present economic system are not sound, and no good reasons for changing it have been given.
————	————	5. If, when visiting any foreign country, we break the laws of that country, we should expect to pay the consequences.
————	————	6. Those who really believe in democratic or representative government should oppose all attempts to change our form of government, even if changes are demanded by a majority of the people.
————	————	7. Labor is responsible for the high standard of living which Americans now enjoy, because without workers goods cannot be produced. Since this is true, we must support labor unions in order to maintain this high standard.
————	————	8. Truth is the best guide to action. Since all newspapers do not give us accurate accounts of current events, we should

Help-   Not
ful   Helpful

> not depend on them for information on which to act.

_____   _____   9. Murder is recognized by most people as socially and morally wrong. But this does not mean that people think it wrong to kill in self-defense, because killing in self-defense is usually not considered murder.

_____   _____   10. No one wants bureaucracy, and efforts should be made to decrease it. But if bureaucracy means the "red tape" which is usually involved in operating the bureaus and departments of any large organization, then efforts to reduce it should not be confined to government. There will be a great deal of it in business organizations also.

_____   _____   11. To preserve freedom of speech, we must forbid Fascists, Communists, and other dictatorial groups to hold meetings and publish papers.

_____   _____   12. An honorary certificate is to be awarded to the best student in school. The judges will base their decision on the school marks of candidates. Although Helen does not always do what her teachers tell her to do and is often absent from school, she should get the award, because she has higher grades than any other student.

_____   _____   13. People who really believe in peace will, if necessary, go to war to defend peace.

_____   _____   14. The more business activity there is, the more goods and services are produced. Therefore, all consumers benefit when business men make good profits.

_____   _____   15. Many of the American people want our army and navy to be only large

Help- ful	Not Helpful	
		enough for the defense of this nation. Since the best defense is an offense, however, they should support enlarging our army and navy so that they will be able to carry on an offensive war against any possible combination of enemy nations.
————	————	16. John's father told him not to buy an expensive suit, because the family's bank balance was low. John did not disobey his father when he bought a suit which cost twice as much as he usually spent. Since the suit he bought was of excellent quality, it was not really expensive.
————	————	17. The state law provides for the punishment of all criminals. Bankers who illegally use depositors' funds for personal investment are certainly criminals and must be punished if the law is to be enforced.
————	————	18. Productive activity, both by business and government, built America. Politics did not. Therefore, we should encourage governmental activities which contribute to the general welfare, and not allow politics to interfere.
————	————	19. Since all young people want to be successful, they should try to avoid getting work in the trades or agriculture. Those who engage in such work have little chance of obtaining footholds in business or the professions and thus have little chance of being successful.
————	————	20. Progress has been responsible for the rapid rise in the standard of living of the American people. If we want to continue to raise our standard of living, we must uphold progress by opposing all attempts to change our ways of doing things.

For Further Reading

Chase, Stuart, *The Tyranny of Words*. New York: Harcourt, Brace and Company, Inc., 1938.

Hayakawa, S. I., *Language in Thought and Action*. New York: Harcourt, Brace and Company, Inc., 1949.

Hayakawa, S. I., *Language in Action*. New York: Harcourt, Brace and Company, Inc., 1941.

Johnson, Wendell, *People in Quandaries*. New York: Harper & Brothers, 1946.

Kaulfers, W. V., G. N. Kefauver, and H. D. Roberts, *Foreign Languages and Cultures in American Education*. New York: McGraw-Hill Book Company, Inc., 1942.

Kaulfers, W. V., *Modern Languages for Modern Schools*. New York: McGraw-Hill Book Company, Inc., 1942.

La Brant, Lou, *We Teach English*. New York: Harcourt, Brace and Company, Inc., 1951.

Lee, Irving, *Language Habits in Human Affairs*. New York: Harper & Brothers, 1941.

Progressive Education Association, *Language in General Education*. New York: Appleton-Century-Crofts, Inc., 1940.

Roberts, H. D., *et al.*, *English for Social Living*. New York: McGraw-Hill Book Company, Inc., 1943.

Walpole, Hugh, *Semantics*. New York: W. W. Norton & Company, 1941.

Chapter 6. DEVELOPING READING AND LISTENING ABILITIES IN THE SECONDARY SCHOOL

READING IN THE HIGH SCHOOL PROGRAM

Reading emphasized in modern schools. The development of reading abilities remains one of the most important responsibilities of the school. The current emphasis upon the overall development of youth and the inclusion of many types of nonreading activities in the secondary school curriculum have tended to stimulate rather than discourage efforts to improve the reading abilities of young people. The modern activity school is characterized by an increased diversity and quantity of good reading materials.

Reading ability important today. Reading competence is important, not only because it underlies success in all areas of study in the high school but because it is essential to personal enrichment and the development of intelligent citizenship. A literate society is not necessarily a democratic society, but an uninformed people cannot long continue to be a self-governing people. Democracy, more than any other kind of society, demands literate and enlightened citizens. Never has the need for intelligent readers in a democratic society been so keenly realized or so frequently insisted upon as today.

Need for improvement in reading programs. Nevertheless, it is becoming increasingly apparent that the schools have been unsuccessful in raising the level of genuine literacy in the United States to satisfactory heights. Gray has estimated that one-half of the adult population is "functionally illiter-

161

ate"—that is, unable to read with ordinary comprehension those books and magazines which have been designed for unselected lay audiences of today. It is probably true that the absolute levels of reading ability have risen in the past quarter-century, but it is likewise true that the range and complexity of modern reading materials have increased even more than the public's ability to read. The result is a net loss in the relative abilities of people to read printed matter.

Educational facilities inadequate. The present widespread illiteracy is due in part to the lack of adequate educational facilities in many parts of the United States. Recent figures indicate that more than 3 million children of school age in many states of the Union are denied the opportunity to attend school. Others attend schools which operate only three to six months per year, are lacking in adequate equipment, and are taught by poorly educated and underpaid teachers. Equalization of educational opportunity through Federal aid to schools should do much to decrease the percentage of illiteracy throughout the country.

High school pupils' need for help in reading. Many boys and girls who do complete elementary programs, however, enter high school with inferior reading ability, even in the large cities. In typical ninth-grade groups, as many as 2 per cent of the pupils score below the fourth-grade norms in reading ability, 30 per cent below the seventh-grade norms, and 48 per cent below the eighth-grade norms. Numerous causes have been advanced for this situation: large classes, inadequate reading material and equipment, lack of attention to individual differences, particularly with respect to reading readiness, inappropriate teaching methods, and a curriculum unsuited to children's needs and interests. Probably all these factors are responsible in varying degrees. In any case, it is clear that the high school has the obligation of developing an effective program of reading improvement.

Reading instruction an all-school task. The responsibility for teaching reading belongs to all teachers in the secondary school. It cannot be left to the teacher of English alone.

Sweeping improvements in the reading abilities of young people could be achieved if the reading problem were made the subject of a school-wide attack. Reading habits, good or bad, are being developed whenever reading is carried on, whether in common learnings, English, the social studies, science, mathematics, or any other subject area. It is essential that all members of secondary school faculties be aware of the significance of the reading problem, and that they be qualified to provide young people with intelligent guidance in reading.

Teachers' need for help in providing guidance in reading. Many teachers in the so-called subject fields fail to give their students proper guidance in reading because they do not regard themselves qualified to do so. They believe that reading instruction belongs to specialists and experts, and that they themselves have a sufficient task in teaching their subjects.

While it is true that specialists and clinicians are needed, effective assistance can be given young readers by any teacher who will be patient and thoughtful and who will take time to observe the reading behavior of individual learners. If the task is conceived as developmental rather than remedial, it will lose much of the forbidding and mysterious aspect which has discouraged many teachers from giving instruction in reading. The following paragraphs deal with some of the factors which all teachers can recognize in their efforts to improve young people's reading abilities.

ELEMENTS IN THE READING PROCESS

Reading a part of total child development. Good reading is based upon the operation of many factors. It calls for physical and mental health, sound vision and hearing, a wide experience background, adequate language development, a strong interest in and a purpose for reading, familiarity with printed symbols, and skill in dealing with various types of printed matter. When all these factors are present in sufficient degree, we say the learner is "ready to read." Reading readiness is essential not only in the initial stages of reading but in all stages of human development. To read any passage of print successfully, a reader must be "ready," *i.e.*, the various factors that have been mentioned must be present. It is the *whole* child who reads, not just his eyes or a part of his mind. When any of the readiness factors fails to operate sufficiently, good reading instruction undertakes to build that factor. Maturation in reading means growth in *all* the factors essential to good reading.

Physical and mental health essential. While some learners become good readers in spite of physical ill health, malnutrition, poor teeth, or infected tonsils, good physical health is necessary to maximum growth in reading. The distractions and discouragements resulting from discomfort, fatigue, and depleted energy frequently interfere with success in reading. Alert teachers may often observe the symptoms of general listlessness and irritability which call for the attention of a physician. Poor performance in reading may require, not additional pressure or assignments from the teacher, but a suggestion to parents that a physical examination is indicated. Rest may be more important than stimulation or rebuke.

Perhaps even more important than physical health is the factor of mental health. Children and young people who are afraid and insecure do not learn well and cannot make satisfactory progress in reading. A recent study of a number of poor readers [1] revealed that a leading cause of reading deficiency among the cases studied was an unhappy home condition—loss of one or both parents, maladjustment, or conflict in the home. Clearly the emotional effects of unsatisfactory conditions in the home had a seriously adverse effect on children's reading. Adolescents as well as younger children require an atmosphere of affection and security for progress in reading.

When mental and emotional problems interfere with

[1] Helen M. Robinson, *Why Children Fail in Reading.* Chicago: University of Chicago Press, 1946.

growth in reading, the teacher by himself is usually not in a position to remove the causes of retardation. The school guidance officers and social case workers may often be of assistance. In some instances it is impossible to remove the causes completely, and it becomes necessary to compensate as much as possible by adjusting to the situation. Special efforts to provide emotional security for the boy or girl in the school environment, to promote good relations with his classmates, and to give him a sense of success and achievement will pay dividends in the form of improved performance.

Sound vision and hearing essential. Obviously a minimum amount of visual acuity is essential to success in reading. Some investigators have found that visual deficiencies are as numerous among good readers as among poor readers,[2] but in cases of serious visual difficulty, progress in reading may be retarded or made completely impossible. Visual fatigue resulting from improperly corrected vision may be a contributory cause of reading deficiency. The Snellen chart or the Betts Ophthalmic Telebinocular will be useful in screening those cases which should be referred to the oculist for examination.

Hearing loss may likewise interfere with learning in general and with reading in particular. Teachers should be on the alert for evidences of auditory deficiency and refer pupils who exhibit symptoms of hearing difficulty for tests of hearing. Whisper tests and audiometer tests may be administered by trained clinical workers.

Wide experience background essential. Reading is not a matter of sounding words. It consists in gaining meaning, rapidly and accurately, from the printed page. If the printed symbol is to convey meaning to the reader, there must be in his mind a background of impressions which may be evoked by the symbols. If the printed matter includes reference to a locomotive engineer, the reader should have had previous opportunity to observe a locomotive engineer in action. When

[2] Paul Witty and David Kopel, *Reading and the Education Process,* p. 210. Boston: Ginn & Company, 1939.

reading growth is retarded because of the reader's limited experience background, instruction may often best take the form of field trips, observation of experiments, laboratory work under careful guidance, and various forms of audio-visual aids such as films and filmstrips, maps, charts, graphs, radio recordings, and phonograph records.

Not merely the reader's total stock of impressions but the effective organization of ideas are important as preparations for reading. The skillful teacher can help the reader bring to mind many earlier experiences which bear upon the subject of the reading material in such a way as to make the printed matter more meaningful. Reading guidance should therefore usually be accompanied by exploratory discussions which will most effectively focus the reader's fund of experiences upon the material to be read.

Adequate language development a part of reading readiness. To read materials in English or any other language it is of course necessary to be familiar with the language in question. Boys and girls from bilingual homes frequently exhibit reading difficulties because of insufficient knowledge of the English language. Direct experiences, to be helpful in promoting reading growth, must be accompanied by abundant contact with language which can identify and interpret the experiences.

The development of reading abilities, therefore, calls for a concurrent development in language expression. It implies numerous opportunities on the part of students for oral and written communication. It implies frequent attention to the derivation and structure of words. It implies particularly an understanding of the varied meanings of words and the importance of context in the determination of meaning. Some of the most familiar words possess many different meanings in contemporary English speech.[3] Only a considerable skill

[3] The *American College Dictionary* lists 104 meanings for the word *run;* 14 for the word *idle;* 30 for the word *level;* 74 for the word *open;* 25 for the word *read;* 36 for the word *beat;* 55 for the word *out;* 42 for the word *put* with its compounds. Each of these meanings includes numerous shadings which can be perceived only in context.

in the use of context for determining the meanings of words can bring about the kind of language mastery that is needed for reading.

Interest and purpose important elements in reading development. Effective reading is not a passive process of absorbing facts or ideas from the printed page. It is rather a reaching out of the mind for meaning—for the answer to a question, for the outcome of a story, for facts related to an existing interest. Reading guidance should provide for the active approach to the printed page, for the attitude of expectancy or of seeking. New reading material must be related to what has been read previously. The reader must actively seek relations between each new passage with what has gone before.

The task of the teacher is to arouse or discover the reading motive—the inner driving power that makes the book a servant and not a master of the reader. Good readers may discover their motives as they read, or recognize interests which have been previously aroused. The average reader in school cannot successfully approach the reading materials "cold"; he should prepare himself or be prepared for what is to be read.

It has been shown that many boys and girls are capable of reading materials which are beyond their normal comprehension level if the materials deal with subjects highly charged with interest for them. Thus a slow reader in the fifth grade may be able to read with understanding a sports story in the daily newspaper if he is an ardent baseball fan. The fact that he has a background of experience in the playing or observation of baseball, that he knows the jargon of baseball, and that he has a keen desire to learn what has transpired, accounts for his unusual performance in reading.

Need for familiarity with the printed symbols. Reading instruction in schools is frequently confined to drill in word recognition, speed of reading, and related skills in interpretation of printed materials. As we have seen, reading is a much broader process than mere symbol perception. Nevertheless, the ability to recognize visual symbols on the printed page is essential to good reading. The analogy has been drawn between reading and viewing a landscape through field glasses. When the lenses are well adjusted and the view is clear, the spectator is almost unconscious of the glasses, particularly if the view is an exciting one. If the view is blurred, however, the spectator is interrupted in his preoccupation with the distant scene and turns to the instrument to secure a better focus. So in reading, under conditions of perfect comprehension, the reader's thoughts are fixed on the action or the thought; but when unfamiliar words or constructions obtrude themselves, the reader is perforce distracted by the mechanical problems of word recognition and interpretation.

Basic reading abilities are developed naturally through close and constant association between meaning and symbol. Sight vocabulary normally grows rapidly, without memoriter methods or much word analysis and consultation of the dictionary. Specific instruction in independent word recognition should be supplementary rather than basic to the program in reading guidance.

An excellent list of abilities in the development of a reading vocabulary is found in the *Research Bulletin* of the National Education Association for January, 1942, "Reading Instruction in Secondary Schools":

1. Recognition and understanding of the general meaning of a stock of words appropriate to the student's age and grade, and continuous growth in acquiring new sight words.

2. Knowledge of the meaning of technical words in each field of study.

3. Ability to discriminate between words that are quite similar in appearance.

4. Ability to select the correct meaning of a word which has more than one meaning according to the context in which it appears.

5. Ability to detect shades of meanings for words that are related but not synonymous.

6. Ability to sense the figurative use of words and to interpret figurative meanings.

7. Skill in attacking unfamiliar words to determine their pronunciations or meanings or both. This implies (a) appropriate phonetic knowledge and skill, (b) ability to divide words into syllables, (c) command of common prefixes, suffixes, and root words, and (d) ability to use the context as a clue to the pronunciation and meaning of new words.

8. Independent use of the dictionary in learning the pronunciation and meaning of unfamiliar words.

9. Habit of using newly acquired words in the student's own written and oral expression.

Young people in high school classes often benefit from some assistance in the phonetic analysis of words. Relatively few will require instruction in the sounds of individual letters, although their attention may need to be called to initial and final letters. Some will not have fully learned the sounds of diphthongs and such common letter combinations as *ough, tion,* or *str.* For most students, however, the great need in word analysis is familiarity with the more common stems, prefixes, and suffixes.

Specialized meanings of technical words require particular attention. Intelligent use of the dictionary, with its pronunciation key and other helps, has served as an important technique in the teaching of vocabulary. The use of context clues, such as substitute words, synonyms and antonyms, typographical aids, direct explanations and appositives, and phrase or sentence structure, have proved especially valuable, particularly in combination with other methods.

Generally speaking, however, a combination of intensive study of significant passages along with emphasis upon extensive, well-motivated reading provides the most satisfactory base for the building of a large recognition vocabulary. English and all other classes should be characterized by a wholesome "verbal" environment, in which the fascination of words may be shared by all students, the accelerated and retarded alike.

Employing appropriate techniques with many types of reading matter. Young readers must learn how to attack reading material which calls for slow careful reading and meticulous attention to details, that which should be read rapidly, that which should be skimmed, and that which calls for rereading and mental outlining. They need to learn how to find the central thought of a paragraph, how to distinguish between major and supporting ideas, how to follow printed directions, how to assemble and summarize information, how to draw conclusions from the material read.

Increasing speed of reading certain types of materials is important at a time when the sheer volume of printed matter places special demands on cultivated persons. It has been shown that, in general, comprehension tends to increase with increased rate, although accelerated speed of reading in itself may be undesirable in the case of reading matter calling for careful attention to details. Speed may be increased by putting students under time pressure in the reading of specific exercises, and especially by encouraging readers to phrase intelligently and to read in thought units.

Attention to the various skills involved in word recognition, comprehension, and rate of reading should in no case obscure the importance of laying the physical, emotional, experiential, and linguistic bases of good reading. Reading is valuable only in so far as it contributes to the wholesome personality, the enrichment of life, and the building of intelligent, democratic citizenship.

PROVIDING FOR INDIVIDUAL DIFFERENCES IN READING ABILITY

No principle of learning is so well established as the principle that it is normal for learners to vary widely in their ability to learn. Perhaps even more significant is the fact that differences are accentuated as a result of effective teaching. The efforts of teachers to bring "retarded" pupils up to a "norm" are therefore as futile as they are unnecessary. The responsibility of the teacher is simply to aim at maximum progress for all the pupils in a class, regardless of their level of achievement. An unselected high school group may vary six or more grades in reading ability. The range is not narrowed by instructional effort. Teachers find it difficult to look upon these differences as normal and to accept them as a basis for their educational planning.

Grouping according to reading ability as revealed by standardized tests. In these cases, students in English and other subjects are assigned to special classes for slow, medium, and advanced learners. The chief argument advanced for such segregation is the fact that accelerated pupils will not be delayed in their progress by the lower standards which must be set for the slow learners. On the other hand, slow or inefficient readers may escape discouragement caused by failure to achieve standards of accomplishment which are beyond them. Under the plan of segregation, teachers avoid the necessity of making differentiated assignments and are able to concentrate on the needs of "homogeneous" pupils.

Opponents of segregation point out that pupils who are relatively homogeneous in reading ability still differ widely in other important characteristics, including reading interests. Some boys and girls, for example, are able to make good scores on reading tests but do not enjoy reading, make no effort to read, and prefer other kinds of activity. Even when they are assigned to "homogeneous" classes, they require individual guidance. Moreover, segregation on the basis of reading ability assumes that this characteristic is the most significant among all the qualities of young people. Actually it is possible that the personal needs of youth, which vary widely even in the most homogeneous class, may be much more important than the level of reading ability. It is argued also that ability grouping creates levels and strata which are repugnant to the ideals of a democratic society.

Segregation essentially represents an effort to escape the need for individualized guidance. Perhaps the conditions of mass education necessitate some measure of escape from individual differences. Sound education, however, requires that we meet and provide for differences instead of attempting to avoid them. Homogeneity in important respects is impossible to achieve, even if it were desirable. The only fundamental solution for differences is an instructional program which accepts them and provides suitable individualized guidance.

Objections to systematic segregation of learners do not necessarily apply to the temporary organization of special groups for slow readers. Special interest and ability groups may, particularly under conditions of mass instruction, prove helpful, provided they do not imply the stratification of the school population on the basis of the specialized skill of reading.

Providing differentiated reading materials and individual guidance for pupils of varying abilities, interests, and needs in reading. No two pupils, even in homogeneous groups, have precisely the same needs, interests, and abilities. For this reason it becomes necessary for the teacher to acquaint himself thoroughly with the characteristics of the learners in his charge. Standardized tests represent only one means of discovering certain of these characteristics. Too often a great deal of time and effort is expended in the administration, scoring, and recording of standardized reading tests, without sufficient application of the findings to the instructional process. Standardized tests may be supplemented with informal quizzes and teacher-made tests of comprehension, speed, and reading interests. Listening to the oral reading of young people frequently gives clues as to their ability to recognize words and gain meaning from the printed page. For such purposes the Gray *Oral Reading Paragraphs* and the Gray *Oral Reading Check Tests* have proved helpful by revealing mispronunciations, omissions, substitutions, insertions, and repetitions. Individual conferences with students about their reading will reveal many ways in which the reader may need help. Observation of pupil behavior is also an important means of discovering needs. Not only can the teacher take note of such phenomena as lip reading, irregular eye movements, and the rise of line markers, but he can observe the degree of absorption displayed by the reader and the voluntary selection of books and magazines from the shelves and racks. Cumulative record cards should be kept for each student so that the various types of evidence may be brought together and interpreted.

With the aid of data gathered by various means, the teacher is in a position to provide the kind of reading guidance which each learner requires. In order to provide such guidance, however, the teacher will find it necessary to organize the instruction in such a way as to make individualization possible. Uniform textbooks for an entire class should, wherever possible, be replaced by a diversity of titles representing many levels of maturity and many interests. When assignments are made, they should be differentiated so that all students may read materials which are within the range of their comprehension. Better still, topics under discussion may be analyzed into subtopics to be investigated by small groups within the class, and the teacher may assist each individual to find suitable reading materials on the subtopics during the research period. Conferences with individual students, carried on while committees are at work, will provide opportunities to assist individuals who require special help in coping with the reading material. When textbooks are used, it becomes especially important to supply supplementary materials of varying difficulty, so that there may be opportunity for all to read with understanding. Books will be supplemented with an attractive array of magazines, newspapers, pamphlets, and pictures. The more successful readers may have opportunity to give assistance, on some occasions, to those whose reading level is lower. And, of course, there will be an abundance of nonreading activities which will enrich and provide background for the reading.

The exclusive use of the textbook, particularly in the "content fields," offers unusual difficulty in providing for individual differences. Many textbooks have readability indexes far beyond the grade level for which they are intended. Even when the reading difficulty of a textbook has been properly adjusted to the grade level, almost half of a typical class will normally have difficulty in reading it. The new vocabulary load of some high school textbooks has been found to be equivalent to the first-year vocabulary load of a foreign-language textbook. Many words familiar in other contexts acquire technical meanings in high school textbooks and need to be taught as new words. It becomes necessary, therefore, for the teacher of history to supply numerous biographies and other interesting nontextbook materials now available for use at all school levels in order to enrich the program in reading. The teacher of science may likewise find in current periodical literature and elsewhere a wide variety of reading materials which may effectively supplement the textbook.

In this whole process of individualizing the reading experiences of young people in school, three major principles should be kept in mind: (1) Students develop good or bad habits and attitudes in every reading situation. Individual guidance is necessary, therefore, in every class or subject which involves reading, not merely in English classes. (2) Reading is only one avenue to learning. The learner himself remains the prime consideration. If pressure to read or to remember results in fears, frustrations, or other detrimental responses, instruction should be so modified as to avoid such results. The purpose of reading is to strengthen and enrich the quality of the learner's present living, not to supply high scores for the school's reading records. (3) *All* learners need help of some kind in reading. There is perhaps more relative retardation among the superior students than among the retarded ones.

PLANNING FOR THE SLOW READER

Causes of reading problems. Retardation in reading is not an evidence of inability to learn, natural perversity, or inherent incapacity for the reading task. Generally speaking, children with a Binet IQ of 50 or over can learn to read materials of varying levels of difficulty, and they can improve in their reading ability. When we encounter cases of reading disability, our task is to attempt to discover the causes of disability and so far as possible to remove them.

There is of course a high correlation between reading ability and what is commonly called "intelligence." Children and youth of high intelligence normally find it easier to learn to read, and they can reach higher levels of reading ability than those of low intelligence. It is likely, too, that the reading experience itself may have an effect upon "intelligence" as measured by existing instruments. We do know that many children of high intelligence do not read so well as their abilities would permit.

The causes of poor reading are interrelated and complex. When children or youth fail to read as well as they can, one or more of the elements essential to good reading are lacking in some degree. These elements include good physical health, good visual and auditory acuity, a sense of security, a broad language and experience background, many favorable experiences with the printed page, strong motivation, and a genuine desire to read. Diagnostic measures should include an examination of these elements. Remedial procedures should consist in supplying these elements to the degree that they are lacking.

Remedial procedures stressing the whole child. Too often the teacher's efforts at improving a young person's reading are confined to drills with the printed page. Often some experience such as a visit to a newspaper plant, with intelligent discussion of what has been planned, is more valuable in the improvement of reading than performing many pages of exercises in a workbook. In estimating the reading needs of the learner, the teacher should take into account the total pattern of the learner's development as a human being. Some young people need more rest at home instead of added homework for maximum progress.

Need for the experience of success. By definition, every retarded reader is lacking in one of the most important factors which contribute to effective learning: a sense of achievement and confidence. The poor reader is in greatest need of the one element he lacks most: successful experience in reading. It is necessary, therefore, to provide the slow reader with reading tasks which he can accomplish successfully, and he must be made conscious of his successes. A certain proportion of failure is inevitable in every person's life, and every learner must know how to accept failures. However, even superior students cannot be expected to accept continuous failure and yet be emotionally prepared to make the kind of progress of which they are capable. Proper preparation for the reading act and intelligent selection of the reading matter for the individual are therefore essential procedures in dealing with retarded readers.

Need for a wholesome emotional climate in which to learn. Classrooms in which teachers and students feel great pressure to meet certain arbitrary standards of achievement are not conducive to progress in reading. The atmosphere of friendliness and relaxation is essential to success in reading, as in all learning. Relaxation is not equivalent to lack of effort. On the contrary, the most successful golfers, public speakers, surgeons, and artists are those who are free from extraneous anxieties and tensions. The teacher of the retarded reader should therefore strive to create in the classroom a cheerful environment and establish personal relations of confidence and friendliness between teacher and student.

Using all available methods of arousing genuine, keen interests in reading. The retarded reader, even more than the highly successful one, requires an environment rich in opportunities for the reading of books, magazines, posters, charts, and other reading materials of high interest value. Attractive magazine racks, bookshelves, and book displays should be provided in the classroom for him. An abundant supply of phonograph records and films, as well as opportunity to listen to selected radio programs, is an important means of arousing strong interests in reading on a variety of subjects. Exchanging oral reports of reading experiences, dramatizing scenes from favorite books, and keeping cumulative records of books read are devices commonly employed by teachers in the building of permanent interests in reading. Unless the desire to read is kindled within the reader himself, very little value is derived from exercises and pressures which emanate from the teacher. Only abundant, highly motivated experience in reading can produce genuine growth in reading ability.

Developing skill in dealing with the wide variety of reading material. Not all reading material should be approached in the same way. Some material calls for rapid reading to follow the course of a story. Other material requires careful attention to details and, therefore, a slower rate of reading. Some reading matter calls for skimming, in which the eye ranges over the printed page with alertness for some fact or idea, or for some cue which may reveal the nature of the material or the trend of the author's thought. The manner in which the reader approaches the material is determined in part by the reader's purpose and in part by the nature of the material itself. Young readers need to be made aware of these differences in the appropriate approach to the printed page.

Learning to develop independence in recognizing new words. The young high school student will encounter many new words in the work of the various high school subjects. Often these words are so numerous and difficult as to cause confusion and discouragement in his mind. Unless he is given concrete help in dealing with them, he may develop an increasing sense of frustration with respect to reading, not only in English but in all his other subjects. As has been pointed out, the study of printed words as such is a futile undertaking. Experiences and concepts must be built in preparation for the encounter with the printed word. However, the recognition of the visual symbol is based upon skills which frequently require systematic teaching. The ability to analyze words into their elements, to employ context clues, and to use the dictionary to find specialized meanings for words should be developed by teachers in all subjects involving reading. Both individual and group consideration of words and their meanings in a variety of contexts can be of inestimable aid to young people who have difficulty in reading.

Individual help for retarded readers. Since the causes of retardation in reading are diverse and complex, no two readers will present exactly the same difficulties. Diagnosis and remediation of reading difficulties must therefore proceed on an individual basis. In cases of extreme disabilities, of course, clinical study and the assistance of experts are needed. In most instances, however, common sense, a sympathetic attitude, and individual guidance are all that is required to promote growth in reading. Special groups for slow readers formed within the class for brief periods of special instruction may frequently prove valuable, but they cannot take the place of the individual interview and individual help.

Speed of comprehension. Since reading has no purpose apart from understanding what is read, it is fundamentally incorrect to speak of speed *and* comprehension as separate disciplines in evaluating reading ability. Instead, it is preferable always to think in terms of *speed of comprehension.* In diagnosing an individual's strengths or weaknesses as a basis for providing appropriate types of developmental work, however, it is often advisable to record speed, in terms of number of words read per minute, apart from the per cent of comprehension for the same material. Comparisons between rate and degree of comprehension are often of value in answering such questions as: Would the reading needs of this particular student be served best by stressing speed at this point, or by concentrating his attention on comprehension until a "speed *of* comprehension" adequate for his purposes is achieved?

If, for example, a ninth grader's comprehension is 95 per cent, but his speed is less than 100 words per minute, it may be desirable to emphasize speed to the extent of letting comprehension temporarily drop to 70 per cent until new reading habits have become established to the point where comprehension can again be stressed without loss in speed. If both speed and comprehension are seriously retarded, more appropriate and more appealing materials, much less difficult in vocabulary and sentence structure, are obviously required at the start. Except as an aid to the reading teacher in situations of the kind just described, "speed of comprehension," rather than speed and comprehension, is the chief concern.

It should of course be remembered, also, that different rates of reading are appropriate to different types of reading mate-.rial. It has been observed that excellent readers, who are capable of rapid reading, will read very slowly when difficult or technical material calls for meticulous attention to details. A teacher should, therefore, not encourage speed at all times. Especially science, mathematics, and other highly theoretical reading matter should ordinarily be read for precision of understanding rather than speed.

Reading, an enabling objective. Even this goal, however, must be regarded only as an enabling objective in the service of the more important aim of building purposeful and discriminating life interests in reading. For this reason, the importance of choosing appropriate and appealing content, suited to each student's background in experience, interest, and needs, cannot be overemphasized. Inasmuch as reading handicaps are often associated with a strong dislike for reading, the first step is often the development of an interest in learning to read well. This requires starting where the learner is and providing a graded sequence of inviting steppingstones to higher levels of achievement. Where reading disabilities are associated with unpleasant recollections, the environment in which special instruction is given should be the most attractive room that the school can afford.

Good morale indispensable. There is probably no better way to develop resistance to any type of remedial or corrective instruction than to label it as such among students and parents. The use in public of such terms as "remedial," "corrective," or "clinical" advertises the fact that those who participate in work so labeled have "something wrong with them." No matter how deficient the student may be, no good can be served by publicizing the fact or "rubbing it in." Surely no one, no matter how humble his station, cares to appear dense in public. All terms that imply inferiority should, therefore, be rigorously avoided in connection with any program aiming to strengthen reading skills and interests. The concept of *developmental* reading—that anyone can improve his reading ability—is preferable to the concept of "remedial" reading. Similarly, the term "reading center" is preferable to the term "reading clinic."

The profession of teaching might well show the same regard for mental differences that physicians show toward physical differences in their patients. Until this point of view is more widely shared, teaching will continue to be the only profession in which mental differences are often disparaged in terms that would be considered in poor taste, ill-bred, or crude if applied to physical ones.

Reading, not a single skill. Reading is not *a* skill, but *a set of distinct skills,* as are swimming, golf, or piano playing. Teaching students only to read orally is not unlike teaching people only one stroke in golf, or the use of only one set method of fingering entirely different progressions on the piano. Unless the term "reading" is used in a very abnormal sense, *no one can be considered a good silent reader today unless he can comprehend ordinary printed material several times as fast as he could possibly read it aloud.* Such effectiveness in the most important of the reading skills is obviously not attained by methods that eventually make it impossible for people to comprehend faster than they can vocalize. If practice is limited to oral reading exclusively during the elementary and intermediate stages, normal rates of comprehension in silent reading can often be attained later only at the expense of special clinical treatment to break down mental word-reading fixations.[4]

[4] Guy L. Bond and Eva Bond, *Developmental Reading in High School.* New York: The Macmillan Company, 1941.

Paul Witty and David Kopel, *Reading and the Educative Process.* Boston: Ginn & Company, 1939.

Albert J. Harris, *How to Increase Reading Ability.* New York: Longmans, Green, & Co., Inc., 1947. For grade norms of ability in silent reading in English.

Oral and silent reading. The following suggestions are recommended to teachers of English and foreign languages who wish to avoid building up one skill at the sacrifice of another:

1. Limit oral reading exclusively to the following types of materials: material that is obviously designed for dramatized oral reading, especially printed speeches, radioscripts, playlets, and poems; materials that are taken up for discussion or correction in class; newspaper clippings, minutes, excerpts from letters, quotations, announcements, etc., used by individual students in reports to the group.

2. Reserve other content for developing ability in silent reading.

3. Make students aware of the fact that *reading is not a single skill* but a combination of skills like golf, tennis, swimming, or playing the piano, and that they should make every effort to *avoid saying the words to themselves* when they are reading silently by trying to get the meaning two or three times as fast as they could possibly read aloud.

4. In the case of a foreign language, rigorously *avoid translation as a test of comprehension in silent reading.* Instead, stress ability to summarize the information or ideas of a paragraph or passage in the *students' own words,* without looking back at the book.

5. If the same material is to be used for both oral and silent reading, always introduce the work in *silent* reading first; otherwise the material cannot later be used as a fair test of speed of comprehension. Moreover, if oral reading is practiced first, the word-for-word reverberations carry over into the silent reading exercises in such a way as to block progress and to fix, rather than correct, wrong habits of subvocal articulation. If only oral reading is practiced, only a plodding, mental form of oral reading is likely to result.

6. Time comprehension in silent reading at least once weekly, starting as early as possible in the first semester, and have pupils figure out both their rate and per cent of comprehension.

EVALUATION

Self-evaluation preferable to teacher evaluation. If ability
in silent reading is the dominant objective of the program,
rather than ability to use the spoken language, silent-reading
tests will be given at least twice weekly, and the results kept
by the students in the form of a graph showing their progress
both in speed and degree of comprehension over ten- to fif-
teen-week periods.

If progress is being made, a curve roughly connecting the
modal points [5] on the chart will show the probable true rate
of progress. Students should be forewarned of "plateaus"—
periods of ups and downs during which no real gains are
visible because new habits are being formed that are not yet
sufficiently developed to be used efficiently. If old habits of
word-for-word reading have to be broken before new efficient
habits can be strengthened, the student may even expect a
temporary *decrease* in comprehension, followed by a fairly
rapid gain as soon as the strangle hold of word-reading fixations is definitely overcome. Where gains are delayed beyond
normal expectations, the student may need the services of an
oculist or psychologist, or he may be so far below the standard for his grade in ability to read ordinary English that work
in developmental reading would serve his immediate educational needs far more effectively than any other kind of work
in school. Avoid drawing conclusions regarding "problem
cases" just from one or two tests, however. All interpretations
of a graph must be based on *trends shown by a succession of
tests over a period of time,* never by any single score. Real
growth is not achieved overnight.

*Pupil self-evaluation charts are valid for all practical pur-
poses.* How valid and reliable are self-evaluation charts of
the kind described on the preceding page? From a careful
statistical analysis of pupil-made reading evaluation charts

[5] Modal points include *all except extreme variations,* such as unusually high or unusually low scores.

Thornton C. Blayne [6] obtained coefficients of .69 and above for the correlation between the graphs and the teachers' grades, and between the former and scores on standardized silent-reading tests.

DEVELOPING KEEN INTERESTS IN READING

A major purpose of all instruction in reading, whether in English or in the "content fields," is the development of continuing and diversified interests in the reading of books and magazines. The teaching of literature, social studies, science, or other subjects will, if successful, eventuate in continued reading in these areas after the student leaves school. In order that voluntary reading may occur in afterschool life, it should be stimulated during the period of school attendance. Coercive methods and formal assignments will not accomplish this result.

Since the interests of young people differ widely, much of the reading guidance must be individual. Interest inventories such as those devised by Witty and Kopel are helpful in discovering young people's interests and in providing subjects for individual interviews. Cumulative reading records, such as the Skinner reading record cards will aid both teacher and student in observing the reading choices over a period of time and in determining the extent and variety of a student's reading interests. Such records ordinarily consist of large cards or folders with spaces for titles, authors, and brief comments on each book, and are filed in a box to which both teacher and students have access.

Students who do not like to read may often discover deep satisfactions in reading when they are directed to books dealing with some special interest such as sports, adventure, radio, aviation, or natural science. Once the student has discovered that "books can be fun," it is often possible to direct

[6] Thornton C. Blayne, "Results of Developmental Reading Programs in First-year Spanish," *Modern Language Journal*, 30 (January, 1946), 39–43.

him to those dealing with other topics and so to assist him in developing a balanced pattern of reading interests. One commercial form for cumulative reading records, called *My Reading Design*,[7] stresses the element of diversity of types of reading by means of a pie graph in which students record the books they have read.

Promoting genuine interests in reading calls for a classroom environment rich in reading stimuli. The English classroom, especially, should be a bright, cheerful room, its walls made colorful with posters, book jackets, and other illustrations, and lined with magazine racks, bookshelves, and exhibit tables. Radio and phonograph instruments should be on hand to offer their aid in opening new areas of interest. The room bulletin board might exhibit book reviews from current newspapers and magazines as well as other announcements and pictures relating to the world of books, or students' creative products inspired by stories and poems they have read.

The classroom climate, too, should be conducive to pleasurable reading. The relaxed atmosphere, the sense of anticipation which should precede the storytelling or dramatization period, and the opportunity to exchange book experiences are essential factors in the encouragement of voluntary reading. And, most important of all, there must be frequent opportunity for everybody to read silently in class, perhaps as often as a whole period or more every week, while the teacher quietly discusses books and reading with individual students.

Providing effective guidance in reading requires familiarity on the part of the teacher with young people's books. Knowledge of the classics of English, American, and other world literatures remains important, but the modern teacher is conversant also with so-called nonliterary young people's books which possess great merit. The stories of John R. Tunis, Joseph Gollomb, Kate Seredy, Frances Lattimore, and Nina Baker are examples of this type; in fact, some of these are thought by many to have high literary quality. Reading lists such as those published by the American Library Association, *Your*

[7] Published by the *News-Journal* of North Manchester, Ind.

Reading (for senior high schools), *Books for You* (for junior high schools), *We Build Together,* published by the National Council of Teachers of English, and *Reading Ladders,* published by the American Council on Education, may serve as guides to both teachers and students in the selection of good books.

Obviously an effective free reading program requires a well-stocked library and the aid of a competent librarian. A good central library, equipped with the best in classical and current books, a wide variety of magazines, pamphlets, and pictures, as well as projection and listening rooms (in the larger schools), is of the greatest importance. In addition to the central library, moreover, there should be a well-chosen room collection, frequently changed and adapted to the interests and the events of the classroom. It will help, too, if there is close cooperation between the librarian and the teacher, so that the former may be on the alert for materials appropriate to the interests and needs of students who come to the library. If the librarian can spend some time in visiting classrooms, she will be in a better position to aid the teacher and to provide expert guidance to students.

Study and Library Research Skills

While the development of strong, continuing interests in reading constitutes a major objective in most of the subject fields and should be central in classroom planning, the ability to read for information on specific topics is an aim of equal importance for all teachers in secondary schools. Improper study habits and the lack of skill in attacking printed materials are responsible in great part for pupil failures in many of the subject fields.

Need for help in learning how to find information in books and magazines. Students need to learn how to use the library card index, such periodical indexes as the *Reader's Guide,* and such reference books as almanacs, atlases, dictionaries and thesauruses, encyclopedias, concordances, and biographical indexes. They need to learn how to use the table of contents, index, and chapter and paragraph headings of books. They need to learn how to skim, to recognize cue words, and to follow cross references and footnotes efficiently. Many students learn these techniques through unguided experience. but others require special instruction.

Skill in finding information may be taught in a special reading period, but the more effective way is to provide the necessary help in relation to real questions on which students, individually or in small groups, seek information. When the skills are taught in isolation from situations in which they are needed, there is no guarantee of genuine carry-over, and what is worse, there is no assurance that students will develop the habit of consulting reliable sources in finding answers to questions in real life. Skill in locating information develops best under the conditions of a problem-centered curriculum in which young people grow in their ability to recognize significant problems, in their desire to find answers to questions, and in their knowledge of sources of information on a variety of subjects.

The locale for guidance in the discovery of information is first the classroom itself, where textbooks, reference books, general works, maps, globes, magazines, and other aids are available and their uses demonstrated. Next, the school and public library should become the scene to which students are introduced in the course of their explorations. Of great assistance in this regard is the school or public librarian, who may give students individual assistance in the library itself and group assistance through talks to the class. Even the simplest devices in finding information should receive attention, since in the case of many students it is not safe to take these devices for granted.

Need for learning how to interpret what they read. The interpretation of the printed page calls for a sufficient stock of afterimpressions to give significance to the printed symbols. As Professor Bobbitt has pointed out,[8] printed words are

[8] Franklin Bobbitt, *The Curriculum of Modern Education,* p. 119. New York: McGraw-Hill Book Company, Inc., 1941.

not little packages of meaning which the reader may acquire by observing them. Rather they are symbols of meanings which are already present in the mind of the reader. Previous experiences with concepts, people, and things are therefore essential to the interpretation of words, sentences, and paragraphs. Young people must learn to recognize not only the meanings of words in their contexts, but also the relationships of words and sentences to each other. Instead of dwelling upon individual words that may give difficulty, they must be encouraged to examine the larger elements—sentences and longer passages—to follow the larger pattern of which individual words are but a part. They must learn to vary their approach in accordance with the purposes they have in mind. The attack on words, phrases, sentences, and paragraphs will vary according to whether the reader is seeking specific details, or reading for the general significance of a passage, or sharing a mood the writer is trying to create, or following directions, or comparing the conclusions or viewpoints of different writers. It has been found also that even twelfth-grade students can benefit from specific instruction in the interpretation of such aids as graphs, tables, and charts.

Need for learning how to organize what they read. Reading, particularly of the study type, is not a passive process. The young reader must constantly relate in his own mind the major and subordinate ideas he encounters on the printed page. He must learn how to recognize the ideas which represent general principles and those which are examples or specific applications of the principles. Outlining, mentally or on paper, is an essential part of this process. When the research involves the use of many sources, the student must learn how to classify the facts and ideas under their appropriate headings. Learning how to take notes and to arrange these notes in logical sequence may contribute to the larger and important skill of organizing the material that is read.

The practice of requiring a research paper in advanced classes in English and the social studies has value in teaching students to organize what they read. Certain cautions should be observed, however. Young people differ widely in their ability to deal with materials calling for complex organization. For some it will be sufficient if they learn how to write a brief paper based on three or four magazine articles on new developments in aviation, or a paper calling for a reference in *Who's Who,* the *World Almanac,* and a current biography. Others will be able to write a coherent summary of the current opinion about a new book, based upon reviews found in several newspapers and magazines. Still others may learn how to use two or three references at the end of an article in *Current Biography* and construct from these references a brief, coherent story.

Experiences in organizing material that is read may be provided in less formal ways than in the conventional research report. The wise teacher will frequently call on young people, either individually or in committees, to summarize the reading matter by enumerating the major conclusions that they have drawn from their reading, along with the necessary supporting details or reasons. Such experiences should be helpful in improving the organization, clarity, and persuasiveness of their own floor talks or contributions to the class discussions.

Cultivating Powers of Discrimination in Reading

Critical reading as selective reading. The process of critical reading may be defined as selective reading, in which the element of acceptance-rejection plays the most prominent part.

Acceptance-rejection may be on a predominantly emotional or a predominantly intellectual level. The reader may accept a story emotionally because it harmonizes with a passing mood, or because it provides a kind of emotional security, as when a character meets and overcomes a difficulty shared by the reader. Or the reader may reject a solution to a human problem on the ground that it contradicts what he knows, or thinks he knows, about people.

Selectivity, of course, tends to operate in most instances of efficient reading. There are certain types of reading, particularly in the case of highly fanciful materials, such as fairy tales and imaginative poetry, in which the reader gives himself over to the "willing suspension of disbelief." Good reading generally, however, involves the active rather than the passive approach to the printed page, a reaching out for facts and ideas which meet a specific need.

Employing valid bases of selection. In order to be intelligently selective in his reading, one needs to be in possession of at least a tentative *basis* of selection. Such bases may be of several kinds. Consciously or unconsciously, the reader asks himself such questions as these:

1. Does the material supply information or ideas for the purpose I have in mind?

2. Does the material conform to what I know from direct experience to be true?

3. Does the material conform to what other competent sources declare to be true?

4. Is the writer qualified to report accurately and to draw valid conclusions?

5. Does the material harmonize with my mood or present emotional need?

6. Does the material harmonize with my sense of values?

7. Does the material deal with a real problem, does it present a false alternative, or does it fail to get at the basic problem?

8. Does the material suppress essential facts or arguments?

9. Does the material exaggerate or minimize the importance of the problem?

10. Is the material intended to advance the self-interest of an individual or group?

11. What implications does the writer's position have for other problems or for action on my part?

12. Has the issue as presented been correctly analyzed into subissues or subproblems?

13. Does the writer make his fundamental position clear?

Do his facts add up to a significant generalization? Do the facts justify the generalization?

14. Is the writer consistent in applying his generalizations to different problem situations?

15. Can the facts that have been cited be verified?

16. Is the author using words to arouse or persuade without taking pains to make clear the realities which they are intended to symbolize?

17. Which statements are reports of objective fact, which are inferences from the facts, which are general interpretations, and which are emotional reactions?

18. Is the solution or proposal offered by the writer superior or inferior to others not mentioned in the reading material?

19. What assumptions present in the reading material are not made explicit?

20. What terms in the material are used without adequate definition?

Rejection does not necessarily imply disbelief on the part of the reader. It means simply that a phrase, a passage, a news story, or a book encountered by him fails to enter favorably into his further thinking or action. The rejected material may or may not influence his subsequent behavior. The reading of a violently rejected editorial may, for example, result in stronger adherence by the reader to a position previously held. On the other hand, he may deliberately pass by a column by Dorothy Thompson or Samuel Grafton because of earlier reactions to the column, without being in any significant way changed by the act of omission.

Learning how to modify the bases of selection. It is clear from an examination of the various bases used by readers for acceptance or rejection that critical reading may be of very high or very low quality, depending upon the nature of the criteria employed. Certain types of genuinely critical reading must assume a greater competence on the part of the reader than on the part of the writer, or at least a comparable competence, as theoretically in the case of a literary critic or the reviewer of a technical book. Obviously, however, the readers of magazines, newspapers, books, pamphlets, and other materials are under the necessity of making judgments regardless of their competence. Voters in an election must make up their minds on questions of far-reaching importance, and they must do so with whatever criteria they may possess. The job of the educator is to help the reader and the listener to increase the number and the quality of the criteria employed.

Some evidence shows [9] that schools have failed to teach children how to use even the most elementary criteria in reading—those relating to the relevancy or irrelevancy of the material to the reader's problems. Experiments in the field of critical thinking, however, suggest that systematic teaching may substantially increase the efficiency with which readers apply defensible criteria to what they read.[10]

More time in literature classes should be devoted to experiences in selecting materials appropriate to the reader's mood or purpose than to the minute analysis of individual selections assigned by a teacher to an entire group. Readers should be constantly encouraged to check what they read against their own impressions and past experiences. If there appears to be a contradiction, not rejection but more careful exploration is indicated. Students should learn to inquire about the value system of the writer. What are the writer's beliefs regarding specific questions suggested by the material? Editorials and columns in newspapers, articles in popular magazines, and fictional materials lend themselves admirably to such analysis. What is known about the competence of the writer, his attitude toward other related questions? What do others say on the same question?

[9] Roma Gans, *Critical Reading Comprehension in the Intermediate Grades.* New York: Bureau of Publications, Teachers College, Columbia University, 1940.

[10] Edward M. Glaser, *An Experiment in the Development of Critical Thinking.* New York: Bureau of Publications, Teachers College, Columbia University, 1941.

It should be noted that no one of these criteria is usually reliable in itself. A writer *may* be right, even though he is contradicted by many other writers. The instruction should lead the reader to use several criteria, and to distinguish between their relative values.

Employing a positive approach to the reading matter. The earlier literature on critical reading stressed the need for defensiveness on the part of the reader. The inadequacy of this approach has since become apparent. Young readers became suspicious of all printed matter and were left without a sense of direction in determining their own courses of action. Mere skepticism and a superior neutrality on all questions with which human beings must struggle in an age of crisis can lead only to intellectual stalemate. Such an approach can produce neither good citizens nor sound thinkers.

A more useful method is provided by the positive, selective approach. The reader must begin with certain tentative, though carefully considered, evaluative criteria. He may be seeking the answer to a pressing question, or an illustration of a principle, or merely momentary escape from a momentary depression. He may seek evidence to support a position already taken on a public question, or he may weigh the arguments for and against a proposal on which he has not made up his mind. He may have certain convictions on some question—for example, the belief that all children should have equal educational opportunity—and accept only such arguments as seem to him to promote the ideal of universal educational opportunity.

Formulating evaluative criteria. The evaluation of reading matter by means of previously determined criteria does not imply a closed mind on the part of the reader. All thoughtful experiences, including those involved in reading, tend to modify the assumptions and beliefs with which one approaches new experiences. Information and insights derived from reading in turn affect the evaluation of new reading experiences.

That the quality of interpretation in reading depends upon

the resources which the reader brings to the printed page is well known. That the reading experience itself enriches the resources which the reader may bring to new reading situations is equally well known. In this reciprocal action between the reader and his reading lies the key to the power of discrimination in the reading process.

The implications of this interaction between past experience and reading for the reading program are far-reaching. They include, of course, the familiar but frequently violated principle that a wide variety of firsthand experiences should be built in preparation for the reading experience. They include also the principle that effective reading is purposeful and selective, and occurs within the framework of previously acquired concepts and attitudes.

Recognizing clear objectives of instruction in critical reading. A number of general principles governing the program of instruction in critical or discriminating reading may now be formulated:

1. From the beginning, the learner should be introduced to multiple sources.

2. The learner should be taught constantly to weigh the nature and competency of the sources.

3. The learner should be taught constantly to compare one source with another, and each new idea with ideas that he formerly held.

4. The learner should be taught constantly to weigh the implications of what he reads, for his own beliefs and actions.

5. In the various subject fields, as well as in the language arts, the aim should be to promote wide and diversified reading of books, magazines, and newspapers, if possible in sources representing diverse views and approaches, rather than reading in a single textbook.

6. The learner should be taught constantly to relate his reading and experience background to the material read. For example, he should be on the alert for "card stacking" by relating information and ideas previously gained on the subject to the new material.

7. The learner should be taught constantly to seek additional information and ideas as a check on the material read.

8. The learner should be taught constantly to distinguish between information and ideas which require further verification and testing and those which may be accepted without further investigation.

9. The learner should be taught constantly to distinguish between statements of objective fact, statements involving facts, statements making interpretations of the facts, and statements expressing emotional reactions. (Distinctions made between such types of statements do not imply that one is more valuable than the other.)

10. The learner should be taught constantly to relate the material read to his own system of values. For example, a reader who believes strongly in the maintenance of civil rights should learn to evaluate a radio speech, a proposed law, or the pronouncements of a Congressional committee in the light of his generalized adherence to the principles of civil rights.

11. The learner should be taught constantly to examine the material read from the point of view of its logical consistency.

12. The learner should be taught constantly to inquire what the basic assumptions of the writer are.

13. The learner should be taught constantly to inquire what special interests or motives may have influenced the writer.

14. In literature, the learner should be taught constantly to compare character and incident with the writer's apparent basic purposes.

Providing many opportunities for purposeful reading. The question arises as to whether the skills involved in critical or discriminating reading can best be taught by means of specially contrived exercises or by means of incidental instruction in connection with more generalized, purposeful learning situations. Objective evidence on this question is still lacking, but it would appear that the most rewarding instructional approach is direct guidance of the reader in the search for information or ideas relating to real problems. Transfer from teacher-invented exercises to purposeful reading situations will probably occur if the exercises are employed to supplement more functional reading experiences and if the teacher carefully plans to accomplish such transfer. Generally speaking, isolated exercises cannot reproduce the fairly complex pattern of relationships which characterizes the editorial, the novel, the biography, or the historical account which the reader may encounter in real life. Moreover, special exercises are less likely to evoke the enthusiastic cooperation of the reader.

Nevertheless, experimentation with systematically planned exercises is urgently needed. Examples of news stories with typically misleading headlines should be used in an effort to determine whether the level of discrimination in newspaper reading can be raised. A number of newspaper columns containing obvious logical fallacies would be suitable material for classroom exercises in the development of sensitivity to imperfect reasoning or "loaded" arguments. Fictional situations involving issues of motivation or consistency of behavior could be presented to a group of young people for the purpose of evaluating their ability to distinguish between valid and spurious characterizations and between logical and whimsical plot constructions. These and other similar activities may serve as a test of effectiveness of isolated exercises in the improvement of the quality of critical reading.

Providing a balance between escape and realism in reading. A clear distinction should be made between the *types* of critical standards that are appropriate for various kinds of reading which is carried on for sheer pleasure and recreation. Even in purely recreatory reading, provision should be made for the exercise of progressively improving standards of judgment. Levels of preference for "escape" literature can be determined by careful scrutiny of young people's reading choices over a period of time. A cumulative reading record of a boy or girl whose reading selections constantly fall within the category of "escape" reading may point to the need for psychological or psychiatric counseling.

The phenomenon of "compulsive reading," characteristic of people who have an appetite for reading which cannot be satiated, even momentarily, by any type or quantity of reading material, has been noted by clinical workers.[11] Such reading is symptomatic of a deep-seated need, in relation to which reading serves as an unsatisfactory substitute for a more fundamental kind of personal adjustment. The condition is comparable to that of an emotionally disturbed person who has recourse to a steady diet of movies in a futile search for relief from emotional stresses. In such cases the critical standards take the form of emotional discernment or personal insights instead of intellectual criteria.

Assuming the existence of a suitable balance between "escape" reading and reading for information or the solution of a problem, it is necessary to examine the degree of refinement reached by individual readers in their standards of preference for purely recreational reading. Recreational reading may range from the comic strip to *The Brothers Karamazov* or the book of *Ecclesiastes* or Plato's *Republic*. The critical standard employed will determine what present mood or emotional or intellectual need must be satisfied, and what kind of creative product is most appropriate at the time. The improvement of such standards consists in making the learner conscious of his own varying needs and moods and in extending his direct acquaintance with the infinite variety of creative products.

Teachers and others have often proceeded in the belief that readers who have developed a taste for aesthetically or intellectually worth-while reading materials can never again be satisfied with the trivial, the crude, or the juvenile (in the pejorative sense). Observation of young people's or adults'

[11] S. J. Conrad, "Compulsive Reading and Its Psychiatric Significance," *Twelfth Yearbook of the Claremont College Reading Conference*. Claremont, Calif.: Claremont College Curriculum Laboratory, 1947.

reading habits does not support such a belief. Some excellent readers oscillate indiscriminately between the Superman or Lone Ranger stories and Dickens or Scott. Many adults read 'Lil Abner and Ellery Queen's stories with apparently the same absorption, though probably not the same kind of emotional response, which they give to a book by Louis Adamic or a poem by Archibald MacLeish. Unless the highly developed taste results in active dislike for the less "acceptable" kinds of literature—such as a reader of Lillian Smith's *Strange Fruit* might feel for Margaret Mitchell's *Gone with the Wind,* or a lover of Willa Cather might feel for Zane Grey, or an admirer of Elizabeth Page's *Tree of Liberty* might feel for Kenneth Roberts' *Oliver Wiswell*—the teacher will probably be wise to accept such catholicity of taste in literary levels as a normal condition.

Providing a variety of reading materials. If our tastes, preferences, beliefs, and attitudes are the product of our previous experiences, our standards for discrimination in reading will not usually rise above the quality of reading materials to which we have had ready access. If our familiarity with world events is limited to the daily newspaper and the radio news broadcast, our critical evaluation of the news will be limited by what the major newsgathering agencies will release or emphasize to the public. The obvious conclusion is that schools must make accessible to readers the greatest variety of types and levels of reading materials. No longer should we be satisfied with great files of two or three popular news magazines or monthly digests on our library tables. Books, magazines, pamphlets, newspapers representing the viewpoints of many groups—religious, business, labor, scientific, consumer, and others—should be readily accessible to youth and introduced to their use.

THE TEACHING OF LISTENING

Of the four facets of language communication—speaking, listening, reading, and writing—listening consumes most time in the daily life activities of people. Nevertheless, it has until recently received little or no attention in educational literature. Thousands of research studies have been made in the field of reading, but the evidence on how we listen and how listening can be improved is still extraordinarily meager.

No doubt reading and listening have many problems and processes in common. Attitudes toward words, recognition vocabulary, the capacity to exercise critical judgment, and the range of interests affect reading and listening alike. On the other hand, the listening situation differs from the reading situation in important particulars. A reader can retrace his steps at will; he can vary the speed of apprehension with the difficulty of the material; he can stop to reflect over a line or phrase, or he can skim and skip and race along the lines that are familiar or uninteresting. The listener is completely dependent upon the tempo of the speaker and upon the enunciation and the modulations of his voice. The listener must learn to guard against the seductiveness of the propagandist and to enjoy the intonations of the actor and the poetry reader. Listening is the great unexplored area for educational research.

Some of the few findings on growth in listening ability have been summarized by James I. Brown, who has pioneered this field.[12] He reports that, according to some studies, reading becomes a more efficient medium than listening for learning at about the seventh grade. According to the same studies, listening ability apparently does not improve significantly after the seventh grade, perhaps because we give little systematic instruction in listening. Moreover, we appear to be less critical when we listen than when we read—again, perhaps we have not been taught to listen critically. Brown further reports tentative evidence that for average and below-average students listening is more efficient than reading. Nevertheless, tenth-grade reading material is probably about

[12] James I. Brown, "The Measurement of Listening Ability," *School and Society*, 71 (Feb. 4, 1950), 69–71.

twelfth-grade listening material. Brown [13] believes that we need "listenability" formulas comparable to the readability formulas recently devised.

Typical instructional situations in school do, of course, involve a great deal of listening. The difficulty is that (1) most of the listening is compulsory listening, (2) most of the listening occurs while the teacher speaks, and (3) little help is given students to listen efficiently. Too often, also, the purpose of the listening is to acquire and retain information for its own sake rather than to get help in finding solutions for problems. One writer [14] has addressed the following questions to teachers relative to the teaching of listening:

Do you talk too much in school? Do you listen more than you talk during a school day? Do you stimulate children to speak more than a single word or thought in response to a question? Are your questions so thought-provoking that your question time is less than your answer time? Do children in class discussion follow each other spontaneously without directing each comment to you? Is the purpose of each listening activity understood by all the students? Do your classroom environment and activities promote purposeful listening? Do you evaluate the quality of listening by observing changes in pupil behavior, habits, attitudes, and ideals? Do you teach good listening habits in all classroom activities?

Listening means hearing with comprehension. One student of the subject has coined the term "auding," which will probably not gain popular adherence but which stresses the need for more than mere awareness or perception of sound.[15] Caffrey [16] illustrates the distinction between hearing and listening by citing case studies in which patients exhibit ability to recognize the sounds of running water, crumpling

---

[13] *Ibid.*, p. 71.

[14] Miriam E. Wilt, "What Is the Listening Ratio in Your Classroom?" *Elementary English*, 26 (May, 1949), 259–264.

[15] Don Pardee Brown, cited in John Caffrey, "An Introduction to the Auding Concept," *Education*, 70 (December, 1949), 237.

[16] *Ibid.*, p. 239.

paper, bells, or footsteps, but fail to comprehend their native tongues or respond to their own names. These studies clearly illustrate the distinction between hearing and listening (or "auding") and perhaps serve to underline the need for assisting learners in the comprehension of spoken language.

Practical suggestions for classroom procedures in the teaching of intelligent listening are meager. One of the best articles on this subject has been written by Althea Beery for the elementary school teacher.[17] Her suggestions are of value to the secondary school teacher as well. Miss Beery lists six ways in which teachers can improve the listening activities of young people:

1. Sensing the relationships of listening to other phases of communication.

2. Understanding the psychological process of listening.

3. Providing general conditions conducive to listening.

4. Utilizing opportunities for children to listen.

5. Understanding the developmental levels of listening—the goals toward which teachers and pupils should work.

6. Keeping alert to new inventions and equipment which will aid the program.

The principles governing the teaching of listening, according to Miss Beery, include:

1. Pupils read better when they have a purpose. Surely they will listen better when they expect to use what they hear.

2. Reading results in greater learning when it is combined with other modes of learning; listening, too, needs to be re-inforced by other forms of experience.

3. Reading readiness is essential to successful attainment in reading; listening readiness should be similarly explored.

4. Comprehension improves when pupils are encouraged to check themselves on the ideas gained from reading; listening probably needs similar checks.

Practical suggestions for the teaching of listening offered by Miss Beery include the following:

[17] Althea Beery, "Listening Activities in the Elementary School," *Elementary English,* 23 (February, 1946), 69–79.

1. Keeping a record of the types of radio program to which young people listen outside of school.

2. Conducting class discussions to improve young people's discrimination in out-of-school use of the radio.

3. Setting up goals toward which to work in the improvement of listening.

4. Keeping a log of the listening activities of the class for a day or a week.

5. Describing the conditions under which effective listening takes place.

6. Experimenting with tape recorder in the improvement of speech and oral reading.

7. Experimenting with various interpretations of material heard by the class.

8. Observing young people outside of class to determine what they listen to in voluntary and unsupervised situations.

9. Providing a diversity of listening situations:

   a. Conversation and telephoning.
   b. Discussion.
   c. Reports.
   d. Directions and announcements.
   e. Story-telling and dramatization.
   f. Poetry and choral speaking.
   g. Oral reading.
   h. Listening to music.
   i. Introductions.
   j. Programs.
   k. Listening to the radio in school.
   l. Listening to recordings and transcriptions.
   m. Broadcasting by students.
   n. Sound films.
   o. Sounds around us.
   p. Listening to other students.

Among the objectives named by Miss Beery are the following: to show courtesy in disagreeing with the speaker, to watch for transitional phrases, to hold the thread of the discussion in mind, to discount bias in a speaker, to listen to content that does not affect the listener directly, to take notes during a speech or report, to write a brief summary of an oral report, to show by remarks that the listener has been considering what has been said, to reserve judgment in listening to different viewpoints in discussion.

The capacity to appreciate a wide variety of literary and musical selections is one objective commonly mentioned in discussions of the teaching of listening. A group of teachers in the Phoenix (Ariz.) Union High School have described classroom experiences in the development of appreciative and critical listening abilities, in a mimeographed document edited by Alexander Frazier, a member of the Committee on Listening of the National Council of Teachers of English. The pamphlet is called *Projects in Listening* and is available from the Superintendent of Schools, Phoenix, Ariz.

FOR FURTHER READING

On Reading

Betts, Emmett A., *Foundations of Reading Instruction.* New York: American Book Company, 1946.

Blair, Glenn A., *Diagnostic and Remedial Teaching in Secondary Schools.* New York: The Macmillan Company, 1946.

Blayne, Thornton, "Building Comprehension in Silent Reading," *Modern Language Journal,* 29 (April, 1945), 270–276.

Bond, Guy L., and Eva Bond, *Developmental Reading in High School.* New York: The Macmillan Company, 1941.

Gray, William S. (Ed.), *Classroom Techniques in Improving Reading.* Supplementary Educational Monographs, No. 69. Chicago: University of Chicago Press, 1949.

Gray, William S. (Ed.), *Reading in an Age of Mass Communication.* New York: Appleton-Century-Crofts, Inc., 1949.

Gray, William S. (Ed.), "Reading in the High School and College." *Forty-seventh Yearbook of the National Society for the Study of Education,* Part II. Chicago: University of Chicago Press, 1948.

Harris, Albert J., *How to Increase Reading Ability* (Rev. ed.), New York: Longmans, Green, & Co., Inc., 1947.

Kottmeyer, William, "Improving Reading Instruction in the St. Louis Schools," *Elementary School Journal,* 45 (September, 1944), 33–38.

LaBrant, Lou, and Frieda M. Heller, *An Evaluation of Free Reading in Grades Seven to Twelve, Inclusive.* Columbus: Ohio State University Press, 1939.

McKee, Paul, *The Teaching of Reading.* Boston: Houghton Mifflin Company, 1948.

"Reading Instruction in Secondary Schools," *Research Bulletin of the National Education Association,* Vol. 20, No. 1, (January, 1942).

Witty, Paul, *Reading in Modern Education.* Boston: D. C. Heath and Company, 1949.

Witty, Paul, and David Kopel, *Reading and the Educative Process.* Boston: Ginn & Company, 1939.

On Listening

Adams, Harlen M., "Teaching the Art of Listening," *Nation's Schools,* 34 (November, 1944), 51–52.

Anderson, Harold A., "Teaching the Art of Listening," in "Educational News and Editorial Comment," *School Review,* 57 (February, 1949), 63–67.

Beery, Althea, "Listening Activities in the Elementary School," *Elementary English,* 23 (February, 1946), 69–79.

Caffrey, John, "An Introduction to the Auding Concept," *Education,* 70 (December, 1949), 234–239.

Coulter, U. C., "Reading and Listening," *Education,* 65 (February, 1945), 375–382.

Steiner, Alice, *et al., Skill in Listening.* Chicago: National Council of Teachers of English, 1944.

Wilt, Miriam E., "Listening in Classrooms," *Elementary English,* 26 (May, 1949), 259–264.

Chapter 7. LITERATURE FOR HUMAN NEEDS

Values of Literature

What do boys and girls want that literature can give them? That is the decisive question to answer in planning a course and in choosing all reading material.

How can boys and girls learn from literature to be the best people they are capable of being? That is the question to answer in planning lessons and classroom procedure and activities.

We know that literature is valuable only as it is a part of life, as it contributes to our lives and helps us to live with others. The only value literature has is a human value.

Literature consists of what people have found out about life. Literature is written experience. We can share the experience of people who have lived in all parts of the world for thousands of years. Through reading we inherit what they have learned.

Reading is vicarious experience. We can experience through it what we should like to find in life—adventure, love, and friendship. We can experience through books what we cannot do ourselves—experimenting in laboratories, discovering new lands, living in different countries, building bridges, working on farms and in a large city. We prefer to learn from some experiences vicariously in books rather than in real life—causing an automobile accident, injuring another's feelings or reputation.

How does thinking of literature in this way guide us in choosing material for English classes?

The books we want. Should we teach the old classics or modern books, magazines, and newspapers?

That is not the way to ask the question about what we should read, because as long as we try to answer it, we stay in a confused state and get nowhere in our thinking. We must begin with live boys and girls if we want to help them grow. We do not begin with a book, saying, "Here is a great classic that has been in the traditional course of study, and for that reason we must put it into the heads of boys and girls." We ask what it has to tell boys and girls. We do not teach books; we try to help boys and girls learn how to use them in their daily lives. If we confine ourselves inside a bound book, we may not get out of it into life, but if we begin with live boys and girls, there is no limit to possible human growth.

Do we read one type of writing for a while and then another type? That is, do all the students read essays for, say, two weeks and then short stories and then poetry? Classes have been organized on this unit plan. Teachers have said that students should learn how to read essays, short stories, novels, poetry, and biography. This classification of reading according to form is mechanical and without vitality.

All people are interested in what they find in literature but not in types for the sake of types. When students are asked why they like a book, they say that it tells them what they want to know about a subject that interests them—dogs, airplanes, nursing.

An intelligent person integrates his reading and other activities. A man could read two books a week for forty years and still be unhappy and a bore if there was no connection between his books and his living. Our purpose is not to have students read books just to read books. Our purpose is to guide students in acquiring reading habits that will carry over into their lives.

Literature for social living. What do boys and girls want that they can find in books? We know that everyone has personal problems and everyone wants companionship.

"The use of literature in the solution of personal problems may at the same time aid us in our search for ways to develop keen and enduring interests in literature. No problem is so interesting to an adolescent as his own problems. If he can find ways of projecting them to a fictional prototype, he will have the additional satisfaction of dealing with them with an objectivity and clarity impossible in the context of his own personal situation. For many youth, the key to the world of books is the opportunity to find companionship and a sense of comradeship with others who must grapple with obstacles and perplexities comparable to their own." [1]

How can a teacher know what the students' problems are? Deborah Elkins in "Students Face Their Problems" [2] describes the way she went about finding what difficulties her students were having in the process of growing up. To determine the extent of acceptance and rejection of each student she administered a sociometric test and had interviews with the boys and girls. The students wrote about their worries and wishes, and they kept diaries for two-day periods. She used sociodrama in which the students revealed their difficulties in relation with others. She found that the problems of her boys and girls were family and peer relationships. This accumulated information was the basis for selecting reading material.

Reading Ladders for Human Relations [3] gives tested ways of using books and annotated lists of books under these classifications: patterns of family life, community contrasts, economic differences, differences between generations, adjustment to new places and situations, how it feels to grow up, belonging to groups, experiences of acceptance and rejection.

The authors of *Literature for Human Understanding* [4] say that teachers using literature to deal with immediate student

[1] John J. DeBoer, "Literature and Human Behavior," *The English Journal*, 39 (February, 1950), 81.

[2] Deborah Elkins, "Students Face Their Problems," *The English Journal*, 38 (November, 1949), 490.

[3] *Reading Ladders for Human Relations*, Washington: American Council on Education, 1949.

[4] *Literature for Human Understanding*. Washington: American Council on Education, 1948.

problems should recurrently ask themselves these important questions:

"First, is my diagnosis of the needs of these children or young people adequate? Second, has my diagnosis been checked against what I know of their community and family life, as well as against psychological studies of human growth and development? Third, do I make flat, unthoughtful translations of behavior into objectives, such as: Johnny punches, therefore, he needs to learn not to punch? May there not be other ways of expressing his energy, and could his aggressiveness be used in the interests of constructive purposes? Fourth, and in conclusion, how can students be led from the consideration of their own felt concerns to greater self-knowledge, deeper appreciation of human behavior, and greater interest in the common problems of all mankind?"

Young people need to see their personal problems in relation to the common problems of all mankind today. Until common problems are solved, individual problems cannot be really solved.

If young people leave our high schools burdened with racial or religious prejudice, or without a sense of collective responsibility for slums, poor schools, inadequate hospital facilities, eroded soil, and the threat of war, we have to that extent failed them. It is true that many of these problems which are undefined in the minds of youth are traceable to others which are in clear focus in their consciousness. Thus, for example, a boy or girl who discriminates against Negroes may do so because of a basic insecurity or feeling of personal inadequacy. Treatment of prejudice must therefore extend to causes as well as symptoms.[5]

Introducing Students to Books

There are men and women who, even though they have passed through the courses of educational institutions, wait till books are put into their hands. They read what their friends read and have no reading programs of their own. If they acquired that habit of waiting for books to be put into

[5] DeBoer, op. cit., p. 79.

their laps in school, then perhaps it was the teaching method that kept them passive, weak, dependent. We want independent readers in our country.

An independent reader spends a good deal of brain power in deciding what he will read and in finding his books. Helping boys and girls to know what they want and to find it is an important part of educating them to be self-directing adults. Finding reading material should be an important part of the reading program. We must be careful not to force books upon students. A student must not be pursued by a book, or the game will be to escape. He must go after the book. He must want a book, or he probably will not like it.

Students may cooperate in finding material. After they have decided what they want to find in books, they may contribute to a record that will be useful to all of them and perhaps to classes that follow them.

Author and title	Relations with parents	Relations with brothers and sisters	Relations with peers	School problems
Daly, *Seventeenth Summer*	X	X	X	....
Forbes, *Mama's Bank Account*	X	....	....	X
Meredith, *Ordeal of Richard Feverel* ...	X	....	X	....
Turgenev, *Fathers and Sons*	X	....	....	....

Planned freedom for reading. Boys and girls should have all the freedom possible so that they can learn to be independent and grow from where they are. They should have all the guidance they want—and none forced on them. They need recognition for what they do, and encouragement and appreciation.

A teacher must be interested in what the students read in order to encourage them. A teacher need not limit the reading of the students to the books she has read nor even think of trying to read all the books the students read. In fact, a student may be more interested in reading a book if the teacher has not read it. He will like to tell her something she does not know and wants to know.

The custom of giving credit for the number of books read has resulted in abuses. If it is the number of books that counts, some students will choose the smallest books to get the credit in the easiest way.

If a teacher tries to test students to give them credit for reading the books, she sets up a contest game that some students will play for all it is worth. To be checked on the details of a book takes the pleasure out of reading. Such a system does not carry over into life. Unless people can find a different method for themselves, they do not read. Adults do not read in fear that someone will ask them questions; they read to get what they want to get. We must let boys and girls learn to read that way.

If a student must finish a book to get credit for reading it, he will hestitate to begin it. It was a long time ago that Francis Bacon said some books are to be tasted, and yet we act as though every book should be thoroughly chewed and digested. Adult readers discover for themselves ways of sampling many books. We must help boys and girls to be the kinds of adult readers they want to be. There are many books that we may never get around to digesting, but we like to know about them, see them, and read here and there in them. Among these are *Don Quixote, Paradise Lost,* Darwin's *Origin of Species,* and *The Descent of Man,* Gibbon's *Decline and Fall of the Roman Empire,* De Tocqueville's *Democracy in America.* We do not need simplified digests of these books. We want to handle the originals to know what to find in them of special interest at any particular time.

It is necessary to know what students are doing in order to help them. We want them to develop ways of working systematically. For any particular undertaking, there can be a method of reporting that will allow each individual the most freedom. The following plan can be adapted for different kinds of work. For example, there might be such variations as these: What I did, What I accomplished, The most interesting information I found, What I want to do next.

A teacher can have a sheet of paper for each student with this form repeated to fill a page:

Date.........................
Title and author..
Number of pages read..............Time spent.............
How I read...

The teacher will keep the papers and give them to the students every day to record what they have read. By this method she can keep a daily check of what students are doing.

Keeping track of the time spent and the number of pages read helps a student to keep at his reading. In writing "How I read" he can say that he skipped the descriptions or other parts that did not interest him or that he read only the special information he wanted. This plan lets him report that he has read parts of books.

There are reasons for spending class time in reading. Time for reading in this modern day is limited. Reading in class says in action that reading is important and worth precious time. Students who read childish books are stimulated to grow up in reading more by seeing their classmates with grown-up books than they would be by anything a teacher could say.

Personal and social interests. How shall we discuss literature in class, and what shall we ask students to write about it?

First and most important, we must know what not to talk about. We must have due respect for persons as individuals with a right to private thoughts and feelings that we will never allow to be violated.

As literature is concerned with the relationships between people, with deep human feelings, sensitivities, and taste, the teacher needs to be sensitive to the feelings of boys and girls. Social sensitivity, which is what we learn from literature, means a delicate respect, for others. It is a sense that tells us what other people would like to talk about in groups and what they would not like to talk about. It means not intruding on any one's personality. It means respecting each person's right to dream his own dreams.

To intrude upon a young person's sensibilities, to violate them, does more harm than can be estimated. It turns the sweetness and light of literature sour and dark. As we love literature, we must guard against spoiling it for others.

Teaching of poetry. It is in the teaching of poetry that we must be most delicate. Poetry that is personal and intimate should not be taught as a vocabulary drill, a geometry analysis, or a cop-and-robbers game to catch the fellow who did not get his lesson. We must not ask a boy to dissect a beautiful love poem in the cold light of a classroom, before his fellow students who grin and giggle because they are embarrassed. Their embarrassment is evidence that they really do care about love and poetry.

A red-headed, full-of-fun tenth-grade boy left a note on a teacher's desk, "Please let us like poetry." When the teacher asked the class what they wanted to do for the poetry unit, they said they would like to read any poetry they wanted to for homework and not to talk about it in class. They said if they could do that, they would spend more than the usual time on homework.

If the adults who love poetry look back to their school days, do they find that they liked poetry because of their teachers or in spite of them? Did they like the poems their teachers prescribed and talked about in class or those they found for themselves?

To what extent have teachers killed the life poetry might have given by talking when a due respect for the sensibilities of mankind would have kept them silent? The mistreatment of poetry in the schools has robbed generations of much that poetry might have given them. We may see our situation in perspective in what an Englishman says about the teaching of poetry in English schools.[6]

Before we can begin to think constructively about poetry in the classroom, we have to face a very unpleasant fact.

Young children, when they come to school, show a natural aptitude for poetry. They love rhythm in words, they are readily moved by it, they often write rhymes and jingles which have a fresh spontaneous quality. At the lowest, they have no prejudice against poetry.

Yet the great majority of adults in these islands are indifferent to poetry, if not actually hostile to it. It disgusts them, embarrasses them, or produces no effect on them whatever.

What has happened? What has gone wrong? What have the schools done, in order to produce this disastrous result? How has the first innocent capacity for pleasure been corrupted and destroyed?

Here some teachers will protest. Anxious to avert the charge of having mishandled this part of their job, they will object that the change is due, not to anything that happens in the classroom, but to the nature of the young British animal. He or she, they assert (but more particularly he), grows out of the first liking for poetry, and develops a natural resistance which no teaching can overcome.

The answer to this is that it is not true. At schools where poetry is handled with tact and understanding, by teachers who love it and *are able to communicate their love of it,* boys and girls do not develop the traditional British hostility to this form of art, but retain an unashamed pleasure in it which grows with them and which they take away with them into adult life.

[6] L. A. G. Strong, in *The Teaching of English in Schools.* A symposium edited for the English Association by Vivian De Sola Pinto, pp. 1–2. London: Macmillan & Co., Ltd., 1947. (By permission.)

It is because poetry has been mistaught and mishandled by teachers unfit to deal with it that we, as a nation, fail to get pleasure from the art in which our literature is richest. We have the finest storehouse of poetry in the world, and ninety-nine per cent of us neither know nor care anything at all about it.

For this state of affairs the schools are to blame.

In America how could a general knowledge, understanding, and love of poetry enrich our private lives and improve our social life? How far do we fall short of realizing the full possibilities that poetry has for us? When in a lifetime does a person need poetry more than during adolescent years?

Much of the finest poetry for adolescents is delicate sensitivity, and therefore teachers of poetry should be very sensitive to the feelings of young people. Some poetry is for solitude or to be shared with a friend in quiet moments. To know when not to talk is a social sense and sensibility needed especially by teachers.

Sometimes students are as loath to talk about parts of novels as about poetry. Writers of novels and poetry reveal personal delicacies as no other writers do. They write what they would not say out loud to anyone and everyone. They write in confidence to those who understand, and it is an offense, even an outrage, to betray that confidence by talking except under fitting circumstances to those who will understand.

Students say they do not want to talk in class about the stories they like. When asked whether they would rather read novels to themselves or talk about them, they vote almost unanimously to read. Surely their feelings should be respected.

Parts of poems and novels are for silence and for solitude. In deciding what to talk about and what not to talk about a teacher can remember that to intrude upon personal delicacies is far worse than to omit the teaching of the facts that examinations are made of.

We must distinguish between literature for silence and literature for social activity. There are more kinds of experience in literature than any one of us has in life. Literature has the variety of experiences of the human race. We must learn how to use those experiences for the improvement of social life.

Many reading experiences, like other experiences, are for social use and enjoyment. They are valuable as they are shared with others. Suppose, Cicero said, that a man were taken high into the heavens so that he could look down upon the earth to see it in perspective, in vast beauty. Suppose that which is beyond possibility should happen. The experience would be without meaning or pleasure unless the man had a friend with whom he could talk about it.

SOCIAL LIVING IN THE CLASSROOM

Literature and life. How can boys and girls share the experiences of literature and correlate them with life for the best kind of growth?

An English class is a social unit of young people learning how to be social beings, learning to be integrated within themselves and with society.

A class should be conducted so that each student can contribute his best and in so doing learn as much as he can. Students should come to class, not on the defensive lest they be caught by their ignorance and tortured, but with contributions for the group thinking, conversation, and enjoyment.

The teacher can help boys and girls be interesting people by making it possible for them to be interested in each other and by being interested in them. She should be more interested in what they say than in what she says. She must continuously learn the art of speaking in such a way as to invite a response. She may have to remind herself that her motto is, Don't teach; let them learn. The communicative arts are reading, writing, speaking, and listening, and the greatest of these is listening. Of all the arts listening is the most creative, and it is the one that a teacher needs most.

A principal said, "As I walk through the halls, if I hear

the teacher's voice, I think she is not so good a teacher as she might be. If I hear quick exchange of student voices, I know the teacher is pretty good. If there is spontaneous, happy laughter several times during the period, I know the teacher is A–1."

Getting student participation. The amount of learning possible varies directly with the amount of student participation. Learning is an active, not a passive, process. It is more blessed to give to a group undertaking than to receive a lecture.

To make a class a social unit requires thinking and planning. The room should be arranged so that students can talk with each other as people talk together in regular life situations. Since we look at people when we talk to them or listen to them, the chairs in the classroom should be arranged so that every student can look at every other student.

Such an arrangement makes it possible to learn to speak to a whole group and to speak so as to be heard across the room. The art and practice of group conversation so that all contribute to group thinking have not yet been developed in social history. There are many adults who can talk with only one person at a time at the dinner table, at a party, or in a conference. They do not know how to include all those present in the conversation. They speak *to* or *at* one person or an audience, but never *with* several people. Rare indeed is the speaker who can make each individual in a group feel that his mind and the speaker's are moving together. The development of history may be measured by the way people have learned to talk and think together in larger and larger groups. Aristotle said in the *Poetics* that the number of actors was first increased to two by Aeschylus, and Sophocles learned to let three actors talk on the stage. American audiences are passive and inarticulate; some day they will learn how to express themselves. A class can be an experimental stage with thirty actors learning to talk with each other. So in the classrooms of our country we can learn the art that society needs.

Students learn to talk with groups if they can take charge of the class as often as possible. Whenever even a few students have something special to tell the class, one student can take the chair and call on them. It will increase participation and interest if the teacher, instead of appointing the chairman, asks, "Louise, will you suggest a chairman?" At first the chairman will be afraid to do more than announce the names of the speakers. He should be encouraged to talk a little to make the speakers feel at ease. When the duties of the chairman are over, there are two questions to ask. Ask the chairman, "Did you feel that the class was supporting you and helping you to be the best chairman you could be?" Ask the class, "Did the chairman encourage you and give you an opportunity to make your best contributions?"

Panel discussions, both planned and extemporaneous, advance learning. A few students sit around a table to discuss any subject of mutual interest.

TALKING AND WRITING TO LEARN FROM BOOKS

Panel discussions are a method of thinking with the authors of books to learn about life. Several students who have read the same book may discuss it. Several students who have read different books may tell each other about them and ask each other questions. The students should have progressed beyond the primitive stage of retelling the story of a book or of telling why they liked or did not like it. Each student should try to think how to ask a question or pose a problem that will stimulate the widest possible discussion. That means presenting a real life problem.

A teacher will find *Reading Ladders for Human Relations* [7] a source of constant help in using books to solve problems. The following selection from Chap. IX, "Experiences of Acceptance and Rejection," shows a method that may be adapted to solve different kinds of problems.

[7] *Reading Ladders for Human Relations, op. cit.,* pp. 87–89.

The discussion of stories like these is important to children because they should understand the feelings of inadequacy and loneliness common to all people. They need to recognize their own attempts at compensation when they are left out. They need also to learn to read the behaviors of other people so as to understand what inner feelings of insecurity or loneliness they may be expressing.

The idea of being rejected or left out will probably never be the major topic around which a book discussion is organized. Instead, such questions and problems will be injected into the discussions of many books until children and young people recognize the theme of acceptance and rejection as one that runs through all fiction that describes human problems realistically. In developing this concept through discussion, certain questions should occur again and again. In response to questions like: "Were there any characters in this story who felt left out? Under what circumstances? What did the person want that he could not have?" children may recall and perhaps reread certain episodes and passages of the story. Such questions as: "Have you known anyone who felt this way? How did it happen?" bring out more concrete descriptions of actual situations of rejection. Thus, the incidents of the story become a way of getting at experiences from real life.

The second step is to analyze the reasons why a person is left out. In considering both the episodes in the book and the situations from real life, such questions as these are helpful: "Was some personal inadequacy the reason for being left out? Was there a lack of social skills—inability to speak the same language? to play the games? to do the right thing? Was membership in a certain racial, religious, or cultural group the reason for rejection in this case? Did a stereotype limit people's ability to know the person as he was?"

Finally, questions can point up analysis of the behavior which indicated hurt feelings or loneliness; "How did the person show that he wanted only to withdraw? Was there any behavior like boasting, bragging, strutting that was a demand for approval? Are there any signs that this person tried to learn to do the things that would give him group approval?" The discussion of such questions is especially important where "chip-on-the-shoulder" attitudes are often ascribed to racial or religious groups. They are also important to individuals whose feelings of inadequacy prevent them from making a resilient and wholesome reaction to rejection.

Consideration of experiences of acceptance and rejection is particularly important in'those elementary school situations where children are seeking to belong to groups and where cliques make for broken hearts and a sense of being left out. Discussions of this kind are also very helpful to teen-agers who find it hard to be accepted in certain social clubs because they lack family prestige or social skills. In school situations where the striving to belong is of great importance, both those who are accepted and those who are rejected benefit from considering how traumatic experiences of rejection influence personality development and growth. Finally, these discussions are basic to an understanding of the feelings of those who are underprivileged or belong to so-called minority groups since these people may often be forced to stand apart from the main stream of American life and to suffer rejection because of the "in-group's" prejudices rather than from a lack of personal worth.

Cultivating student initiative. In so far as possible the students, and not the teacher, should ask the questions and propose the subjects for discussion. They should be encouraged to talk about the characters in a story as though they were people in real life and to compare them with people they know. These questions may be made more specific to fit particular characters. What is the chief character's main problem? How did the characters get into the situations they are in? What made them the kinds of people they are? Does a character take hold of a situation and manage it, or does he wait, trusting that luck will fix up everything? Does he let calamity overtake him? Does he manage his own life or let himself be pushed around? Does he think of everything as it affects him, or does he think of himself as a member of a social group? How much is his friendship or love worth? Does he know what friendship is? How would he define friendship?

To encourage students to have something to say about what they read, the teacher may ask them to write in ten minutes what they think is the most interesting idea, situation, or problem. The students' papers can serve as the basis for discussion.

To start a discussion, the teacher may ask the students at the beginning of the period to write their answers to a question. If the class is reading stories or plays, the question might be one of these: What does a character do or say that shows what kind of person he is? What problem does one of the characters have to solve? Why is the problem a character has to solve particularly hard for him; that is, harder for him than it would be for a different kind of person? Does the author show why the criminal is the kind of person he is? Is he naturally a bad person, or did his environment make him bad? What likable qualities do we see in the criminal that show us that he might have been a better person under better conditions? How are two characters different? How do we understand one character by seeing why he is different from another character? How does a character get into trouble when, with the best intentions, he is trying to help someone? How does a character make trouble for himself and others by failing to act at an important time? How did a character get into trouble because he did not understand the situation in which he happened to be? How did a character help himself by helping others? In what ways is a character a better person than he realizes?

To focus attention and interest upon a subject, a teacher may say that after a discussion each student will write for five or ten minutes. He may write his answer to a question or his analysis of a situation. For example, if the lesson is Cassius' first conversation with Brutus in *Julius Caesar*, the students may be told at the beginning of the period that they will write briefly how Cassius shows that he understands Brutus very well.

Discussions based upon comments made by the students can accomplish much more than writing book reports and book reviews. Book reviewing is a highly specialized profession for which all high school students do not need to be trained. Book reports have taken a lot of joy out of reading. They have neither personal nor social interest for students or teachers. They have been burdens to all concerned.

READING ALOUD

Reading aloud is a social activity, as well as an art, that needs developing in high school. All people may at any time in their lives be called upon to read to others.

If all the students in a class have copies of the same book and the students take turns reading aloud, there is no challenge to give the meaning of the printed words because everyone can look at them for himself. There is a totally different situation when two, three, four or five students are the only ones to have copies of a story or poem, and they take turns reading. They are responsible for giving the other members of the class all they will get from the reading. One can be the leader to tell the others when to start and stop. It is easier and more fun to read with others than to stand up alone to read, and it is less monotonous and more interesting to listen to a variety of voices than to listen to one reader.

If some students, even though they can yell across a playground, seem unable to speak above a faint murmur in the classroom, the teacher cannot help them by talking to them. She must provide a situation in which they will speak out. It is good if the English class can meet often in the school auditorium or theater. The ability to speak and read distinctly develops suddenly on the stage. A school auditorium might be scheduled for use every hour of the day.

Most plays were written for the stage. A student can direct a play, and with even one rehearsal the student actors can read their parts on a stage with pleasurable learning for themselves and the rest of the class. Reading a play on the stage with as much costume and scenery as desired comes nearer giving the satisfaction that producing a finished performance does than we are apt to think.

Many poems can be understood best and enjoyed most

when read aloud. A stage is a stimulating setting from which to read them.

Using choral speaking. Some teachers, because they have had no special training in conducting verse-speaking choirs, hesitate to have their students do group or choral reading. There are no absolute rules as to how choral reading should be done. Any one may experiment with methods. A student may be given the responsibility of arranging a poem for group reading and of directing the reading. In group activity, students lose their self-consciousness and improve their ability to read aloud.

Intensive Reading of the Classics

Perhaps some day we can learn how to conduct classes in literature so that the students are not studying just one classic at a time but many books all the time. Thirty people cannot be expected to be interested in reading the same book at the same time in the same way. No two people want to get exactly the same thing from any one book. Because we do not know a better method, we follow the old tradition of studying a few classics intensively. We know that some people have been harmed by this method. If a person never wants to read again what he has read in school, then the school has killed a part of life for him. If a person leaves school because he is not interested or because he finds life outside school more interesting, then the school has failed him and the society of which he is a part.

If we study one book at a time, we can try to have a variety of activities. We can try to apply the motto *e pluribus unum,* that is, to bring a diversity of abilities into a social unit and to encourage a diversity of abilities to develop. We must plan for all the students, not just for those we call the brightest in our subject.

The more group activities there are in a class and the more varied they are, the more opportunities there are for poor students to take their parts and so work themselves up to being good students. A teacher needs to be always alert to think how to let poor students do what they can do. Even the poorest student has some special abilities. He may, for instance, read poetry aloud very well though he shows no interest or ability in explaining the meaning. He may read a short, humorous part on the stage though he does not read well in his seat. If he cannot read, he can set the stage or manage the sound effects. He can choose the cast for a play as well as any one else and be an important person while doing it. When there are two or three things to be done, he can be the one to decide which to do first. He can take charge of the class when there is nothing to do but call on the others to speak or read. In the discussion of a story he can tell whether he thinks a character acts as a person in a similar situation in real life would act. He can usually compare situations in stories and in movies. The more he does, the more he will want to do. If he is an important member of the class, he will want to live up to his position. The teacher and he may both be surprised how soon he will be a good student.

In choosing the classics to study, we need to remember that there are no essential classics and no best books for all classes.

There is no one way or best way to teach any classic. The only thing we can do is to help students find in the classics what has meaning for them. A teacher should not say, "This is the way I teach *Macbeth* (or any other classic)." She could say, however, "We tried this last year when we were studying *Macbeth*." A teacher needs a reserve supply of methods from which to choose. The following suggestions are examples of what may be done. Though they are applied to definite classics here, they may be adapted for use with others.

Learning about life with Shakespeare. Shakespeare holds the mirror up to nature or up to life in action. We must remember that the play's the thing. It is not a vocabulary workbook.

A play should be presented so that it can be understood as easily as possible. People have said that we must understand Shakespeare to enjoy him. It would be better to say that if we enjoy him, we will understand him.

Students need help in starting a Shakespeare play. Probably a teacher should never send them into a play by themselves but tell them the main plot or problem and introduce them to the characters. Theater managers do that when they print a synopsis of a play on a program. If the audience knows what to expect, they can enter into the whole play from the beginning.

Students may enjoy Shakespeare's language if they are not bogged down by it. When students have difficulty with Shakespeare, they often say that they do not understand his old-fashioned language. A teacher will not begin with obscure words. As soon as students understand what Shakespeare is saying, his vocabulary, which seemed so baffling at first, can be a delight. No one has ever put words together so effectively. His word combinations are in the fabric of our language. Here is an assignment that will cultivate a sense for apt phrases and so will increase the vocabulary. It will help students to read Shakespeare by giving them something to do with their pens as well as their minds.

Copy twenty-five short phrases from each act. Choose phrases that you like and that you might use in conversation without attracting attention. For example, you might copy these phrases from *The Merchant of Venice*: Believe me, no; I thank my fortune; peep through their eyes; laugh like parrots; you are marvelously changed; worthier friends; you grow exceeding strange; let me play the fool; dumb wise men; not worth the search; speechless messages; her sunny locks; my little body is aweary; hears merry tales; let him pass for a man; I dote on his very absence; my foolish eyes.

Parents and teachers can give many reasons for memorizing passages from Shakespeare, and students can give many reasons for not memorizing them. Students may gain appreciation of Shakespeare as a poet if they learn not only to repeat passages but to write them in poetic lines. Learning to count the five feet in a line will help them to do that. A teacher can save a good deal of time in checking papers if she gives each student a copy of parts of a passage with blanks to be filled in where words, phrases, and lines are omitted. For example,

> The .... of mercy is ....,
> It .... heaven
> .... beneath. It is .... blest.

Recordings of Shakespeare's plays are as reliable as a teaching aid can be. No matter how they are used, they are valuable, but a teacher will find every year she uses them that she discovers a few more ways of helping students to learn more from them and to enjoy them more.

A teacher will find that it is better not to introduce a play by playing several records because the students cannot understand them even though they have the books that go with the record in front of them. The teacher may tell what is in a record before it is played, or the class can study the text with the teacher's help. Once the students get into the play, they can follow the records with no difficulty at all.

If students spend two or three weeks analyzing a play scene by scene and speech by speech before they hear the records, they are too tired of it to enjoy the records.

A teacher needs to be very sensitive to the rising and flagging interests of a class to catch the tempo for maximum understanding and enjoyment. There can be a variety of ways of interspersing discussions and listening to records. Several students may read a famous speech; then the class can listen to it on the record and talk about how the lines can be spoken most effectively. There might be a contest in delivering Antony's speech in *Julius Caesar* before the class hears the record. The class might make a record of a part of a play and then compare their record with the record made by professionals.

At the end of the study there is great advantage in listening to the entire play without interruptions. The play was written to be acted all at once. Stretching the study of it over days or weeks pulls it out of shape; the records bring it back into shape.

How can students learn from Shakespeare the ways of human life? The following assignments are suggestions:

While studying *Julius Caesar* the class may be interested in discussing these subjects and perhaps in writing essays on them:

Is any character in the play the kind of person you would like to have as a friend?

How do all the parts of Cassius' character fit together?

What does Caesar think of Cassius? What do you think of Cassius?

What does Caesar think of Brutus? Dante put Brutus in the lowest depths of his inferno because Brutus betrayed his friend. What do you think of Brutus?

If a famous actor were playing in *Julius Caesar*, which character do you think he would choose to be?

Compare the speeches of Brutus and Antony to explain why Antony's speech was more effective.

Two members of the class may be willing to read the parts of Plutarch's *Lives* of Caesar and Brutus that Shakespeare used for his play and tell the class how carefully Shakespeare followed Plutarch and where and how he changed the stories as Plutarch told them. Other members of the class may be willing to read about Caesar in Roman history in an encyclopedia or in a history book and report to the class. If any members of the class are studying Caesar in Latin, they might tell the class what Caesar himself wrote and might teach the class to read a sentence or two that Caesar wrote in Latin.

While studying *Macbeth*, students may learn to understand life a little better and to appreciate Shakespeare as an interpreter of life by thinking how they would answer this question: *Macbeth* is recognized as a very great piece of literature. How is it different from a murder story in a daily paper? Why should we spend precious school time in studying this murder story written three and a half centuries ago when we do not discuss the details of the latest murder in class? This is a way of asking what makes great literature great. Of course there is no authoritative final answer. It is a question to keep thinking about.

Macbeth is a complete story and a completely motivated story. A newspaper story of a murder is not a complete story in itself, and many of the parts are not motivated; it excites interest and emotions but leaves them in a state of excitement, undirected and hence devastating and dangerous. If students can understand the principle and practice of motivation in *Macbeth,* they can grow in ability to analyze literature and life. They can keep asking at various stages of the play why a character does what he does, and they can see that Shakespeare has explained the reason for every action. In life if we know the causes of troubles, we can do something about them; we can take positive action, and to do that keeps a mind healthy. In our own lives and in the lives of those about us we see only fragments of life; we do not see the complete stories. We are baffled and worried by what we do not understand. If we see a complete pattern of life in a piece of literature, we can see how life works out and learn a little about how to make our lives work out the way we want them to.

Learning to enjoy novels. If novels are to be studied intensely there should be great care not to press the life out of them but to keep them alive so that the boys and girls can know them at their best.

Assigning so many chapters a day and then retelling the story is about the surest way to kill a novel. But what can a teacher do? The class meets every day, and there must be an assignment and something to fill up the class hour.

Students often need help in starting a novel, and so the first chapters may be assigned and discussed in class so that everyone will understand what the main problem is and will get acquainted with at least some of the characters. After that the assignments for home work may be merely to read. Not having an assigned number of pages is a freedom that brings its rewards. Every day the teacher may note the page to which each student has read. Knowing that they will report how far they have read is an incentive to the students to read as far as they can. There is great psychological difference between assigning work and checking it and recognizing it. The teacher will know the parts of the novel the class is prepared to talk about. At least some of the class hours may be spent in reading. A novel should be read as rapidly as possible. A novel becomes dull and heavy in proportion as its reading is prolonged.

Every novel, of course, is a different problem for every class because individuals are interested in different problems of their own. No two novels are alike. There is no one way to teach any novel. Possible ways of teaching two novels may suggest other methods.

A Tale of Two Cities is one of the most satisfactory, if not the most satisfactory, novel for intensive study. Students at the end of their high school careers often list it as the best piece of literature they read during their four years. It is a novel they might not read by themselves, and it is one they are glad to have read. It is a concentration of a great deal of human life and history.

The plot is so tightly interwoven that it is one novel that can be discussed chapter by chapter. A teacher after several years will find connections between the parts of the story that she had not noticed before. If it takes a teacher so long to discern all the threads, it is evident that students in their first reading will need help in getting the maximum from the story. It is strands of characters that make the story; therefore to know the story of every character is to know the whole story. A list of the characters may be kept on the board, and the story of each reviewed every time he reappears.

A Tale of Two Cities is a story of personal friendship and love and of loyalty to humanity. Some of the questions we can ask are these: How does each character help us to understand people? To know Sidney Carton helps us to see beneath the surface the really valuable human qualities in people. The story is the emerging of a new society, a better life for the majority of the people. There is a conflict of loyalties to the old way of life and the new way of life. Which characters knew that their loyalty was on the side of humanity and progress? Charles Darnay, Dr. Manette, the Defarges, others? Which characters had to learn where their loyalties belonged? the mender of roads, others? Which characters were not loyal to progressive humanity and so were destructive forces and were themselves destroyed? Roger Cly, Gabelle, the Marquis, others?

Silas Marner is left in the curriculum perhaps because it has been there so long. Teachers of English in England are surprised that American teachers should give it so much attention and say that, if they were to choose a novel by George Eliot, they would choose *The Mill on the Floss*. It may not be necessary to have any book by George Eliot in the curriculum. She wrote about an age that is past and about a society that is quite different from ours; therefore, though her books are of great interest historically, there might be other novels that could tell our boys and girls what they want to know about life.

If *Silas Marner* is a prescribed novel for intensive study, the teacher must think what the story has to communicate to boys and girls in America today. It is not the story of an adopted child because social agencies with their scientific knowledge would not trust a little girl with a man like Silas. It would be the story of the girl that would interest boys and girls, but it is not Eppie's story; it is the story of a queer man. Why should boys and girls, with all they want to find out about life, be interested in him? There is one thing that can appeal to every one: it is the story of a man who had to adjust to a new way of life when his old life was swept away. We all see versions of that story all around us; we all live through a similar story many times. The main plot is eternally true: when old friends forsake us, we must find new friends. There can be no life in isolation; to live we must live with others, love, and be loved.

Tenth-grade students in one high school have what is called a novel unit. According to a schedule made out in September a supply of novels (many more than one for each student) is brought to the classroom. For two or three weeks the students read the novels at home and in class. A great deal of thought is given to getting a variety of novels that the boys and girls will enjoy.

For Further Reading

Broening, Angela M., *Conducting Experiences in English*, pp. 13–120. Chicago: National Council of Teachers of English, 1939.

Burton, Dwight L., "There's Always a Book for You," *The English Journal*, 38 (September, 1949), 371–375.

Carlsen, George Robert, "Literature and Emotional Maturity," *The English Journal*, 38 (March, 1949), 130–138.

Elkins, Deborah, "Students Face Their Problems," *The English Journal*, 38 (November, 1949), 498–503.

Hatfield, W. W. (Ed.), *An Experience Curriculum in English*, pp. 17–82. Chicago: National Council of Teachers of English, 1935.

Loban, Walter, "Evaluating Growth in the Study of Literature," *The English Journal*, 36 (June, 1948), 277–283.

Mirrielees, Lucia B., *Teaching Composition and Literature in Junior and Senior High School*. New York: Harcourt, Brace and Company, Inc., 1943.

Neville, Mark, *Books for You*. A book list for the senior high school. Chicago: National Council of Teachers of English, 1945.

Neville, Mark, *Your Reading*. A book list for grades 7, 8, and 9. Chicago: National Council of Teachers of English, 1946.

Poley, Irvin C., "English as a Help in Developing Mature Personalities," *Bulletin of the National Association of Secondary School Principals*, 30 (February, 1946), 163–169.

Rollins, Charlemae, *We Build Together* (Rev. Ed.). Chicago: National Council of Teachers of English, 1948.

230   TEACHING SECONDARY ENGLISH

Rosenblatt, Louise M., *Literature as Exploration*. New York: Appleton-Century-Crofts, Inc., 1938.

Taba, Hilda, *Literature for Human Understanding*. Washington: American Council on Education, 1949.

Taba, Hilda, *Reading Ladders for Human Relations*. Washington: American Council on Education, 1949.

Van Til, William, John J. DeBoer, R. Will Burnett, and Kathleen C. Ogden, *Democracy Demands It*. New York: Harper & Brothers, 1950.

Chapter 8. WORLD LITERATURE FOR WORLD SURVIVAL

LITERATURE FOR SANITY IN HUMAN RELATIONS

In *Education and World Tragedy*,[1] Howard Mumford Jones tells us that between 1900 and 1930 the world's civilized nations have killed one-third more human beings than were killed by war in the previous eight hundred years. "If the entire population of the United States were wiped out tomorrow, their number would be less than the number of human beings who have died of violence, disease, or starvation in war or as a result of it during the last half century." Indeed, when the direct and indirect casualties of wars fought since 1900 are totaled in terms of the best available estimates, the unique distinction of our age will probably be that of having destroyed more human beings in fifty years than lost their lives as the result of war in all previously recorded history. Since the leadership of mass destruction has been furnished almost exclusively by the world's most educationally advanced countries, it is important to reflect upon the tragic humor in the verses

> This world is a marvelous place
> Its wonders never cease;
> All civilized nations arm for war,
> All savages are at peace.

In an age in which science has made the brotherhood of man the only long-range alternative to mass suicide, the study of the literatures, languages, and cultures of other

[1] Howard Mumford Jones, *Education and World Tragedy*, p. 7. Cambridge, Mass.: Harvard University Press, 1946.

231

peoples deserves every encouragement that the modern school can give. Inasmuch as a world problem cannot be solved by any one group of teachers working alone, the cooperation of all teachers of every subject is required throughout the period that the child is in school. Since the need for understanding peoples and cultures other than our own is plain enough for all to see, the neglect of world literature in the large majority of high schools is a matter for genuine concern. Examination of courses of study in English reveals that literature beyond the elementary and intermediate grades is limited very largely to that of England, especially books produced at a time when very few young people, outside sons of the gentry, were able to read. If the aim in the teaching of literature were to prepare American young people to take their seats in the House of Peers as it was constituted a hundred years ago, such a reading program would be admirably suited to the purpose. If the aim, however, is more effective and enlightened living in the present century, such a narrowly restricted emphasis comes very close to sabotage.

At the college and university level, where leadership might be expected to receive training and encouragement, the preparation of teachers of literature is the most deficient of all. In the large majority of institutions of higher learning, even students preparing to teach in American schools are so overloaded with required courses in English classics of the past that the opportunity to become acquainted with the literature of their native land is all but crowded out from the undergraduate program. In view of the educational needs of the second half of the twentieth century, such a constricted emphasis could easily be misinterpreted to mean that the aim of the program is to make prospective teachers narrowly educated so that they may be the more broadly ignorant.

Nor has the graduate program for advanced degrees in English been of a type designed to produce effective leadership for schools dedicated to the advancement of the American way of life. Among the severest critics of American scholarship in English is Oscar Cargill. In *Intellectual America—Ideas on the March,*[1a] he presents the following outspoken diagnosis of American scholasticism:

Idolatrous worship of the pure intellect and its fanciful constructions is one of the ties that binds a large group of American scholars to the other continents of the Intelligentsia and creates American scholasticism. Devotion to the technique of research without much concern as to the utility of their results is typical of these scholiasts. . . . It is their privilege to be beyond good and evil, but not, in any vulgar way, like throwing kisses at the bishop's wife; rather, in judging their own results and in denying the right of society to hold them to an accounting. Properly understood, American scholasticism is completely amoral. Pure art and pure scholarship are sisterly Narcissans under their translucent skins. . . .

. . . Aryanism, completely rejected by one body of scholars, was completely accepted by another and much larger body—the teachers of literature. . . . The graduate study of literature would be the study of philology, or what was generously termed "Anglo-Saxon literature." So, despite the fact that there was hardly a piece of writing in Old or Middle English before 1370 that had as much aesthetic merit as *Ten Nights in a Bar Room,* the scientific analysis of this stuff was begun. . . . Now, while it is true that the commonest words in English speech have Anglo-Saxon originals and these in turn have Gothic counterparts, not one of these scholars has demonstrated that the ideational content of these limited Northern vocabularies was a heavy burden for the intellect of a moron. Words like *the, is, have, sleep, drink,* and *eat* represent the profundity of primitive Anglo-Saxon thought. Pundits of whom the revered Walter W. Skeat, Litt. D. LL.D., D.C.L., Ph.D., F.B.A., of the University of Cambridge is typical, have laboriously traced *Ha* (interj. E) back to Old Friesic *haha* to denote laughter!) and to German *He*; but it is said that Caligula quite unethically uttered a similar sound when he ordered Pomposo, the philologist, thrown to the lions. In all the Northern vocabularies there are no equivalents for such words as *democ-*

racy, politics, morals, aesthetics, and—horror of horrors—*scholarship!* The wolfish pursuit of moronic vocabularies and the ghoulish unearthing of the pennings of the Northern barbarians diverted young students from the true historical fount of wisdom. . . . Before long there were no classical scholars in the old sense in America, but only philologists, papyri readers, and robbers of tombs. On every front save that of history the triumph of *Kultur* over culture was complete. . . . The chairman of the department of English [at a famous American university] reported in 1938 that the average time spent by doctoral candidates in that institution is ten years. What a dehydrating process that must be! If the purpose of American education is to take young men and women out of circulation, the monastic discipline of factualism and of philology has much to commend it. . . .

. . . The future may draw from such diverse figures as Mencken and More the Emersonian axiom that thought is never truth until it is tested by action. The Intelligentsia—all types and kinds— lived too much out of the world to instruct the world in much of anything. Just as German scholarship did nothing to save Germany, so our intelligentsia have done nothing for us. We shall muddle on—with, or without, them.

Because foreign language teaching in this country has, until recently, also been dominated by scholasticism—with blighting effects upon enrollments and outcomes in high school language offerings—the curriculum of secondary education is inadequately prepared to serve the needs of the present generation in the field of literature for enlightened human relations. In a country representative of all the major and minor cultures of the earth, in which the defenses of peace are ultimately no stronger than the morale that prevails at home, it is extraordinary that most people still have to rely on the movies or the bookstands in drugstores for an acquaintance with world literature. As a means for building an understanding of the cultural meaning of America in terms of the contributions and backgrounds of her people, world literature, properly defined and selected for the purpose, would seem to .deserve a central place in the curriculum. Exclusive emphasis upon the literature of one European country because its language happens to be English is poor psychology, and even worse public relations, in a land whose largest population centers house enough people from non-English-speaking homes to fill a sizable city in almost any of the countries from which they came.

BASIC CONSIDERATIONS IN TEACHING WORLD LITERATURE

Obviously, if world literature is to contribute its just share to the achievement of a significant societal purpose, it cannot be taught purely as a scholastic discipline or end in itself, on the theory that literature exists for literature's sake and that people are secondary. In fact, a broader conception of the term than has heretofore been dominant in academic circles is almost imperative if the offering is to meet the needs of so large a number of teen-age young people as should be served. Only a conception of world literature as including everything effectively written—without regard to time or place of origin—that has real meaning for present-day life, is likely to be broad enough to have the range of appeal and adaptability that are indispensable in serving students of widely different backgrounds, abilities, and maturity levels in reading. The overcrowding and competition that have already become serious in the high school curriculum doom to failure or impotence any program in world literature designed exclusively for young people with purely aesthetic interests in belles lettres. A safe slogan here is the observation previously quoted from Mary Weeks, "If the matter does not count most, the manner will not count at all."

Some basic principles of instruction in world literature. If an effective, influential program in world literature is to become securely rooted in the curriculum of the American secondary school, attention must be given to such fundamental considerations as the following:

1. Inasmuch as the leadership of destruction since 1900 has come almost exclusively from those countries which have provided the most education to the most people, the answer

to the world's problems is not to be found just in more and more education, but in more *education of the right type.* In other words, the *amount* of education is important only in relation to the *kind.* In terms of this analysis, merely compounding the ineffectual would hardly offer a promising solution. Despite the conspicuous inadequacies of "education as usual," however, the guiding slogan of many schools seems to have been "when you are sure it doesn't work, do it some more." That this slogan has often been operative in the teaching of literature no one acquainted with the results can easily deny.

2. Since no one can be a leader without a following, the intensive education of a few to the neglect of education of the many has often led to class cleavage within society, often to the displacement of trained leadership by dishonest incompetence. General education for all, adapted to their varied backgrounds, abilities, and potentialities, thus becomes essential in every basic field of education. For the teaching of literature, this means that improved and more varied means for reaching those large numbers of people who do not readily respond to the deaf-mute approach to literature exclusively through silent reading must be capitalized. Sound films, recordings, and transcriptions are now available in such abundance and increasingly convenient form that exclusive reliance on an approach to literature which in the entire history of mankind has never proved successful, except among a very small number of human beings, can no longer be justified as either necessary or desirable.

3. Since the value of a book to the living generation does not depend primarily upon when or where it was written, but upon the light which it throws upon problems that are crucial in our own lives, the organization of offerings in world literature by chronological periods, or geographical areas, is appropriate only for very advanced students desiring to make a profession of literature in college or university teaching. Although every foreign classic that has endured

through the centuries deserves to be evaluated to see whether the problem with which it deals is important in our own day, the mere fact of its antiquity cannot be accepted as a justification either for its incorporation or exclusion. The age of a classic, per se, may as easily give proof that it no longer has significant meaning for our time as evidence of a direct contribution to active, cultivated living in the present. Inasmuch as the number of classics which the world has to offer in translation far exceeds the number that can be read in high school, the selection must be made in terms of such criteria as the following:

a. Does the book throw light on issues that are basic and real in the lives of today's young people, or does it merely serve as an escape from responsibility?

b. Does the language of the book block comprehension, or does it help the high school reader to sense the atmosphere, mood, or emotional impact of the author's creation? Inasmuch as young people vary widely in reading ability and maturity of reading interests, assignment of the same book to all members of a particular class is rarely practical.

c. Is the book's bearing on present-day life sufficiently clear that it can be made to illuminate today's problems by way of comparison or contrast with the past—without strenuous efforts on the part of the teacher? Unless a book's purpose or message can be grasped by the reader without laborious dissection, it is beyond his present level of maturity, and more likely to contribute to a dislike for the reading of good literature than to the development of discriminating and enduring reading interests in out-of-school life. Surely the use of taxpayers' money to create a lifelong dislike for great books is not an intelligent investment. It is likely to be defended only by those whose interests in literature have unconsciously become commercialized on the professional level. The value of a book to a consumer is not necessarily the same as to one who receives a salary for teaching it.

d. Does the book stress a purely resigned, passive type of

neutered goodness, or does it emphasize the strength of goodness, reinforced by ability, and actively exercised in constructive cooperative action with others? In as highly inter-
dependent a world as the one in which the present generation is now living, passive individual goodness is inadequate
for the solution of problems that are clearly beyond the
power of any single person to overcome. For this reason, if
a work stressing passive resignation in the form of a homey
little doodlebug philosophy of life is used, the results of this
view, as visible in the kind of society that has evolved among
those sharing it, deserves serious consideration. Intellec-
tualized, neutered goodness has consistently been cherished
in class-crystallized societies opposed to almost everything
that the American way of life has formerly stood for in the
way of equality of opportunity, progress toward humanely
great goals, or democratic form of government. It has had
no greater vogue than among those who favor "the costume
parade of a caste society with themselves as Brahmins."

e. Is the story, novel, epic poem, or play available in other
forms than the original in translation? If a literary work is
of such timely significance that more than a few students
for whom it is likely to have special value can profit from it,
the availability of adaptations, condensations, recorded excerpts, or dramatizations in the way of sound films is a
matter of practical importance in reaching young people
representing varied degrees of reading ability and different
backgrounds or levels of social maturity. Indeed, if a work
has had more than a purely local or temporary appeal, the
probability is strong that it has been converted into an opera,
song, moving picture, or play, or dramatized on recordings,
or retold in short-story form. Examples of famous contributions to world literature that have been popularized and preserved largely in adapted form include such works as the
following:

> Goethe's *Faust*, now known to nonspecialists in literature
> chiefly as an opera by Gounod.

Gutiérrez' *El Trovador,* now seldom performed except as the opera, *Il Trovatore,* by Verdi.

Cervantes' *Don Quixote,* known to many the world over only as a moving picture, opera by Jules Massenet, or retold story.

The *Don Juan* legend, as dramatized by the Spanish poets, Tirso de Molina and José Zorrilla, now known chiefly in story form, or as the opera, *Don Giovanni,* by Mozart.

Saavedra's play, *Don Álvaro o la fuerza del sino,* hardly known outside Spanish-speaking countries except as Verdi's opera, *La Forza del Destino.*

Corneille's famous drama, *Le Cid,* known to the modern world chiefly as an opera by Jules Massenet.

The early Germanic legends and myths, known to non-German-speaking people chiefly as the plots of operas by Richard Wagner.

The foregoing are not cited as titles that every offering in world literature should include, but to illustrate the preservative and popularizing power of adaptation—especially dramatization integrated with music. Who can deny, for example, that Goethe's poem, *Der Erlkönig,* would today be known only to a few monastic scholars, working in the silent vaults of a large research library, had it not been set to music as a song by both Schubert and Loewe? The point is that a program in world literature, to reach as many young people as could profit from it, cannot afford to neglect the means by which the originals have been popularized and preserved for posterity. To limit the approach to literature to silent reading in a form that, for want of use even among educated adults, has to be dusted every week in a library or museum, is to limit its appeal and effectiveness to so small a fraction of the secondary school population that enrollment sufficient to guarantee a strong continuing program cannot be achieved. A more aristocratic attitude toward literature can be maintained among university specialists in professional courses required of candidates for advanced degrees, but it is fatal to the teaching of literature to teen-age young people. The ability to interpret and present literary works in broader terms than one's own personal or professionalized interest is an indispensable qualification of the effective teacher of world literature in high school. Although the reading of a book in the original language and form in which it first appeared doubtless has great advantages, the point should not be pressed so far that even teachers of foreign languages must blush to admit that their acquaintance with the most influential book in western culture—the Holy Bible—is based exclusively on a *translation!*

f. Does the material stress the oneness of human nature? A book whose appeal is to be found exclusively in its emphasis upon superficial external differences, without affording any insight into their causes, has no rooting in either good science or good religion. Good literature, as Henry Grattan Doyle once put it, places its stress on those things that bring men together, and not on those things that drive them apart.

g. Does the material give insight into the reasons why different culture groups think, talk, dress, or behave as they do?

h. Does the material give insight into the fact that our standard of living, as well as civilization itself, is the product of contributions from all the major and minor cultures that have populated the earth, and that these contributions can continue to our advantage in the present and future?

i. Does the material give insight into the mutual interdependence of human beings in the family, community, nation, or world, in such a way as to indicate that ability to enjoy working with people for the common good is not merely good religion, but a modern essential to survival itself?

j. Does the material afford insight into the tragedy that has often been inflicted upon individual and group life by treating human beings as *means* rather than as *ends* only?

OFFERINGS IN WORLD LITERATURE

Although adequate representation of world literature in the reading program deserves encouragement at all grade levels of elementary, secondary, and higher education, the need is urgent enough to warrant the introduction of offerings placing special emphasis on the significant, timely contributions of literature from all those parts of the world with which our future is inextricably woven. Indeed, in view of the social composition of the United States, and its potentialities as a world leader, every reading program may well be a program in world literature, using the contributions of our own country as a basis for comparing and contrasting our problems and ways of life with those of other cultures. Clearly composition, spelling, and usage can be taught as easily in a course that includes readings in world literature as in one that stresses English and native American authors exclusively.

As early as 1937, the Santa Barbara Senior High School, under the leadership of E. Louise Noyes, began converting its first-year courses in English to a community-centered offering in world literature carrying the title "Builders Together." Participation in the program was voluntary for both pupils and teachers. Because of the careful preparation that preceded the inauguration of the program, and the forethought given to public relations, the enrollments in the new-type alternative courses soon exceeded those in the traditional English classes. The success of the innovation from the beginning was assured by first trying out experimental units in the regular English classes to gauge their effectiveness and to stimulate interest among students; by explaining the proposal to the administration and to fellow teachers (with concrete examples of possible materials, activities, and methods), and then inviting the participation of volunteers to conduct added sections as enrollments increased; by explaining the choice of two equally accredited types of English courses to the graduating classes of the local junior high schools; by describing the nature of the innovation, as a purely voluntary alternative, to parents, and inviting their suggestions and criticisms; and finally, but most important, by rooting the offering in the backgrounds of the students and life of the community.

In the following quotation from *Conducting Experiences in English*,[2] Miss Noyes describes the nature of the course and some of the activities apart from the individualized reading of literature in terms of personal or special group interest:

Santa Barbara may perhaps be particularly fortunate in the variety and type of her foreign-born citizens, but it seems that almost any community could find a large amount of material at hand for such activities. Every one was friendly and interested in the work the youngsters were doing. In itself this brought grown-ups back to school with the growing interest and belief in world friendship and appreciation of what other cultures contribute to American life. During the study of Italy, classes visited a city park which was the former home of Dr. Franceschi Fenzi, the great Italian Botanist, a man of world-wide reputation. They visited also one of the city parks in which almost every tree is a rare specimen brought here by this same Dr. Fenzi. Individuals visited two of the large city fish markets, both run by Italians of long residence in the city. They learned there of the fishing industry of the city. They learned that it was lárgely manned by this same group. A Montecito estate which is a perfect replica of an Italian garden was visited. Since one world famous Italian sculptor is a resident of the city, this lent point to the discussion of that branch of art.

The study of the Scandinavian countries found a number of residents ready to help the students. A physician was very willing to talk of his boyhood days in Norway; another man was willing to share with them very beautiful snap-shots taken on a trip back home just the year before. Many people brought books and pic-

[2] Angela M. Broening, *et al.*, *Conducting Experiences in English*, pp. 242–248. A publication of the National Council of Teachers of English. New York: Appleton-Century-Crofts, Inc., 1939.

tures sent from the old country. Luncheon at the Viking restaurant, whose proprietor was most generous, proved a high spot in the experience of one group. A Swedish Christmas party was a culminating activity for another.

Finally came the question, "What kind of a community do we wish Santa Barbara to be?" And after that, "What kind of state, nation, world do we wish for the future?" How have foreign-born groups helped to build American culture, and how may they help in the future?

One large part of the year's work has not yet been mentioned even though it has been started first and then carried on through the entire year. The first six weeks were spent in definite work on the improvement of reading skills. This work was begun, but all the teachers concerned in the experiment wish the next term to begin the work of the course first. This plan will permit the students to begin reading along their own special lines of interest and to use much of their reading as testing material for each individual.

Suggested Activities

I. What is our Community?

Trace your own background through both great-grandparents, if possible, at least through grandparents.

Bring an anecdote of your background to share with us all.

Find some one way in which your parents or grandparents had a share in building the community in which they lived. Tell us about it.

See how students are helping to build this school, this community.

What plans, if any, have you for your share in building the community in which you hope to live?

Find out, through a census, what the racial make-up of the present 10B class is.

Plan the questions for this census and discuss your plans with other members of this same group.

Plan, as a class, for the same type of census of the whole school.

Tabulate the material obtained. Work for accuracy.

What work are people doing in Santa Barbara to·build a better city? List the people who are best known for such work. Are they the only ones who are thus working? Who are some of the unnamed ones who are contributing a full share?

Through what agencies are these people doing their civic work?

Plan interviews with some of the people in each of these groups. Let various church groups . . . plan a collective interview; possibly carry it out collectively. This same type of thing can be planned for the school community.

Make a map or a graph, or both, of our community for racial elements and for contributing elements, churches, schools, etc.

II. What is the Background of Our Peoples and Relationship to Us?

The what and why of an immigrant. Distinction between immigrant and emigrant.

Find out why your ancestors left their homeland. Find out why they chose to come to America rather than to some other country. Discuss the meaning of "The Land of Promise" and "America, the Melting Pot."

Find out what agencies and situations in New York helped them to think of this country as the land of their dreams and what things, if any, disillusioned them. (Edmund Steiner is good here; also rather specially *They Who Bring Dreams* and Schauffler, *Scum of the Earth*.)

How and when did your ancestors make their way to California? Did the journey add to their dreams or take from them?

Plan an exhibit of things brought from the homeland. (Culminating activity) Discuss how the home in the Old World influenced the one in the New: furnishings, habits, attitudes, etc.

There are said to be five main ways in which immigrants have contributed to American culture: Manual work (see Panunzio specially), old customs, the fine arts, science and invention, and journalism. Can you think of other ways in which immigrants have contributed to our culture?

Newcomers have perhaps a harder time, with more obstacles to overcome, in getting an opportunity to help build than do oldtimers (natives). Discuss some of these obstacles. Find out how people you actually know or know of have overcome them. Find out what has helped.

Try to construct a whole community built just of immigrants. What nationality would you choose as the best for each piece of constructive work? Build a composite citizen. Build a composite town. (This is a good culmination for the whole work.)

Study the musicians, painters, sculptors, actors, producers, writers, etc., of our town, then of the nation, who are foreign-born. Try to see what their contributions have been to our culture. A modern problem is those who come over as "guest artists" only. Investigate a bit on this. Find out whether we are now sending American-born artists of all sorts back to other countries as "guest artists." Try to contrast the results, both on the countries and the artists.

Make a similar study of scientists and inventors.

Make such a study of newspaper men, of whom there has been a surprising number (Bok, Bennett, Schurz, McClure, Pulitzer).

Read biographies of immigrants to our country. There are many of them. Read from two angles: for the type of work that the person did after he came to America, and for the type of struggle that the person had in adjusting himself to America.

Make a list of such books, with comment appended of your opinion on each.

Write a story of yourself as an immigrant to one of these countries; make it accurate by finding how such countries receive immigrants; try to see yourself in this situation as the immigrants you have been reading about were in our own country.

Make a bibliography of books about immigrants by talking to friends and neighbors who are of foreign descent. Try for both biographies and novels. Try for both individual and collective biography, for both individual and collective experience. Such novels, for instance, as Bojer's *The Emigrants,* Cather's *My Antonia,* Rolvaag's *Giants in the Earth,* and *Peder Victorious* give collective experience. Books are legion on these topics; you will enjoy asking people what ones they have read and liked in addition to going to the card catalogue for your facts. Some of you may be able to read a book in some language other than English that bears on this same problem.

Many of our holidays and our manner of celebrating them have much that has come from the old countries. Choose some one or two, such as Christmas or Easter or Thanksgiving and show some part of our celebration that has come from one of the older nations.

We take many conveniences in our homes for granted today.

Find out for which of these we must thank some nation other than ourselves. Compare and contrast modern ways of housework with those of earlier days and with those of the countries from which your ancestors came.

Many people today are keenly alive to the beauty (or lack of it) in our natural surroundings and in the conservation of our natural resources. How have foreign-born helped in this? Are we ahead of or behind other nations in our attitude toward such things?

Write a story of a typical day in the old country home and then one of such a day in the new country for some family.

Plan, if possible, a festival day in the country of your greatest interest. Perhaps you will be able to exhibit a real costume from your country or at least to draw a typical one.

Compare and contrast our treatment of the aged poor with the treatment accorded the same groups in some other country.

Compare and contrast the local governments of two towns or cities.

Plan a picnic in _____ and in Santa Barbara. Perhaps you can prevail on some of the cookery classes to help you supply a little of the actual food for us, enough for samples.

Go to church in the two countries, in _____ and in Santa Barbara, and tell what was different. Go to a Christmas service particularly.

Go to school for a day in the two countries.

Go to a Boy or Girl Scouts meeting. Compare and contrast. Perhaps some of you have actually belonged to such groups somewhere else or have been to a Scout Jamboree.

Go to a wedding celebration in _____ and in Santa Barbara, with all the old ceremonies carried out as they were in the old country.

Illustrations of all the above, either crayon drawings on the board or bulletin board ones large enough to be seen from a distance, or large tempera paintings will be always helpful and welcome.

III. What Kind of Community Do We Wish Ours to Be?

Men have always striven for an ideal community. Find out about some of them. Perhaps some of your ancestors helped at Brook Farm or at the Oneida Community in our country. Some of you will like to look up something about one of the earliest stories of an ideal community. It is written by a man named More and is called *Utopia*. Modern writers also have played with the same idea. See what you can find about such communities.

One basic idea is at the back of all such ideas. Can you guess what that idea is? Must it be at the back of any plan for a planned Santa Barbara? Find out whether we have already taken any steps in that direction.

Many agencies are at work to make Santa Barbara the kind of city we wish it to be. Do all of them agree as to what is best?

Foreign-born groups have already made many contributions to the growth of Santa Barbara. Find out about all of these. Are they all working in the social field? In the religious? In the civic? List and evaluate as many such contributions as you can.

If any groups are working today, find out about them also. Do you know what the Tokalon Club is? Do you know the work that the Sons of Herman are doing? These are only examples. Find others, just as many as possible. Are all these groups working alone, or is there any unifying agency?

What is a community survey? Is one desirable here on this problem? Can we as a tenth-year group do it? If so, how? Can we help actually to make Santa Barbara a better place in which to live?

That world literature can be drawn from life as well as from books is convincingly proved by Frances Unapher of the Froebel School, Gary, Ind., in "Experiencing Poetry of Fourteen Nationalities." [3]

EXPERIENCING POETRY OF FOURTEEN NATIONALITIES

A ninth-grade class in a foreign district was reading narrative poetry. The pupils noted that *The Pied Piper* is an old German story. A member of the class contributed the information that her parents had told her many stories in the verse of another country. Most of the pupils, it appeared, themselves knew poems which they wished to recite or to sing. "But what do the poems say?" asked the teacher. A little Czechoslovakian boy translated his song: "A child has returned home after visiting a neighbor cousin.

[3] *Ibid.*, pp. 14–15.

'What did you do at your cousin's?' asks Mother. 'I had a glass of wine and now my heart hurts.'" A Greek boy concluded his translation:

> How long, my followers,
> Will we be living in the mountains
> Alone just like lions,
> In the caves of the mountains?
> It is better to have one hour
> Of free and happy life,
> Than to have forty years
> Of slavery and imprisonment.

After a number of recitations had been given, the teacher called attention to the fact that although few in the class (there were fourteen nationalities present) could understand the poems, all found the poems pleasant to listen to. It was obvious even if the words were foreign that poetry has rhythm, melody, emotion.

To make a collection of well-known poems in other languages and to translate them for the benefit of their classmates now appeared to be the wish of the class. In this they needed the help of their parents. So for the next few days parents and friends in the community were kept busy reciting and writing out and helping translate the poems that they learned when they were in school in the old country. Interesting comments were brought in. A Rumanian mother said, "When I was in school I learned all the great poems of my country. Boys and girls in American schools do not learn enough poetry." Pupils checked this statement at home with their parents and came back reporting general agreement with it. Most of their parents knew more poetry than they did. "My dad knows a lot of patriotic poems like this one. Are there any patriotic poems in America?" asked Greek Harry Thanos.

Meanwhile the reading of narrative poems went ahead in class: "Incident of the French Camp," "Hervé Riel," "Sohrab and Rustum," "The Highwayman," and all the old favorites.

The little excursion into the literature of other lands helped develop an understanding of and an appreciation for the riches that come to us in America with our foreign citizens. It gave parents and children, who in a new world environment are too often at odds, a chance to bend heads over the same paper in happy collaboration. It gave opportunity for interviewing, translating, and oral reading in the best sort of audience situation. As for poetry, it made clear the fact that rhythm, emotion, and imagination are common to poetry of all nations.

For the junior high school level, the following unit from *An Experience Curriculum in English* [4] is indicative of possibilities in the use of world literature for education in human relations.

Exploring the Social World

1. *Primary Objective:* To make our lives richer by recapitulating some of the experiences of our predecessors.

Enabling Objectives: To experience vicariously the early world of man; to compare present-day life and thought with those of the people of other ages.

Typical materials: In the Light of Myth (Baker); Tale of Indian Heroes, Being Stories of the Mahabharata and the Ramayana (Steel); Story of the Cid (Wilson); Children of Odin (Colum); Book of King Arthur and His Noble Knights (MacLeod); Wonder Book of Old Romance (Darton); Orpheus and His Lute (Hutchinson).

2. *Primary Objective:* To participate vicariously in the mental growth of our ancestors.

Enabling Objectives: To gain an understanding of the mental growth of various peoples through an acquaintance with their literature; to realize how the results of social and scientific progress affect our lives today; to understand present-day social institutions in the light of the continuous contributions of the past; to participate with peoples of other times by experiencing vicariously their social, cultural, and economic expansion.

Typical materials: Old English Ballads, *Beowulf, Story of Roland; Boy of the Lost Crusade* (Echols); *Early Men of Science* (Nida and Nida); *Up from Slavery* (Washington); *Ulysses* (Tennyson); *Elegy Written in a Country Churchyard* (Gray); *Lincoln, the Man of the People* (Markham); *Golden Tales of Our America* (Becker); *One Hundred Narrative Poems* (Teter).

[4] W. Wilbur Hatfield, *et al., An Experience Curriculum in English,* pp. 47–48. A publication of the National Council of Teachers of English. New York: Appleton-Century-Crofts, Inc., 1935.

In the junior and senior years of the high school, a semester or year course stressing more mature literature in English translation is desirable, provided the concept of literature is not restricted to fiction or belles lettres, but interpreted to include all effectively written works that have both a timely significance for our time and a real personal meaning for the student. The notion that effectively written books on aviation, scientific discovery, or sports cannot be considered literature has done much to narrow the appeal and influence of the reading program in many senior high schools. Where the total school enrollment is limited, an upper division course in world literature, sponsored jointly by teachers of English and the modern and ancient languages, is often possible. When such cooperative sponsorship is operative, students can be given the choice of doing their reading either in English translation or in the original language, and of receiving credit in whichever language their reading is done. Since it is unlikely that many students will wish to read books in a language that is not taught in the school, the problem of evaluation is negligible. Even if the number of such students were large, it would not be difficult to delegate the evaluation of their reading to responsible members of the community who have a fluent reading knowledge of the language in question. Reports of their reading to the class would give the teacher an adequate supplementary basis for judging depth of comprehension.

The foregoing possiblity is especially recommended for small schools in which advanced classes in foreign languages cannot be offered, as a means for enabling especially interested young people to maintain contact with the language that they have learned at home or in school, and to enrich the program in world literature with contributions from students whose reading has been done in the original tongue. A teacher of foreign languages who is also a part-time teacher of English should be especially qualified to conduct such a course. The most important qualification, however, is a strong conviction concerning the importance of the offering and enthusiasm in sponsoring it. Ability and interest in the work may well be weighted heavily in the appointment of new teachers of English and foreign languages to replace those who withdraw from the school.

METHODS IN TEACHING WORLD LITERATURE

Inasmuch as the methods, devices, and activities described in the chapters on reading, evaluation, and literature are for the most part equally appropriate for world literature courses, only those procedures that are especially applicable need be reviewed here. In general, offerings in world literature cannot be expected to serve the needs of as many young people as should be reached unless a high degree of differentiation in content and methods is assured. Such a differentiation can be provided in the following ways:

Surveying the social composition of the school, neighborhood, and community to determine which culture groups are represented. A census conducted by the students themselves, early in the course, will provide a basis for the selection of reading materials that serve local needs most directly. The census should yield a card index giving the names, addresses, and possible contributions to the class program of speakers, painters, sculptors, musicians, dancers, writers, and business or professional people among the various culture groups represented in the community and environs.

Selecting a unifying theme for the semester, with subtopics suitable for differentiated committee work, or for organizing the program into two- to six-week units. Pupil participation in the selection of the unifying theme and in the organization of the course in broad outline, under the teacher's guidance, is essential to the success of the undertaking. Examples of unifying themes, and of group procedures in deriving them, are contained in the quotation from E. Louise Noyes, cited earlier in this chapter.

Organizing the class into groups. The students may be grouped under their own chairmen, according to common

interests as revealed during the discussion of the census
returns and unifying theme, or according to data from such
questionnaires regarding reading interests, social attitudes,
and the like, as the teacher may wish to use.

*Discussing the availability of reading materials in the
classroom, school, and neighborhood libraries.* A reading
guide. in the form of a mimeographed sheet giving simple
directions for locating references, as well as a list of the most
widely useful collections of translated works and of anthologies containing selections from world literature, will prove
a valuable aid. If many students are new to the school, a
visit to the school and neighborhood libraries is desirable as
a means of acquainting them with the resources of these
facilities and for giving them practice in locating and charg-
ing out materials.

*Setting aside at least two class periods each week as read-
ing periods under the teacher's supervision.* While the students are reading silently, the teacher can confer with individual students or committees. Although some students will
have to be excused from the class occasionally to go to the
school library, this number will be small if the group is cau-
tioned to bring essential reading materials to class. Their
number can be reduced even farther by securing permission
to move books relevant to the course into the classroom as a
kind of reserve library for two- to six-week periods if a separate classroom library cannot be established. Bookshelves
mounted on wheels are the most convenient means for trans-
porting and storing books that are to circulate for limited
periods.

*Providing opportunities to meet able representatives of the
culture group whose literature is included in the reading program.* If the census mentioned earlier has been conducted by
the students under proper guidance, the selection and invitation of visitors from a roster acceptable to the teacher and
class should be delegated to the students themselves, once
their plans have been reviewed and approved. Since, in the
final analysis, there is no completely satisfactory substitute

for actual practice in meeting people on common ground, if education in human relations is a central concern, the suggestions offered here are especially important.

Where the opportunities to meet representatives of other cultures are exceedingly limited, sound films and recordings that bring the world into the classroom acquire added importance. In schools in which effective cooperation exists between teachers of English and modern languages, correspondence with young people who are studying English abroad is desirable. It is not necessary that the students write in a foreign language if they are willing to receive replies in their correspondent's native tongue. In such cases, however, the cooperation of intermediate and advanced students of modern languages in making translations may be needed. In many communities, local organizations of Americans of foreign origin, as revealed by the class survey, will be willing to assist in making translations.

In general, foreign correspondence tends to die out unless it is guided by a group purpose. Such cooperative group activities as conducting an informal public opinion poll via letter on topics of common interest, *e.g.*, living and working conditions abroad, reasons for differences in customs, most widely known books, stories, or plays, etc., help to give correspondence a significant purpose, especially if an audience is provided in class for the reading and discussion of returns. The opportunity for motivated practice in composition that this activity provides is too obvious to require special emphasis.

Choosing methods of evaluation appropriate to the program. In an individualized reading program, in which few students read the same book, the problem of evaluating, or checking up on what each student has done, can become unwieldy unless appropriate, practical means are selected. Although class discussions, oral presentations, and written work afford ample bases for judgment in most cases, some students will read more books than can be discussed during the class hour. When it seems desirable to test their claims to extra credit, the citation test described in *Modern Languages for Modern Schools* [5] will be found a simple, yet practical, "open-book" device. It requires, however, that the student have with him the exact copy of the novel, play, story, or epic poem that he claims to have read.

For the measurement of comprehension in independent reading (when each student reports on a different book) the citation technique is equally practical. It is often useful as a check on actual reading, for when translations, previous book reports, abundant critical comment, or moving-picture versions exist, few other techniques afford so simple a check on firsthand acquaintance with the foreign text. As many as six students can be examined simultaneously within twenty to thirty minutes during a free-reading period in class. Thus while pupil A, who had read *Tamango*, locates the exact passage in which the hero dies, pupil B locates the exact passage in *La Parure* that states that the necklace was made of paste. Such a generalized application naturally presupposes some degree of acquaintaince with the material on the part of the instructor. When the content of a story, play, or book is vague in the instructor's mind, or unfamiliar to him, a brief individual report substantiated from time to time by direct reference to the text is the only alternative. For example, the teacher may say:

Teacher: I see that you have read the *Life of Sir Basil Zaharoff* in Spanish. Who was he?

Pupil: He was a famous munitions king, who became one of the world's most influential and richest men.

Teacher: What does the author of the book think of Sir Basil? Does he make him out to be a hero, a villain, a victim of circumstances, or a benefactor to humanity?

Pupil: I think he describes him as a clever and not-too-honest politician.

Teacher: Can you find a passage in the book that reflects this attitude on the part of the author?

Anticipating needs in the way of audio-visual aids and equipment. As soon as the program has taken form, the selec-

[5] W. V. Kaulfers, *Modern Languages for Modern Schools*, pp. 124–127. New York: McGraw-Hill Book Company, Inc., 1942.

tion of appropriate recordings and sound films becomes important, since orders can rarely be filled without considerable advance notice. Inasmuch as relevance and timeliness are decisive factors in the use of audio-visual aids for educational purposes, a definite calendar of presentations is essential. Thanks to the radio, music, drama, and commentary have become so much a part of life in the United States—from washing dishes to reading in bed—that a film or recording introduced without preguidance, *i.e.*, giving the listener something specific to look for, and follow-up in the way of discussion and critical evaluation by the audience, is likely to be regarded as an occasion for superficial entertainment instead of pleasurable learning.

Source Materials for World Literature

Several anthologies containing selections from world literature are available, but the use of any one as a uniform basic text invites the danger of limiting the appeal and value of the course to young people with special interests in literature for its own sake. Although two to five copies of each of the better anthologies might well be made available, collections of translations, as well as individual works that are available in translation, are to be preferred in conducting an individualized reading program. The foregoing may well be supplemented with effectively written, reliable books about foreign countries, as well as with biographies of their most distinguished contributors to the arts and sciences. For bibliographies of literature in translation the reader is referred to *Foreign Languages and Cultures in American Education*,[6] the

[6] Walter V. Kaulfers, Grayson N. Kefauver, and Holland D. Roberts, *Foreign Languages and Cultures in American Education*, pp. 351–391. New York: McGraw-Hill Book Company, Inc., 1942.

Library Literature. New York: The H. W. Wilson Company. See *Translations* in recent editions of this "author and subject digest to current books, pamphlets and periodical literature relating to the library profession."

Book Review Digest, Library Literature, Readers' Guide to Periodical Literature, Helen R. Sattley's *Children's Books about Foreign Countries,* Dorothy E. Smith's *The Four Freedoms and the Atlantic Charter: A Reading List for Young People, Books for You: A High-school Reading List Arranged by Themes and Types,* and *Your Reading: A List for Grades 7, 8 and 9.* In addition to the foregoing, the *Education Index* [7] occasionally yields helpful leads under the captions *Bibliographies, Anthologies, World Literature, Translations,* etc.

Inasmuch as many foreign novels, stories, and plays have been competently dramatized on sound film, the resources of the moving picture are not to be neglected. Among the distributing agencies that specialize in 16-mm adaptations, including foreign films with English subtitles, are Brandon Films, 1600 Broadway, New York; the International Film Bureau, 6 North Michigan Ave., Chicago 2, Ill.; the Film Classic Exchange, Fredonia, N. Y.; and Association Films (Y.M.C.A. Motion Picture Bureau), New York. For a comprehensive listing, see *The Educational Film Guide.* [8]

Helen R. Sattley, *Children's Books about Foreign Countries.* Chicago: National Council of Teachers of English, 1949.

Dorothy E. Smith, *The Four Freedoms: A Reading List for Young People.* Chicago: National Council of Teachers of English, 1943. Out of print but still available in many libraries.

Books for You: A High-school Reading List Arranged by Themes and Types, pp. 76–99. (Other Lands and Peoples—Their Life and Literature.) Chicago: National Council of Teachers of English, 1945.

Your Reading: A List for Grades 7, 8 and 9, pp. 78–105. (We the People.) Chicago: National Council of Teachers of English, 1946.

Book Review Digest. New York: The H. W. Wilson Company. Published monthly, except in July, with a six months' cumulation in August and a cloth-bound cumulated annual in February. See *Fiction-Translated Stories,* etc.

Readers' Guide to Periodical Literature. New York: The H. W. Wilson Company. Lists translations published in periodicals. Poems are listed by author and under *Poems.* See especially *Translations.*

[7] *Education Index.* New York: The H. W. Wilson Company.

[8] *The Educational Film Guide.* New York: The H. W. Wilson Company.

Where close cooperation exists among teachers of English, foreign languages, and social studies, public showings of feature-length films to which the public is invited, can help carry the program in world literature into the community on a self-sustaining basis. Under the leadership of teachers of foreign languages, Pasadena in California has been particularly successful in bringing foreign classics to the screen through the cooperation of a local moving-picture theater with school clubs and teachers in the subject fields.

More convenient for classroom use than films in most cases are the recorded dramatizations and vocal 'interpretations, with musical background, of great pieces of world literature. The number of recordings featuring poems, great speeches on democracy, condensations of novels, stories, and plays, etc., is now so great that only a few examples can be cited here:

Ronald Colman, *Tales of the Olympian Gods*, Decca Records, Album No. DA-475.

Orson Welles, *No Man Is an Island*. Great speeches and poems stressing the interdependence of man, and the democratic tradition since the days of Pericles. Suitable for the junior and senior years in high school.

For sources of world literature on records, the classified catalogues of the various recording companies are especially helpful. For literature interpreted by native voices, the transcriptions available from the Linguaphone Institute, 30 Rockefeller Plaza, New York 20, are unsurpassed. Teachers who wish to dramatize adaptations of well-known classics as play readings or radiodramas for school assemblies, Parent-Teacher Association meetings, and the like, will find the fifteen-minute scripts available on loan from the Educational Radio Script Exchange, Federal Security Agency, Washington, especially useful. A catalogue will be sent on request.

Opportunities unlimited. Because of the range and scope of world literature, and the innumerable ways in which its resources can be adapted to serve special needs, the possibilities indicated on the preceding pages are but illustrations that will, in time, suggest even better procedures to all who subscribe to the saying "where there's a will, there's a way." None of the illustrations represent the maximum that the school *should* do. They are but the minimum that it can *afford* to do in a world in which it is no longer possible to keep either ideas or guided missiles from crossing boundary lines— in a day and age when "ships sail on clouds." [9]

For Further Reading

Barnes, J. R., "World Literature," *The English Journal*, 26 (November, 1937), 734–739.

Carlson, G. R., "Creating a World Outlook through Literature," *The English Journal*, 30 (December, 1944), 526–537.

Cross, N. M., "World Literature for High School," *Secondary Education Bulletin*, 5 (January, 1936), 7–10.

Dowler, C. X., "World Literature, a Required Course," *Secondary Education Bulletin*, 13 (February, 1947), 5–6.

Lucas, H., "The Type Approach to the Study of World Literature," *The English Journal*, 36 (December, 1947), 533–535.

Middlesworth, L., "Literature as an Illuminator of Dark Corners in Geography," *Ohio Schools*, 18 (June, 1940), 280–281.

Montgomery, M., "Global Pattern—Life and Literature," *The English Journal*, 34 (November, 1945), 504–506.

Pease, K., "World Literature in the High School," *Secondary Education Bulletin*, 7 (February, 1938), 38–39.

Petitt, O. J., "Peoples of the Modern World; Unit in Literature," *The English Journal*, 37 (October, 1948), 404–408.

Pirhalla, J., "Adventures in World Literature," *Junior College Journal*, 9 (March, 1941), 247–250.

Sattley, Helen, Chairman, *Children's Books about Foreign Countries*. Chicago: National Council of Teachers of English, 1949. Reprinted from *Elementary English*, 26, January–May, 1949.

Stolper, B. J. R. "English Literature in the High School: A Project in World Literature," *36th Yearbook of the National Society for the Study of Education*, Part II, pp. 63–70.

[9] Walter V. Kaulfers, "Targets for Our Aims—The Role of World Languages in Secondary Education," *Modern Language Journal*, 33 (March, 1949), 171–178.

Chapter 9. MASS MEDIA OF COMMUNICATION: MAGAZINES

America may be said to be a nation of magazine readers. For every book reader in the United States there are at least two magazine readers. Americans read magazines for amusement, for information, and for inspiration. They turn to them for interpretation of the news, for side lights on interesting characters, for humor, for advice on practical problems, for adventure and excitement, and for personal and religious guidance. Magazines supply readers with fiction, history, political analysis, child psychology, news of sports, hobbies, and scientific developments, suggestions for interior decoration, home building and maintenance, clothing, health care, choice of schools and vacation spots, as well as scores of other types of informational and recreational materials. They present these materials in the form of words, photographs, cartoons, charts and graphs, drawings, and other visual symbols. Magazine communication has become a highly developed art and is today one of the most interesting and effective reflectors of American life.

Approximately 6,000 magazines, with a total circulation of 240 million, are published in the United States. They range from low-grade comic books, cheap pulp magazines, and lurid adventure magazines to such sophisticated journals as *The New Yorker*, quality magazines like *Harper's*, and learned periodicals like the *Journal of Genetic Psychology*. Within a given field of interest, they range from such an excellent popular magazine as *Science News Letter*, to the *Scientific American*, to the highly technical magazine *Science*.

There is a magazine for every level of reading ability, interest, taste, and political opinion.

How well prepared is the American public to read magazines with intelligence and pleasure? Generally speaking, the American school has been much more interested in books than in magazines as media of communication. As in so many other ways, the school has been slow to adjust itself to this development in American life. Clearly in the field of magazines, the school has both a great opportunity and a great challenge.

Objectives for Magazine Study

The study of magazines in school should be guided by a number of clear objectives. Mere reading of them at home or in school cannot in itself result in the improvement of the quality of magazine reading by American youth. The following objectives are suggested as possible directions for educational efforts in this field:

Expansion of magazine reading interests. One of the fundamental purposes of the secondary school is to prepare young people for the constructive use of leisure time. The magazine offers a wide variety of opportunities to adolescents, not only for the pursuit of their present interests but also for the development of many worth-while new interests. Boys and girls whose tastes in magazines are limited to the pulps, adventure magazines, or one or two popular publications can learn to enjoy many other periodicals which will open new fields of interest and activity to them. Hobbies, sports, athletics, fashions, public affairs, science and nature, humor, education and child care, occupations, worth-while fiction, and many other areas of interest are represented by many magazines of which the typical youth is unaware and which are usually not available at the commercial magazine stand. It is the responsibility of the school to make these available to him and to encourage him to explore them.

Improvement of reading tastes. We have frequently heard the complaint that public tastes in books, radio and television programs, photoplays, and magazines are deplorably low. No doubt this complaint is justified. But tastes, like other human characteristics, are in large part learned, and it is possible for the home, the church, the school, and other social institutions to do something about them. Teachers can, by creating a favorable environment and providing happy experiences with high-grade magazines, substantially improve young people's tastes in magazine reading.

Understanding of personal and social problems. Magazines offer an excellent means of providing young people with personal and vocational guidance. Martin, in an excellent article on this subject,[1] has called attention to the value of such magazines as *Hygeia* and the *Journal of Public Health Nursing,* as well as numerous bulletins of the American Medical Association, for the girl who is considering nursing as a profession, or the *Architectural Forum* and *House Beautiful* for the boy who wants to know something of the opportunity and challenge to be found in the profession of architecture. She cites *Crisis, Opportunity,* the *American Hebrew,* and *Common Ground* as examples of periodicals which may help boys and girls to develop a greater appreciation for various minority groups in American life. Such·magazines may frequently be much more effective in combating prejudice than many books. Young people who experience only frustration in their efforts to read literature and history may discover that the reading of such magazines as *Air Trails, Popular Aviation, Building America,* and *Field and Stream* can be very rewarding. Many young people now lost to the schools at the legal school-leaving age could perhaps be retained if the reading fare provided were within the range of their interests and capacities.

[1] Laura K. Martin, "Personalizing Magazines," *The English Journal,* 31 (November, 1942), 660–663.

Development of independent judgment in magazine reading. In a democratic society, ultimate decisions about public policy must be made by the people. It is of the greatest importance. therefore, that the people have access to as many sources of information and opinion as possible, and that they learn to make up their own minds after careful examination of many points of view. When young people read magazines which reflect only one basic view respecting public policy, they are likely to be influenced by the particular person, persons, or agencies which publish the magazines. For this reason, high school youth should be introduced to many viewpoints in the magazine world. They should learn how to compare these viewpoints, to recognize the bias of the writers, and to make up their minds independently.

Many magazines are produced on a mass basis. For example, eleven publishers control roughly one-fourth of the total magazine circulation in the United States, with seventeen magazines out of the total of 6,000 magazines published. They are DeWitt Wallace (of *Reader's Digest*), Curtis Publishing Co., Crowell Publishing Co., Hearst Publications, Coronet-Esquire, Inc., J. Howard Pew, *Time,* Inc., Gardiner Cowles, Atlas Corporation, T. M. Meuller, and McCall, Inc. Five publishers—Curtis, Time, Crowell, Hearst, and McCall —with ten magazines, represent one-fifth of the total magazine circulation in this country. Since these publishers hold essentially the same views on most public questions, it is important that students become acquainted with opinions held by publishers of other than those who produce the popular mass magazines. The opinions expressed or implied in these mass magazines should be considered in the light of the special interests of the publishers, many of whom belong to the group described by the Hutchins Commission on a Free and Responsible Press as "big business," just as other smaller magazines should be read in the light of their own biases. Chapter 6 discusses in considerable detail the methods by which independent judgment in reading can be developed.

MAGAZINE READING INTERESTS OF YOUTH

Boys and girls of all age levels like to read magazines. In the elementary school, such periodicals as *Child Life, Boys' Life, American Boy, Open Road, Boy Scout, Calling All Girls, American Girl, Popular Science, Popular Mechanics, Youth's Companion, Jack and Jill,* and *American Junior Red Cross News* are widely read. Already in the seventh and eighth grades, *Life, Reader's Digest, National Geographic,* and *Collier's* are very popular. Bright children in the elementary school will undertake to read *Radio News, Scientific American,* and *American Magazine,* while dull children show preference for *Photoplay, Film Fun, True Story,* and *Argosy.* And of course the comic magazines, of which more will be said presently, are read by children of all ages, regardless of intelligence level.

By the time a boy or girl reaches high school, his interest in comic magazines is beginning to wane. In the course of the ninth year of school there is a sharp decline in young people's interests in them, although a number of youth persist in reading them throughout high school and into adulthood. However, interest in magazines generally continues strong. Estimates vary as to the number of magazines the typical high school student reads regularly. One investigator sets the number at from two to three, while another finds that students will average as many as four. One writer reports that the average high school student spends nearly three hours per week in reading magazines. While this figure is substantially below that for radio listening, it is much higher than is commonly supposed. Could it possibly be higher than that for voluntary textbook reading?

High school youth differ widely in their magazine preferences. Boys have different favorites from those found among girls. Bright students choose titles different from those preferred by slower learners. Only certain magazines show a universal appeal to young people regardless of age, sex, or intelligence. These include *Reader's Digest, Life, Saturday Evening Post,* and *Collier's.* Table I lists fifteen magazines which Witty and Coomer found most popular among high school students, while Table II lists favorite magazines of junior high school pupils as found by Ashby. Girls, of course, tend to turn to women's monthly magazines, even as early as age fifteen, especially magazines of romantic fiction, society, and fashions, while boys respond to the themes of adventure, sports, and mechanics. Magazines designed specifically for boys continue popular in the ninth grade but tend to be out of favor in the later years. Such magazines apparently should be made available to boys and girls in the early high school years. Boys seem to be more varied in their interests in magazines than girls are.

Both boys and girls in high school exhibit interest in the themes of adventure, humor, and love (according to Sterner), regardless of the medium in which they are found. Apparently the theme is more important to them than the medium. They will utilize radio, motion pictures, books, or magazines with equal enthusiasm, provided they can find the type of information or entertainment which appeals to them.

USING MAGAZINES IN SECONDARY SCHOOLS

Many teachers have reported classroom experiences with magazines which have resulted in improved reading tastes and extended reading interests on the part of high school youth. It seems clear that the reading tastes of the American people could be materially altered for the better, particularly in the field of magazines, if all schools were to provide youth with the opportunity to become acquainted with the many good materials available.

Comparison of the present magazine reading interests of high school youth with a list of magazines ranked according to cultural level will reveal the degree to which the schools

TABLE I

RANKINGS GIVEN BY HIGH SCHOOL STUDENTS TO THE FIFTEEN MAGA-
ZINES, OTHER THAN COMICS, READ MOST FREQUENTLY BY
BOTH SEXES *

Name of magazine	Rank—both sexes
Reader's Digest	1.0
Life	2.0
Saturday Evening Post	3.0
Ladies' Home Journal	4.0
McCall's	5.0
Good Housekeeping	6.0
Collier's	7.0
National Geographic	8.0
Scholastic	9.0
Popular Science	10.0
Time	11.0
Popular Mechanics	12.0
American Magazine	13.0
Esquire	14.0
Look	15.5

* Paul Witty and Anne Coomer, "Reading the Comics in Grades IX
to XII," *Educational Administration and Supervision,* 28 (May, 1942).

TABLE II

FAVORITE MAGAZINES OF PUPILS IN THE DENNIS JUNIOR HIGH SCHOOL,
RICHMOND, INDIANA *

Boys	Girls
1. Newspapers	1. Newspapers
2. Comics	2. American Girl
3. Popular Science	3. Life
4. Boys' Life	4. Comics
5. Popular Mechanics	5. Look
6. Open Road for Boys	6. Good Housekeeping
7. Life	7. Collier's
8. Collier's	8. American Magazine
9. American Boy	9. Weekly News Review
10. Liberty	10. Ladies' Home Journal

* From L. W. Ashby, "What Periodicals Do They Read?" *School
Executive* (October, 1941).

have thus far failed to develop suitable standards of preference. Table III ranks forty-nine well-known magazines according to the judgments of competent readers to whom Morgan and Leahy submitted them. The rankings correspond closely to those obtained by Kerr and Remmers, who used a similar method. While one might disagree with individual

TABLE III

CULTURAL LEVEL OF MAGAZINES *

Yale Review	1	Good Housekeeping	26
Saturday Review of Literature	2	Vogue	27
Forum	3	Ladies' Home Journal	28
Nation	4	Popular Mechanics	29
Harper's Magazine	5	Saturday Evening Post	30
New Republic	6	Life	31
Current History	7	Woman's Home Companion	32
Living Age	8	Collier's	33
Asia	9	American Magazine	34
American Mercury	10	Pathfinder	35
National Geographic	11	McCall's	36
Scientific Monthly	12	Redbook	37
Scientific American	13	Cosmopolitan	38
Travel	14	Liberty	39
Time	15	Argosy	40
House Beautiful	16	College Humor	41
Reader's Digest	17	Physical Culture	42
House and Garden	18	Photoplay	43
Nation's Business	19	Short Stories	44
Better Homes and Gardens	20	Real Detective	45
Parents' Magazine	21	Western Story Magazine	46
Hygeia	22	Breezy Stories	47
Field and Stream	23	True Story	48
Harper's Bazaar	24	True Confessions	49
Country Gentleman	25		

* Adapted from a table in *Communications Research* 1948–1949, p. 133, by Paul F. Lazarsfeld and Frank Stanton. The table is based on studies by W. L. Morgan and A. M. Leahy, "The Cultural Content of General Interest Magazines," *Journal of Educational Psychology*, 24 (1935) and W. A. Kerr and H. H. Remmers, "Cultural Value of 100 Representative Magazines," *School and Society*, 54 (1941).

rankings, it is probable that the table suggests a possible scale against which a student's magazine preferences might be evaluated.

Of course, many teachers of English and the social studies in American high schools have made effective use of magazines in their classes. As long ago as 1935, Mabel A. Bessey and her committee made a study for the National Council of Teachers of English, in which they reported a widespread interest in magazines among teachers of English. More recently, however, Mallon reported that "there appears to be little solid conviction among schools concerning the use of periodicals and their place in the school program." Mallon based his conclusion upon a nation-wide survey of school practices in the selection and purchase of magazines. Smith had reported similar findings from the schools of New York State. While it is true, therefore, that a growing number of teachers are interesting themselves in the improvement of magazine reading, as Miss Bessey's report and numerous professional articles on the subject would indicate, schools and teachers generally have thus far failed to recognize the significance of the problem or to take systematic steps to solve it. Not only Mallon's findings, but the limited range revealed by studies of young people's interests in magazines, would support this conclusion.

CLASSROOM ACTIVITIES IN MAGAZINE STUDY

If one aim of magazine study in secondary schools is to extend the student's range of interest in magazines, it would seem that the common practice of requiring subscriptions to a single magazine like *Reader's Digest* or *Coronet* is an inadequate means of attaining our goal. Although these and other magazines have made great strides in simplifying their vocabulary and thought content, Bessey's conclusion in 1935 that no one magazine is ideally suited to classroom use probably is valid today. The magazines specifically designed for the classroom, like *Scholastic, The American Observer,* and others, are perhaps exceptions to this rule, but when group subscriptions are taken to these, they should be supplemented with a wide variety of titles from the commercial field.

There is general agreement among investigators in this field that the major technique in the development of magazine interests is the provision of desirable magazines in quantity. As in the case of books, young people tend to prefer those magazines to which they have easy access. La Brant and Heller, Witty, Allen, Woodford, and many others have reported that high school youth, when constantly confronted with desirable magazines under favorable circumstances, will respond by developing keen and continuing interests in these magazines.

Naturally, it is not sufficient to mount the magazines attractively on easily accessible magazine racks or to arrange them neatly on shelves or tables. It is necessary to provide a great variety of challenging and interesting activities calling for explorations in the magazines. It is necessary also to devote a considerable amount of class time to browsing among them, either in the classroom or in the school library, to silent reading of articles and stories, and to individual informal interviews between teacher and student concerning the material read.

Continuous, informal contact with many magazines can bring gratifying results in the form of improved reading interests. However, a growing number of teachers have undertaken the systematic study of magazines with their classes—the types of periodicals available, the nature and influence of magazine advertising, financing, and control, magazine audiences, types and levels of magazine fiction, and similar topics. These units on the magazine have usually been organized around some central purpose, such as the production of a class magazine, the selection of a list for purchase by the school library, or the classification of magazines according to educational level of the audience or the political and social views of the publisher. In the pursuit of these purposes, students carry on a great variety of subsidiary activities.

The following list of activities includes many which have been reported by teachers in the professional literature. Many of them are appropriate only for certain age levels or for the achievement of specific objectives. The selection of the activities should be determined by the needs of a given class, by the materials available, and by the over-all organization of the unit.

SUGGESTIONS FOR INDIVIDUAL AND GROUP ACTIVITY

1. Bringing magazines of interest to school.
2. Looking for pictures, stories, and articles related to the work of the class.
3. Reading poems or other quotations from magazines to the class.
4. Making a class booklet or individual scrapbooks containing pertinent clippings from magazines.
5. Conducting simple experiments in science suggested by a magazine article.
6. Dramatizing a story found in a magazine.
7. Preparing a magazine display.
8. Listening to the school librarian giving a talk on magazines.
9. Listening to a magazine editor discussing his problems.
10. Finding stories about people of other lands.
11. Finding favorable stories about members of minority groups.
12. Finding stereotypes, situations, and expressions in stories which hold members of minority groups up to contempt or ridicule.
13. Preparing a classification chart of magazines, using such headings as the following:
   a. Price.
   b. Frequency of issue.
   c. Size.
   d. Illustrations (many or few).

    e. Advertisements (many or few).

    f. Size of print.

    g. Quality of paper.

    h. Political or social bias.

14. Comparing a current issue of a magazine with an old copy to note changes.

15. Reporting on an article from a hobby or a science magazine.

16. Reporting on a single magazine, telling

    a. Why the speaker likes or dislikes it.

    b. Whether it is too "old" or too "young" or just right.

    c. Whether it is worth the price.

    d. What feature(s) the speaker enjoys most.

    e. Whether boys or girls would enjoy the magazine most.

    f. What the general point of view of the magazine is, if it is a news magazine or journal of opinion.

17. Finding out how much money can be saved by buying a particular magazine by the year instead of the week or month; in groups, rather than individually.

18. Comparing accounts of the same news story by magazines representing different political and social views.

19. Sending poems, stories, or letters of opinion to the contributors' column.

20. Finding answers to specific questions in bound volumes or current issues of magazines, with the aid of the *Reader's Guide.*

21. Conducting a "magazine hour," for the presentation of original poems, stories, or other material, or quotations from current magazines.

22. Visiting a printing shop in which magazines are published.

23. Posting references to interesting magazine articles on the bulletin board.

24. Designing the cover, sectional headings, etc., for the class magazine.

25. Preparing attractive advertisements for the class magazine.

26. Making a survey of the magazine reading habits of the community.

27. Making a study of the magazine reading of the country as a whole and its probable effect upon the national thinking.

28. Presenting an assembly or P. T. A. program reporting with graphs, charts, and other visual aids the results of a study of community or national magazine reading.

29. Establishing class standards as to what makes a good magazine.

30. Organizing a magazine club.

31. Writing letters to subscription agencies, members of other classes, editors, and advertisers, discussing the contents of an article or story or of a magazine as a whole.

32. Keeping a card file of magazine articles read, naming the title of the magazine and of the article, the name of the author, the subject, and the date of the issue.

33. Writing reviews of articles or stories which have an especial appeal.

34. Keeping a bulletin board record of current materials in magazines, especially those which are not widely known.

35. Interviewing community leaders as to their interests and preferences in magazines.

These activities should be amplified by suggestions found in the magazines themselves and by ideas contributed by the students. Emphasis should always be placed on the current magazine interests of the students.

Topics for Committee, Panel, and Class Discussions

A major activity, and one which is likely to attract the interest of most high school boys and girls, is the discussion of topics related to magazine reading. Discussions may occur in small groups dealing with a specific aspect of magazine publication, in panels before the class, or in the class as a whole. They may in some instances follow symposia in which certain members of the class present a series of floor talks on the topics under discussion. The following list includes topics which have been discussed in a number of high school classes:

1. What magazines are easy enough for us to read?

2. How can we find an article or story that has appeared in a recent issue of a magazine?

3. How can we interest father or mother in getting a magazine we like, or in reading a magazine which we think is interesting?

4. If we could choose just one magazine for our home, which one would we choose? Why?

5. What would be a good magazine for our father? Our mother? Our brother? Our sister?

6. How can one spend most advantageously a magazine budget of $15 for a family for one year?

7. If we were editing a magazine for the general public, what kinds of articles and stories would we publish?

8. What are the chief differences between the "pulp," "slick," and "quality" magazines?

9. What magazines are not published to make money? Does a nonprofit magazine necessarily operate in the public interest?

10. How can magazines help one to decide upon an occupation?

11. In what magazines should one look for books to buy? What movies to see?

12. How can one discover the viewpoint of a magazine on social, economic, and political questions?

13. Is the reading of comic magazines harmful?

14. Do pictures in magazines always tell the truth?

15. On what basis are articles chosen from the *Reader's Digest* or other digest magazines? (If you cannot determine from the contents, write to the editors.)

16. Have magazines (including comics) influenced your way of living? How?

17. How does your family choose its magazines? What magazines do you wish your family would take regularly? Why?

18. Circulation figures show that the most widely read magazines are owned by a very few individuals or corporations. Discuss the effects of centralized control of magazines upon public opinion.

19. How does publicity differ from propaganda? How does propaganda differ from education?

20. Discuss examples of propaganda in current magazines.

21. What are the values of magazine advertising to the reading public? What is needed for intelligent reading of advertisements?

22. Discuss ways in which some magazine articles or stories deal unfairly with certain minority groups, such as foreigners, Jews, Mexicans, Negroes, and others, by character selection, attitudes, and phrases such as "to jew down" or "that's white of you."

23. What standards of judging a magazine should a reader employ?

24. What responsibilities do magazines have to the general public?

25. To what extent do magazines *reflect* public opinion? To what extent do they *create* public opinion?

Care should be taken that students spend ample time in preparation for the discussions. Mere talk about most of the topics that have been suggested is valueless. A great deal of thought and study should precede a panel or general class discussion. Examination of the magazines themselves and of references about the magazines is essential to good discussions. Such magazines and references should be made available to students. Some suggested references are listed at the end of this chapter.

The "Comic" Magazines

Most "comic" magazines are not comical. They are serial stories of mystery, adventure, and horror. They represent a relatively new medium for public entertainment. Relying chiefly upon colored illustrations, they make a strong appeal to readers who find conventional reading difficult. People of all ages read comics. Of the approximately 40 million readers of comic magazines, probably a majority are adults, belonging to every level of educational background. The comics present a real challenge to the schools.

As a new form of communication, they should be welcomed by the schools. Any medium which facilitates the communication of ideas must be received warmly as an ally of the schools. Resistance to new forms of communication is not new. The novel and the motion picture were resisted at first as instruments of the Evil One. Perhaps by utilizing this new medium it may be possible for the schools to attain objectives which thus far have proved to be difficult if not impossible to attain.

It is true that the contents of most comic magazines are objectionable. Many appeal to tastes even lower than those to which the pulps and the worst movies appeal. They accentuate violence, prejudice, and in some instances the more lurid and sensational aspects of sex. The fact that parent groups, and in recent times even state legislatures, have expressed concern over comic magazines and have undertaken to suppress many of them should occasion no surprise.

Nevertheless, a mere negative attitude toward the comics will be unavailing. Whether the teacher approves or not, young people will read them openly or surreptitiously. Suppressing the reading of them will not change the reading habits of boys and girls, and it is the actual reading preferences of boys and girls that we wish to influence. Moreover, if we can utilize young people's interests in comics to develop more intelligent and critical attitudes toward reading, we should seek every means to do so.

Actually, there is no evidence that the reading of comics has serious effects upon young people. Heisler, for example, compared pupils who read comics to excess with those who did not indulge in such reading. She found no significant differences between the two groups, although she considered educational achievement, mental age, socio-economic status, social adjustment, and personal adjustment in her comparisons. She pointed out that, if significant personality differences were ultimately discovered, it would still be necessary to determine whether maladjusted children preferred to read comic books, or whether the comic books caused the maladjustment.

Nor is there apparently any relation between intelligence or reading ability and a liking for the comics. Sperzel failed to find any relationship between the reading of comic books and vocabulary growth. Thorndike analyzed the vocabulary of *Superman, Batman,* and *Detective Comics,* and found a considerable range in the vocabulary employed. From a technical point of view, the chief criticism to be raised against the comics is the poor legibility of the reading material, which has been confirmed by a number of studies.

Indeed, one writer (Yuill) reports that in her judgment some of the comics are "growing up," that they are presenting good stories, often illustrating current social problems and participating in campaigns in the public interest, with a medium the masses will accept. Yuill referred to some of the best selling comics which she studied in a circulation survey—*Batman, Superman, Action, True, Calling All Girls, Captain Marvel, Captain Midnight, Famous Funnies,* and *Magic Comics.* She found in them an educational weapon which we should not be afraid to use.

The objection to the comics, then, is not primarily that they are harmful in themselves, but that their contents are inferior to reading materials which could be much more rewarding. The obvious inferences are that (1) we should use the comic magazine form for worth-while purposes, and (2) we should provide young people with an abundance of excellent books and magazines by way of competition with the worthless type of comic magazines. Most teachers are not in a position to do the former, but as a rule they can do a great deal to make suitable reading materials available to high school youth. The need in children's lives which the comics are filling, and which are unsatisfied by real life—the need for fantasy, adventure, and identification with heroes— should be filled by means of more substantial and more desirable reading materials until the comics themselves have reached suitable levels of quality.

Even when young people have developed strong interests in good books and magazines, they are likely to continue to read comics. Witty and Coomer found that comics hold high rank even in a high school rich in opportunities and motivation for wide reading. Arbuthnot, after commenting upon the phenomenal sale of comic magazines and the fact that "young America is reading the comics and liking them," declares there is probably little cause to worry about children and their comics as long as they are also enjoying good books. It appears, therefore, that the mere reading of comics by boys and girls should cause no great concern, provided they also read books and magazines of high quality The teacher who accepts the fact that many young people read the comics and aids them in developing a critical attitude toward them is wiser than the teacher who merely ignores the existence of this type of reading and forbids it in the classroom.

NEWSLETTERS

A new type of publication, which is neither newspaper nor magazine, has recently been growing in popularity. It is the so-called newsletter, which, because it stresses interpretation rather than reporting of the news, is here considered under the heading of magazines. It was originally designed as a confidential report by an expert to a selected clientele. Since its beginning, it has gradually attained wide popularity, and today there are newsletters for almost every business, social, political, or economic interest. Since they represent a wide range of outlook on public affairs, they serve as a valuable corrective to the tendency toward monopoly in the magazine field. Schools should make much wider use of newsletters than they do at present, in order that students may be confronted with a greater diversity of opinion on current problems.

For Further Reading

On Magazines in America

Allen, Frederick L., "The Function of a Magazine in America," *University of Missouri Bulletin*, 46 (Aug. 10, 1945), 23.

Bainbridge, John, *Little Wonder or the Reader's Digest and How It Grew*. New York: Reynal & Hitchcock, Inc., 1945.

Berelson, Bernard, *et al.* "Majority and Minority Americans: an Analysis of Magazine Fiction," *Public Opinion Quarterly*, 10 (Summer, 1946), 168–190.

Brown, John Mason, "The Case against and for the Comics," *Saturday Review of Literature*, 31 (Mar. 20, 1948), 31.

Curti, Merle, *The Growth of American Thought*, pp. 698, 703, 711, and 743. New York: Harcourt, Brace and Company, Inc., 1943.

DeBoer, John J. (Ed.), *Education and the Mass Media of Communication*. Chicago: National Council of Teachers of English, 1950.

Frank, Laurence K., "Status of the Comic Books," *New York Times Magazine*, Feb. 6, 1949, p. 36.

Lazarsfeld, Paul, *et al.*, *The People's Choice*. New York: Columbia University Press, 1948.

"Magazines for Your Information," *Scholastic*, 52 (Feb. 9, 1948), 18.

Miller, Merle, "Freedom to Read: Magazines," *Survey Graphic*, 35 (December, 1946), 462.

Roulett, L. Felix, "Magazines for Tens and Teens," *Hornbook*, 20 (July, 1944), 271.

Wood James P., *Magazines in the United States*. New York: The Ronald Press Company, 1949.

On Magazines in the Schools

Carney, Elizabeth, "An Effective Newspaper and Magazine Unit," *The English Journal*, 25 (November, 1936), 752–756.

Heisler, Florence, "A Comparison of Comic Book and non-Comic Book Readers of the Elementary School," *Journal of Educational Research*, 40 (February, 1947), 458–464.

LaBrant, Lou L., and Freida M. Heller, "Magazine Reading in an Experimental School," *Library Journal*, 61 (Mar. 15, 1936), 213–217.

Martin, Laura K., *Magazines for School Libraries*. New York: The H. W. Wilson Company, 1950.

Masser, Isabel, "Magazine Reading at the Junior High School Level," *California Journal of Education*, 16 (December, 1941), 485.

Simmons, Josephine, "A Semester of Current Literature," *The English Journal*, 30 (January, 1941), 47–53.

Smith, Dora V., *Evaluating Instruction in English*, p. 96. Chicago: National Council of English, 1941.

Smith, Mary E., "Periodicals in the Classroom," *The English Journal*, 27 (May, 1939), 372–378.

Sterner, Alice P., *Radio, Motion Picture, and Reading Interests: A Study of High School Pupils*. Teachers College Contributions to Education, No. 932. New York: Teachers College Bureau of Publications, Columbia University, 1947.

Strang, Ruth, *Exploration in Reading Patterns*. Chicago: University of Chicago Press, 1942.

Tyler, I. Keith, "Developing Discrimination with Regard to Mass Media," Chap. III of a report of a subcommittee on Audio-Visual Education of the North Central Association. *North Central Association Quarterly*, 22 (October, 1948), 196–226.

Witty, Paul, and Anne Coomer, "Reading the Comics in Grades IX to XII," *Educational Administration and Supervision*, 28 (May, 1942), 344–345.

Woodford, Mary E., "A Reading Course for Juniors," *The English Journal*, 30 (January, 1941), 24–31.

Zimmerman, Helen, "Making Magazine Study a Vital Part of the Curriculum," *Minnesota Journal of Education*, 15 (December, 1934), 142–143.

Chapter 10. MASS MEDIA OF COMMUNICATION: NEWSPAPERS

In spite of the rapid development of other means of communication, the newspaper remains the people's chief source of information regarding current affairs. According to Lazarsfeld,[1] neither the weekly news magazine nor the radio newscast has reduced the total amount of newspaper reading. The 328 morning newspapers in the United States aggregate a total circulation of 21,081,905; the 1,453 evening newspapers account for a circulation of 31,203,392; and the 530 Sunday newspapers are bought by 46,308,081 people. Many copies of the newspaper are, of course, read by more than one person. Clearly the intelligent reading of the newspaper continues to be a primary objective of the schools.

The problem is not merely one of creating the ability to comprehend what is in the newspapers and to utilize their numerous and excellent services, but of developing independent judgment with respect to biases present in their news and, editorial columns. In most American towns there is no newspaper competition.[2] Of the 1,781 daily newspapers in the United States approximately 375 are owned by a few large chains controlling more than one-fourth of the total daily circulation.[3] The growth of the great news services and syndicates, which have enabled American journalism to match

[1] "The Daily Newspaper and Its Competitors," *Annals of the American Academy of Political and Social Science*, January, 1942, p. 219.

[2] "One-Newspaper Towns in the United States, 1910–1940," *N.E.A. Journal*, 36 (February, 1947), 118.

[3] R. K. Eichelberger, "Freedom to Be Well Informed," *Senior Scholastic* (Teachers' Edition), 51 (Oct. 27, 1947), 22–23.

the efficiency of our other mass-production industries, has at the same time created the danger of monopoly in the realm of ideas. The need for critical reading abilities is therefore more acute today than in any previous period in our history. Examples of distortion and suppression of the news in favor of the economic and political interests of the publishers (real or imagined) could be enumerated at length. Inasmuch as the viewpoints advanced in the daily press are frequently supported by propaganda materials distributed in large quantities to the schools, the need for providing a balance of opinions in the reading matter available to children and youth becomes apparent.

Newspaper Reading Interests of Children and Youth

Newspaper reading interests of elementary school children. The great majority of studies dealing with newspaper reading have been conducted at the high school level. It would be wrong to assume, however, that elementary school pupils are not interested in newspapers, or that their interest is confined to the comic strip. Several investigators have found that both boys and girls in the elementary school devote a considerable amount of time to the reading of newspapers. Others have found that children read books in greater quantity than adults, and that both adults and children read newspapers about thirty-five minutes daily. If the time spent in listening to the radio (generally estimated at two and one-half to three hours daily),[3a] the time spent at the movies, and the time spent in reading magazines are added to this figure, it becomes apparent that children spend approximately as much time with the mass media of communication as they spend in school. It is clear that the school cannot afford to ignore the educational effects of these communication media.

While comic strips lead in popularity among the various features of the newspaper, general news, sports, and local news appear prominently among the sections which ele-

[3a] More in the case of television, where it is available.

mentary school pupils read. The comic section, according to Witty, is very popular among children. The average number of comic strips read regularly by the groups in his study was twenty-one. The studies of newspaper reading by children of elementary school age that have been reported are extremely limited in number. Further research in this area is urgently needed.

Newspaper reading interests of high school youth. A large number of investigations have been made in the field of high school students' interests in newspaper reading. Such studies as have been made of the time devoted to newspaper reading by high school students suggest that young people generally spend from fifteen to thirty-five minutes daily, and adults thirty-five to sixty or more minutes daily. Comic strips lead all features of the newspaper in popularity, with sports and general news (foreign and national) following closely. Boys, of course, give high priority to sports news, girls to fashion news. Front-page news, as opposed to news stories on the inside pages, achieved high rank among the sections of the newspaper most widely read by both boys and girls in high school and by adults. Local news likewise commands great popularity.

One investigator observes that students tend, after graduation, to drift into indifference and apathy with regard to current affairs. He attributes this fact to a number of factors: (1) unfamiliarity with newspaper vocabulary (72 per cent of more than 500 students did not know that "probe" means "investigation"), (2) inability to distinguish between news stories and editorials, (3) inability to detect instances of journalistic license, embodied in such overused expressions as "It has been reported, alleged, or surmised," (4) inability to discover discrepancies when newspaper stories flatly contradict their headlines, and (5) inability to distinguish between desirable and undesirable newspapers. This investigator recommends that schools give systematic instruction in critical thinking, in the meaning of newspaper jargon, and in the development of criteria for evaluating newspapers.

Newspaper Reading in the Schools

One study of school activities in promoting more intelligent reading of the newspaper revealed that twenty-nine of forty-one schools addressed made efforts to provide guidance in the reading of newspapers, and that all the schools believed that such efforts are desirable. Judging by the extensive bibliography of school units on newspapers, one may reasonably conclude that secondary schools, at least, are giving considerable attention to the problem of newspaper reading. Whether they are giving effective guidance on a sufficiently large scale is difficult to say. Little evidence has been reported on this question. The results, in terms of young people's reading interests in the field of the newspaper, would suggest that present efforts are insufficient.

Objectives for the Teaching of the Newspaper

One of the clearest statements of desirable objectives in the improvement of young people's newspaper reading has been made by Dale. He asserts that intelligent study of a good newspaper can help us lead rich lives by (1) showing us what work in the world we can help do, (2) helping us to get the most for our money, (3) helping us to see the crime problem clearly, (4) helping us to have a good time on a small income, and (5) helping us to make up our own minds. In another place, Dale lists three objectives for the teacher of English in the development of discrimination in newspaper reading: (1) familiarizing boys and girls with the best examples of modern journalism, (2) helping boys and girls get a richer and much more comprehensive understanding of the role that the press might play in community life, and (3) developing the capacity for close, careful reading.

Three major categories of objectives emerge from the literature in this field: (1) the expansion of young people's interests in newspapers, (2) the development of an awareness of the major trends and events in current affairs, and (3) the development of powers of discrimination with respect to newspaper reading.

Expansion of young people's interests in newspapers. Newspapers at their best provide a variety of services which are not adequately utilized by young people, many of whom restrict their newspaper reading to the comic strips, sports pages, and possibly the front-page headlines. By availing themselves of other parts of the daily newspaper, young people can find amusement and entertainment, information concerning present hobbies and suggestions for new ones, guidance in the selection of motion-picture and radio programs, business and vocational information, and many other kinds of aid. In many instances young people need merely to be introduced to newspaper features to start them on the road to fuller utilization of what the newspaper has to offer.

Development of an awareness of the major trends and events in current affairs. Studies of knowledge of current events on the part of young people and adults, including teachers, reveal that many people have only the vaguest knowledge of men and events in our own time. Regular newspaper reading is essential to an elementary acquaintance with the happenings in the world today. With all their limitations, newspapers, along with radio newscasts, are our chief source of knowledge concerning the contemporary scene. A list of the major events recorded in the newspaper in the course of two or three days of news reporting yields a large volume of information regarding such fields as politics, economics, commerce, sociology, science, religion, education, art, music. It would appear that the school could and should utilize more fully and more skillfully the resources provided by the daily newspaper for the preparation of well-informed citizens.

Development of powers of discrimination with respect to newspaper reading. While the press performs an indispensable service as an educational agency, and while American journalists are among the most efficient in the world, newspapers are not, in the main, completely reliable as sources of information. Most newspaper-reading adults in the United States express lack of confidence in the factual accuracy and impartiality of newspaper reports.

The fact that the publication of a newspaper, or a chain of newspapers, involves heavy financial investment quite naturally tends to create in the publishers a bias in favor of the viewpoint of the large industrialist. The social and political outlook of the advertiser will also necessarily affect the treatment of the news. The need to win and maintain large circulation will often cause newspapers to favor a viewpoint thought to be popular among large sections of the readership. For this reason it is necessary to provide young people with skills that will enable them to read newspapers with discrimination.

Pitfalls in the reading of newspapers take many forms. Least common of these is the deliberate misstatement of fact. Much more common is the distortion of the news by means of emphasis upon certain items and by means of underplaying or suppressing others. This practice is probably unavoidable. It is followed by newspapers of every political, economic, and social complexion. It results from the necessity of making choices among available news stories and from exercising judgments which inevitably involve some prejudices. Some newspapers, of course, make greater efforts than others to present the news impartially. Some are more successful than others in eliminating "editorializing" from the news columns.

Developing discrimination in reading the newspaper is not a mere process of cultivating skepticism. It is a process of building a broad background of information about the topics under discussion, of inducing an awareness of a given newspaper's bias, and of confronting the reader with a variety of viewpoints on public affairs. In practical terms, this process involves bringing into the classroom a variety of newspapers, magazines, newsletters, pamphlets, and books which will enable the reader to approach the local newspaper with greater intelligence. Reliance upon a single source, or type of source, leaves the reader helpless in the face of whatever purposes may move the publisher.

PROCEDURES IN NEWSPAPER STUDY

A great volume of material has been published on the subject of classroom procedures in the improvement of newspaper reading. Many of the techniques reported are duplicated in the various references listed below, but the total number of different activities is very large. Some of the more promising of these activities are listed here, including suggestions for both elementary and secondary schools.

Projects and Class Activities

I. Write a class book on the newspaper. Chapters may be devoted to these or similar topics:
   A. The ways in which the printing press has changed man's life.
   B. How the newspaper affects our daily lives.
   C. The industries connected with newspaper publishing.
   D. The contributions of the "fighting journalists" (Dana, Garrison, Zenger, etc.) to present-day newspaper journalism.
   E. Some of the outstanding services to the country performed by newspapers during the past war.

II. Prepare a class exhibit on the newspaper. Invite other classes and your parents to visit the exhibit at an "open house." The exhibit may consist of projects such as these:
   A. Charts showing
      1. A comparison of the amount of space given to various subjects or types of stories in a tabloid newspaper and more conventional newspapers such as the *New York Times,* the *St. Louis Post-Dispatch,* the *Kansas City Star,* or the *Christian Science Monitor.*
      2. The percentage of your town paper which is devoted to advertising and the percentage given to

news. (Measure by column inches. Is the paper primarily an advertising or a news medium?)

3. The special features that can be found in ten of the leading newspapers of the country. Show what can be found in one but not in another, and perhaps compare your findings with your local paper.

4. The sources from which news generally comes.

B. Caricatures, or cartoons, which explain

1. The duties of a newspaper editor, publisher, reporter, copyreader, headline writer, and foreign correspondent.

2. The meaning of the following terms:
Rotogravure.
News syndicate.
News vs. a feature story.
Tabloid.
A newspaper chain.
Yellow journalism.
Jingoism.
Facsimile newspapers.

C. Diagrams showing

1. A newspaper plant layout.

2. The ways news is gathered.

3. The route news follows, from source to reader.

D. Models, in clay, wood, or papier mâché.

E. Paintings, pencil sketches, or water colorings.

III. Present an assembly or P.T.A. program about the newspaper. Activities such as these may be included on the program:

A. A living newspaper [4]

B. A skit depicting the editor and his staff preparing the day's edition for press.

C. A monologue or pantomime showing the "average reader" reading the "average newspaper." Perhaps this could be portrayed in two scenes: (1), how he actually reads it and (2), how he should read the newspaper.

IV. Visit a newspaper plant.

V. Visit a paper mill or newsprint plant.

[4] See Spencer Brown, *They See for Themselves*, pp. 57–77. New York: Harper & Brothers, 1945.

VI. Visit a radio newsroom.

VII. Visit an advertising agency.

VIII. Prepare a class newspaper using and following rules set up by the class as to what a good newspaper should do and contain.

IX. A class survey to find out the class's favorite (1) news columnist, (2) reporter, (3) comic strip author, (4) sports columnist, (5) features columnist. Determine if their choices have been the wisest and best.

X. Make a study of what a reader can expect to find in various types and sizes of newspapers (by using copies of these papers): large metropolitan dailies, tabloids, religious newspapers, papers published by various national or ethnic groups, labor newspapers, newspapers published by companies and corporations, Sunday newspapers, weekly newspapers, and, if possible, newspapers published in other languages.

XI. Try to find some answers to this question: What effect does the reading in our community have on our thinking?

XII. Bring to class articles to be judged by Dale's "canons of journalism."[5]

XIII. Briefly study the history of newspapers in the United States.

Small Group Projects

XIV. A panel discussion: The ways in which radio news and newspaper news are similar, and the ways in which they differ.

XV. Compare the way in which news articles in newspapers and news magazines (*Time, Newsweek, Business Week, New Republic,* and *United States News*) are handled. In what major ways do they differ?

XVI. Make a class survey, using the families of the class members as guinea pigs, of what is read by the different age groups, separating them by sexes.

XVII. Compare your local newspaper with the *New York Times,* the *New York Herald-Tribune,* the *Christian Science Monitor,* etc.

[5] Responsibility, freedom of the press, independence, sincerity, truthfulness, accuracy, impartiality, fair play, decency. Edgar Dale, *How to Read a Newspaper.* Chicago: Scott, Foresman & Company, 1941.

XVIII. Select several newspapers and determine how much space is devoted to crime stories and other sordid happenings of the day. Compare the amount of space with the amount given to national news, international news, art, movies, books, and the theater.

XIX. Determine the community and welfare projects that have been undertaken in your community during the past year. To what extent did the local paper participate? On the basis of its role in these campaigns, would you say that the paper is, or is not, performing a community service?

XX. Make a comparison of radio columnists with newspaper columnists.

XXI. Make a comparison of newspapers from different sections of the country.

XXII. Make a comparison of newspapers from different types of communities (farming, residential, industrial, etc.).

Individual Projects

XXIII. Find out all you can about the author of your favorite comic strip: his philosophy of life, his political, social, and economic affiliations, his views on contemporary affairs. To what extent are these views reflected in his work? Present your findings to the class in a talk: "A Personality Profile of _____."

XXIV. Pick stories which you believe contain a definite bias. Tell the class what you believe this bias is, and what you think the effect of this bias will probably be.

XXV. Read several issues of *Quill and Scroll, Scholastic, Tide, Editor and Publisher,* and *Broadcasting* to become familiar with the current issues and problems connected with school newspapers, advertising, commercial newspapers, and radio news.

Topics for Panel, Class, and Small Group Discussions

1. Should newspapers suppress news harmful to the country? [6]
2. Should newspapers omit names of first offenders in minor crimes?

[6] Items 1 to 17 are from J. A. Thalheimer and J. K. Gerberich, "Reader Attitudes toward Questions of Newspaper Policy and Practice," *Journalism Quarterly,* 12 (September, 1935), 266–271.

3. Should newspapers be licensed by the Federal government?
4. Should newspapers be permitted to criticize the government?
5. Should newspapers publish beer advertisements?
6. Should newspapers publish whisky advertisements?
7. Should newspapers publish patent medicine advertisements?
8. Should crime news be put all together on a certain inside page?
9. Should crime news be omitted entirely from newspapers?
10. Do newspapers usually suppress news which will reflect on advertisers or prominent citizens?
11. Do papers in general purposely falsify the news?
12. Are papers generally unfair to labor?
13. Do papers generally publish too much sensational news?
14. Does publication of crime news lead to more crimes?
15. Do papers usually present a fair treatment of opposing political parties?
16. Do newspapers usually present a fair treatment of legislative bodies of the government?
17. Do newspapers usually present a fair treatment of religion?
18. Ask the following questions about any paper you read:
   a. Who owns the paper?
   b. What groups in the community is the newspaper eager to attract?
   c. Who are the advertisers?
   d. What are the principal factors in the newspaper's editorial policy?
   e. What groups in the community are likely to benefit from this editorial policy?
   f. What groups are likely to be harmed by this editorial policy?
   g. In what ways is this policy expressed throughout the paper?
   h. Are important items of news repressed?
19. Are the headlines an accurate summary of the news article, or are they merely glaring fictions to attract readers?
20. What is the point of origin of foreign dispatches?
21. Does the paper have too many pictures?
22. Does the paper have too many cartoons?
23. Apply to the newspaper Dale's "canons of journalism":
   a. Responsibility.

    b. Freedom of the press.

    c. Independence.

    d. Sincerity, truthfulness, accuracy.

    e. Impartiality.

    f. Fair play.

    g. Decency.

24. In analyzing newspapers these factors should be brought into account:

    a. Who are its competitors?

    b. How many pages and sections does it usually have?

    c. For what feature(s) is it outstanding?

    d. What are the outstanding features of outstanding newspapers in the United States and in foreign countries?

    e. Who are, if any, the outstanding writers, reporters, analysts, cartoonists, and photographers who contribute to it?

25. Does the paper present news accurately, interestingly, adequately?

26. Does it interpret the news?

27. How does it interpret the news?

28. Does the newspaper comment and editorialize upon the news in its "news" articles?

29. Does the advertising in the paper help the community carry out its business?

30. Does the newspaper help solve business, family, or economic problems?

31. Does the newspaper entertain and amuse, but not have this as its sole, or most important, reason for being published?

32. Does the newspaper show what reforms or changes in society are needed?

33. Does the newspaper help you get the most for your money?

34. Does the newspaper help you see the crime problem clearly?

35. Does the newspaper help you have a good time on a small amount?

36. Does the newspaper help you make up your own mind (not, make it up for you)?

37. Is the source of news, as given in the news story, a reliable one? Is it a specific person or agency? Does the person hold a responsible position? Does he serve any specific or special interest?

38. Which type of news is more accurate—radio or newspaper?

39. Would a newspaper without advertisements present the news more accurately?
40. In what sense is a newspaper a business enterprise, run for profit for the owner?
41. Is propaganda found in newspaper advertisements? What is the function, good or bad, of "public service" advertising?
42. How important is freedom of the press in a democracy?
43. What are the inventions that have made our newspapers the complex enterprises that they are today?
44. How much money is involved—the cash outlay—in publishing a newspaper?
45. What are the differences (how does the paper change) in the various editions published during one day?
46. Are newspaper headlines usually accurate?
47. How much can be learned by reading headlines alone? (Try a class game: Each pupil submit stories, with headlines cut off. Mix them up and try to match stories with headlines.)
48. What is a good definition of "news"? What are its characteristics?
49. What are the functions of advertisements?
50. Why can some advertisements be grouped together without any display (classifieds) while others must be attractive and showy?
51. What stories are usually found on the front page?
52. Why are advertisements in a newspaper usually grouped?
53. How does the composition of a newspaper *news* story differ from that of nonprofessional news stories?
54. What is the function of the editorial page in a newspaper?
55. What are the ways in which the function, type, and intent of editorials differ today from those of fifty years ago?
56. In what important ways do news stories and feature stories differ?
57. Many towns have only one newspaper and one radio station with a single owner. Other towns have a morning and an evening newspaper, both with the same owner. Does this agree with what is usually thought of as freedom of the press, or with what is usually thought of as freedom of competition?
58. What differences can be noted in by-line and non-by-line news stories?
59. What are some ways in which news is gathered?

60. What are the meanings of these words which are often found in news stories: "alleged," "it is reported," "from an unknown source," "from good authority," "it is felt in some circles," "an unconfirmed report," "no comment," "a press conference"?
61. How may propaganda be defined? recognized? combatted?
62. Can propaganda be found in comics, sport news, feature articles, and editorials?
63. In what ways is your family provided for, or not, in the make-up of your local newspaper?
64. How does your family usually interpret, or discuss, the daily news?
65. What are slanted headlines?
66. In what ways can the gist of news be obtained hurriedly from newspapers?

For Further Reading

Anderson, Esther M., "A Study of Leisure-time Reading of Pupils in Junior High School," *Elementary School Journal*, 47 (January, 1948), 258–267.

Andrews, Katherine, "A 3B Class Studies the Newspaper," *The English Journal*, 35 (November, 1946), 497–500.

Billet, Roy O., "The Unit on the Reading of Newspapers: A Group Project," *The English Journal*, 31 (January, 1942), 15–31.

Brink, William G., "High School Pupils' Interests in Magazines and Newspapers," *School Review*, 48 (January, 1940), 40–48.

Burton, Philip Ward, "Newspaper Reading Behavior of High School Students," *School and Society*, 63 (Feb. 2, 1946), 86.

Chamberlen, Maude, "The Improvement of Newspaper Reading," *The English Journal*, 29 (October, 1940), 639–647.

Dale, Edgar, *How to Read a Newspaper*. Chicago: Scott, Foresman & Company, 1941.

Feingold, Gustave A., "Newspaper Tastes of High School Pupils," *School and Society*, 59 (Apr. 29, 1944), 316–319.

Fendrich, Paul, "Newspaper Interests of High School and College Students," *Journal of Educational Research*, 34 (March, 1941), 522–530.

Harvey, C. C., "A Unit of Work on the Newspaper," *Bulletin of* the *National Association of Secondary School Principals*, 33 (January, 1949), 65–75.

Hill, George E., "Word Distortions in Comic Strips," *Elementary School Journal*, 43 (May, 1943), 520–525.

Horn, Gunnar, "The Newspapers," *Clearing House*, 18 (May, 1944), 539–541.

MacDougall, Curtis D., "Journalism Teaching," *Journalism Quarterly*, 22 (December, 1945), 349–352, 392.

Mitchell, C., "Attitudes of High School Pupils toward the Public Press," *School Review*, 50 (February, 1942), 107–111.

Staudenmayer, Maude S., "Study of the News," *Clearing House*, 21 (January, 1947), 288–291.

Tinker, Miles A., "Illumination Intensities for Reading Newspaper Type," *Journal of Educational Psychology*, 34 (April, 1943), 247–250.

Witty, Paul, and Anne Coomer, "Reading the Comics in Grades IX to XII," *Educational Administration and Supervision*, 28 (May, 1942), 344–353.

Chapter 11. MASS MEDIA OF COMMUNICATION: MOTION PICTURES

The Commercial Motion Picture as a Concern of the School

We have seen that the average person in America probably spends more time in contact with the mass media than he spends in school. Probably one-fifth or more of his waking hours is spent in viewing, reading, or listening to these media. When one remembers their powerful appeal, their skillful use of sound, color, anecdote, and dramatic effects, their educative potentialities become apparent. Since the school is deeply concerned about the concepts, attitudes, and behavior of adolescent youth, conditioned as these are by many influences, it must take account of the media of mass communication. Moreover, newspapers, magazines, radio, television, and motion pictures are produced primarily for profit rather than for public enlightenment, and they may therefore be competitors as often as they are allies of the school. The school may learn much from their techniques; it must utilize their resources of entertainment and information; but it cannot identify itself with all their purposes.

Motion pictures present peculiar problems for the secondary school. Professor Edgar Dale, who has perhaps explored the educational implications of the mass media more than any other writer in this field, points out that (1) commercial films usually deal with subject matter in a harmfully superficial manner and (2) too often they portray the good life as the acquisitive life, "with undue emphasis upon luxury,

fine homes and automobiles, swank and suavity . . . urbane
and super-sophisticated living." [1]

The influence of the movies on the attitudes and emotional
life of young people has been amply demonstrated.[2] One
writer describes their effects in the following words:

Cecil B. DeMille's movie bathtubs left their mark on modern
plumbing. Clark Gable minus undershirt in *It Happened One
Night* set off a slump in the men's underwear business. . . . Greta
Garbo's smoked glasses and Joan Crawford's padded shoulders
are still with us. Veronica Lake's over-the-eye hair-do prompted
an entire generation of girls to peek at the world through their
tresses.[3]

Many, if not most, commercial motion pictures glorify
false values and present a distorted picture of human life.
Rose Terlin writes:

The dominant philosophy of the typical movie scenario is that
all problems are solved by romantic love and that success in life
consists in getting to the top by any means whatever. Movie hero-
ines are either exquisitely gowned occupants of luxurious resi-
dences or Cinderellas magically whisked into the arms of the
handsome, wealthy Prince Charming of their dreams.[3]

Perhaps a more serious criticism of the commercial motion
picture is its tendency to present members of minority groups
and citizens of other countries as stereotypes rather than as
individual human beings. Except in a remarkable series of
recent films, such as *Gentleman's Agreement, Lost Boundaries,* and *Pinky,* the movies have commonly caricatured
rather than characterized the Negro and the Jew. Negro
characters particularly are presented as clowns or menials

[1] Edgar Dale, *Audio-Visual Methods in Teaching*, p. 210. New York:
The Dryden Press, 1946.

[2] Ruth C. Peterson and L. L. Thurstone, *Motion Pictures and the
Social Attitudes of Children*. New York: The Macmillan Company,
1933.

[3] Rose Terlin, *You and I and the Movies*, p. 18. New York: The
Woman's Press, 1936.

instead of human beings who share the talents, aspirations, and weaknesses of members of all other races. Orientals are often represented as sly and treacherous, Italians as hot-headed, Mexicans as moonstruck serenaders, Russians as uncouth and murderous. Honest portrayals of minorities and foreigners remain relatively rare on the American screen.

The fact that the motion picture is so effective a medium intensifies the problem for the educator. Leon Reisman points out that

the cinema has unique powers for encouraging an audience to surrender its critical detachment. First of all, the intense light of a projector demands a kind of hypnotic attention to what is occurring on the screen. Second, the control which a director can exercise over an audience through the use of his camera is much more autocratic than a novelist or a dramatist can hope to possess. This is because visual symbols, used in an elementary and literal fashion, are clearer, more concrete, and less ambiguous than even the simplest words. Third, the clearly defined boundaries of the screen and the darkness outside those boundaries emphasize the importance and the truth of the film; the screen seems to displace the whole world. Fourth, the clear-cut dimensions of the screen and the mobility of the camera unerringly combine to show only what the director wants you to see.[4]

Critical-mindedness, therefore, becomes peculiarly important as an objective in the education of movie-going youth.

MOTION PICTURES IN AMERICAN LIFE

The magnitude of the motion-picture industry as an educational agency will become apparent from some recent figures relating to production, distribution, exhibition, and attendance. The Department of Commerce reports that more than 2 billion dollars is at present invested in the industry. Profits for seven companies aggregated about 53 million dol-

[4] Leon Reisman, "Cinema Technique and Mass Culture," *American Quarterly,* 1 (Winter, 1949), 317–318.

lars in 1948.[5] The foreign market alone is estimated to have grossed 100 million dollars in the same year. Total receipts of American motion-picture theaters for the year, exclusive of Federal admissions tax, exceeded 1½ billion dollars.

Estimates of attendance at motion pictures vary. Earlier estimates by the Motion Picture Research Council of an average of 77 million persons—28 million of them children— are perhaps less accurate than that of Gerald M. Mayer, managing director of the International Division of the Motion Picture Association, who places the figure at 90 million, and the weekly attendance for the world at 250 million.

A recent development in the industry is the increase in drive-in theaters, which in 1948 numbered 743—137 of them on all-year basis.

That some effort is being made by the industry to accept responsibility for its child audience is revealed in the organization of a children's film library in 1946 by the Motion Picture Association of America, to make available suitable films to children aged eight to twelve at special Saturday showings. According to the Britannica Book of the Year (1949), children's programs were given in more than 2,500 theaters in 1948.

Attendance at the motion pictures is confined largely to the middle-income groups. Costs interfere with attendance on the part of members of low-income groups, while the availability of other, more expensive types of diversion probably tends to keep members of the upper income groups away from the motion-picture theater.

In recent years, attendance at motion pictures seems to be declining somewhat.[6] Causes for the decline appear to be changes in people's tastes and possibly a falling off of the quality of the productions. What effect the growth of television will have upon movie attendance is as yet too early to determine.

[5] U.S. Treasury, National Income Supplement.
[6] "The Fortune Survey," Fortune, March, 1949, 39–44.

CONTROL OF THE FILM INDUSTRY

Even more than in the case of the other mass media, the control of motion pictures is concentrated in the hands of a very limited number of financial groups. According to Reisman,

five companes control the field; they have decisive power in the trade, do the largest business, make the most profit, and have invested the greatest share of the 2.7 billion dollars capital in the industry. These five are Loew's Inc. (Metro-Goldwyn-Mayer), Paramount Pictures, Inc., RKO Corporation, Twentieth Century-Fox Film Corporation, and Warner Brothers Pictures, Inc.[7]

The "little three" are Columbia, United Artists, and Universal Pictures. In 1936, the following investors exercised financial control over these major film companies: Morgan (through A. T. and T. and Western Electric), Dillon, Read (a Wall Street investment company), Lehman Brothers (another investment company), Standard Capital, H. H. Giannini, and Rockefeller (through Chase National Bank and the Radio Corporation of America).[8]

However, in 1946 there were 100 independent producers. The following six of the ten greatest "box-office" pictures were made by independents: *Birth of a Nation* (D. W. Griffith), *Gone with the Wind* (D. O. Selznick), *The Best Years of Our Lives* (Samuel Goldwyn), *Duel in the Sun* (D. O. Selznick), *The Bells of St. Mary* (Leo McCarey), and *Snow White and the Seven Dwarfs* (Walt Disney).

The "big five" exercise a vast amount of control over all three branches of the business—production, distribution, and exhibition. Their ownership of motion-picture theaters is revealed in the accompanying table, taken from the *Hollywood Reporter* for Mar. 4, 1948.

[7] Reisman, *op. cit.*, p. 315.

[8] Helen Rand, and Richard Lewis, *Film and School*, p. 103. A publication of the National Council of Teachers of English. New York: Appleton-Century-Crofts, Inc., 1937.

Paramount .... 1,565 theaters
20th Century-Fox ....   485 theaters
Warner Brothers ....   465 theaters
Loew's (MGM) ....   116 theaters
RKO ....   104 theaters

The major companies produce nearly all the pictures cost-
ting a half million dollars or more to produce and grossing
from a million dollars up. They have under contract practically all the "big name" producers, writers, technicians,
and actors and, through the Central Casting Corporation,
dominate the supply of extras. As in the case of television,
the costs involved in producing major feature films is too
great to permit a large number of small, competing independents to enter the field. The resultant problems for education in the discriminating use of commercial motion pictures must be apparent.

All this is not to imply that commercial motion pictures
systematically engage in propaganda in behalf of the economic interests of the investors in the industry. The production of such excellent films as *David Copperfield, The House
We Live In, Monsieur Verdoux, Abe Lincoln in Illinois, Louis
Pasteur, Zola, The Informer, Madame Curie, The Three
Musketeers, The Snake Pit,* and literally hundreds of others
which have brilliantly interpreted the classics or presented
artistic original screen plays for millions of people whose
reading experiences are extremely limited, is testimony to
the wonderful potentialities of this medium and to the solid
contributions which the industry has made.

Pressure groups have a profound effect upon the nature
of the propaganda found in the movies. To a considerable
extent these determine what may or may not be included in
a film. In some cases the pressure group is the producer himself, as in the case of the filming of *An American Tragedy,*
which, over the protests of the author, Theodore Dreiser,
made no reference to the social emphasis of the book. In
other cases, the pressure group may be a government agency,
such as governments of states or cities which exercise censor-

ship over films. Religious groups exert pressure upon the movies by undertaking to prevent the exhibition of pictures which they regard as injurious to the faith and morals of the spectator. Thus the Catholic-sponsored National Legion of Decency boycotts "objectionable" pictures and the theaters which show them. Both the Legion of Decency and the Protestant Motion Picture Council issue weekly or monthly listings and evaluations of pictures. Political, professional, social, labor, business, foreign, and other organized groups exert pressure from time to time in order to prevent unfavorable representation of members of their groups in motion pictures.

NEWSREELS

The newsreels, which are controlled and distributed by five companies—20th Century-Fox (Movietone News), Hearst and MGM (News of the Day, formerly Hearst Metronome News), Pathe and RKO, Paramount, and Universal—present perhaps the most serious problems for the educator because of their partial and often distorted reporting of the news. The newspapers often "bury" or suppress news items which are unfavorable to the policies of the publishers or the interests of the advertisers, but they include each day a wide range of types of news stories, and the better newspapers make a genuine effort to report most of the significant happenings of the day. When they report public speeches, they generally attempt, with varying degrees of success, to select for quotation those parts which in their judgment represent the speaker's central ideas. Because of the limitations of time and the nature of their medium, newsreel producers and directors are obliged to make a very narrow selection from the week's news. This selection is made on the basis of the producer's present judgment concerning the public taste and preference, and on the basis of fairly well-defined views regarding public affairs.

Dale's analysis of the content of motion pictures in 1935

is probably substantially valid for newsreels today. He found that military themes occupied 26 per cent of the total, political themes 22 per cent, economic themes 6 per cent, and sports and gossip the rest.[9] Pictorial value and the audience's desire for excitement are often the chief criteria for the inclusion of news shots. Congressional investigations, parades, visits by foreign dignitaries, performances by swimming, golfing, baseball, and football stars and other athletes, fires and floods, and other spectacular materials are the chief stock in trade of the newsreels today. Speeches generally are represented by brief excerpts—often so edited as to change the essential idea of the speaker. Occasionally the on-the-spot coverage of the newsreel camera provides valuable evidence, as illustrated by shots of disputed plays in football and baseball, and in such incidents as the Chicago Memorial Day demonstration before the Republic Steel Company plant, movies of which were used by a Senate committee investigating police brutality.

Documentary Films

The commercial "documentary" films—those which portray some phase of science, nature, industry, or other aspect of contemporary life—deal chiefly with travel, sports, hobbies, popular science, and occasionally history. Many basic activities of living which are less dramatic or spectacular are commonly neglected. Harap reports that

the commercial documentary film is often a highly dramatic and absorbing presentation of a business organization or an industrial process. When the sponsor is not too obtrusively present in the film, it is a satisfying and exciting screen experience. It dramatizes everyday life without falsifying it.[10]

[9] Edgar Dale, *The Content of Motion Pictures*. New York: The Macmillan Company, 1935.

[10] Henry Harap, "The Motion Picture as Communication," *Social Education*, 7 (January, 1943).

The United States government, as well as business, labor, and educational groups, has produced numerous documentary films of various levels of quality. Perhaps the best known documentaries are those in the "March of Time" series, which often deal with controversial subjects. The government film, *The River*, produced in the thirties, still ranks as one of the most artistic and effective of the documentary films produced in the United States. *The Plow That Broke the Plains* similarly illustrates the value of the medium of the documentary film in creating a deeper insight into the spirit of American life.

OBJECTIVES FOR MOTION-PICTURE STUDY

Because of their unique appeal to young people, motion pictures provide ideal material for instruction in English classes. However, mere discussion of motion-picture experiences may not necessarily possess educational value. The school should formulate specific objectives for its work in this field. Motion-picture study should be, not a mere excuse for practice in speaking, writing, reading, and listening, but an undertaking worthy in its own right. The result of such study should be genuine changes in behavior and attitude on the part of young people toward the movies.

Dale suggests three possible objectives for motion-picture study: (1) teaching students an awareness of the effects of movies on individuals, (2) enabling students to select movies more thoughtfully, and (3) developing more varied and critical standards of motion-picture viewing.[11] He points out that it is just as important to be able to select a movie wisely as to make judicious selection of a book, and that the ability to evaluate and enjoy a movie requires as much guidance as does the development of appreciation.

Learning to view motion pictures critically does not mean developing a fault-finding attitude. It should involve a growing capacity to derive profound pleasure from good movies,

[11] Dale, *op. cit.*, pp. 211–215.

through a greater understanding of dramatic techniques and the technical qualities of pictures, and a greater sensitivity to the themes and issues with which the pictures deal. The critical attitude, moreover, should not interfere with the enjoyment of fantasy on the screen, in which the spectator gives himself over to the "willing suspension of disbelief." What has been said in another chapter on critical reading abilities applies with equal force to the other media of communication.

One may add to Dale's list of objectives the use of motion pictures in aiding young people to solve some of their personal problems. A number of feature pictures, many of them now available in shortened form for classroom use, deal seriously with boy-girl relationships, standards of values, intercultural relations, and other problems of great significance for adolescents. A teen-age girl viewing the picture *Alice Adams* or the picture *Little Women* may gain greater insight into personal values than she might from reading many books. Like literature, films should be used as instruments in meeting human need, not made an end in themselves. Activities in reading, speaking, listening, and writing in connection with motion-picture study will certainly improve the quality of young people's communication, but they too should be treated as means to understanding, not as ends in themselves.

SUGGESTIONS FOR CLASSROOM PROCEDURE

Miss Harriet J. Baldwin, a teacher of English in the Clinton, Ill., High School, has assembled many valuable suggestions for class activities in connection with the study of motion pictures. These activities are designed to achieve the objectives discussed in preceding paragraphs, and incidentally to develop the students' own competence in the various facets of language communication, including skill in the mechanical aspects of expression and in reading. The following suggested activities represent a slightly modified and expanded presentation of Miss Baldwin's list.

CENTERS OF INTEREST RELATING TO THE MEDIUM OF THE FILM

1. The Advertising of Movies

Reading	Writing	Speaking	Listening	Problems in evaluation
Reading newspaper advertisements of many movies. Reading advance publicity displayed by motion-picture theaters.	Rewriting movie advertisements as students think they should be written from the point of view of accuracy.	Discussing a specific movie from the point of view of its newspaper advertising.	Listening to the discussion with the idea of offering criticism and experiences of one's own.	Are the pictures what the advertisements say they are? What devices are used for getting people into the theater?

2. History, Costs, Investment, Control, Censorship

Reading	Writing	Speaking	Listening	Problems in evaluation
Dividing the class into small groups for research on the various problems.	Compiling class book containing the findings of the research group.	Conducting panel discussions on various phases of industry control.	Asking questions about points brought out in the panel discussion.	What effects do ownership and control of the movies have upon their content?

3. Motion-picture Reviews

Reading newspaper and magazine reviews of a movie before a student or the class attends it. Study various movie reviews in the same magazine	Writing reviews of a movie after viewing it, for possible use in room, school, or local newspaper. (If possible, a movie should be seen twice—once for content, once for direction, acting, etc.)	Discussing reviews in class, considering the audience needs, standards of judgment employed, soundness of assumptions, etc. Giving oral reviews before the class.	Listening to views of others in the class, and agreeing and disagreeing with them.	Evaluating a picture on the basis of a movie review. Comparing the movie reviewer's judgments with one's own. Deciding whether a movie is fair, critical, or mere "ballyhoo." Comparing different reviews of the same movie. Comparing reviews with advertisements in the same paper or magazine.

4. The Script or Scenario

Reading various sources on what makes a good story or plot. Reading stage plays, classic and modern, and comparing their structure with scenarios.	Selecting a scene from a play that has been read and rewriting it for a movie.	Discussing the merits—plausibility, effectiveness, etc., of the story.	Listening to the views of others and adding one's own.	Judging the story in the light of standards set by the class. Comparing movies made from books with the books themselves. Was the change, if any, an improvement?

5. Acting

Reading good books about acting and actors, and stories of motion-picture people like *Good Night, Sweet Prince* and *Dressler's Story of My Life*.	Taking notes on discussion about acting. Making outlines for lists of standards. Writing letters of commendation to screen players who have made good performances.	Developing standards for good acting, with examples from movies or plays.	Acting out scenes from movies and on final skits, while the class observes and evaluates.	Rating several movies on the basis of standards for acting.

6. Photography

Reading books and articles on motion-picture photography and learning about various kinds of "shots" and their use.	Writing to the studios or the Eastman Co. for unusual pictures. Writing to movie cameramen for answers to specific questions about photography.	Group reports to class, followed by general discussion, on problems of lighting, double exposure, etc., and the effect of good photography on the spectator.	Listening to a guest speaker on motion-picture photography.	How might camera angle shots in a specific picture be improved? Was lighting used to good effect? Evaluate still pictures collected and make a display.

7. Setting

Reading about what is involved in designing and constructing a movie set. (Magazine articles are likely to offer the best material.)	Writing studios for pictures showing settings of various movies. Writing designers for information about their work. Writing descriptions of effective settings seen in the movies.	Constructing a setting for a scene in a play, and explaining it from the standpoint of what will show in shots from certain angles. Discussing authenticity.	Listening to the explanations and offering suggestions on the basis of standards already formulated.	Formulating standards of judgment about settings.

8. Sound, Music, and Dialogue

Conducting research in small groups, each selecting one problem—sound effects, music, or dialogue.	Writing a review of the dialogue and sound effects of a motion picture in the light of specific standards.	Reading some of the reviews in class and following the reading with a class or panel discussion.	Illustrating the use and effect of music and sound by means of records, *Burlap Bags* and *Radio Is Here to Stay*; also by showing the movie *Fiddle-de-de* first with and then without sound.	For a specific movie. 1. Did dialogue intensify and promote action of the play? Give examples. 2. Did it seem real? 3. Where could action have been substituted for dialogue with better effect? 4. What unusual sound effects did you notice? Unnecessary ones? 5. Was music used as a sound effect? How? 6. Was any of the dialogue too long?

307

9. Direction

Reading about the importance of direction and the role of the director. Newspaper reviews of motion pictures may furnish good material.	Writing letters to well-known motion-picture directors asking questions about their work. Writing minutes of class or committee discussions on this topic.	Discussing a motion picture from the viewpoint of the director's interpretation of the story.	Listening to group discussion to get the views of others.	How well did the actors seem to know what the play was about? Did the director handle all types of scenes well? (Tragedy, comedy, farce). Was the movie well edited? What scenes would you have omitted? What scenes should have been added, if any? How did the director use photographic effects?

10. Newsreels

After seeing several newsreels, reading about the controls, scope, and purpose of newsreels.	Writing summaries of group discussions.	Discussing certain newsreels which individuals or the class have seen, determining whether and how the news has been "slanted."	Deciding whether the news commentator's tone of voice had anything to do with the effect of the newsreel.	Does the selection of material reveal any bias in behalf of a specific political or social ideology? What is the role of sound and music in newsreels?

11. Documentaries

Reading about the nature and influence of the documentary film, using the *Reader's Guide* to locate articles on the subject.	Writing to producers and distributors for lists of documentary films.	After viewing a documentary at a motion-picture theater or in school, discussing its purposes and techniques.	Listening to the narrator in the film or films and noting voice quality, humor, dramatic effects, and timing.	Does the film contain propaganda? What is the motive for the propaganda? Is it skillfully handled? Is it justified, from your point of view?

12. Exhibition and Audience Reaction

Reading about ownership of motion-picture theaters, finding out about control of local theaters, "block booking," and other problems of exhibition of films.	Writing reports on interviews for a class newspaper or class book.	Interviewing local theater managers on policies of film selection, racial discrimination in admissions, and ways of theater-school cooperation. Interviewing friends and others on their preferences in motion pictures.	Arranging a field trip to a local theater and requesting the manager to explain equipment used, procedures in exhibiting films, and skills needed for the purpose.	Does the local community have any control over what movies are shown? Does the exhibitor suppress any movies? Can the exhibitor exercise any control over selection of movies?

CENTERS OF INTEREST RELATING TO THE CONTENT OF THE FILM

1. *Life Goals*

Reading	Writing	Speaking	Listening	Problems in evaluation
Reading books on which certain movies are based, and comparing book and film to determine whether characters in the film pursue goals described by author.	Prepare a script for a movie reflecting one's own goals in life, with respect to community service, money, marriage, vocation, etc.	Reporting, individually or in committees, on life goals implied in specific movies. Presenting skits illustrating conflicting goals for living.	Listening to group reports and skits to determine how they compare with one's own conception of worthy goals for living.	Comparing or contrasting goals implied in certain movie characterizations with those familiar book characters from Helen Keller's *Story of My Life*, *Little Women*, and others.

2. *Crime*

Reading	Writing	Speaking	Listening	Problems in evaluation
Reading articles in magazines about the ways in which crime is treated in the movies.	Writing an editorial for the room or school newspaper on the way crime is treated in the motion pictures.	Presenting group reports on crime in movies through real or mock radio programs, forums, panel discussions or socio-dramas.	Listening to the reports critically, preparing to make suggestions for improving the effectiveness of the reports.	Do the movies reveal the causes of crime? Is the criminal made glamorous? Are solutions suggested? Are the characters convincing?

3. Love and Marriage

Reading	Writing	Speaking	Listening	Problems in evaluation
				Does the picture represent physical beauty and luxury as the major ingredients of a happy marriage? Does it leave basic conflicts or differences between husband and wife unsolved in what is represented as a happy marriage? Does it emphasize joint responsibilities in marriage? What other assumptions about love and marriage do you find in the picture, and do you accept these assumptions?

In this and subsequent sections, supply activities of categories similar to those in the preceding sections: reading of books, magazines, and pamphlets, panel discussions, forums, class discussions, committee research, radio programs, exhibits, and the like.

311

4. Wealth and Class

Do movies generally present stories in luxurious settings? Do they leave a correct impression about the way most people live? Why do movies tend to restrict themselves to scenes of wealth? What does this tendency have to do with their mass appeal? Are the wealthy fairly and accurately represented in the films? Do working people and their organizations receive attention on the screen? Favorable or unfavorable? What is the attitude of the films toward government and the governmental agencies? Do you think this attitude is sound? Why or why not? Do you believe that movies can be a "drug" to prevent social change? How?

5. Violence

Is violence, either in terms of individual conflict or war, shown as a desirable method of settling disputes? Do movies and newsreels make any assumptions as to causes of war? Do these assumptions harmonize with your own as derived from reading, discussion, and thinking?

6. Intercultural and International Relations

Are members of minority groups, particularly Jews, Negroes, Italians, Mexicans, and Orientals, portrayed as individual human beings or as stereotypes? Is the Negro generally shown as a comic character or a menial? Are Jews generally represented as aggressive and money-mad? What movies deal seriously with the problem of intercultural education? Are the characters in these movies convincing? Do they tell the truth?

313

7. Personal Problems

Do the films deal honestly with the personal problems of people? What films have helped you to understand some of your own problems—such as getting along with your parents, maintaining good relations with your age mates, adjusting yourself to your own physical development, developing self-confidence, finding pleasure in a variety of wholesome recreational activities and the like? What films, in your opinion, suggested undesirable solutions to these problems? Is the humor in the pictures wholesome or does it reflect unfavorably upon people?

All these activities are, of course, merely suggestive. The films that come to town and the boys and girls themselves will supply the occasion and the subject matter for motion-picture study. Nor should the categories that have been presented be taken up in sequence. Many of them can and should be discussed simultaneously. It need not be emphasized that no effort should be made to introduce *all* the suggested activities in the unit on the photoplay.

The skills of communication, such as those involved in reading and library research, in the mechanics of written expression (including spelling), pronunciation, vocabulary, and the like, can be effectively taught in relation to the actual use of language, to which this unit admirably lends itself.

For Further Reading

Bailey, Thomas, *The Man in the Street.* New York: The Macmillan Company, 1948.

Dale, Edgar, *Audio-Visual Methods in Teaching,* New York: The Dryden Press, 1946.

Dale, Edgar, *Children's Attendance at Motion Pictures.* New York: The Macmillan Company, 1935.

Dale, Edgar, *et al., Motion Pictures in Education.* New York: The H. W. Wilson Company, 1937.

DeBoer, John J. (Ed.), *Education and the Mass Media of Communication.* A publication of the National Conference on Research in English. Chicago: National Council of Teachers of English, 1950.

Grey, Lennox, "Communication and the Arts," *The Communication of Ideas,* pp. 119–142. New York: Harper & Brothers, 1948.

Inglis, Ruth A., *Freedom of the Movies.* Chicago: University of Chicago Press, 1947.

Lewin, William, *Photoplay Appreciation in American High Schools.* Monograph No. 2 of the National Council of Teachers of English. New York: Appleton-Century-Crofts, Inc., 1934.

Rand, Helen, and Richard B. Lewis, *Film and School.* New York: Appleton-Century-Crofts, Inc., 1937.

Reisman, Leon, "Cinema Technique and Mass Culture," *American Quarterly,* 1 (Winter, 1949), 314–325.

Schramm, Wilbur L. (Ed.), *Communications in Modern Society.* Urbana: University of Illinois Press, 1948.

Stecker, H. Dora, "Some Desirable Goals for Motion Pictures," *Proceedings of the National Conference of Social Work.* Chicago: University of Chicago Press, 1927.

Van Til, William, John J. DeBoer, R. Will Burnett, and Katherine C. Ogden, *Democracy Demands It!* New York: Harper & Brothers, 1950.

Waples, Douglas (Ed.), *Print, Radio, and Film in a Democracy.* Chicago: University of Chicago Press, 1942.

Chapter 12. MASS MEDIA OF COMMUNICATION: RADIO AND TELEVISION

RADIO AS A MASS MEDIUM

Like the motion picture, radio broadcasting has become one of the great industries of the United States. The net time sales in 1948 for radio programs in this country, exclusive of agency commissions, were about 417 million dollars. Incidental revenues swelled this figure. Approximately 81 million radio sets were in use in 1949, including 14 million car radios, plus 4,500,000 FM receivers, plus 3,200,000 television sets.[1] Morris Ernst reports that 15 million more families have radios than have magazines, 6 million more have radios than have bathtubs.[2]

Radio succeeds not only in reaching great masses of people but in reaching them in a singularly effective way. The announcer, the actor, and the singer have access, through radio, to the intimacy of our homes and establish a direct, human contact with us.

Listening is a friendly activity, usually more enjoyable and more interesting than reading. It depends upon other human beings. We are usually sympathetic when we listen; at least we are on our good behavior. Through long training we have learned to listen patiently; the plethora of platitudes reaching our ears during the day would be unbearable if we encountered them in print. And so it is that whatever is human, personal, or intimate seems favored by auditory communication—humor, for example, and suggestibility. The listener seems as a rule to be friendly, un-

[1] *Broadcasting Yearbook.*
[2] Morris Ernst, *The First Freedom*, p. 125. New York: The Macmillan Company, 1946.

critical, and well disposed toward what he hears. The reader, on the other hand, tends to be more analytical and more critical, and in the long run probably more accurate in his knowledge and better informed.[3]

ACHIEVEMENTS OF RADIO

The advent of radio has made available to the American people cultural resources which were formerly denied to all but the more privileged economic groups. Shakesperean drama, for example, which formerly was reserved for those who were able to pay the fairly high admission prices to legitimate theaters, or occasionally to "road show" movies, is now frequently brought into the homes of the lowest income groups, presented by professional players. The finest symphony orchestras, soloists, and choruses perform for all who can afford some kind of radio set. The following programs are taken at random from a current listing recommended by the Federal Radio Education Committee (FREC):

This Is Europe (MBS). Famous artists and composers interpret a different country each week. A different orchestral work composed for the program is presented each week.

Mutual's Choral Series (MBS). This program presents outstanding college and university choruses.

Piano Playhouse (CBS). Solos, duets, and improvisations by outstanding pianists in both jazz and classical music.

N. Y. Philharmonic Symphony (CBS). America's oldest symphony orchestra in its nineteenth consecutive season on CBS.

Carnegie Hall (ABC). Featuring a thirty-five-piece orchestra, the program presents both classical and semiclassical musical selections.

Theater Guild on the Air (NBC). Adaptations of notable stage successes with leading stage and film stars in the major roles.

Author Meets the Critic (ABC). Timely, uninhibited half-hour discussions in which an author is interviewed by two critics. Recent and controversial books are discussed.

[3] Hadley Cantril and Gordon W. Allport, *The Psychology of Radio*, p. 180. New York: Harper & Brothers, 1935. (By permission.)

Meet the Press (MBS). An unrehearsed "press conference of the air," in which four reporters from the nation's leading newspapers question the most prominent person in the news for the week.

Memo from Lake Success (CBS). Weekly presentation by United Nations Radio Division. Reports human interest stories and UN activities on all fronts.

Voices That Live (ABC). Such artists as Caruso, Melba, McCormick, and Tetrazzini are played in a collection of recordings dating back to 1895.[4]

These are but a few of the large number of excellent programs which the American radio brings to the people. There are programs for every taste, for every educational level. The programs recommended by the FREC illustrate the tremendous educational potentialities of the medium of radio. They embrace the finest in music, drama, public discussion, information, and humor. At its best, radio brings to us some of the most significant products of American thought, art, and culture. It serves also as a reflector of the myriad facets of American life. It does not succeed in reproducing the nuances which were so eloquently described (in depression years) in the following passage from an address by Dr. Howard W. Odum, but in its variety it succeeds in suggesting some of them:

Who, then, are these Americans in the new radio picture? What are they doing, and which way are they going? What are the names and nature of those who pass across the stage—a vast multitude, mass and class, from the ends of the earth—some planted deep in the soil of the New World, some fallen on barren ground, some crowded out by the luxurious growth of unplanned bigness and complexities of modern life? Over there in cities they speak forty tongues and know nothing of the regions of the national domain. Over here in the vast plains some toil and spin in the heat of the day, some in the backway places, some on the mountainsides and the flatwoods, some in the richer soils of limitless land. And in between, on highways and byways, the millions of

[4] From "Look and Listen," *Elementary English*, 26 (December, 1949), 490.

folk of village and smaller industry cling to the old dreams of opportunity for the common man and pray for the prophet of the new day. Other thousands move hither and yon—fruits of the new mobility and of the too rich harvests of unplanned achievements —homeless wanderers, farm squatters again, national nomad paupers, hitchhikers and freight-train riders in multitude; mass on mass by wayside, in flophouses, anywhere, everywhere. Other hundreds of thousands restless and dissatisfied, recruited from every class and type, maladjusted in the new crisis; and massed round about millions of unemployed, common man and intellectual; white and black, Jew and Gentile, urban and city, with haggard faces and staring eyes, strained nerves and flashing tempers, loyalty to life, liberty, and loved ones straining loyalty to law and order.

And, in the shadow of the great American pageant, stragglers and clusters of marginal folk—gangsters and racketeers, kidnappers and crooks, gunmen and thugs, bank robbers and holdup confederates, incredible armies of the underworld, organized criminals, leaders and privates, entrepreneurs of a new economic traffic; a new generation of specialists, of artists and technicians; luminaries for the Star Spangled Banner. And still other dimmer shadows silhouetted against a quick changing background, challenging radio and all its parts to match speed with speed.

Yet not all of America is one, or North, or South, or East, or West; or farm, or backwoods, or submarginal folk. It is not Wall Street, or Fifth Avenue, or Lake Shore Drive, or Hollywood, or cotton-mill village, or mining town, or men in prisons, or Negroes in chains. America is not all industry; neither all urban or all rural; not all white, not all black; neither young nor old, male nor female. Life in the United States is still of, for, and by the people who are neither all scoundrels nor saints, neither all morons nor geniuses. America is not the same yesterday, today, and tomorrow. Nor is all of America American; part of it is of other lands and people; so yesterday, so today, perhaps more so the day after the morrow of economic nationalism.

But, whoever the American people are, whatever they do, wherever they be, they appear as never before both creators and creatures of the great mass power—the perfect laboratory for the limitless reaches of radio. And surely there must be not only education for information and instruction but some cultural direction and equilibrium for the impatience and immaturity of intellectual and common man alike; restless, resistless tides of people, resurging spiritual power of youth and race; mass emotions and folk impatience nigh unto flood tide.[5]

CRITICISMS OF RADIO PROGRAMS

These, then, are among the achievements of this miraculous new medium of communication. What are some of its shortcomings? Many serious criticisms have been directed against the radio industry. Particularly, the children's programs have been subject to unfavorable reactions from parents and teachers. The chief objection by parent groups has been the emphasis upon excitement, horror, and excessive stimulation in children's programs.[6] DeBoer found in his study of children's responses to radio drama that some children's pulse rate rose as much as fifty beats per minute during especially exciting incidents in the radio stories, and that these changes were accompanied by sudden and extreme fluctuations in blood pressure.[7] But perhaps the most serious criticism leveled at American radio for children is its vacuity. Radio's opportunity to aid children in arriving at a better understanding of themselves and each other and the world round about them is enormous. In large measure it has failed to utilize this opportunity and has frankly planned its programs to reach the largest possible juvenile market for its sponsors.

That there is no necessary conflict between the objectives of maximum entertainment and education was demonstrated when Superman undertook to combat racial and religious

[5] Howard W. Odum, "The Implications of Radio as a Social and Educational Phenomenon," *Educational Broadcasting 1936*, pp. 94–95, edited by C. S. Marsh. Chicago: University of Chicago Press, 1937. By permission.

[6] Dorothy Gordon, *All Children Listen*, p. 58. New York: George W. Stewart, 1942.

[7] John J. DeBoer, "Radio and Children's Emotions," *School and Society*, Sept. 16, 1939, p. 369.

prejudice and went to the top in the Hooper ratings. Studies of the sources of child interest in radio have further established the possibility of arousing vigorous listener response with dramatically presented interpersonal situations with educational significance.[8] The problem appears to be one of finding sufficiently talented script writers who know something of the problems of children and who know how to deal with them effectively in the context of a dramatic continuity.

In the realm of adult programs—to which, incidentally, children begin to listen increasingly from approximately the age of ten—similar reflections upon lost opportunities are in order. It is true that the best in radio programs, illustrated by those listed above, command the unstinting admiration of thoughtful listeners. But for every Norman Corwin masterpiece there are scores of fatuous "soap operas," and for every symphony concert there are hundreds of cacophonous disk-jockey programs, counterfeit hillbilly performances, and idiotic quiz shows.

Radio must, of course, appeal to every type and level of taste. But there is room on the air for instrumental and vocal music, both classical and popular, addresses, forums, debates, sports events, mysteries, religious broadcasts, quiz programs, variety programs, and many other forms of entertainment. It should be possible for the listener to make a free selection from among many of these kinds of programs both during the day and in the evening. Radio offers no such choice. In some cities, on a summer Sunday afternoon, the listener has a choice of six to eight broadcasts of the same baseball game, and the symphony normally heard is withdrawn in favor of the sports show. During most hours of the day the choice is from an array of the most fantastic potboilers with such intriguing titles as *Life Can Be Beautiful, John's Other Wife,* the *Second Mrs. Burton, Young Widder Brown, Road of Life, Portia Faces Life, Stella Dallas,* and *Backstage Wife;*

[8] John J. DeBoer, "The Psychology of Children's Radio Listening," in *Radio and English Teaching,* p. 41, edited by Max J. Herzberg. New York: Appleton-Century-Crofts, Inc., 1941.

57.4 per cent of daytime programs consist of this sob-sister drivel. Twenty million American women listen each day to the more than forty soap operas on the air.[9] The editors of *Fortune* estimate that the average soap-opera fan listens regularly to 5.8 of the soap operas, while some listeners follow as many as 28. A University of Chicago graduate student, in surveying the listening habits of housewives, found that "not one of the women interviewed listened less than five hours a day, the mean listening hour a day being slightly more than eight."[10] Some farm comment, recipe programs, interviews, news summaries, Arthur Godfrey, and give-away programs offer the only "relief" from this fare. First-rate music, drama, and political or literary commentary, except on educational stations (which operate chiefly during daytime hours)[11] are practically unknown on the radio during the daytime hours. Even the evening hours in which choice radio programs can be heard are confined to certain days of the week. Those who desire popular music need never wait until Thursday evening. Those who want good drama, even good mystery drama, must wait until certain evenings of the week. As for Saturday evening, the producers have apparently abandoned the period after 7 P.M. almost completely to the jitterbugs and the barn dancers.

Soap operas, of course, reflect the special economic predilections of the sponsors and producers. Waples reports that "in forty-five serials carefully followed up for three weeks, not one character was found from the laboring class."[12]

Many excellent broadcasts, of course, are produced by the

[9] Jerome H. Spingarn, *Radio Is Yours*, p. 6. Public Affairs Pamphlet No. 121. New York: Public Affairs Committee, 1946.

[10] Ruth Palter, "Radio Attraction for the Housewife," *Hollywood Quarterly* 3 (Spring, 1948), 249.

[11] Dallas W. Smythe, *An Inventory of (Non-Commercial) Educational Radio Programming*. With assistance from Jennie N. Smythe and Howard H. Hyle. Urbana, Ill.: Institute of Communications Research, University of Illinois, August, 1949. (Mimeographed.)

[12] Douglas Waples, *Print, Radio, and Film in a Democracy*, p. 67. Chicago: University of Chicago Press, 1942.

schools themselves, either over their own stations or in co-operation with commercial stations. Cleveland, Chicago, Detroit, and many other American cities have pioneered in putting this powerful medium to educational use. School children, in both large and small communities, are being granted access to the microphone, often to a greater extent than the schools have been able or willing to accept. University radio stations have performed notable service in bringing educational and cultural materials to the public. But the audiences reached by all of these are relatively small in comparison with the huge audiences of the great networks.

CONTROL OF RADIO

The air waves belong to all the people.[13] No private citizen or corporation owns any of the radio channels. Government, representing the people, periodically grants the use of these channels to individuals or corporations. It has the power to grant, withhold, or withdraw the use of the air waves. The United States, unlike Great Britain, Canada, and other countries, follows the policy of extending broadcast privileges to private agencies instead of operating radio stations by means of governmental agencies. Nevertheless, it reserves the right of supervision and a degree of control over the private operators. This supervision and control are exercised through the Federal Communications Commission (FCC).

The FCC, which was established in 1934, is composed of seven men, appointed by the President of the United States. The Commission grants broadcasting licenses which are renewable every three years. It has no power to censor programs, but it may, though it does not, regulate the types of programs produced. According to its "bluebook," the FCC requires stations to include a certain proportion of "sustaining" (unsponsored) and educational programs, to eliminate advertising excesses and the advertising of liquor, to avoid defamatory statements, obscenity, and indecency, to give

[13] Communications Act of 1934, as amended.

equal opportunity for both sides of controversial questions to be heard, to avoid offending religious sensibilities, and to include a reasonable proportion of "live" programs. These requirements, particularly with respect to the proportion of sustaining programs, are, however, rarely enforced or interpreted in favor of the radio stations.

The interpretation and enforcement of these regulations depend upon the integrity, intelligence, and public spirit of the members, and upon the pressures which influential groups are able to bring to bear upon the Commission. Some of the FCC members have been noted for their exceptional competence and devotion to the public interest. Others have been mediocre or worse. The "regulation" concerning sustaining programs, for example, is frequently circumvented by scheduling them at times when the audience is smallest—on Sunday mornings, when millions are in church, or late at night, when millions are in bed. Lobbies in Congress always represent a threat to effective regulation of the air waves. Jerome H. Spingarn declares,[14]

Ever since its creation, the Federal Communications Commission has been a storm center. It has always operated under pressure—from the industry, from Congress, and from the press. . . . When rebuffed, Congressmen have sometimes attempted to harass the FCC by investigations, by speeches on the floor, by sniping at FCC appropriation bills, and by impugning its employees.

Control within the industry itself is vested largely in the big four networks: the National, the Columbia, the American, and the Mutual broadcasting systems. The NBC, oldest and largest of the networks, is owned by the Radio Corporation of America, whose subsidiaries include the RCA Victor Distributing Corporation and numerous foreign corporations engaged in broadcasting and the manufacture and sale of radio equipment. RCA's 13,881,000 shares of common stock

[14] Federal Communications Commission, *Public Service Responsibilities of Broadcast Station Licenses*. Washington: Federal Communications Commission, March, 1946.

in 1940 were in the hands of about 25,000 persons.[15] Registrar for the preferred stock was Chase National Bank; for the common stock, the New York Trust Company. NBC embraces (as of 1947) 167 affiliated AM stations.[16] In 1947, CBS included 162 affiliated stations in the United States and its possessions.[17] ABC has 252 affiliates in the continental United States.

Advertisers, who ultimately pay the bills for radio, exercise control over the nature of its offerings. The big advertisers are relatively few. Former Commissioner Clifford J. Durr of the FCC asserts,

> One eighth of NBC's entire advertising business comes from one advertiser, and two advertisers provide almost one fourth. Ten advertisers accounted for nearly 60 per cent of its business. One seventh of Blue's (the Blue Network, since disbanded by court order) advertising business came from one advertiser and two provided approximately one fourth. Over 60 per cent of its business came from ten advertisers. To a slightly less degree the same situation prevails in CBS and Mutual.[18]

If radio news, commentary, and even drama tend to favor the economic interests of powerful groups in American life, Mr. Durr's figures should provide at least a partial explanation. Says S. E. Frost,

> Under the present system of American radio, and within limits set by the Federal Communications Commission and the ideals of the station owner, the advertiser actually "calls the tune." It is his interests that are considered, even when a particular advertiser is barred from the air.[19]

[15] T. P. Robinson, *Radio Networks and the Federal Government*, p. 10. New York: Columbia University Press, 1943.

[16] John Moody, *Moody's Industrial*, p. 2690. New York: Moody's Investor's Service, 1948.

[17] *Ibid.*, p. 667.

[18] Spingarn, *op. cit.*, p. 19.

[19] S. E. Frost, Jr., *Is American Radio Democratic?* p. 94. Chicago: University of Chicago Press, 1937.

OBJECTIVES FOR RADIO STUDY

The first of the objectives for the study of radio in secondary schools arises from the nature of the control of the industry. In a democracy the best defense against monopoly in the field of communication is an enlightened public; and the schools, which constitute one of the few educational agencies operated not for profit, have a major responsibility for providing enlightenment. It must do so by making available all pertinent information on controversial issues, impartially and systematically.

Spingarn offers some valuable suggestions as to what the public can do about radio, and by implication what the schools can do in preparing youth for dealing with the problems which radio presents. One of his suggestions is to form listeners' groups for the purpose of safeguarding listener interests.[20] He points out that many civic organizations and parent-teacher groups have active radio committees, and that in a few cities community-wide radio councils have been established to aid local groups in bringing about better radio programs. The Community Radio Council in Winston-Salem, N.C., for example, produces attractive programs for welfare agencies and helps to recruit audiences for them. In other cities "monitoring" groups, consisting chiefly of housewives, volunteer to keep records of changes in radio schedules, particularly of the appearance and nonappearance of news commentators, some of whom are often quietly dropped when their views offend powerful interests. These monitoring groups serve as pressure groups in behalf of viewpoints which the radio might otherwise be tempted to neglect. By writing letters to the stations and especially by asking for hearings by the FCC (which are rarely reported in the press), these monitoring groups succeed in speaking for the interests and desires of the listening public. In encouraging voluntary action of this kind, the schools can serve

[20] Spingarn, *op. cit.*, p. 28.

effectively in raising the general level of civic participation and in making radio more democratic.

A second major objective of the schools in the area of radio study is the elevation of the listener's taste. This objective can be achieved (1) by frequent analysis and comparison of the various radio programs now available and (2) by consideration of the almost limitless possibilities of radio as a medium of communication. The fact that millions of American men and women are willing to tolerate programs of the soap-opera level is an indictment of the kind of instruction, or lack of instruction, given in the schools. Introducing young people in secondary schools to programs of high quality and developing group standards for radio listening may serve measurably to improve the kind of radio fare which will be offered the American public in coming years.

The method of improving young people's tastes in radio is not the method of coercion. Levenson declares,

Enduring standards and tastes cannot be imposed from without, but must be developed from within. A genuine continuous growth begins first with an understanding of the levels at which tastes exist. Consequently, as applied to radio, before the teacher attempts an abstract discussion of comparative standards, it is well to know to what programs the children are listening. What programs are available in the community? When do they listen? Does anyone aid them in their selections? What are their preferences and dislikes? Such a simple survey of the listening habits of the class is a good preliminary step in guidance. It will not only provide the teacher with the information she seeks, but if parents' reactions are solicited also, the enterprise can serve to promote further interest in parental guidance at home.[21]

A third, and perhaps the most important, objective for radio study in secondary schools is the development of the ability to evaluate news reports and commentaries on the air. Evaluation of the reliability of the news and its interpretation calls for a knowledge of the special interests of the program

[21] William B. Levenson, *Teaching through Radio*, p. 377. New York: Rinehart & Company, Inc., 1945. (By permission.)

sponsor, the broadcast agency, and the speaker; a familiarity with the various propaganda techniques; and a broad background of information concerning the topic or topics under discussion. While this third objective is probably the most difficult of the three, it is at the same time also the most essential.

SUGGESTIONS FOR CLASSROOM PROCEDURE

Some of the objectives listed by Wrightstone [22] for school broadcasts may be applicable to any study of radio programs:

Functional information: Objectives dealing with the acquisition of facts, information, concepts, and principles in various fields.

Powers of critical thinking and discrimination: Objectives dealing with ability to infer, to analyze, to apply generalizations, principles, or standards.

Attitudes and appreciations: Objectives dealing with the quality, direction, and consistency of beliefs, convictions, opinions, and choices.

Interests: Objectives dealing with the building of broader, deeper, and growing interests and preferences in each area of the curriculum.

Creative expression: Objectives dealing with self-expression in any media, including self-purposed experiments or investigations.

Personal-social adaptability: Objectives dealing with emotional, personal, and social values and patterns of behavior.

Skills and techniques: Objectives dealing with conventionally accepted "tools" or skills peculiar to a subject or discipline.

Woelfel and Tyler list the following activities in radio study which are especially applicable to English classes:[23]

Classroom Discussion

Discussing out-of-school radio programs in class.
Discussing the characteristics of good radio speech.
Discussing examples of propaganda in everyday programs.

[22] J. Wayne Wrightstone, "Evaluating the Production and Use of School Broadcasts," *The Phi Delta Kappan,* 22 (March, 1939), 333.

[23] *Radio and the School,* pp. 176–178. Copyright 1945 by World Book Company. Reproduced by special permission.

Comparing radio "news" and newspaper "news."
Discussing radio personalities.
Analyzing techniques used in radio programs.
Appraising the radio quality of various broadcasts.
Establishing criteria to be used in criticizing radio drama.
Discussing vocational opportunities in radio.
Explaining the psychological appeal of different broadcasts.

Writing

Adapting stories or plays for radio presentation.
Writing radio dialogue and continuity.
Writing original radio plays.
Writing letters to broadcasters.
Writing radio "commercials" or advertisements.
Writing reviews of radio programs.
Analyzing personal listening habits and preferences.
Making an inventory of popular programs.
Keeping a radio "log" of listening.
Preparing a bibliography of books and magazine articles dealing with radio.

Speech and Dramatics

Producing a radio play or skit in the classroom.
Practicing correct pronunciation and careful diction.
Delivering radio news reports or interpretations.
Criticizing the speech of well-known radio personalities.
Presenting panel and forum discussions in class.
Burlesquing radio announcements and advertisements.
Imitating well-known announcers.
Imitating popular comedians and M.C.'s.
Using spot-broadcast techniques for dramatizing personal talks.
Presenting a radio production in the auditorium.

Reading

Reading radio plays or scripts.
Reading books on script writing or production.
Reading radio articles in current magazines and newspapers.
Reading *Radio Guide* or *Variety*.
Reading stories and plays dramatized on radio programs.

Other Activities

Visiting a radio station.
Listening to transcriptions in the classroom.
Listening to "live" broadcasts in the classroom.
Interviewing radio technicians, personalities, etc.
Demonstrating radio equipment.

Miss Phyllis Stump, teacher of English in an Illinois high school, has prepared three units on radio study: "What Is the Organization of Radio?" "How Does Radio Operate?" "What Does Radio Offer?" In these units she suggests, among others, the following class activities useful in the teaching of English (adapted):

1. *Letter writing.* To the networks, local stations, the Federal Communications Commission, radio performers, sponsors, regarding quality of programs, elimination of commentators, requesting schedules, etc.

2. *Library research.* Consulting school and community libraries for material on the networks, biographies of radio stars, information on FCC activities, and the like. Investigating specific types of programs: drama (serials, radio theaters, mysteries), comedy and variety, audience participation, news, music, talks, and others. Cyclopedias, yearbooks, and references listed at the end of this chapter, in addition to trade and popular magazines could constitute the major references.

3. *Interviews.* Interviewing local broadcasting executives about the organization and problems of radio; interviewing representative citizens on their views about radio programs.

4. *Class and panel discussions.* Discussing the nature of controls upon radio, with the effects of such controls on the character and content of radio programs. Discussing a class trip to a radio studio, considering such questions as the following: What new ideas do you now have about broadcasting? How many different people are necessary for presentation of certain programs, such as newscasts, a play, a musical program? What are some rules for the use of the microphone? What phase of broadcasting appealed to you most? With our present school facilities, would it be possible for us to do some radio work? What types of programs would you like to do?

5. *Oral reports.* Reporting of findings on investigations described above, on the role of the advertiser in the radio industry, the role of the newspaper in the radio industry, the effectiveness of the FCC and the NAB, and the relation between the local station and the network.

6. *Organization of a radio club.* Electing officers, deciding purposes, choosing prepared scripts for class broadcasts (some are available from the U.S. Office of Education), assigning students to phases of broadcasting which appeal to their individual interests, adapting stories or plays for radio presentation, writing original scripts, presenting programs to the class or in the assembly, or in a local radio station, evaluating the radio play and the presentation, dividing into committees responsible for such parts in the broadcast as announcing (studying enunciation, pronunciation, variety in and enrichment of voice quality, through recording one's own voice, listening to successful radio speakers, and practicing speech skills), investigating various types of radio scripts by listening to the radio and using printed scripts from the networks and the local library, noting sound effects on the radio, visiting radio stations, interviewing the person in charge of sound effects, reading suggestions for sound effects in books and articles on radio, utilizing information on working out suitable effects for class broadcasts, conferring with technicians at local radio stations, learning rules of parliamentary procedure, developing skills in writing, speaking, listening and radio techniques.

7. *Radio listening.* Filling in the following questionnaire:

(*Write 1, 2, or 3 in the right-hand column to indicate which type of program seems to you superior in quality.*)

Type of program	Rating
Comedy, variety	
e.g., Bob Hope, *Duffy's,* Red Skelton, etc.	
"Sophisticated" detective	
e.g., Thin Man, Mr. & Mrs. North	
"Family" drama	
e.g., Aldrich, One Man's Family, etc.	
Evening action serials	
e.g., Lone Ranger, etc.	
Action, detective drama	
e.g., Gang Busters, etc.	

"Thriller" drama ....
   e.g., Inner Sanctum, Suspense, etc.
Popular orchestras ....
"Serious" drama ....
Children's afternoon serials ....
   e.g., Captain Midnight, Superman, etc.
Quiz and audience participation ....
Children's once-a-week programs ....
   e.g., Let's Pretend, Youth on Parade, etc.
Semiclassical and classical ....
Musical programs ....
News broadcasts ....
Forums and round tables ....

Analyzing the results of the questionnaire, reporting the results to the class, discussing reasons for the choices.

Monitoring radio programs for a period of a week to find out whether viewpoints on public affairs are reasonably balanced among the various networks, stations, commentators, and forums. Each student might select some one station or some one evening and report his findings to the class.

8. *Reading about radio.* Reading collections of radio plays, like Corwin's; reading books on radio play production; studying network radio schedules; reading radio magazines and magazines containing selections from recent radio addresses (like *Talks*); reading radio reviews in magazines and newspapers.

9. *Dramatizing.* Presenting a radio play for the class, school, or local station: selecting the play, electing a student director, trying out for the cast, volunteering for such committees as announcing, sound effects, and script writing, recording and criticizing the program before final presentation, evaluating the presentation.

10. *Writing.* Writing radio scripts, writing radio reviews for the room, school, or community newspaper, posting recommended radio programs on the bulletin board.

TELEVISION

Although television as a mass medium of communication has been anticipated for many years, it has not exhibited signs of rapid growth until the present time. As these lines are written, television—or TV, as it is now commonly called—is available over an area representing a population of about 75 million people.[24] At the end of 1949, there were ninety-four active TV stations in fifty-four cities, with others in preparation, as compared with nineteen stations in early 1948. Television sets, numbering 3,200,000 as of February, 1950, have multiplied ten times in two years, and are continuously and rapidly increasing in number. Chairman Coy of the FCC has predicted,

Eventually there will be one or more television sets in every one of the 39,000,000 homes in America. . . . I foresee the day when television will be the most powerful instrument of communication ever devised, the most universal and most effective purveyor of education, information, culture, and entertainment.[25]

Smythe [26] believes that AM (standard) radio will progressively decline with the growth of TV, calling attention to the fact that at present nearly all owners of television sets listen less to radio because of TV. He reports further that other forms of entertainment are likewise suffering as a result of competition from TV, though to a milder degree. Movies rank second to AM radio, books third, magazines fourth, and newspapers fifth in order of their decline because of TV. What effect the advent of TV has had and will have upon conversation and creative activities in the home is not known, but it may be assumed to be considerable, considering the estimate, reported in various sources, that families average four hours per day in TV viewing.

Certainly the advent of television is likely to have profound influence upon family life in America, and upon the ways in which ideas and attitudes will be formed. The enormous expense involved in producing television programs and operating its stations may sharply restrict the number of programs

[24] Dallas W. Smythe, "Television and Its Educational Implications," *Elementary English*, 27 (January, 1950), 42.

[25] Address to the Theatre Owners of America, Chicago, Sept. 25, 1948.

[26] Smythe, *op. cit.*, p. 46.

available and the range of viewpoint represented by TV shows in America. The Milton Berle slapstick program, for example, is reputed to cost $20,000 per week to produce, and Philco is said to spend more than $15,000 per week on its weekly "theater" program.[27]

The significance of these facts for schools is effectively expressed by Smythe in the excellent article already cited:[28]

What can the schools do about it? They can orient their pupils toward the real world we live in to a greater degree than is now done. A conspicuous opportunity lies before teachers in the humanities, especially in the field of English. Our curricula in these fields are heavily weighted with literature—prose and poetry—and with drama. But our population, once it leaves school, pays precious little attention to such material. Instead, we find that reading rates low on all studies of how people spend their leisure time . . . In terms of hours, average radio listening exceeds magazine reading in the order of 10 to 1. It exceeds newspaper reading by a very wide but flexible margin (depending on the city). It exceeds book-reading more than it does magazines. . . . Increasingly our "literature" and "drama" will grow to consist of what is seen over TV.

The objectives are simple. Selective use of the media should be encouraged, based ultimately on respect for the dignity of man. And the pupils should be encouraged to make known to the stations . . . their considered judgments on the program fare they are offered. . . . It goes without saying that before they can teach such things, teachers should practice such rights and responsibilities themselves.

FOR FURTHER READING

Allen, Harold B., "Mass Pressure on Radio and Journalism," *English Journal*, 38 (October, 1949), 447–453.

Corey, Stephen M., "Audio-Visual Materials of Instruction," *Forty-eighth Yearbook of the National Society for the Study of Education*, Part I. Edited by Nelson B. Henry. Chicago: University of Chicago Press, 1949.

[27] *Ibid.*, p. 45.   [28] *Ibid.*, p. 52.

DeBoer, John J., "Radio and Children's Emotions," *School and Society*, Sept. 16, 1939, p. 369.

Herzberg, Max J., *Radio and English Teaching*. New York: Appleton-Century-Crofts, Inc., 1941.

Levenson, William B., *Teaching through Radio*. New York: Rinehart & Company, Inc., 1945.

Public Service Responsibilities of Broadcast Station Licencees. Washington: Federal Communications Commission, March, 1946.

Smythe, Dallas W., *An Inventory of (Non-Commercial) Educational Radio Programming*. With assistance from Jennie N. Smythe and Howard H. Hyle. Urbana, Ill.: Institute of Communications Research, University of Illinois, August, 1949. (Mimeographed.)

Smythe, Dallas W., "Television and Its Educational Implications," *Elementary English*, 27 (January, 1950), 41–52.

Spingarn, Jerome H., *Radio Is Yours*. Public Affairs Pamphlet No. 121. New York: Public Affairs Committee, 1946.

Woelfel, Norman, and I. K. Tyler, *Radio and the School*. Yonkers-on-Hudson: World Book Company, 1945.

Chapter 13. AUDIO-VISUAL AIDS IN THE ENGLISH CLASSROOM

OVERVIEW

A survey of the development of educational practices and procedures reveals that the use of audio-visual aids, or multisensory aids, has always been an integral part of good education. Good teachers have always recognized that education and life are one and have used everything at their command to vitalize the learning process through the five senses. Realizing that anything the eye sees or the ear hears, anything that impinges on the other senses—all are aids to instruction—they made use of the blackboard, pictures, excursions, models, charts, slides, dramatizations, and graphs long before the terms audio-visual or multisensory were used to designate them; and they continue to use them wherever they serve the learning process, along with the newer technological advances made by our civilization, such as movies, radio, recording devices, and television.

Although instruction at the junior and senior high school levels is more highly specialized than at lower levels, the basic objectives of instruction in language arts remain the same: communication and appreciation. Because of their wide range of abilities and background, the members of these heterogeneous groups are not equally capable of interpreting verbal symbols. Multisensory aids, properly utilized to enrich and supplement the curriculum, are potential sources of great power in the hands of a skillful teacher to extend the range of vicarious experiences for all students. In providing perceptual and auditory experience as a basis for language development, these aids enable those students who are not facile verbally to bring experience to the printed page.

Brief visits to various classrooms in America revealed the following activities as typical of work being carried on in the English classroom:

In classroom A, students had set up a newspaper staff. They were practicing what they were learning about a newspaper by putting out a newspaper of their own.

In classroom B, a committee reported animatedly on the results of a field trip to a local settlement house, part of a unit on knowing the community.

In classroom C students in makeshift costumes were presenting a modernized version of *Julius Caesar* to an enthralled class. Even the window washers had paused in their labors to watch and listen.

In classroom D, students were presenting a marionette show depicting scenes from a favorite book.

In classroom E, students were watching a film for the second time. The film was stopped at points where the class raised questions, and at the conclusion, the instructor helped them to summarize their findings.

In classroom F, the instructor was showing a filmstrip on the relationship of words within a sentence. When students asked questions, she quickly turned the frames backward and forward to clarify points.

In classroom G, students were rehearsing talks which they had prepared to accompany slides (borrowed from the public library) illustrating their favorite book characters. The program was to be presented in the auditorium.

In classroom H, colorful book jackets which adorned the bulletin strip above the blackboard on three sides of the room called attention to the latest library releases. Posters, made by the students, illustrated their favorite books. The class was listening to book reviews presented and illustrated by their own members.

In classroom I, a teacher was showing postcards and photographs on a screen by means of an opaque projector. She was telling about her travels in the British Isles to enrich the background of students who were becoming acquainted with English poets and writers.

In classroom J, students were using the tape recorder to listen to their own voices in the interpretation of poetry. In another corner of the room, a student was ready to play recordings made by the poets themselves, or by professionals.

On the door of classroom K was a sign, "Please do not disturb. We are listening to a radio broadcast."

In classroom L, students were presenting a simulated radio script. The "dummy microphone" consisted of an eraser poised on a yardstick.

In classroom M, a student was pointing out places in the news on three maps: a world map, a map of the United States, and a state map.

In classroom N, students were reading books, pamphlets, and brochures to find information on a group project.

In each classroom, student interest was high; in each instance the class was making use of multisensory aids to learning. As Edgar Dale [1] has pointed out so ably in presenting his "Cone of Experience," the learning process is most direct when we provide opportunities for direct experience, and it is most abstract when we use verbal symbols or abstractions of experience. In between, moving from the concrete to the abstract, we find the contrived experience, dramatic participation, demonstrations, field trips, exhibits, motion pictures, radio, recordings, still pictures, charts, graphs, maps, and diagrams.

Availabilities

It is a common misconception that there is a dearth of audio-visual material available for use in the English classroom, but a glance at a listing of motion pictures, slides, filmstrips, and recordings compiled by Rita J. Kenny and Edward T. Schofield [2] should dispel this concept. Prepared as a service

[1] See bibliography at the end of this chapter.
[2] See bibliography.

to teachers of English in junior and senior high schools, this listing includes those materials which will assist in the teaching of basic skills in the use of oral and written English, as well as those materials which will help to develop an understanding and appreciation of literature. The list is presented in eight sections: English literature; American Literature; Literature of Other Lands and Times; The Mechanics of English; Books and Libraries; Modern Media of Communication; Business English; Biography.

The teaching of Shakespeare, for example, has been the subject of controversy among members of the profession, as well as among lay critics, largely because of those methods of presentation based solely on structural analysis and interpretation. How much more meaningful, and how fascinating, the world of Shakespeare would become to a student whose teacher made available to him these audio-visual aids to learning:

Coronet Instructional Films, 65 E. South Water St., Chicago 1.
England: Background of Literature (10 min., sound). Shows London as the inspiration of Chaucer, Dickens and Browning; the countryside, which was so meaningful to Shakespeare, Keats, and Kipling; and the sea, as Coleridge, Conrad, and Masefield wrote of it.

British Information Services, 30 Rockeller Plaza, New York 20.
Julius Caesar, Act III, Scene 2 (19 min., sound). Screen version of the forum scene, presenting the speeches of Brutus and Antony. An unforgettable example of rabble-rousing.

Teaching Film Custodians, Inc., 25 W. 43rd St., New York 18.
Master Will Shakespeare (11 min., sound). A brief story of the life of Shakespeare which includes scenes from *Romeo and Juliet* and other plays.

Romeo and Juliet (39 min., sound). Excerpts from the MGM production. The film follows the love story from the first meeting through the final scene in the tomb.

Hoffberg Productions, Inc., 620 Ninth Ave., New York 19.
Memories of Shakespeare (30 min., sound). The life of Shakespeare: his birthplace, the school, the Globe Theater, the Memorial Theater, his retirement at Stratford-on-Avon.

Eastin Pictures Company, Davenport, Iowa.

Othello (40 min., sound). An excellent cast in the principal scenes from this famous play.

Young America Films, Inc., 18 E. 41st St., New York 17. Filmstrips.

As You Like It (50 frames). A pictorial synopsis of the play based on scenes from the United Artists motion picture, with Laurence Olivier.

Hamlet (60 frames). A pictorial synopsis of the play based on the Laurence Olivier screen version.

Introduction to William Shakespeare (41 frames). A brief survey of the life and times of Shakespeare.

Macbeth (45 frames). A pictorial synopsis of the play based on scenes from the Orson Welles screen version.

A Midsummer-Night's Dream (53 frames). A pictorial synopsis of the play based on scenes from the Warner Brothers motion picture.

Romeo and Juliet (62 frames). A pictorial synopsis of the play based on scenes from the MGM motion picture.

Shakespeare's Theater (43 frames). Illustrates the nature and structure of the Elizabethan theater by showing how a group of students reconstructed Shakespeare's Globe Theater as one phase of their introduction to his plays.

E. L. Morthole, 2216 Greenwood Ave., Evanston Ill. Filmstrips.

The Macbeth Country (58 frames). Includes scenes of Cawdor Castle, Inverness, Dunsinane, and MacDuff's Castle.

Stratford-on-Avon with Warwick and Kenilworth (57 frames, color). Shows interiors of Anne Hathaway's cottage, castles of Warwick and Kenilworth.

Columbia Recording Corporation, 1473 Barnum Ave., Bridgeport, Conn. Recordings.

An Album of Shakespearean Song (3 records, 78 rpm, 30 min.). Songs from *As You Like It, Twelfth Night, The Tempest, Love's Labour's Lost, Measure for Measure, Much Ado about Nothing.* Sung by Mordecai Bauman, baritone, accompanied by Ernst Victor Wolff at the harpsichord.

Hamlet (6 excerpts, 3 records, 78 rpm, 30 min.). Readings by Maurice Evans.

Julius Caesar (11 records, 78 rpm, 1½ hours). Recorded by

Orson Welles and the Mercury Theater Players. Orson Welles also acts as narrator.

RCA Victor, Camden, N. J. Recordings.

Hamlet (3 records). Reading by Laurence Olivier.

Studidisc: Audio-Visual Division, Popular Science Publishing Company, 353 Fourth Ave., New York 10. Recordings.

A Midsummer-Night's Dream (78 rpm, 10 min.). Contents include Act II, Scene 2; Act III, Scenes 1 and 2.

On Shakespeare (78 rpm, 1 min.) by John Milton. An effective reading of this sonnet.

Linguaphone Institute, 30 Rockefeller Plaza, New York 20. Recordings.

Shakespearean Records (5 records, 78 rpm, 50 min.). Famous speeches from *King Richard the Second, Merchant of Venice, As You Like It, The Tempest, King Henry the Fifth, Othello, Hamlet,* and *Midsummer-Night's Dream.*

If in addition, the teacher employed dramatization of various scenes, supplemented by a recording of student attempts; had available maps and pictures of the Shakespeare country; had a model of the Shakespearean stage—the possibilities are endless—how could Shakespeare be termed "dull stuff"?

If the class is interested in word study, how much enrichment can be gained from these sources:

Coronet Instructional Films, 65 E. South Water St., Chicago 1. Films.

Build Your Vocabulary (10 min., sound). Mr. Thompson, who finds himself at a loss for words at a meeting, takes a cue from his son and embarks upon a systematic campaign for vocabulary improvement.

Do Words Ever Fool You? (11 min., sound). False impressions created through misuse of words in advertising and at home. Shows how words, if not used carefully, may become confusing.

How to Judge Facts (10 min., sound). This film helps students to establish a judicious mental attitude toward fact finding. They learn to guard against platitudes, false analogies, assumptions, and double meanings as well as to gain a new clarity in mental perspective.

Improve Your Pronunciation (10 min., sound). Walter begins to realize his pronunciation shortcomings. He formulates a program for improvement by using three basic rules: pronounce each sound correctly, pronounce each syllable, use accepted pronunciation.

Spelling Is Easy (10 min., sound). Five rules for learning to spell, built around the story of a boy who is writing a report.

We Discover the Dictionary (10 min., sound). In writing a letter, students learn about guide words, spelling, definitions, diacritical marks, and kinds of dictionaries.

Who Makes Words? (10 min., sound). In a practical situation, students learn that some words are borrowed, some are invented, and some come about through changes in spelling or meaning. They learn the important ways by which our language grew.

Curriculum Films, Inc., 1775 Broadway, New York 19. Filmstrips.

How to Develop a Good Vocabulary (48 frames, color). A student learns to develop a formula for vocabulary building: keep a notebook for new words, look up the new words in the dictionary, and use them correctly.

Importance of Vocabulary in Communication (56 frames, color). The experience of a French child who knows no English and is lost in New York illustrates the importance of an ever-growing vocabulary.

Radio Arts Guild, Wilmington, Ill. Recordings.

Drama of Everyday Words (78 rpm, 10 min.). Alexander McQueen tells informative and entertaining anecdotes about the derivation of English words.

Greek Words in Our Language (78 rpm, 5 min.). Alexander McQueen tells anecdotes about the derivation of words from the Greek.

Latin Words in Our Language (78 rpm, 5 min.). Alexander McQueen tells anecdotes about the derivation of our words from Latin.

Sounds That Make Sense (78 rpm, 5 min.). Alexander McQueen tells anecdotes about the enrichment of our language through sound.

Words That Got into Trouble (78 rpm, 5 min.). Alexander McQueen tells anecdotes about the derivation of some words.

Further sources of information which must include releases of current materials are listed in the bibliography.

UTILIZATION AND EVALUATION

If the teacher has determined his basic objectives and purposes and knows the materials that are available, the use of multisensory aids becomes a part of his whole, integrated approach to teaching. Limitations exist only in the skill and imagination of the teacher. Procedures that are basic to effective teaching with any instructional aid are basic in the use of multisensory aids: preparation, presentation, and follow-up. Within this concept, the teacher should train students to utilize these aids as they would use a library book, another supplementary aid to learning.

The following outline has been prepared in the hope that it will serve as a guide to good utilization and evaluation, for the two go hand in hand.

PREPARATION

A. Selection of the material.
   1. Is it authentic?
   2. Is it up to date?
   3. Will it help to attain the objectives set up?
   4. Is it available at the time it fits the lesson?
   5. Is it understandable to the students at the grade level where it is to be used?
B. Integration with the total learning situation.
   1. Is the purpose for using the material clear in the mind of the teacher?
   2. Is the purpose for using the material clear in the minds of the students?
   3. Is the material being used at the time that it fits the lesson?
C. Physical aspects of the environment.
   1. If pictures, posters, models, or exhibits are used, is provision made for pupils to move about freely to view and study them?
   2. If radio broadcasts, records, or transcriptions are used, are

arrangements made for students to sit in informal group-
ings near the loud speaker?

3. If projected materials are used, are provisions made for
room darkening, adequate ventilation, proper seating for
good vision, safeguarding the equipment?

PRESENTATION

A. Physical arrangements relegated to unobtrusiveness.

B. Use of the aid as often as instructional needs dictate.

FOLLOW-UP

A. Discussion of the material presented.
1. Did students find answers to points they were to look for?
2. Did it clarify points not understood?
3. Is further clarification necessary?

B. Further activities stimulated by this learning experience.
1. Are there ways of applying what has been learned?
2. Have further research and learning been stimulated?

C. Evaluation of the material.
1. Did students indicate that the objectives had been
achieved?
2. Could these objectives have been achieved equally as well
or better by any other means?

BIBLIOGRAPHY

Because of space limitations, it is impossible to include a complete listing. However, the following, it is hoped, will be helpful
in giving an overview of the numerous sources of available information and materials.

General

"Audio-Visual Materials of Instruction," *Forty-eighth Yearbook
of the National Society for the Study of Education*, Part I,
Chicago: University of Chicago Press, 1949. Pp. 320.

Dale, Edgar, *Audio-Visual Methods in Teaching*. New York: The
Dryden Press, Inc., 1946. Pp. 546.

Dent, Ellsworth C., *The Audio-Visual Handbook*. Chicago: Society for Visual Education, 1946. Pp. 226.

Kenny, Rita J., and Edward T. Schofield, "Audio-Visual Aids for the English Teacher," Part I, October; Part II, November, 1949. Newark, N. J.: *Audio-Visual Guide.*

McKown, Harry C., and Albin B. Roberts, *Audio-Visual Aids to Instruction.* New York: McGraw-Hill Book Company, Inc., 1949. Pp. 605.

Periodicals

AER Journal, Association for Education by Radio, 228 North La Salle St., Chicago 1, Ill. Published monthly except June, July, and August.

Business Screen, 157 E. Erie St., Chicago 11, Ill. Eight issues a year.

Educational Film Guide, The H. W. Wilson Company, 950 University Ave., New York. Published from September through April.

Educational Screen, 64 East Lake St., Chicago, Ill. Published monthly except July and August.

Film and Radio Guide, 172 Renner Ave., Newark, N. J. Published from October through June.

See and Hear, 157 E. Erie St., Chicago 11, Ill. Published nine times a year.

Newsletters published by the universities of Indiana, Illinois, Iowa, Kansas, Minnesota, Missouri, Nebraska, Ohio State, and Wisconsin.

Films

Coronet Instructional Films, Inc., catalogues. 919 N. Michigan Ave., Chicago 11, Ill.

Educational Film Guide. New York: The H. W. Wilson Company, cumulative annual catalogue with supplement service. Title, index, subject classification, brief descriptions, frequent comments.

Educators Guide to Free Films. Randolph, Wis.: Educators Progress Service. Listing of films and slide films revised annually. Title, index, subject classification, cross index, and brief descriptions.

Encyclopedia Britannica Films. Catalogue. Wilmette, Ill. Free catalogue of available films by subject and title.

Film Council of America, 12th at Lamarr, Austin, Tex.

Films from Britain. British Information Services, 30 Rockefeller Plaza, New York 20.

Falconer, Vera M., *Filmstrips*. New York: McGraw-Hill Book Company, Inc., 1948. A descriptive index by title and subject classification. Descriptions.

Keystone View Company. Catalogues. Meadville, Pa. Free extensive listing of 3½-by-4-in. slides; materials and directions for slide making.

One Thousand and One, The Blue Book of Non-theatrical Films. Chicago: Educational Screen, 64 E. Lake St. Annual listing of films, classified in subject groups.

Selected Educational Motion Pictures, A descriptive Encyclopedia. Washington: American Council on Education, 1942. Pp. 372.

S.V.E. Educational Motion Picture Catalog. Chicago: Society for Visual Education, Inc. Free. Brief descriptions of educational films, film strips, and 2-by-2-in. slides under topical headings.

United States Government Films, Castle Films, Division of United World Films. New York: 30 Rockefellei Plaza. Free. Catalogues describing the U.S. Office of Education Visual Training Units, Army and Navy Training Films, and U.S. Department of Agriculture Films.

Teaching Film Custodians, 25 West 43rd St., New York. Listing of literature films—excerpts from feature photoplays—available for English classes.

The best sources of information for teachers will be found in the film libraries of the local school system, state university, or state department of education. Current news about film releases will be found in periodicals, listed above.

Radio

Levenson, William, *Teaching through Radio*. New York: Rinehart & Company, Inc., 1945. Pp. 474.

Listenables. Recommended listing prepared by Radio Committee, N.C.T.E., Leon Hood, Chairman, 61 Lafayette Ave., East Orange, N. J. Weekly during school term. Includes annotations, comments, and occasional reviews.

"Look and Listen," *Elementary English*. Monthly column devoted to current news in audio-visual field with emphasis on classroom utilization.

Radio Network Listings. American Broadcasting Company, Rockefeller Center, New York. Columbia Broadcasting System, Inc., 485 Madison Ave., New York 22. Mutual Broadcasting

Company, 1440 Broadway, New York. National Broadcasting Company, RCA Building, Radio City, New York.

Radio Script Catalog, 5th Ed., Educational Radio Script and Transcription Exchange. Washington: Federal Security Agency, U.S. Office of Education.

Radio and Television Bibliography. Washington: Federal Security Agency, U.S. Office of Education.

Reid, Seerley, and Norman Woelfel, "How to Judge a School Broadcast." Available on loan from Educational Radio-Script Exchange, U. S. Office of Education, Washington.

Sterner, Alice P., *Radio, Motion Pictures and Reading Interests*, A Study of High School Pupils. New York: Bureau of Publications, Teachers College, Columbia University, 1947.

Sterner, Alice, *A Course of Study in Radio Appreciation*. Newark, N. J.: Audio-Visual Guides.

Waller, Judith C., *Radio, the Fifth Estate*. Boston: Houghton Mifflin Company, 1946.

Woelfel, Norman, and Keith Tyler, *Radio and the School*. Yonkers-on-Hudson, N. Y.: World Book Company, 1945. Pp. 358.

Recordings

Bernstein, Julius C., "Recording and Playback Machines: Their Function in the English Classroom," *The English Journal*, 38 (June, 1949), 330–341.

Company Catalogues. Columbia Recording Corporation, 1473 Barnum Ave., Bridgeport, Conn. Decca Records, Inc., 50 West 57th St., New York. General Records Company, 1600 Broadway, New York. RCA Victor Records, Inc., Camden, N. J.

Killgallon, P. A., "Recorded Sound Aids," *Elementary English*, 27 (March, 1950), 171–181.

Miles, J. Robert, *Recordings for School Use: A Catalog of Appraisals*. Yonkers-on-Hudson, N. Y.: World Book Company, 1942. Annotates and appraises the recordings listed. Deals with utilization of recordings, facts about records and equipment, as well as the selection and operation of record players.

Transcription Exchange Service, U. S. Office of Education, Washington. Free. Catalogue of transcriptions and recordings available to schools for rent or loan; many recorded broadcasts.

Free and Inexpensive Teaching Aids

Aids to Teaching about the United Nations, Office of Press and Radio Relations, National Education Association, Washington 6.

British Information Service, 30 Rockefeller Plaza, New York 20. Beautiful pictures, maps, pamphlets, on various aspects of the British Empire. Some free, some at nominal cost.

Catalogue of Business Sponsored Educational Material. New York: Committee on Consumer Relations in Advertising, Inc., 1945. Annotated lists of pictures, posters, movies, exhibits, etc., which are distributed without cost.

Educators' Index to Free Materials. Randolph, Wis.: Educators Progress Service. Comprehensive annotated listing organized under subject headings.

Sources of Free and Inexpensive Teaching Aids. Bruce Miller, Ontario, Calif. Sources of all types of aids, including those the pupils and teacher can make.

Heimers, Lili, Director, *Teaching Aids Service of the Library.* Upper Montclair, N. J.: New Jersey State Teachers College. Mimeographed listings on various subjects, giving annotated listings of pictures, exhibits, recordings, films, charts, publications, etc., with prices indicated. Listings range in price.

Chapter 14. ENGLISH IN THE
UNIFIED STUDIES COURSE

WHY AN INTEGRATED COURSE?

Why are an increasing number of schools experimenting with integrated courses?

Information is valuable only as it is integrated in the lives of people. The integration of learning for living is the whole of education; therefore we must give attention to it.

"Do you teach subjects or boys and girls?" was asked decades ago. We know that education is not amassing or covering blocks of facts or information or areas of learning. Facts are worth nothing in themselves; they are valuable only as they are used in life. The ability to integrate information for use is the ability to use the mind. This ability needs to be trained and developed.

Advantages of the integrated course. When two or more traditional subjects are combined, the possibilities are increased for integrating the subject matter and integrating it with life.

A fresh start with a new kind of course can mean freedom from the debris of traditional courses; it can mean progress just as being free from the moats and walls and social classifications of feudalism was an advantage to our pioneers. Indeed, we can take the pioneer spirit as our guide. We may call it experiment and find that it is continuous adventure. The bell that rings for the integrated course can be a liberty bell—liberty to learn.

An integrated course has human advantages. Students who have chosen it rather than two traditional courses have

given as a reason that it is easier to adjust to one teacher than
to two. The teacher, of course, can know the boys and girls
better. Perhaps the chief advantage is that the boys and girls
have more time to learn to work with each other.

Learning and working with others may be the most important part of education. People in our modern society need to
know how to get along with others. We want people to be
integrated within themselves and with society. Book learning or theory by itself cannot provide all that is needed. When
boys and girls are together in school and naturally interested
in each other, there is an opportunity for learning to cooperate. We must learn how to use this opportunity. High school
boys and girls are full of life, and we should help them to
make the most of it. They should prepare not merely for
living in the future. Their life now is very important. Living
in the present can be the best preparation through planned
practice for living in the future.

When two or more traditional courses are integrated, the
students should learn more than they could learn in separate
courses. The subject matter of history or other social studies
can mean more if the students talk and write about it. They
can learn to talk and write more effectively if they talk and
write about substantial material.

The combined course is not merely the addition of two or
more courses. When two courses are combined, there is a
different quality just as there is a different quality when two
chemicals are combined. It is, therefore, a mistake to judge
an integrated course by the same standards that are applied
to the traditional courses. Teachers in traditional English
courses in one school were critical of the integrated courses
because the students who came into their classes after a year
or two in integrated courses did not know the subject matter
that these teachers had been teaching. A teacher said that a
boy had not learned anything in his integrated course because
he had not even heard of her pet grammatical terms.

Evaluation in the integrated course. When students in
integrated courses take the same objective tests at the end

of the year that the students in the traditional courses take, there is usually a greater variation in the scores of the students in the integrated courses. The reason may be that, with greater freedom and diversity, the individuals have acquired different kinds and degrees of learning. The students in the integrated courses do very well on reading tests. The reason probably is that they do more reading and more kinds of reading. In mechanics of composition tests, even though they have studied very little formal grammar, they may do as well as the students who have been drilling all year. In a history test of matching and identifying names, dates, and facts in a prescribed text the students in an integrated class did very poorly. It would be unfair to say that that in itself proved they had not learned so much history as the other students had.

We might think of the tests in this way: What have the students learned that these tests did not check? The students had grown in readiness and flexibility in talking and writing. They could talk about the problems of people in history. They might have done very well on a test requiring thoughtful interpretation. How well might the students in the traditional courses have done on tests that gave the students in the diversified course an opportunity to register what they had learned? Probably we shall have to have new types of tests for integrated courses.

There was a boy who ran into a real test during his summer vacation. He worked in the office of one of his father's friends whose avocation was history. The employer said to the father,

How can a boy his age know so much history? He has read part of Plutarch's *Lives* and Gibbon's *Decline and Fall of the Roman Empire*. He not only knows what the *Koran* is, but he has had a copy and has read parts of it. Listen to the subjects we have been discussing: Why the murder of Pompey in Egypt is a better subject for a tragedy than the murder of Julius Caesar in Rome. The Crusades as a solution of an unemployment problem and an advancing stage in international relations. Why the Reformation did not take place until after the invention of printing. What five or six bragging explorers might have said to prove they deserved to have this country named for them. What a pope meant when he said, "If there is a future life, Richelieu has much to answer for; if not, then he lived a successful life." How truly did Gandhi speak when he said, "Time runs always in favor of the sufferer (oppressed) for the simple reason that tyranny becomes more and more exposed to it as it is continued."

A girl in an integrated class said of a friend, "She reads pages and pages just to answer questions. She never wants to talk about history."

An interest in talking about history ought to be one of the tests of a history course. An English teacher pondered that idea for a number of years while she was teaching Stephen Vincent Benet's *John Brown's Body* to eleventh graders who were studying United States history with another teacher. Though she tried in every way she knew, she never found that the students could talk about the historical background of *John Brown's Body* in a way to help the English class. The individual students may have correlated the subjects in some ways unknown to her, but she began to question the assumption that students will correlate what they learn and to reflect that knowledge is valuable in proportion as it is correlated.

She noted that other teachers find their work hampered because the students are unable to read and write about their subjects. The fact that there is so little carry-over from one course to another indicates deficiencies in the curriculum. The carry-over is the hardest and most important part of education, and that is what we have neglected. It is too much to expect students to do it by themselves. There are many different study skills they need which we have not helped them learn.

Teachers who decide to organize an integrated course look for a plan or course of study to follow. They should not expect to find one ready-made. The essential quality of the integrated course is its life. It must live for boys and girls and be an integral part of their lives; therefore it will always be flexible and will always be changing. It will be continuous exploration.

If two subjects are combined in one class that meets two periods a day, can the students learn more about both subjects than they could learn in separate courses? A description of a week's work in one class will show the interlacing of two subjects. It is not an example of integration at its best but at low ebb when it is just two subjects put together.

A TEACHER-PLANNED PROGRAM BY STUDENT REQUEST

The students in a tenth-grade class that was a combination of world history and English had been giving reports and wanted a change. They had no suggestion except that the teacher plan the work and give them the assignments a week in advance. The teacher was disappointed in the lack of student initiative. The teacher of such classes must expect disappointments; she needs a fortifying philosophy.

She submitted this plan, which the students accepted without protest or interest:

BARBARIANS

World History, pages 151–159, 176–183

Vandals
Goths
Huns, Attila
Franks, Charlemagne
Norsemen, Vikings, Norse mythology—Thor, Odin . . .

Monday, Tuesday, and Wednesday hand in the pages of your notebook to show how you are working and how much you have done. Have essential information on all the subjects and as much interesting information as you can find. Look up every subject in more than one book besides the text. Copy as much as you wish, and be sure to put quotation marks around everything you copy. Give the sources of your information.

Friday, hand in the section of your notebook on the barbarians. All the work will be judged for the quality of the information, the organization of the material and the mechanics of writing (sentence structure, spelling, etc.).

On Friday there will be a test on the barbarians.

"How can you give us a test," the students asked, "when we don't all know the same things?"

She said, "I'll try to think of a test that will not catch you for what you do not know but will give you an opportunity to tell what you know."

On Friday the teacher said, "The title of this test is *As You Like It*. The first question is on the board. You may write on the subject in general or in particular in any way you like. If you do not write on the first question all the period, you may write your own questions and answer them."

The first question had been on the board since Wednesday, and the teacher had suggested that the students think about it, but apparently they had not done so. Some said they had never heard of a pure race or a mixed race and had no ideas whatever on the subject. The teacher said that a pure race would be one in which there had not been marriages with other races. The purpose of the question was to stimulate their thinking about what they had read, to correlate and organize information in their own minds to see how it applied to modern world conditions. This was the question:

Judging by what you know about the barbarians, do you think there could be a pure race in Europe in modern times? If there is not a pure race, could there be a superior race? How likely is it that the ancestors of some Americans were barbarians? Do you think that belonging to a pure race or to a mixed race would be anything to be proud of?

The test papers were interesting reading. The teacher resolved to try never to ask students to write what is not interesting. A few quotations will show that the students were using their minds:

1. I think I can truthfully say that there are no pure races in Europe because of migrations and wars and intermarriage. The barbarians naturally fierce and warlike would find occasion to

fight and, if they won, naturally they would settle down to keep their prisoners from defiance, and naturally they would probably marry. If they married, there probably would be little half-barbarians and little half-something-elses.

2. To be a superior race, there must be a pure race.˙ Myself, I defy anyone to define the word "superior." Superior in what?

3. There is no pure race in Europe. In order to prove this, I will write a short essay on what I have read, using the barbarians as an example.

Years ago there were many tribes of barbarians. Each one of them at some time or other conquered some other races of people. In turn, these races were also conquered. And so went on the history of the world. As these races of people were conquered, their tribes split and intermarried with other people of the world. Thus, there could *not* be a pure race.

I think that belonging to a pure race is not half so wonderful as belonging to a mixed race. It's hard to explain, but the Lord would never give everything perfect to one race of people. In a mixed race you have everything the Almighty will give you. This is the only way I can put into words what I mean.

Yes, I think that some Americans may be descended from the old barbarians. In fact, I think many people are descended from the old barbarians.

People could be proud of barbarian ancestors because every race or tribe has contributed something to the world.

I don't think that belonging to a pure race would be anything to boast about. It would prove that your race was unsociable in not being able to get along with other races.

4. There were many thousands of migrations. This means that different races overlapped in territories so that there could not likely be a pure race.

The barbarians were people with no culture. They didn't care for anyone else. They got there own food for themselves, and if any other person came around they would fight. It was not until they began to have a community that they really were getting out of the barbarian stage.

5. There can be no pure race, because of the Barbarian. The Barbarian sweeping over all of Europe and Asia. And the Tale if true of the Viking coming into the America's.

If there is a pure race, it would have to be in the darkest part of Africa. The most impentral part. Where there might not have been any people. So there is still nothing that say's wheter anyone has entered the darkest part of Africa.

One Barbarian on having entered that place could make a whole colonie impure. Which would mean that there would be no pure race there.

Hitler said that the Germany was a pure race. If any race was pure it could not be pure. Because of all the fighting going on in that neighborhood of the country. As the Huns and Goths and the Romans fought in that vicinity.

With all the warfare and steeling of Women, and the Barbarian going all over the Continanite and into Asia and Asia Minor there is no possible way that any one race could be pure. Even if there were reaching into the darkest Jungul.

Since there is no pure race there could be no Superior Race. Which means that all races are equal. And there can be no rating of one race over another.

6. I think a mixture of race is very good for all people would become more tollerant, no more people like Hitler could induce a Country that they are the master race. If all the people had a pure race then everone would be better than everyone else and wars would be spouting all of the time. If there were half pure race and half mixed races the pure races would persecute the mixed races and the mixed races would feel under the rest and would never amount to much. If everyone thought everyone else was equal to them then the world could unite and wars and differences of government and religion could be made tollerent.

The individual questions were as different as the interests and abilities of the students who wrote them. Thirty students in a few minutes thought of more questions than the teacher could have formulated. The variety reinforced the teacher's theory that if students have the freedom, they can find what interests them. A few of the questions and answers will show how alert the students were while reading.

1. What could people learn from the barbarians?

People could learn from them that war and slavery does not work. They might have used barbarism as a steppingstone to civilization.

One good thing about the barbarians is that they believed in freedom. When a tribe was defeated, it hardly ever stayed that way. The people would rise against the government and start out where the old government quit.

There was one thing wrong with them. They would make the same mistakes they fought against.

2. Did the Visigoths fight for the fun of it?

The Visigoths were the kind of people that liked a home better than fighting. Yes, the Visigoths left their home once and had a few battles but what they really wanted was a peaceful home and a good living. A lot of people think they just wanted to fight but I don't think so. They fought for their homes and living and liberty.

3. Were the Huns smarter than the Romans?

Yes I think they were because they were the first to leave there home for something better. They had battles that proves the men were smart, they had to be smart to defeat the Romans. At one time they worked for the Romans and they captured so much territory that the head of it by Attila recieved 21,000 lbs of Gold. But the Huns made a mistake like the Germans and were defeated.

4. Do you think the Norsemen discovered America?

Yes, I do because 986 Bjarni set sail from Norway and was going to greenland to see his father on the way a big storm came up and he lost his way and he went by some strange territory but he did not land because he was in a hurry to see his father in Greenland to celebrate Christmas. He finally got to Greenland and there he say Leif Erickson and told him about his voyage so Leif said when I grow up I would like to explore this new land and some years later, when he was a man he did go out and explore. 1000 A.D. he left Iceland and travelled for days and finnally he landed in what is now called New Foundland he didn't explored it much then he went past what is now know as Novia Scotia. He kept on going Southward and landed in what is now know as New England for the winter he went inland on some river, which I don't know the name of. Their he builts some huts and lived for the winter. In the next few years he made a few trips back to Iceland and Greenland and brought back some people. there was his 2 brothers and a sister. A brother didn't like the sister and treated her cruley so she told her other brother to kill him. So they end up both dead and they other people went back to the old world.

5. How did the Huns live?

They lived on horseback, and they didn't even cook their food. At nite time they would just lean forward and go to sleep.

6. Where were the Vikings buried?

They were buried in the ships.

7. What did the Vikings like best?

Their ale and eels.

The students were not repeating what had been said in class. There had been no class discussion. The teacher makes a mistake when she thinks she must cover everything in class. The only classwork on the barbarians had been a series of short dramatic presentations on Wednesday.

What about the use of language in the student writing? There is a sense for vivid, direct expression, and there are many errors. The teacher said to one boy, "You can write more accurately than that, can't you?" He said, "Oh, sure. I wasn't thinking how I was writing. I was just thinking about what I was writing." Ideas come first and then ways of expressing them accurately. He will be ready to learn the ways of accuracy if he realizes he has something to say. He will be ready to learn from a teacher who has discriminating appreciation for his ideas. With his positive attitude he can teach himself accuracy of expression.

Student Reports

We know that young people learn more readily from each other than from an older person. We often hear that the best way to learn a thing is to teach it. Then why do we not let boys and girls learn by teaching each other?

It is hard for a teacher to sit still through poor reports, to suppress the old habit of taking command. She is bored when she is inactive. Let her reflect that every student is like her in that respect. One day after two months of student reports the teacher became impatient with what seemed to her dull and superficial reports. She asked this question: Can you learn more from a student at his worst than from a teacher at his best? Here are the answers of two students.

A student at his worst is better than a teacher at his best!

I think this statement is very true. A teacher talks as she would to an adult and often times far above our heads. Whereas a student talks more in our language. He uses words we understand, and when he uses a new word, most of the time he explains what it means. A teacher is stiff and formal when he talks. Kids usually are informal and the kids aren't afraid to interrupt sometimes to comment or ask questions.

I think we learn just about as much from a teacher as from a student if [underlined three times] we listen.

If a dull teacher starts to talk, I get bored and don't learn anything, but if an interesting student gets up, I listen and learn.

A teacher, after several years of experience with student reports, wrote:

Don't pupils and teachers get "terribly sick" of report after report? Haven't you been able to develop some new way of presentation?

In spite of efforts to discover new methods of presentation, the *report* remains our chief way of transmitting information after it has been gathered and organized. Of course, the old-fashioned stereotyped methods of reporting may become almost as uninteresting as the traditional recitation. While we still seek other methods, some of us have become convinced that there is no other way of oral presentation. The solution of this difficulty seems to be in the elaboration of the techniques of the report. Good illustrative material, especially if it is prepared for the occasion, always commands attention. A report will usually get attention if it makes good use of human-interest material. This may come in the form of narration, or may make use of a movie, a class trip, or brief dramatization. The panel, symposium, and discussion group are frequently used.

Creative pupils frequently interject excellent showmanship into their reporting. One committee reporting on the winning of Texas prepared a radio script that presented the episodes in the life of a family that moved to Texas from east of the Mississippi River while Texas was still a part of Mexico. The skillful unfolding of the story of this family was also the unfolding of the story of Texas. The broadcasting effect was obtained by the use of a microphone in an adjacent room, which was connected to a loudspeaker in the core room. Sound effects and music helped make the program sound "regular."

Last year a boy and girl who were reporting on slave life on a Southern plantation costumed themselves as carefully as for the stage and, staying entirely within character, told of the life and customs on an ante-bellum plantation.

A recent effective report was on the flags of the Latin-American republics. A sophomore girl made the flags accurately of colored paper. She displayed them, made necessary explanations, and answered questions. Later she conducted a quiz by showing a flag and asking that the name of the country which it represented be written. It should be noted that her oral presentation was reduced to a minimum, but that she had spent hours in research and construction.

A junior girl reporting on the development of democracy in America filled three large blackboards with simple line drawings like those so often shown drawn on the old-fashioned school slate. A man was represented by a circle for a head and simple lines drawn for trunk, arms, and legs. A house was simply two roof lines, with other lines that suggested the outside dimensions of sides, doors, windows, and so on. There were dozens of labeled drawings showing step by step various democratic developments. One label read, "The constitution provides: that no 'Title of Nobility shall be granted by the United States and . . .'" Above was a group of figures with noses tilted upward. Obvious tears of the aristocrats fell to the ground. Another drawing was labeled, "Women were granted the right to vote in the territory of Wyoming, December, 1869." Inside an outline of the borders of Wyoming a skirted figure dropped a ballot into a slotted box.

This girl's graphic presentation was a type of report very different from those that most of us remember in our own school days. Thus she made a contribution to the technique of the report and thus do we learn from year to year new ways of presentation.[1]

[1] MacConnell, Charles M., Ernest O. Melby, and Christian O. Arndt, *New Schools for a New Culture, Experimental Applications for Tomorrow*, pp. 66–67. New York: Harper & Brothers, 1943.

Giving a report is a social activity. As such it is learning democratic skills and techniques through practice. It is communicating with a group. It is successful or valuable as it communicates; therefore the student's purpose is to tell his classmates what he thinks will interest them and be valuable to them. A student should never give a report to exhibit his own erudition. That would not be communication, and it would breed antisocial characteristics.

"How do I know what will interest the class?" a student may protest. The answer is that learning what will interest the class is an important part of the assignment and valuable training for life activities.

The student who gives a report learns in the process to find, select, and present information. He learns by practice to integrate the skills of communication for a real purpose.

How about the students who listen to the reports? They have the social responsibility of helping the speaker to do as well as he can. They can learn to be active listeners. Many teachers have found that the students can learn most by taking notes. The teacher also takes notes, and then makes a test based on her notes. This method stimulates the responsibility of the speaker and gives finish and dignity to the whole process.

There is, of course, not just one way of planning student reports. A teacher may learn from the experiences of others who describe their methods in the books listed at the end of this chapter, but no one should look for ready-made plans because the essence of the integrated program is that it begins with the students as people. The boys and girls have different interests every day of the year.

Student planning of a program is an important part of student learning through participation. It is one of the arts of human relations that can never be caught in a tight formula but is always challenging because it is democracy in action.

A description of some programs of reports will show how students can work together. The teacher should keep reminding herself: Never do anything that the students can do.

The members of a world history-English class suggested in October that each student should tell something about a country. The class chose a chairman for the reports. He posted the program on the bulletin board and every day was chairman. The students had these instructions: Choose your country or part of a country and report on the people of the country at the present or at any time in the past. Do not try to tell everything at once. The following notes may give you suggestions:

The people. Who are they?
How do they make a living?
Living conditions:
   Standards of living for the majority of the people—houses, food, clothing.
   Social welfare.
   Health, sports, amusements.
Education for the total population.
Religion.
The background of history that explains why the people are what they are.
The famous people.
Art, architecture, music, literature.
Government.

The teacher was skeptical. This was superficial and scattered. For years she had advocated the chronological study of history. Her idea was to begin with primitive man and follow the textbook, but be ready to branch off at any time on subjects that interested the students. She had tried that for a year, and the students had not been as interested in the main line or the branches of history as she had hoped. She resolved this time to let the students take the lead. As she observed the way they worked, she admitted they were right and during the rest of the year noticed how many interests they had generated in this apparently superficial way. It really is good sense to get a panoramic view of any new subject.

The teacher resolved to follow the lesson revealed in the story of the boy who wrote, "Dear Aunt Ruth, Thank you for the book you sent me for Christmas. It tells more about penguins than I am interested in knowing." A teacher must put the outlines of her college courses and her old ideas about what students should cover in the background, while the students must be constantly asked, "What are you interested in knowing?"

After the reports on subjects scattered over the world, the class decided to organize the next set of reports around a central subject and chose the religions of the world. Then a boy asked, "Could I report on Ivan the Terrible? I have always wanted to know about him." He said he would be interested in hearing the reports of the others about religions, but he would rather spend his time on what he wanted to know. Several said they would like to hear about Ivan the Terrible but did not want to read about him. It was agreed that any one who did not want to read about religions would report on people. "Why can't we choose our own subjects all the time?" they asked. "Then if we miss any parts of history, you can tell us what they are and we will learn them." The teacher asked, "Could each of you find subjects and direct your own work for the rest of the year?" Diana said, "Oh, yes! There are so many things I want to know." She seemed to be speaking for the whole class.

"Now," the teacher said to herself, "we have discovered the way of freedom in learning. This method of self-motivation and group learning will accomplish everything we want."

The fall was sudden. Within two weeks it was Diana who led the complaint that the reports were boring. A boy said, "A teacher's business is to teach, not just to sit back and learn from the pupils." A girl threw this remark at the teacher, "If you ever knew anything, why didn't you tell it?"

The teacher took solitary refuge in reviewing history. All pioneering is difficult. Democracy in the history of the world has been opposed by those who would benefit from it and even by those who said they wanted it. If it took the feudal serfs so many hundred years to take their destinies into their own hands and come to America to be our ancestors and citizens, how can we expect boys and girls to pass from a "purely teacher-directed classroom" to democracy in two months?

Within three weeks, the fall turned into a bounce. The student committee in charge of the study program, without any prompting from the teacher, suggested student reports. The students said they must find a way to make the reports interesting. A girl said, "The reports would be interesting if they were on subjects that are interesting to us. Everyone is interested in sports; therefore I think we should study about sports from an historical point of view." Several students protested vehemently, saying that they were learning all they wanted to know about sports in other ways and that this was the one year in their lives, so far at least, to learn world history. The class agreed, and the teacher reflected that if students are free to choose their learning, they want to learn. The students decided that their next three studies would be (1) Palestine at the present time and its history and the crusades, (2) Russia, (3) famous scientists and their contributions to history. There would be a variety of group reports and single reports.

The students gave the teacher outlines of their reports, and she made copies on the duplicator in the office. Some made their own carbons for the duplicator because they wanted to illustrate their reports with charts or drawings. When a student gave his report, everyone in the class had a neat outline. He could add notes as he wished. This was note taking made easy. Each student gave the teacher one or two questions on his report to add to the general test. The students did most of the brain work, and the teacher did the mechanical work.

CLASS ORGANIZATION

The teacher should be an executive.
One class had this statement about committees:

The purpose of having committees is to make it possible to conduct the class in a democratic way and by so doing to learn the ways of democracy. To learn to think, plan, and work with others is to cultivate one of the abilities most necessary in civilized society. The possibilities for learning in a class are increased in direct proportion to the practice of democracy by the class. This means that the aim of all committees is to make the possibilities for learning as great as possible.

Executive Committee. The class officers are the Executive Committee. It may refer questions to other committees and may consider any questions that do not come within the province of other committees. [The class called this the Red Tape Committee.]

Progress Committee. This cφmmittee is responsible, with the teacher, for making the lessons as valuable to the students as possible. The Progress Committee will be trying constantly to answer these questions: How can the students learn most in the least time? How can they get the most experience in talking with people, in writing, in understanding the significance of what they read, in finding information that is interesting to them and will be useful to them?

Freedom Committee. This committee is organized on the basic principle of American life that everyone should have as much freedom as possible. Freedom is everyone's business and responsibility. Everyone needs to learn to manage himself, to discipline himself, to educate himself. A problem that the world is trying to solve and that the Freedom Committee will try to solve for this class is What can we do so that a few will not take away the freedom of the majority? If a class is to be free, one person or a few persons should not be so uncivilized as to take away the freedom to learn from the majority of the class. Everyone should at all times help the class do what it is trying to do.

Program Committee. This committee is responsible for special social activities of the class. It will contribute to the learning program by providing for the practice of English (reading aloud, speaking, etc.) in pleasant, social situations.

These fine words provided the machinery for democracy, but rather often there was chaos. The students took every advantage of freedom; they tried all the old tricks to provoke a teacher to be a dictator. Though they want to be grown up outside of school, they acted childish in school. A teacher will be disillusioned and defeated unless she can see the situation in perspective. She can get that perspective in the history of our country. It would seem as though everyone would have accepted the freedom that democracy gives, but democracy develops unevenly. How far on the road of history from feudalism to democracy is the organization of our schools? Is it like the organization for human relations we want in the life of our country? The provoking tricks of children are signs of retarded social development and evidence that the schools have let them down and that there is a lot of learning to make up. The more students abuse freedom, the clearer it should be that it is the use of freedom that they need to learn. The teacher can realize that there is nothing so important to learn as the practice of democracy.

TEACHER ADJUSTMENT

"Why does it take the students so long to learn that freedom and democracy are not disorder and noise?" the teacher kept saying to herself in despair. Then she noticed that she was slow and clumsy in getting down off her high horse. She recalled that when Lincoln Steffens asked Albert Einstein how he was able to make his great discoveries, Einstein said, "By challenging an axiom," and she allowed herself to challenge axioms of classroom procedure while trying to think what the purpose of education is and how it can be accomplished in an integrated class. She kept turning over these ideas:

1. Order? How important is it? It was important in feudal organization to maintain the *status quo*. We want growth. Growth is movement and constant change. Feudal order was for the benefit of the nobility at the top of the pyramid. Is the traditional kind of order in school for the benefit of teachers? Students say they feel uncomfortable when it is too quiet. They like noise. The best ideas do come out when everyone talks at once. Does assuming that there should be feudal order in school retard adolescent growth? There may be more progress when teachers stop maintaining their kind of order and the students learn to have the order in which they can learn best.

2. The divine right of kings. The king can do no wrong. How long it took the world to recognize and combat that propaganda! How long will it take teachers to admit that they are not omnipotent and all-knowing?

3. Learning rules and following the directions and assignments of a teacher can not provide the training necessary for doing most of the things that people in America want to do.

4. Sitting in rows of seats and answering questions is not a common situation in American life. What does it train people to do?

5. It's quite stupid to ask a person a question if you know the answer. Then why do teachers do it? It's stupid to tell a person what he already knows. Then why do we train boys and girls to tell teachers what teachers know?

6. It's uncivilized in a group to address one's remarks to a single person and exclude all the others present who hear what is being said. It is civilized manners to include everyone present in a conversation; therefore why don't we learn how to do that in a classroom?

7. People succeed in life as they succeed in their relationships with people. Therefore why don't boys and girls learn to think, talk, work, and play together in school?

8. Versatility is a valuable ability. Why don't we try to do different things in different ways in a classroom? We might try to put this ancient preachment into practice: "To everything there is a season, and a time to every purpose under the heaven: . . . a time to laugh; a time to mourn, and a time to dance: . . . a time to keep silence, and a time to speak." —Ecclesiastes 3: 1–7.

CLASSROOM CONDITIONS FOR SOCIAL LEARNING

What is the essential equipment for the classroom? A bulletin board for the use of the students, a speaker's stand, dictionaries and as many other reference books as possible, maps, movable chairs, or chairs and tables.

Whether to have armchairs or tables is a question to consider. It may be a matter of personal preference. A variety of arrangements should be possible for discussions, committee meetings, and other class activities.

The arrangement of the chairs is very important. A teacher who for five years said, "Put your chairs where you want to; that is, where you think you can do your best work," found that in time the chairs were in a single row in the shape of a horseshoe. The advantage of the big horseshoe is that the boys and girls can look at each other while they talk with and listen to each other. They can learn to include everyone in what they say; they can talk with thirty people at once and speak so that they can be heard across the room. These are valuable social qualities. There seems to be a disadvantage, which really is a possibility for learning how to behave in a group. The arrangement encourages the students to carry on little conversations with their neighbors; in fact, it makes it impossible not to do it. The teacher tried it and found out for herself. When a disturbance arose, a student would glare at the teacher and say, "You ought to change his seat and put him between two girls." The teacher always insisted that to be responsible for their own behavior was part of their social training.

There should be all the natural social training possible. One year in September Oscar said to the teacher, "I want to sit by myself. I came to school to learn; the others just want to have a good time." He sat by himself, and he and the teacher had a private line of communication. As his special project, he was doing scholarly research on pre-Darwinian discoveries that led to the theory of evolution. One day in December in a dramatic aggressive manner he plunged his chair into the circle and began to lead a series of revolts against the teacher. He stopped studying. He tried to be a bad boy, but his tricks were amateurish, those of boys much younger than he, and he soon gave them up. In April he was elected president of the class. He was a strong leader. He studied even harder than he had in the fall but in a different way. The teacher meditated that a class is the world in miniature and that it was good for him to realize as early in life as he did that even an intellectual person needs to be sociable.

A Sophomore Core Unit on Theater, Motion Pictures, Radio, and Television [2]

An unusually active group of sophomores in the New School, an experimental division of the Evanston Township High School, planned and carried through with zest a study of "The Theater, Motion Pictures, Radio, and Television." This unit was well adapted to the development of many skills stressed by the New School, skills in cooperative planning, oral expression, and creative work. The real interests and skills developed in this unit carried over into the work of the second semester and into radio and other school activities.

Core, the distinctive course in the New School, is a two-period class in English and social studies, with emphasis on developing skills and attitudes which lead to constructive, creative citizenship and to personal happiness and satisfaction in a modern world. In the first two years the areas for study are pupil chosen and pupil-teacher planned.

In this group the choice was made democratically after several topics had been proposed, examined, and tentatively outlined. It became evident that the girls wanted something in the fine arts; the boys wanted to study industry and inventions. The decision was made, not by a simple majority vote, but after discussion and group thinking, by a consensus with everyone agreeing. The final choice was a combination of drama with radio and television. This combination we believed, would give opportunities for worthwhile plays and programs and for the study of technical and industrial production.

In preliminary planning we decided that half of our time should be spent on historical development and half on the present-day stage and the media of motion pictures, radio, and television. Each person was to give two reports, preferably one in each of the two major divisions. Each student was also to initiate, direct, or

---

[2] Charlotte C. Whittaker, teacher. From *Education in the New School*. A description of the eleventh- and twelfth-grade programs, Evanston Township High School, Evanston, Ill.

participate as a leader in one related activity, to participate in discussions, give minor reports, and do some writing connected with the unit.

Outlining and planning were carried on jointly by a committee, the instructor, and the Core. Individuals outlined parts of the study. The committee members wrote on the board before and after school and during their study periods. During Core class everybody made suggestions and decisions on parts of the outline. This concerted action took a week, during which time, brief get-acquainted hobby or interest talks were a part of each day's session.

The outline committee began its work by using encyclopedias and books on drama to prepare the historical outline. The part of the instructor was to suggest what plays and playwrights from the traditional lists would interest tenth-grade students. Our outline was developed not primarily from the greatest plays, but from those most likely to be a part of the pupils' experience or the experience of their parents. As one girl remarked, it is satisfying to find a reference in a current newspaper or to hear one's parents talk about a play we are reading. As soon as the outline had been finished, reports were chosen. If more than one person really wanted the same report, the decision was left to chance, the fairest system according to an adolescent way of thinking.

After the outline had been mimeographed by the committee, two weeks were allotted for research work and preparation for the first reports. During this period, we opened our study of drama by reading aloud James Barrie's *What Every Woman Knows*, a somewhat obvious play, but one well adapted to a first play reading. Its theme has adolescent appeal and affords a good opportunity for discussion. With good luck in timing, we heard Helen Hayes, who opened her series on The Electric Theater with this play. Next we listened to the recordings by Orson Welles of *Julius Caesar*, another popular, one-plot, uncomplicated drama.

By this time our first reports were ready. A discussion of drama as a portrayal of life and emotion led directly into the contribution of the Greeks. The boy who reported on Greek drama had read Aristotle on tragedy and two Greek plays. His two-period report interested the group and led him into a further study of the Greeks. The instructor added information on another Greek play and reviewed *Medea*. Some pictures of Judith Anderson's performance were shown. Later several pupils saw *Medea* with their parents.

Roman plays left less impression because none were in our environment. However, there was interest in the Roman theater and in the Coliseum, especially on the part of the Latin students. From Rome we took a cursory glance at the medieval period and the revival of drama through the church and guilds.

Although Shakespeare may not be a part of the environment of all adolescents, it is a part of an Evanstonian's environment. In this area Northwestern University presents an Elizabethan play every year; this year *The Taming of the Shrew* was given. Our own drama department played *Macbeth* and one of our group on the lighting crew kept us informed about the costuming, the traditional Elizabethan staging, and the manner of reading the lines. Previously we had heard the *Julius Caesar* recordings. We now had reports on Shakespeare's life, the Elizabethan stage, and *The Taming of the Shrew*. Two pupils presented scenes from *Romeo and Juliet*.

A student of ability presented a report on Restoration drama, including *She Stoops to Conquer, The Rivals,* and *School for Scandal.* Molière, representing French drama, was the topic of the instructor's report, with pupils reading brief scenes from *The Would-be Gentleman.* A German pupil reported on German drama.

Our interest began to be high when we produced Act I of Ibsen's *A Doll's House* in a reading dramatization. A chalked circle in the center of the room was the stage; placards labeled the furniture, and a few properties added to the classroom performance, which was viewed by visitors from a nearby teachers' college. An excellent report on Ibsen preceded the dramatization. Next Chekhov's *The Boor* was dramatized informally by another group. Shaw was represented by *Major Barbara*, viewed at the Goodman Theater by several pupils and reviewed by us, with one scene read aloud. Each dramatization was worked up by a student director; no attempt was made to have parts memorized.

When we had completed the historical background, a pupil secured a speaker, a graduate student at the University of Chicago, who took our outline and developed ideas in discussion with us. Some pupils were reading reviews in the daily papers, weekly magazines, and *Theater Arts*, and keeping our bulletin board posted. The instructor led a two-day discussion on the current theater season in Chicago and New York. Students showed pictures of stars and scenes on our reflectoscope. A scene from *The Winslow Boy* was read. Because we could not have reports on all the famous actors, we selected Sarah Bernhardt, Edwin Booth, Helen Hayes, Gertrude Lawrence, Paul Robeson, Al Jolson, Katharine Cornell, and the Barrymore family. The head of the high school drama department, Haydn Bodycombe, related his experiences as an actor.

Because the Evanston High School produces a Gilbert and Sullivan operetta each year, we included a report on Gilbert and Sullivan, illustrated with records brought from home. At other times our homes provided us with Paul Robeson records and with a movie on Al Jolson.

In American drama we saw a movie of an old-time minstrel show. A report on the Little Theater movement promoted a bus trip to the Goodman Theater to see *Arsenic and Old Lace*. This was the first stage play seen by some of the pupils, although several others saw most of the important plays in Chicago this year. Eugene O'Neill was represented by a reading dramatization of *Ile* on our wire recorder; it was ham acting, true, but interesting for us. Christmas brought not the old time *Christmas Carol*, but a classroom dramatization of *The Exile*. Other American plays were reviewed.

Because we have a serious ballet student in our group, ballet was introduced successfully. The first report included demonstrations of the ballet positions, original drawings as illustrations, and the history of ballet. The second report, with much illustrative material, presented five ballet stars of today.

Strangely enough, we gave the least time to motion pictures. In Core, not all the planning is done in the beginning, but as ideas develop we add activities. Some pupils went to the Museum of Science and Industry to see the Nickelodeon Theater. Others saw the famous revivals at Northwestern's Technological Institute. One girl compared the novel, the stage play, and the motion picture script of *Jane Eyre*. A stimulating discussion was held on the case for and against censorship of the movies. We saw the school movie *Mutiny on the Bounty* and read the book for group discussion. We also discussed current films and had reports on the history of motion pictures.

When we began the study of radio, we secured the help of Pierce Ommaney, head of the high school radio section, in working with our wire recorder and producing radio scripts. Our first scripts were adaptations of the short stories in the short-story book read regularly by sophomores. When we had a stack of adaptations and a few original scripts, the radio instructor gave us some pointers on production. After we had practiced an original radio script, he took over the production of it by our Core over WEAW, on which the high school has a weekly program. We entered ten radio scripts in the *Scholastic* Contest. As a result of our becoming acquainted with the high school studio and radio instructor, seven of us signed up for the radio class second semester. Three more scripts by this group have been produced. In our next unit "Law and Justice" we worked on recordings of scripts on freedom and liberty. Two pupils have gone out for technical radio training, one taking the Red Cross "ham" course.

Radio and television gave an opportunity for those boys who are primarily interested in science to acquire status. For over a week, our already overcrowded room was piled with amateur radio sets; there were technical diagrams on the board; a television cathode caused excitement. The instructor became the learner. Boys who gave mediocre or poor reports on academic subjects became interesting and effective speakers when they held equipment in their hands.

Because the commercials are so large a part of American radio, we discussed radio advertising. A pupil whose father is secretary of a dental organization discussed FCC regulations concerning medical advertising and demonstrated by the use of the wire recorder misleading types of advertisements. The mother of one pupil, head of the copywriting division of an advertising agency, defended advertising and taught us some of the principles upon which copy is based.

Various types of radio programs were discussed and our horizons widened by listening to new programs. Again the status of the instructor and class shifted, for this generation of students has been brought up on radio. Many of them have a listening acquaintance with classics they have not read, and many of them do read classics they hear dramatized on the radio. Also this generation gets its news of the workings of the government from radio. They are impatient with the old methods of the study of government by the method of cataloguing the three departments —executive, legislative, judicial. They study government in action; they discuss current bills in Congress, and present-day Supreme Court decisions.

Television was an exciting new subject. About one-third of the students have television sets at home.

What were our gains?

First of all, we had many stimulating daily sessions. As a result, we acquired greatly improved skill in speaking and reading aloud and a widening of experience to include the legitimate stage. We provided a wide scope for leadership and original creative work by the ambitious abler pupils and opportunity for effective presentation and status for the mechanically minded and sport fans. We had an ideal medium for cooperative effort. We opened a doorway into extra-curricular activities in radio and drama. We interpreted history through some of its potent mirrors, the stage, the screen, and the radio. We found a topic of conversation and an activity in common with the adults of our families.

The skills and interests we have developed through this unit should help us to more creative work in United States History in our third year and should provide interests and satisfaction for a lifetime.

A CORE COURSE IN AMERICAN LIFE [3]

A unique course designed to present a well-rounded picture of American progress has been developed by the New School for third year pupils. It has been evolved by teachers and students over a number of years and not only fulfills the state requirement for American history but illustrates the core technique of cutting across traditional subject matter lines. The course involves a cultural, "slice of life" approach in which we capitalize on the totality of the American experience, as opposed to the more specialized political emphasis that usually characterizes the high school history class.

[3] Leslee J. Bishop, teacher. From *Education in the New School*. A description of the eleventh- and twelfth-grade programs, Evanston Township High School, Evanston, Ill.

The attempt to find unity and cohesion in the fabric of the American tapestry has been assisted by the two-period schedule used for core classes, the background of core experience on the part of the pupils, and the close proximity of the New School library with its 1,600 volumes on various phases of Americana. With these and other books our students have done-research into political histories to fashion an outline—a framework of time and personalities which makes it possible to show all developments in logical time sequences. From economic histories we took the story of how Americans have earned a living; how our great industrial machine grew out of small handicraft beginnings. In other fields we read of man's speculation about himself and his environment as shown in his folklore, superstitions, formal and unorganized knowledge; his strivings to transmit his ideas through painting, sculpture, architecture, music, and literature; the institutions he established to popularize and perpetuate his ideas in schools, libraries, churches, newspapers, and societies of all sorts. We studied the conflicts of personalities, theories, and nations— we studied the America of people, ambitions and ideals. We sought the *real* America.

This year's program started with an examination of

A. The uniqueness of the United States, as contrasted to other countries.

B. The principles of the "American dream" and their meaning.

C. The characteristics necessary for national existence, for our remaining a great nation.

D. The unsolved problems of America to determine their cause, and if possible, work toward their future solution.

To point up our emphases, discussions were held on:

J. T. Adams, *The Epic of America* (epilogue).

Louis Hacker, *The Shaping of the American Tradition.*

N.C.S.S. yearbook, *The Study and Teaching of American History.*

John Gunther, *Inside U.S.A.* (foreword and finale).

Smith, *The Democratic Spirit* (selections).

MacLeish, "America Was Promises" (records).

V. Parrington, *Main Currents in American Thought* (passages).

H. S. Commager, "Who Is Loyal to America?" (*Harper's Magazine*).

E. Wesley, *American History in Schools and Colleges.*

Commager and Nevins, *Heritage of America* (selections).

Civic Education Service, "The Civic Leader" (selections).

Van Wyck Brooks, *The Flowering of New England, The World of Washington Irving,* and *New England: Indian Summer* (passages).

PUPIL-TEACHER PLANNING

One of the important phases of the course was the experience in curriculum planning by both pupils and teacher. In determining the best technique for organizing and presenting an approach somewhat different from the ordinary to the study of history, it was decided to adopt the plan of considering certain time periods, using the horizontal-chronological method of development. To do this we set up a sequence of time periods each of which we studied from every point of view that seemed to make a contribution to its understanding. In the Colonial period, for example, the influence of religion and religious leaders was considered significant in the growth of the American mind, quite as much as the impact of the political, economic, and social structure. On the other hand, literature played an important part in the pre-Civil War sectionalism, while industrialism was significant in the realistic postwar period. Thus we did not operate from any particular subject-matter field, but let the characteristics of each period determine the emphasis.

Four student committees were established to develop outlines on the chief areas suggested for organization of the subject: (1) social and religious, (2) political and economic, (3) science and technology, (4) literature and the arts. Every person in the class was a member of one of these four working committees. Outlines developed by these groups were combined into a master plan and put on the blackboard, where the class acting as a committee of the whole divided the material into problems of approximately equal work which were the basis for individual reports. In the presentation of material the student was free to choose any device or technique best suited to an effective delivery of his topic. Thus speakers, trips, movies, pictures, and board drawings were all found to be useful, depending on the nature of the report.

FOR FURTHER READING

Brameld, Theodore, *Design for America*. New York: Hinds, Hayden, and Eldredge, 1946.

Class of 1938, Ohio State University School, *Were We Guinea Pigs?* New York: Henry Holt and Company, 1938.

Giles, H. H., *Teacher Pupil Planning*. New York: Harper & Brothers, 1941.

Gordon, Elizabeth, "The Little Democracies," *The English Journal*, 39 ,(February, 1950), 82–86.

Kaulfers, Walter V., Grayson N. Kefauver, and Holland D. Roberts, *Foreign Languages and Cultures in American Education*. New York: McGraw-Hill Book Company, Inc., 1942.

MacConnell, Charles M., Ernest O. Melby, and C. O. Arndt, *New Schools for a New Culture*. New York: Harper & Brothers, 1943.

Roberts, Holland D., W. V. Kaulfers, and Grayson N. Kefauver, *English for Social Living*. New York: McGraw-Hill Book Company, Inc., 1943.

Weeks, Ruth Mary, *A Correlated Curriculum*. New York: Appleton-Century-Crofts, Inc., 1938.

Chapter 15. DESIGNING THE CURRICULUM IN ENGLISH

APPROACHES TO CURRICULUM MAKING IN ENGLISH

Communication as a school-wide responsibility. It was pointed out earlier in this book that the communication arts —reading, listening, speaking, and writing—are learned through their use in all kinds of situations. Whether the learning is in the direction of more effective transmission of thought will depend upon the environmental factors that condition the individual's behavior. For this reason, the kind of communication which occurs in the home, in the community, in the gymnasium, on the playground, and in the school as a whole will be decisive in determining the quality of communication in which young people engage.

The school can exercise relatively little influence upon the language environment in a given home or community. Its chief efforts must be directed toward the establishment of a desirable language environment in the school as a whole. The teaching of English is first of all a responsibility of the entire school staff. For substantial results in the field of language learning, therefore, a determined and persistent school-wide attack upon the problems of reading, writing, speaking, and listening is necessary.

A school-wide attack upon the problem of language communication requires school-wide planning. While the teachers of English may and should exercise leadership in the planning, they cannot be the exclusive designers of the school-wide strategy. If all the teachers, administrators, guidance and admissions officers, coaches, counselors, and other members of the educational staff are to have a genuine part in shaping the language environment of the school, they must share in the over-all planning. Failure on the part of teachers in the various subject fields to give adequate attention to the problems of communication is frequently attributable to the fact that they have had no part in defining the goals or the procedures by which the goals are to be attained.

The improvement of reading abilities is one example of a project in which the cooperative efforts of all members of the school staff are needed. Every room in the school, not merely the English room, should be a reading room, in which boys and girls find encouragement and stimulation to read. The science room, the social studies room, the foreign language room, even the mathematics room, should be provided with book bulletin boards, book shelves and book tables, magazine racks, and an abundance of appropriate reading materials attractively arranged and displayed. Teachers in all fields should take time to introduce young people to these materials, selected to meet a wide range of interests and reading abilities, and allow time to students to read them at leisure during class time and to share their reading experiences with each other. Teachers in all fields should give particular attention to the reading problems peculiar to their special subject matter. Techniques of library research should be taught as much by the teacher of home economics as by the teacher of English. The teacher of science has as much responsibility for cultivating critical discrimination in the reading of the newspaper as does the teacher of the social studies. In all instances, the aim should be not only the development of skills, but especially the establishment of keen and enduring interests in reading.

Similarly, all teachers in the secondary school have responsibility for the improvement of language expression on the part of youth. Provision for an abundance of such activities as letter writing, floor talks, panels, group discussions, conversations, and similar forms of speaking and writing should be made in all the subject fields. Opportunity for responsible writing, under sympathetic guidance, with attention to the varying and shifting meanings of words and the emotive as well as denotative qualities of language, can be offered most effectively in relation to the study of the numerous fields of the secondary school curriculum. All teachers should aid individual learners in achieving reasonable standards of literacy and of clarity of expression, without applying puristic and excessively exacting standards.

Teachers of English can contribute effectively to the general quality of communication in the secondary school by initiating the organization of faculty committees, including representatives of the various subject fields, which will survey the various problems of language communication in the school and make specific recommendations to both the faculty and the administration with respect to a school-wide program in communication. Style sheets for reference in all classes should be made with the participation of teachers, students, and where possible, representatives of the community. Expressional needs reported by leaders in industry, commerce, labor, churches, and other community organizations should be considered in the drafting of the style sheet. By these means the objective of a school-wide effort toward improved communication may be converted from a pious hope into a reality.

Curriculum making in English as a cooperative undertaking. In an ever-growing number of secondary schools, curriculum development in English is regarded as one of the responsibilities of the classroom teacher. Teaching competence therefore now includes some understanding of the ways in which a modern curriculum is built.

The first of the skills needed for curriculum development is the ability to work with others in the process. It is true that fundamentally the curriculum in English embraces those experiences which each student has in the classroom in association with his peers and his teacher, and that ultimately the individual teacher is a major determining factor in curriculum making. A curriculum certainly is not a paper course of study or a series of mimeographed resource units. But others besides teachers of English and their students have a stake in the English curriculum. The school staff as a whole, the community as a whole, the teaching profession as a whole, parents and nonparent patrons, and the school administration are vitally concerned with what happens in the classroom. They should therefore participate in the planning.

Curriculum development in English as in other areas has been conducted in recent years by agencies ranging from the Federal government to the smallest local school unit. The U.S. Office of Education, through its current Life Adjustment Program, state departments of education, through their curriculum development programs, city-wide curriculum committees and central research bureaus, as in New York and Chicago, local school faculties and local departmental groups have been actively studying the problems of curriculum development in English and producing curriculum guides, resource materials, book lists, and outlines for basic curriculum studies. Professional organizations of teachers, through such bodies as the Curriculum Commission of the National Council of Teachers of English, as well as state and local organizations of teachers of English, are vigorously advancing the work of developing an English program in harmony with the needs of youth today.

In all these, the classroom teacher plays an increasingly important part. No longer do most school administrators, through hand-picked committees, distribute ready-made courses of study to teaching bodies with instructions as to what subject matter to "cover" in what period of time. Educators are becoming increasingly aware that only as teachers themselves develop new insights and purposes, and as they share in the planning of the program, can genuine progress be made. With universal participation, progress may appear to be slower, but it is far more likely to be real and enduring.

Democratic curriculum planning exemplifies all the skills and complexities of communication involved in the process of group planning and decision. It illustrates the kinds of abilities which teachers of communication attempt to develop among their students. It calls for the development of leaders who know how to secure maximum response from members of the group; how to mediate differences; how to clarify issues which arise in discussion; how to discover points of agreement and narrow the areas of disagreement; how to encourage the timid and tactfully restrain the aggressive; how to make summaries and generalizations; how to encourage action when the group seems ready for action; how to make effective use of the expert, the resource person, and the recorder. It calls for the acceptance of common purposes by members of the group; for respect for divergent or conflicting opinions; for skill in expressing viewpoints dispassionately and impersonally, sometimes with humor and always with careful consideration of the ways in which these viewpoints will be received and understood. The emotive qualities of words and phrases take on particular importance when curriculum problems are discussed.

New proposals for the curriculum frequently challenge school practices established by early training and long experience. Innovations in curriculum organization and practices may by implication seem to discredit methods and materials in which teachers have invested a great part of their lives. Curriculum discussions should therefore emphasize past and present successes on the part of schools and teachers, as well as shortcomings that need correction. Curriculum development must be based on genuine acceptance and initiative on the part of the teachers if it is to be more than merely verbal change or a merely temporary expedient. Moreover, it must rest ultimately on community approval, secured through wise interpretation of school problems to the community, and through active participation in the process by representatives who can speak for all elements in the community. In the end, the school can do only what the community tolerates or demands. For this reason, the community has the right to be fully informed as to the problems, purposes, and procedures which are involved in curriculum change, and to express its wishes with respect to the kind of product which results from the educational process.

The students, too, have a place in the work of planning the school curriculum. The school does not delegate to the community or the students the technical work of designing the curriculum or of choosing instruments and techniques. The administration and faculty are presumably trained to perform these tasks. However, the students are not comparable to the inanimate objects on an assembly line. They are human beings with a right to a voice in the determination of what will happen to them in school. Curriculum makers can learn much from the students with respect to the needs and desires of youth which should be considered in the planning of the school program. Moreover, it is not sufficient to ascertain these needs and desires by means of questionnaires, check lists, and inventories. Only through personal interaction in planning groups including students, at least on frequent occasions, can teachers be certain that they are dealing with actualities instead of mere theories. Nor should curriculum plans be so rigid as to exclude abundant opportunity for teacher-student planning in the classroom.

To secure the genuine, rather than the merely verbal, assent of all members of groups participating in curriculum development, members of working groups must operate on a plane of professional equality. When superintendents, principals, supervisors, curriculum directors, and other administrative personnel meet with curriculum-planning groups, teachers tend to defer to those who in the daily operation of the school possess legal and administrative authority or who speak in behalf of the administration. They tend to be inhibited in the expression of disagreements and to accept outwardly viewpoints to which they do not actually subscribe. Even when administrators succeed in establishing a wholesome, democratic atmosphere in the group meetings, the "status" relationships frequently if not universally interfere with free group process. The effects of such relationships can be minimized if the administrators will make clear in advance that such effects exist, and that each member of the group should feel no hesitation in expressing his own views without fear of criticism or of offending—indeed, that all honest views will be warmly welcomed. The leaders of planning groups should generally be individuals who do not possess the "status" relationships. Obviously those teaching members of the group who express views contrary to those held by the administration or by the majority of the group should not be subjected to disparagement or embarrassment of any kind, regardless of the nature of the opinions expressed. Perhaps on some occasions the planning group should meet without the presence of administrative or supervisory personnel, in order that a greater degree of freedom of discussion may be encouraged.

STEPS IN CURRICULUM MAKING

Need for clear definition of goals. Fundamental planning of the program in English does not consist of a mere rearrangement of traditional subject matter, or of the addition or subtraction of certain classics, or the expansion or contraction of the period devoted to composition or speech. On the contrary, it consists in a rethinking of the purposes of the program in communication and a planning of the kinds of experiences which may lead to the fulfillment of these purposes. In the determination of aims, curriculum groups may be guided in part by the formulations made by such national groups as those discussed in Chap. 1, including committees of the National Education Association and the National Council of Teachers of English. These formulations of aims, however, should be conditioned by the special needs of the local community and the local school population. In order that curriculum development may be powerfully motivated by the real needs of particular groups of young people, it is desirable to conduct systematic studies of the problems reported by boys and girls in school, recent graduates, parents, nonparent school patrons, community leaders, and others. Suggestions for procedures in conducting such studies are available from the State Superintendent of Public Instruction, Springfield, Ill.

Perhaps the greatest obstacle to sound curriculum development is the habit of thinking of certain content as a necessary part of the program merely because it has always been there. Many teachers, for example, think of *Julius Caesar* or *The Lady of the Lake* or the conjugation of strong verbs as essential ingredients of an English program simply because these items have enjoyed such a secure position in the past. Actually no subject matter or drill or class activity has a place in the program unless it can be demonstrated to fill a need in daily living or contribute to the achievement of clear social objectives. Even the so-called "cultural heritage" has no place in the program except as a resource in the fulfillment of the present human need.

Need for organization consistent with stated goals. When the aims of the program in language communication have been defined, it becomes necessary to determine the instructional organization most likely to achieve them. The nature of such organization will depend upon a number of factors. Chief among these, perhaps, is the type of organization employed in the school curriculum as a whole. If planning takes place exclusively within the boundaries of the English field, or independently of the planning in other fields, the problems of organization will relate chiefly to the interrelations of the various aspects of language communication, the relative emphasis to be given to each at the various levels, and the themes, projects, centers of interest, or problems which will serve as substance for the activities in communication. Intradepartmental planning calls for much consultation with other departments for the purpose of avoiding unnecessary duplication of effort. Thus in one school, problems of consumer purchasing were studied in science, business administration, social studies, home economics, and English. The theme was appropriate for all these fields, but proper coordination was needed in order that waste and boredom might be avoided.

One issue which planning groups face at the outset is the degree to which the curriculum will make provision for teacher-student planning. Decisions must be made as to whether the general framework for each year's program, along with a designated sequence of supporting units, should be planned in advance, or whether classes should be free to select their problems and activities in accordance with their current interests and with current happenings. Those who favor the latter course argue that under wise guidance students will over a sufficient period of time include all significant areas of study in the program of class activities, and that the efficiency of learning will be heightened if the subject matter is selected by the students instead of prescribed in advance. "How can we be sure," they ask, "that all students want to study radio programs when the time for the radio unit arrives? Or, if an exciting movie comes to town, why should we not evaluate it, instead of studying vocations just because it is the next unit in the course?" Advocates of this view hold that a variety of resource units and reference books for individual instruction in the skills is all that is needed in the way of curriculum plans.

In most schools, however, some fairly fixed outline of topics or units is laid out for each year's work. Varying degrees of flexibility are permitted within the general framework, but the nature and sequence of topics are specified in advance for all classes in English. Especially in the larger schools, such uniformity is deen.ed essential, not only because the physical properties of the schoolroom and the availability of reading materials make greater spontaneity difficult, but also because teachers feel a greater sense of security when they know with some definiteness what will be taught in the course of a semester. It is thought also that by this means the essential aims of the program in English are more likely to be achieved, at least in part.

A fixed outline should not be permitted to interfere with

the opportunity of a teacher and her students to suspend the usual sequence in favor of some special project that seems promising. One teacher, for example, conducted a unit on housing in a ninth-grade class in a Kansas junior high school. By means of library research, a community survey, interviews, class reports, talks to community groups, and free reading, the boys and girls learned the arts of effective communication in connection with a topic of vital interest to them. The project had no relation to the formal program as described in the school curriculum, but it yielded educational results which probably exceeded any which might have been attained by more conventional means. Freedom to take advantage of new ideas and unforeseen situations should be safeguarded regardless of the type of curriculum organization that has been adopted.

A second issue which faces teachers as they plan the program in curriculum development is the question whether the work is to be organized around types of language organization or problems, centers of interest, investigational activities, and the like. In many high schools, perhaps a majority of high schools, units of instruction deal with such activities as letter writing, reporting, grammar, punctuation, literary types, and similar topics in language expression and literature. Other schools have adopted the plan of selecting topics or problems which are likely to capture the interest of young people and which will provide strong motivation for reading, writing, speaking, and listening. By this means a number of objectives important in general education may be attained, and the activities in communication may take place in the natural context characteristic of everyday living. In schools which retain the traditional subject organization, the choice of topics for units is sometimes complicated by the fact that such subjects as social studies, science, home economics, and art frequently deal with similar topics. While some overlapping cannot be avoided, teachers of English should not hesitate to draw upon various subject fields for material in a stage of curriculum development which is transitional to the unified studies type of secondary school program. Teachers of English should not be disturbed when the objection is made that certain topics discussed in English classes belong to the social studies or some other subject. When suitable relations have been established among teachers in the various subject fields, there should be little difficulty in avoiding undesirable duplication in the subject matter of instruction.

Selection and planning of instructional units based on student needs. The criteria which determine the inclusion of certain units of instruction in the English program are derived from the common needs of young people at the successive stages of their development. Thus, boys and girls who enter the junior or senior high school for the first time frequently have difficulty in adjusting themselves to the increased freedom and responsibility with which they are confronted in the new type of educational institution. Previously they have enjoyed a certain degree of emotional security from contact with a single teacher, who if she was successful in her relations with children, served as a mother substitute. In the junior or senior high school, boys and girls are called upon to exercise a degree of initiative which was not possible or acceptable in the elementary grades. Instead of a single teacher, many teachers and a number of administrative functionaries become a part of their lives. Some boys and girls are unprepared for their new responsibilities. All require a certain degree of aid and guidance. When such assistance is not otherwise provided, the work in English classes may well be focused upon the problems of orientation to the new situations which young people find in the secondary school.

Similarly, in the later years of the secondary school, other themes may dominate the English curriculum. In some institutions the sophomore year is given over to the study of the community or to the mass media of communication; the junior year is devoted to the study of American life through its literature, art, science, music, government, and other forms of group activity; the senior year is reserved for elective courses representing special student interests such as dramatics, forensics, journalism, special types or periods of English, American, or world literature such as the novel, the short story, the play, poetry, Shakespeare, Tolstoy, Victor Hugo, and the like. In each year of the secondary school, the work is concentrated on some phase of human experience which will appeal to adolescents. The English classes in modern secondary schools undertake to assume their fair share of responsibility for meeting student needs in the areas of family relations, intercultural education, social ideals and personal values, etiquette, personal business practices, and the constructive use of leisure time.

Illustrations of major emphases in the successive years of the secondary school might be taken from any of numerous programs which have been developed in recent years. In Waukegan Township High School (Illinois), for example, members of the English Department have taught units on such topics as these:

Leisure Time	Newspapers
Magazines	Radio Programs
Short Stories	Travel
Motion Pictures	Biography
Personal Living	Documents of Freedom

In the Jacksonville, Ill., High School the general theme for the first-year English is orientation. Units of instruction in this year include "Getting Acquainted," "Understanding Ourselves," "Living Together" (including conversation, family living, motion picture and radio appreciation, vocations, hobbies, and the like), and "Knowing All Kinds of People" (including comparisons of different cultures inside and outside America). Second-year English at Jacksonville centers about the theme, "Broadening Our Horizons." It includes units on "The Newspaper in Today's World," "Oral Communication in the Modern World," "The World of Humor," "The World of Science," and "The World of Human Achievement" (with heavy reliance in the last two units on interviews, biography, and biographical fiction). The third-year English is a study of the American scene. The units deal with such topics as "Understanding the People of Various Regions," "The Ideal of Freedom," "Pride in Work Well Done." The fourth-year work is described as "A Senior's Design for Living." While this year's activities include many panel discussions and debates, grammar and usage reviews, library research experiences, and letter writing, a conscious purpose of the teacher is to aid young people in developing for themselves a working philosophy of life. It will be noted that, while the dual interests of the individual and society are recognized throughout the four-year program, the first and fourth years tend to focus on the individual and the second and third years give greater attention to the broader problems of society.

Illustrations of functional units in English programs could be multiplied from many other high schools in all parts of the United States. "Leadership," "American Ideas and Ideals," "What Men Live for," "Exploring Human Nature," "Races and Cultures that Make up America," "Newspapers," "Radio," and "Television," suggest the kind of subject matter with which English classes in modern high schools deal. They offer refreshing contrast to courses of study, unfortunately still the prevailing type, which are based on a list of rather narrow, specialized skills or informational items, with the contents of each unit properly processed and canned in the form of textbooks and anthologies.

Sterility of traditional curriculum organization. An illustration of the sterility of the traditional organization may be taken from a typical eleventh-grade English course of study (1948) used in a large, suburban Middle Western high school.[1] The following excerpt from this course in Junior English presents an interesting exercise in the study of assumptions on which traditional courses are built:

[1] This high school, noted in many respects for the excellence of its educational offerings, has since undertaken a program of curriculum development in English.

OBJECTIVES

In Reading:

1. To teach pupils to read the literature of our country both for its content and for its significance in our heritage.
2. To make pupils aware of the basic concepts which underlie the succeeding periods of American life.
3. To require pupils to know the contribution of our chief American men of letters.
4. To review those literary types studied in the sophomore year —the novel, the drama, and poetry; and to acquaint pupils with the essay and the short story as literary types, particularly as the short story is America's contribution to literature.
5. To develop in pupils a more discriminating taste in their reading of magazines and of novels, and to instil a genuine interest in reading biography and other forms of nonfiction.
6. To make pupils library-conscious.

In Writing:

1. To insist upon the minimum achievements of English I and II with particular review of the outline and the paragraph writing of English II.
2. To require in III^1 and in the first weeks of III^2 a number of expository themes involving related paragraphs, as preparation for the long theme.
3. To eliminate the following persistent errors:
    a. Faulty reference of pronoun.
    b. Lack of parallelism.
    c. Misplaced modifiers.
    d. Faulty and excessive use of "so."
    e. "Is where," "Is when," and "Is because" sentences.
4. To teach certain simple rhetorical patterns, such as:
    a. Balanced sentences ("not only" . . . "but also").
    b. Parallel structure for similar ideas in a series.
    c. Correct subordination.
5. To review the five basic spelling rules (pp. 231–239 in the *Century Handbook of Writing*).

In Speaking:

1. To continue the practices set up in English I and II.

In Grammar:

1. To review, for the individual or for the class, any functional grammar in which the individual or group is notoriously weak.

TEXTS

Minimum Requirements in English.
Anthology in American Literature.
A Writing Handbook.
Tools: notebook, assignment book, fountain pen, pencil, red pencil.

UNITS

First Semester

1. The Colonial Time and The Making of a Nation . . . . 3 weeks
2. The Flowering of the East, Part I . . . . 4 weeks
3. The Flowering of the East, Part II . . . . 4 weeks
4. The Westward Movement . . . . 2 to 3 weeks
5. The Growth of Realism and America in the Modern
   World . . . . 2 weeks

NOTE: An extra week is purposely provided to be used at the discretion of the individual teacher, either for supplementary reading or for any unit which the class had not covered in the specified time.

Second Semester

6. Modern American Prose . . . . 3 weeks
7. The Expository Theme Based on Reading . . . . 6 weeks
8. Modern American Poetry . . . . 2 weeks
9. Modern American Fiction . . . . 3 weeks
10. Modern American Drama . . . . 3 weeks

It will be noted that in this school the curriculum committee has abdicated in favor of the textbook writers. The literature is presented without reference to any particular interests which the students might have, or to any problems or special needs which might exist among the young people in this community. Indeed, the presentation follows the reverse of what student interests are likely to be, since it begins with the colonial period, which for this Middle Western community is the most remote in time and place. If any of the selections in the anthology should arouse student interest, they would do so by the sheerest coincidence. The needs and interests of the youth appear to be a matter of total indifference to the school. Pupils, according to the statement of objectives, are to be made "aware of the basic concepts which underlie the succeeding periods of American life." Are there such concepts? If so, for what reason should awareness of them be made a basic aim of instruction in English? The syllabus does not tell. Quite probably many of the selections in this anthology may give pleasure to its readers; may help them to develop sensitivity to literary excellence; may help them in developing a personal set of ethical values; may give them insight into human motivation, or into the spirit of American democracy. If they do, however, it will not be because of any design on the part of the textbook or the school. The stated purpose of the school, for reasons undeclared, is to acquaint students with certain historical concepts and with certain literary types, including the short story, not because it helps the reader, but because it is alleged that the short story is "America's contribution to literature."

This is not curriculum planning. This is pathetic rationalization for teaching what has always been taught and what the teachers have learned as English majors in college. Teaching adolescents in these times calls for more than a knowledge of literary history, biography, and criticism. It calls for an intimate knowledge of young people and their needs, and a willingness to subordinate the materials of instruction to the varying requirements of the human beings who are to be educated. The tragic fact is that the quoted material still represents the rule rather than the exception.

Criticism of the traditional organization of English courses does not necessarily imply that textbooks and anthologies are valueless. Anthologies particularly are of the greatest usefulness in making available shorter selections of prose and poetry which would not otherwise be readily accessible.

Language textbooks serve an admirable purpose in providing reference material in convenient and logically organized form for use in answering questions about language usages. The chief objection to the anthologies and textbooks is the fact that they are used, and intended to be used, as substitutes for the kind of educational planning which takes account of the current and varying interests, needs, and problems of the students.

Objectives of English instruction broader than the mechanical skills of communication. The organization of instructional units in English around such themes as family living or intercultural relations is not intended merely as a means of providing adequate motive for the various forms of communication. Teachers of English, like their colleagues in other fields, are first of all teachers of boys and girls. The subject is merely an instrument and, as traditionally organized, a fairly crude instrument in meeting the complex needs of growing individuals. A boy who feels insecure or frustrated or rejected needs personal guidance more than he needs rules for punctuating sentences. A story about Haym Salomon may be more needful to a youngster who has been poisoned by anti-Semitic parents than the analysis of a Shakespearean play would be. For this reason, in a unit on the worthy use of leisure the teacher should focus upon leisure time activities with as much concern as she does upon developmental problems in reading. The fact that reading, writing, speaking, and listening develop more rapidly and effectively in the context of such a unit should not obscure the essential validity of the broader objectives of the unit.

Activities in English programs which are not problematical in nature. Not all the experiences of young people in English classes should relate to problems or systematically organized units. A functionally designed curriculum should enrich, not impoverish, the lives of young people. Units of instruction which deal with personal development or human relations or the heritage of freedom do not necessarily provide for the kind of exhilaration which an individual experiences when he reads or hears a lyric poem, or expresses a mood of sadness or contentment in his own "creative writing." The trend toward the introduction of common learnings courses carries with it the danger of making the secondary school curriculum exclusively utilitarian. Teachers of English should jealously safeguard those experiences which bear no relation to the intellectual solution of problems, personal or social, but which are important to cultivated human beings in the pursuit of happiness. Among these are the aesthetic experiences which are in the nature of contemplation and emotional response. These do not necessarily involve library research, or group deliberation, or reporting, or any of the familiar activities associated with instructional units. They may involve sharing an experience with a sympathetic group or with an individual, or they may simply involve quiet individual reading. A teacher should feel under no compulsion, for example, to draw parallels between Julius Caesar and Mussolini if it appears more natural simply to analyze the characters of Caesar and Brutus and Antony and Cassius, and to enjoy the purely dramatic aspects of Shakespeare's story. For some students Wordsworth's *Ode on Intimations of Immortality* or Lanier's *Hymn to the Sunrise* may arouse deep emotion, without posing any problems or even creating a desire for language communication with others. Young people of every level of mental ability or stage of language development may find joy in hearing Sandburg's *Fog* or reading O. Henry's story *The Gift of the Magi* without listening to panel discussions on the weather or the joys of a happy married life.

One method of providing for such nonproblematical experiences is to prepare a flexible schedule for English or common learnings classes, in which a part of the time is devoted to the activities of systematic units such as those described in preceding paragraphs, another part to free reading in books and magazines on a great variety of topics, and another to such miscellaneous activities as literary films, filmstrips, recordings, and discussion of current topics unrelated to the central unit described in the formal brochure for the English program. By this means it is possible both to attack directly the stated objectives of the curriculum in English and to provide for those relatively unplanned activities which contribute to the well-rounded development of cultivated people. Such a distribution of activities may be represented by a schedule like the following:

ENGLISH OR COMMON LEARNINGS PERIOD

M	T	W	Th	F

Unit activities (American life, boy-girl relations, etc.)

Special activities (films, recordings, etc.)

Free reading and sharing of reading experiences

Skills of communication taught in relation to the need for them. The organization of the English curriculum as described in the foregoing paragraphs raises fundamental questions relating to the teaching of communication skills. After all, so long as we retain the traditional subject fields type of curriculum, teachers of English bear primary responsibility for the improvement of skills in reading, writing, speaking, and listening. Should these skills be taught in separate units or incidentally in relation with purposeful activities in communication?

Most of the studies which have been made on the mastery of skills stress the need for strong purposes on the part of the learner. They indicate clearly that skills are learned more quickly and permanently if the learner recognizes the need for them and sees them in relation to actual use. For this reason it would appear that instruction in the various phases of language communication should be given as need arises. Such instruction may and should be given to individuals in connection with the various reading, listening, and expressional activities as they occur in the development of a unit, or it may take the form of intensive classwork when certain needs appear to be common to many students. Incidental instruction need not be unsystematic instruction. In all cases it should be direct instruction, designed to improve the quality of young people's activities in communication. Special units focused upon the skills of grammar, punctuation, reading, and the like, tend to be lacking in adequate motive for the learner and in carry-over value, and to contribute to the frustration which in part accounts for the high mortality among students in English classes.

Unitary organization in the English curriculum need not interfere with varying emphases upon the various types of language skill from one semester to another. Departments of English which include teachers specially prepared to teach speech may well assign certain semesters of work to teachers of speech, not to offer courses in speech, but to provide particular attention, under expert guidance, to the speech activities arising out of given units of instruction. Isolation of any type of language communication in any one semester is unnatural and educationally unsound; but emphasis upon specific kinds of reading or language expression at various stages of the program is highly desirable, especially if it permits maximum utilization of the particular talents of teachers. Supporting skills in relation to the various units of each year of the program may therefore be opportunely described in the English syllabus with a view to improvement in listening, reporting, letter writing, reading, library research, enjoying poetry or plays, and the like, with different skills receiving major attention in different semesters. Care should be exercised, however, to include in each semester a sufficient variety of language activities to ensure continuous and well-rounded development in language abilities.

Smaller teacher load needed for curriculum planning. Perhaps the chief obstacle to progress in curriculum development in English is the amount of time and effort which teachers are required to devote to the process. As has been indicated, curriculum development is everybody's job, not merely that of a small committee of teachers. A teaching body may delegate specific responsibilities to small committees, but if genuine progress is to be made, all teachers should be induced to take part in the work and to accept the results of the planning. Ways should therefore be found to free teachers sufficiently for curriculum work. The preparation of resource units requires extensive library work, much reading, and careful study of the needs of boys and girls in high school classes. Teachers who are called upon to meet class after class, attend to the routines of the home room, supervise extra-class activities, and make periodic reports to parents and administrators, cannot be expected to devote a great deal of time to the preparation of original resource units. Smaller teaching loads, and systematic provision for free time in which cooperative planning and research may be conducted will be needed in order that basic improvements may be made in the English curriculum.

Help should be sought from state curriculum programs, university curriculum laboratories, from individual high schools which make new resource units available, and from such excellent periodicals as *The English Journal,* which publish descriptions of newer practices in English classes from month to month. Teachers who develop new curriculum materials should be encouraged to share them with colleagues in other high schools. At the present time, teachers of English are lacking in an adequate clearinghouse of ideas for instructional plans. But even under the most favorable circumstances, alert teachers find it difficult to carry on their responsibilities with five classes and a homeroom, and at the same time make genuine contributions to the curriculum in English.

If faculty meetings were converted, at least on certain occasions, into planning conferences on curriculum problems, progress might be made in persuading teachers to think in terms of the needs of all students instead of the subject-matter requirements of a limited number who plan to enter college. Specific duties in the preparation of unit materials and in experimentation with new classroom practices would still need to be assigned to small committees of teachers, but it might become possible through the process of large group planning to avoid the conflict which occasionally arises when a minority of teachers proceed on their own to make innovations in the organization and content of the English curriculum. Reduced load for all teachers, and particularly for the smaller working committees, is essential to successful engineering of the newer and more functional type of English program.

Preparing the way for the development of the integrated secondary school curriculum. Slowly, very slowly, a number of American secondary schools, particularly junior high schools, are finding it possible to substitute the educational needs of boys and girls for the vested interests of the subject fields as a basis for curriculum organization. If the new programs in these schools succeed in conserving all the values found in the old subjects, they may substantially reduce the number of students who drop out of school before graduation, and aid those who complete the secondary school curriculum in meeting the pressing personal and social problems of our time.

Efforts to overcome the limitations of the subject-centered organization have taken many forms. In certain schools, a single two-hour course, known as common learnings, or core, or unified studies, is substituted for the separate courses in English and social studies or science. Other schools undertake to correlate the work of such separate courses as American history and American literature. Such efforts are variously known as correlation, fusion, and integration. The chief distinction among them is in the point of departure—the subject matter, as in correlated courses, broad fields courses, survey courses, or the problems and interests of the young people, as in some of the common learnings courses.

An interesting example of a problems course is the Floodwood, Minn., project for the eleventh and twelfth grades, which was inaugurated under the general supervision of Professor Theodore Brameld, at that time of the University of Minnesota. The course occupied two periods daily and extended through two years. The over-all purpose was to study the direction of American life, with particular emphasis upon probable future developments in the field of government, economic life, art, literature, music, and the like. Past and present were used as guides in plotting probable future trends. The Floodwood project was based on the assumption that schools have lived too much in the past, and that the real interests of youth are toward the future. Naturally, the course offered abundant opportunity for analysis of problems of today.

It should be noted that the plan of organization alone will not ensure either subject matter mastery or the meeting of young people's needs. Some teachers of the subject fields have always subordinated their subject matter to the observed needs of individual boys and girls. Some common learnings courses are highly formalized, with the newer type of subject matter dominating both the organization and the method. Nevertheless, the plan of organization tends to focus attention either upon the subject matter to be mastered, or upon the diversified and varying needs of youth. Any plan which will facilitate the utilization of subject matter in the satisfaction of genuine, current need is likely to be superior to one which creates in the teacher a sense of obligation to a fixed sequence of facts and concepts. Particularly in English, any organization which makes room for emotional learnings and the free appreciation of aesthetic values is superior to one which encourages merely the mastery of facts, concepts, and skills.

Plans providing for correlation of independent courses are usually based on the logical organization of subject matter. Generally they have been unsuccessful, because it is difficult to find pairs of teachers who are able to plan together and to relinquish their subject-matter interests sufficiently to make the correlation effective. Such efforts have value in stressing the deficiencies of the series of unrelated experiences which make up the traditional curriculum. If they will serve as steppingstones to a genuinely integrated curriculum which provides for all the common learnings, and at the same time stimulates the development of individual interests which may be pursued as far as the student's capacities warrant, they may make a highly valuable contribution to the development of a genuinely functional curriculum.

Whatever the organization of the secondary school curriculum, it will have responsibility for improving the language expression and the listening and reading abilities of youth. It will have responsibility for contributing to the aesthetic sensibilities of adolescent boys and girls, and to their mental health. This book has emphasized the broader functions of language communication, both in specialized English classes and in the common learnings course. It has documented the general principle that human values, not mere words, grammatical generalizations, historical facts, or verbalistic skills are the criteria by which we measure the success of the educative process.

For Further Reading

Brameld, Theodore, *Design for America*. New York: Hinds, Hayden, and Eldredge, 1946.

Class of 1938, Ohio State University School, *Were We Guinea Pigs?* New York: Henry Holt and Company, 1938.

DeBoer, John J. (Ed.), *The Subject Fields in General Education*. New York: Appleton-Century-Crofts, Inc., 1941.

Giles, H. H., S. P. McCutchen, and A. N. Zechiel, *Exploring the Curriculum*. New York: Harper & Brothers, 1942.

Gray, William S. (Ed.), *Reading in an Age of Mass Communication*, Chap. VI. New York: Appleton-Century-Crofts, Inc., 1949.

Jewett, Ida A., "Gathering Forces in the High School English Curriculum," *Teachers College Record*, 49 (December, 1947), 143–153.

Weeks, Ruth Mary, *A Correlated Curriculum*. New York: Appleton-Century-Crofts, Inc., 1938.

Chapter 16. EVALUATING GROWTH IN ENGLISH

Evaluation is that phase of education which is concerned with appraising the success of the school in attaining the purposes for which it is maintained by society. Although evaluation utilizes evidence in the way of scores obtained from valid and reliable tests, it is by no means confined to this type of evidence. A growing realization that neither knowledge nor skill in itself compels action has shifted the emphasis from the measurement of knowledge and skills as ends in themselves to appraising the changes in human behavior that the learning program has brought about in keeping with the life-centered aims and objectives of the school. Modern evaluation thus does not mistake proficiency on a pencil-and-paper test for either the desire or the ability to apply any of the correct answers in real-life situations outside of class. Although it is self-evident that a severely retarded reader cannot be expected to develop the habit of reading good magazines and books until his deficiency is remedied, it is also true that proficiency on a reading test is not always correlated with discriminating, constructive reading habits in out-of-school life.

In a sense, modern evaluation approaches the learner in a manner comparable to that in which a competent physician approaches a patient. As in modern medical practice, the value of a particular remedy does not reside in the drug,

403

but in the improvement ·that it helps to bring about in the individual. If the results are contrary to expectations, the treatment is changed, even if the "average" patient usually responds favorably. By comparison, educational practice has only begun to emerge from the patent-medicine bottle and bloodletting stage that characterized so much medical practice until well into the nineteenth century. Today, a certain drug as a cure-all, or a particular procedure, such as bloodletting, as a remedy for almost everything, is no longer considered acceptable practice. Modern therapy depends upon a thorough diagnosis of the individual, and upon careful observation of the changes which the treatment brings about in him. Nor is a particular procedure or prescription continued beyond the point of diminishing returns. Since the value of a specific depends upon the improvement that it induces in a particular case, no good physician proceeds on the assumption that because one grain of it is good, ten would be perfect.

Increases in fundamental knowledge about the human mind, while still inadequate, have nevertheless been sufficient to force education to recognize that mental differences are as great as physical ones, and that consequently significant progress can be achieved only through the adoption of differentiate procedures comparable to those used in modern medicine. Where this conception has become operative in forward-looking schools, the parallel between medical practice and modern education is easily recognized. The first step in the instructional process is always a diagnosis of the needs of the individual in comparison with others of his own age, sex, life interests, and potentialities. The second stage is individual prescription in terms of the diagnosis. The third is evaluation of the prescription in terms of the changes which it has produced in the learner. The fourth step is the modification of the learning program in keeping with the findings. Repetition of all these steps, as required, until the maximum improvement that is possible to the individual has been achieved, constitutes the educative process from the instructional viewpoint. Just as a physician, after thorough diagnosis, may realize that his patient's blindness cannot be cured, and recommend him to a school that specializes in the reeducation of the visually disabled, so the teacher will not attempt, much less force, the impossible but, as one acquainted with other alternatives, rely on guidance to secure for the individual the maximum good that is accessible to him.

Obviously, wherever young people of different capacities, abilities, and life destinations are compelled by law to attend school, society is obliged to provide alternatives in sufficient variety and amount to accommodate everyone. There is little point to diagnosis or guidance if, after all, there is only one uniform set of offerings into which the individual can be guided. Although differentiated offerings are easier to provide as separate classes in large schools than in small ones, a high degree of differentiation is possible in almost all courses by replacing uniform learn-and-recite procedures with semi-individualized programs conducted on the supervised workshop plan.

CRITERIA FOR AN EVALUATION PROGRAM

Inasmuch as evaluation is an integral and indispensable aspect of the educative process, the criteria by which its adequacy can be judged are of key importance. In the field of English, such questions as the following deserve especial attention:

1. Does the evaluation program include measurement of the extent to which the offerings in English are compatible with the needs and abilities of the students? High rates of failure and a widespread dislike of English are symptoms of maladjustment. The extent to which such maladjustment prevails can be determined by means of student reactions on questionnaires requesting them to rank, in order, the subjects that they like most and those that they like least. Additional clues can be obtained by requesting them to rank the

subjects which they are taking in the order of their helpfulness or value to them. If such rankings are obtained in neutral circumstances—*i.e.*, outside the English class, by someone not connected with the department, and unsigned—the results are less likely to be influenced by a desire on the part of the pupils to please the examiner. Although a low rating does not necessarily prove that a course is without value, it can safely be accepted as an indication that, as currently offered, the program has not been successful in communicating these values to the learners.

2. Does the evaluation program include adequate means for individual diagnosis of a pupil's needs or difficulties? A valid and reliable measure of speed and depth of comprehension in reading is indispensable for sound guidance in any subject making extensive use of printed materials. Nothing is more absurd than assigning books which are on a tenth-grade level of reading difficulty to tenth-graders whose reading development has not advanced beyond the sixth grade. In addition, inventories of hobbies, recreational interests, preferences in free leisure-time reading and participation in remunerative as well as social activities outside the school are essential to a sound guidance program in English. If a general health record is not available, essential data should be obtained from the student. Since hearing and vision are especially important in language learning, a recheck should be made if the data on the health record are over two years old, or if the student shows evidences of speech difficulties or retardation in reading ability.

3. Does the evaluation program provide for a cumulative record that can be passed on from teacher to teacher as the student progresses through school? An individual folder for each pupil, containing his case history to date, and such insights as succeeding teachers have been able to contribute to it, is especially valuable in guiding a pupil's work. Included in the file should be a cumulative record of the pupil's reading, giving the author and title of books, as well as the names of magazines most frequently read, classified accord-

ing to subject, such as sports, science, aviation, mystery, and adventure. A cumulative record of this kind is almost indispensable for guiding reading interests into more mature or broader channels.

4. Does the evaluation program include tests of special abilities, such as spelling, vocabulary, or usage, as *diagnostic* instruments to assist in locating possible causes of difficulties in using language for purposes of communication? Since nearly all communication situations in real life draw simultaneously upon such abilities as vocabulary or pronunciation, the use of special tests of these components for other than diagnostic purposes is seriously to be questioned. Where scores on subtests are added together into a total score, and interpreted to represent general achievement in English, the results are likely to be misleading. Even statistically, such total scores are of dubious validity. Since reading, for example, involves vocabulary, a total score obtained by adding reading scores to vocabulary scores involves measuring vocabulary twice. The result is a statistical fiction that may yield no significant fact regarding the individual's power and effectiveness in real-life communication. By definition, total scores of this kind can be used arbitrarily to determine whether or not a pupil is eligible to sit in another classroom, but such strictly intramural uses of tests risk the constant danger of widening, rather than bridging, the gap between life and the school. Evaluation is not primarily a grade-labeling process, nor does it assume that schooling and schoolkeeping are synonymous with education.

For an impartial, critical appraisal of the many tests available for measuring ability in English vocabulary, spelling, grammar, reading ability, and knowledge of literature, the reader is referred to the *Mental Measurements Yearbook*.[1] This comprehensive guide contains evaluations of almost all published tests and rating scales by at least two independent critics, along with detailed information regarding their cost,

[1] Oscar K. Buros (Ed.), *The Third Mental Measurements Yearbook.* New Brunswick, N. J.: Rutgers University Press, 1949.

nature, length, publisher, reliability, and validity. When used with due regard for their limitations, these tests can be employed to advantage as diagnostic instruments, to measure the effect which a particular learning procedure has had upon a special language skill. However, since achievement in English, in terms of ability to perform effectively in real-life situations, is simply not synonymous with total scores obtained by process of addition, the use of such tests for other than clinical or diagnostic purposes is to be avoided. Any pencil-and-paper test is best regarded as a measure of latent or potential ability. Whether or not an individual will actually communicate effectively in all the life situations in which language is used—from letter writing and telephoning, to public speaking and conversation at table—can be determined only by observation of actual performance in situations that reproduce life as closely as possible.

5. Does the evaluation program include appraisal of outcomes in the way of reading interests, speech habits (including usage outside the English class), insights into human relations through literature, and other traits or qualifications cited as objectives of the course of study? Since both teachers and students tend unconsciously to give priority to those aspects of the course that are certain to be tested, an aim cannot legitimately be considered an objective until efforts to appraise it, in proportion to its relative importance, are included in the program of evaluation. The fact that habits, insights, and attitudes cannot always be measured satisfactorily on tests scorable by machine has caused many schools to limit measurement to such intramural examinations of ability in spelling, vocabulary, or grammar as yield easily countable results, but which, as means rather than ends, should be reserved for diagnostic or clinical purposes rather than used as measures of achievement in English.

Methods of evaluation. Among the devices that teachers can employ as means for appraising the attainment of the life objectives, as distinguished from the narrower classroom objectives of the English program, are the following:

RATING SCALES. Where the definitions on the scales are studied carefully, and the directions for their administration followed to the letter, the results are more reliable than teachers' grades. For a description and appraisal of published rating scales the reader is again referred to the *Mental Measurements Yearbook*. Since it is impossible, however, for an author, unacquainted with a particular course of study, to devise a measuring instrument that will meet local needs to perfection, the construction of rating scales to appraise special objectives should be an inescapable responsibility of curriculum-revision committees.

Where students and parents have been conditioned to think of evaluation only in terms of subject-matter tests scorable from a key, it is advisable to introduce the scales gradually, perhaps by letting students rate themselves early in the semester and by discussing the results. The support of parents is also desirable. For this reason, any marked change in the evaluation program should not be attempted until after it had been approved by the local parent-teacher association.

TESTS OF ATTITUDES AND INSIGHTS. Owing to the fact that it is easy for young people to give answers that they feel are desired, but that do not necessarily represent their own standards of values, such measuring instruments are best administered in disguised form, in an environment, such as the home room, that does not yield ready clues to the nature of the test. This usually means including the key items among "dummy" items, dealing with a different subject, and repeating the same key item in different form, in another part of the test, to yield a measure of consistency.

ANECDOTAL RECORDS. Observations of student behavior in situations that test growth, in keeping with the life-centered objectives of instruction in English, are a valuable aid in evaluation. Since most teachers cannot rely on their memories in the case of large numbers of students, brief notations on a three- by five-inch card, or slip of paper, can be kept in a special file, or dropped into the folder containing the student's case history, reading record, etc. As reminders, these records are of practical value in counseling your people, in conferring with parents, and in appraising the work of students at the end of the semester. The observations may well include such evidence of growth as ability to get along with people of different national, racial, or religious backgrounds, especially where intercultural understanding is an aim of the English program; growth in tact or initiative in group discussion; increased cooperation or leadership in class or extracurricular activities, and the like.

PRODUCTIONS. Items contributed to the school newspaper, to the class or school yearbook, or to a special class bulletin or magazine, all afford evidence that may desirably be included in an evaluation program. The degree of recognition and approval that these contributions have received from fellow students, as well as from readers outside the class, should be considered in appraising their worth. Such items are also appropriate for filing in the student's folder.

6. Does the program include pupil participation in self-evaluation?

Pupil participation in self-evaluation. Such questions as "Why did I get a C?" or "What do I have to do to get a B?" often show that the student either does not understand the bases on which his grades are based, or that he holds the teacher more accountable than himself for his record in the course. Since a sense of personal responsibility for one's own work and the ability to appraise one's self objectively in relation to others are important educational outcomes in themselves, all methods that contribute to perspective and growth along these lines deserve special attention in English classes. Inefficient outcomes, obtained at the cost of exhausting efforts on the part of the teacher, are to be expected wherever the curriculum neglects the promotion of personal responsibility and ability in self-appraisal on the part of students. Among the means that can be used effectively for these purposes, two deserve special consideration:

a. Self-rating by students, early in the term, on alternate forms of the rating scales or testing instruments that are to be used in appraising outcomes later in the course. Comparison of results obtained on the first self-rating with those obtained subsequently affords evidence of progress or growth in a form easily recognizable to most young people. A week of exploratory self-testing, with discussion of results and time for individual counseling, is not too much to include as an introduction to a year course in English.

b. Computation by students of the per cent of difficulties encountered per 100 written words of their own composition. This implies that students will divide the number of difficulties in spelling, punctuation, capitalization, usage, etc., by the total number of words written over periods of five to ten weeks to see to what extent progress in overcoming handicaps has been made. A record sheet, with subdivisions for legibility, neatness, spelling, capitalization, punctuation, paragraphing, language usage, etc., is useful in helping young people to tabulate their difficulties according to kind and amount, and thus to locate specific weaknesses that deserve attention. If every error or mistake is regarded as a difficulty to be overcome, rather than as a violation to be punished, a more positive and constructive attitude toward written work can be developed than commonly prevails in English classes.

Unless pupils learn from their mistakes, instead of becoming discouraged by them, much of the teacher's time and effort in grading papers is destined to be wasted. For this reason, written work of special importance that has been proofread by the teacher should be reworked by the students, with proper notation of the nature of the difficulties by kind and amount. To be practical in large classes, this self-evaluation plan requires setting aside occasional recitation periods as workshops, during which papers accumulated over a period of time can be revised with the aid of the teacher and of able students appointed as assistants. A folder in which each student's papers, arranged in order of date, can be kept available in the classroom is desirable. Although such folders can be stored on shelves, in groups corresponding to the seating arrangement in the class, a filing case is preferable, even if it has to be constructed from an apple box or strong pasteboard carton. Keeping the folder up to date can well be made the responsibility of the student. To prevent the plan from becoming unwieldy, only papers of special importance need be included.

If the foregoing suggestions are followed, recording of grades in a special grade book is unnecessary, since the teacher has a representative sample of actual work done in the course. Such concrete evidence is far more convincing to parents and pupils than symbols in a notebook. In appraising work in the course, the care with which the student has kept up his folder and corrected misspellings or misusages marked for attention deserves to be considered. If students are instructed to make corrections on the original paper, exactly where the error first occurred, the extent to which they have been conscientious about their progress can be judged at a glance by paging through the folders.

7. Does the evaluation program deemphasize grades as ends in themselves?

Emphasizing progress instead of grades. Since students and parents, as well as teachers, have become accustomed to school marks or grades of some kind, and to value them far out of proportion to their reliability, abandonment of grades without first securing widespread acceptance of a more desirable substitute is likely to meet with opposition. A single teacher who eliminates grades on his own initiative in a highly grade-conscious school may even find students neglecting work in his classes for assignments in other courses in which grades are the only motivation. Although a modern teacher will give support and, if possible, leadership to the gradual adoption of more valid means of evaluation, he will not introduce sudden and sweeping changes entirely on his own persuasion. This does not mean, however, that improvements cannot be introduced from the start within the framework of the local grading system. The recipe for progress here involves three steps: (1) supplementing grades with other means of evaluation of the type suggested in this chapter, and gradually basing grades upon them exclusively, (2) reducing the number of grades given in daily work by substituting other means of evaluation, (3) deemphasizing grades by means of the devices suggested in the following paragraphs.

By placing grades or scores on papers and examinations in an inconspicuous place, such as the lower left-hand corner of the reverse side, where they cannot readily be seen by other students in returning written work, serves to deemphasize grades by making them a matter of private, personal property, rather than a part of the public domain. The advertisement of a high or low grade should be left to the discretion of the pupil himself; it should not be done for him by any teacher who subscribes to the American tradition that the dignity of the individual should be respected rather than belittled among his peers.

Although good work deserves commendation, reference to it by grades is to be avoided. Instead of saying, "Here are three A papers that are worth reading to the class," it is preferable to say, "I think you will be interested in these samples of the papers we wrote last Friday. While listening to them, try to decide which are best, or whether they are all equally good." After reading samples of the work done by the group, the papers that are especially good can be posted on the bulletin board as a form of recognition to the authors. A private word of commendation to them is preferable to public mention of names in highly grade-conscious schools. Because of the competition for marks that many teachers have fostered as their only means of motivation, publicly commending a student by name for superior work might only win him the unenviable distinction of being an "average raiser," "apple polisher," or "teacher's pet."

8. Is the evaluation program appropriately differentiated to accommodate terminal as well as college-preparatory students?

Evaluation of college preparatory work. Because teachers tend unconsciously to favor offerings in high school that enable them to make direct use of work which they have taken in college, the tendency to convert English courses into vest-pocket editions of university offerings, and to evaluate performance only in terms of eligibility to sit in a college classroom, is irresistible in most secondary schools. In fact, there is good reason to believe that in some institutions few young people could risk admitting that they are not preparing for college for fear of losing face in classes in which the emphasis is on little else. Inasmuch as only private schools of the narrow "coaching" type enroll only students who are preparing to pass college entrance examinations at a predictable date, the average secondary school is for most young people a terminal rather than a preparatory institution. Overgeneralizations, such as "all our students go to college," should be challenged at once for specific facts to support them, and discounted if none are available. Obviously, no evaluation program can be considered fair which appraises considerable numbers of young people exclusively in terms of objectives that have no life meaning for them. Indeed, it is a peculiarly warped kind of thinking that favors compulsory school attendance and then provides only for the needs of a favored minority.

In view of the variations in curricula, standards, and requirements among the nation's colleges and universities, it is hardly possible to prepare a student satisfactorily for college in a general, blanket sense. The best that the high school can do is enable him to meet the standards and requirements of *the particular* college or university entrance examination that he has selected. Below the junior year, decisions regarding such matters are likely to be too unreliable to afford a practical basis for guidance or differentiated instruction. Moreover, the results of coaching attempted below this level are destined to become too rusty for use two or more years later. For this reason, exclusive emphasis upon college-preparatory subject matter and evaluation limited to performance in it have little justification in the first two years of high school, even in the case of young people whose abilities, interests, and social-economic backgrounds give every evidence of a successful future in college.

Beyond the sophomore year, however, when evidence of a serious decision regarding preparation for a particular college is confirmed by the parents and school counselor, a differentiation of work, and of bases of evaluation, within the regular classes, is appropriate. In unselected groups, this may mean organizing into working committees those students who give more positive proof of intention to enter college than a mere expression of potential interest. Special assignments can be outlined for them for completion on the contract plan. Tests duplicating types of items likely to be found on modern entrance examinations can likewise be administered from time to time to help orient the students. If the class is conducted on the supervised laboratory-workshop plan at least twice a week, the teacher can guide the work of the college-preparatory committees, as well as of the terminal students, on school time without extra work.

Inasmuch as it should be possible for terminal students to achieve good marks in work appropriate for them, the danger that the college-preparatory students will gain a monopoly of the better grades can be avoided by using such subscripts as A_t or B_r in reporting marks to the school office or university. The symbol A_t can be defined as a grade of excellent in *terminal* work accepted for high school graduation, while the symbol B_r can be defined as good progress in work *recommended* for college.

Since a keen sense of responsibility for one's own work and a capacity for self-direction are indispensable to success in the university, spoon-feeding, coddling, or "mothering" of college-preparatory students is to be avoided. Any grade of A or B achieved in such circumstances is in danger of misrepresenting the true qualifications of the individual receiving it, and to revert to the "unsupported" level of a C or D in college—with embarrassment to all concerned. Inasmuch as a grade of A or B, unless specifically qualified, is commonly understood to mean "recommended for college," no preparatory junior or senior should be awarded these grades unless he can achieve them under guidance in circumstances providing for growth in self-direction and a sense of responsibility for his own work. Providing opportunity, encouragement, and guidance for successful preparation for college is a legitimate responsibility of the secondary school. Passing out college-recommended credits as if they were chewing gum, to the neglect of terminal students or of other equally important responsibilities, is neither a requirement nor a commendable aim.

The fact that requirements imposed by institutions of higher learning are regarded in some quarters as sterile, and even destructive of fundamental educational values, does not justify any teacher in disregarding them on his own initiative. Desirable changes can be effected only through concerted action on the part of parents, teachers, school administrators, and university representatives. That desirable changes are possible, however, is evidenced by the fact that only the recommendation of the principal, based on evaluative data of the kind described in this chapter, is required for admission to the state university in some of our most educationally advanced states. Wider adoption of this principle, through the leadership of the National Council of Teachers of English, Parent-Teacher Association, and other groups in recommending changes to the colleges, would constitute a distinct forward step in American public education. No great hope for the schools can be discerned in the perpetuation of a system of grading and evaluation which, even if it were perfected in terms of the ideals on which it rests, would only transform the teacher from educator into schoolkeeper, or grade labeler in an automatic sausage factory.

FOR FURTHER READING

Buros, Oscar R., *The Third Mental Measurements Yearbook.* New Brunswick, N. J.: Rutgers University Press, 1949.

Educational Testing Service, 20 Nassau St., Princeton, N. J. Publishers of modern achievement tests in English and other subjects.

Greene, Edward B., *Measurement of Human Behavior*. New York: The Odyssey Press, Inc., 1941.

Greene, Harry A., *et al.*, *Measurement and Evaluation in the Secondary School*. New York: Longmans, Green & Co., Inc., 1943.

Kaulfers, Walter V., *Modern Languages for Modern Schools*, Chap. 13. New York: McGraw-Hill Book Company, Inc., 1942.

Remmers, Herman H., and N. L. Gage, *Educational Measurement and Evaluation*. New York: Harper & Brothers, 1943.

Ross, Clay C., *Measurement in Today's Schools*. New York: Prentice-Hall, Inc., 1947.

Smith, Eugene R., *et al.*, *Appraising and Recording Student Progress*. New York: Harper & Brothers, 1942.

Torgerson, Theodore L., *A Diagnostic and Remedial Program for Studying the Maladjusted Child*. Milwaukee: E. M. Hale & Company, 1938. Forty-five pieces in portfolio.

Traxler, Arthur E., *The Nature and Use of Anecdotal Records*. New York: Educational Records Bureau.

Traxler, Arthur E., *The Use of Test Results in Diagnosis and Instruction in the Tool Subjects*. New York: Educational Records Bureau, 1937.

Weitzman, Ellis, and Walter J. McNamara, *Constructing Classroom Examinations*. Chicago: Science Research Associates, 1949.

INDEX